The conclusion of the first chapter of this book raises this question – "Did Christianity meet spiritual needs that the traditional religions were less able to meet?" The answer to this concern is, "Yes." The author of this book has painstakingly explored the reasons and the methods that helped to explain the success story of his grandfather's struggles to carry on the CMS mission enterprise from 1905 to 1970.

Missionary inroads into other religions and cultures are not without some form of difficulties. Baseline hurdles must be encountered in language, belief systems, spiritual disparages, internal conflicts, leadership wrangles and so on. All these are characteristic of the path trodden by the Rev. Canon Omulo throughout his mission agency.

One significant feature of Canon Omulo's contribution to evangelism is the establishment of school education as a vehicle. Up to this point, Anglican church schools sprang up through local initiatives with Omulo himself developing a feeder school that on Sundays became a worshipping congregation.

The Anglican church in Kenya is now well established. Canon Omulo's initiatives covered a vast region which has since birthed several dioceses. Readers who may not be familiar with the geography of Africa in general and that of Kenya, in particular, will appreciate the simple fact that compared to Apostle Paul's burden of traversing Europe and Asia with evangelism, the burden Canon Omulo bore, to where history has reached, was equally heavy.

Philemon Akach, PhD
Senior Lecturer,
Maseno University, Kenya

I have read many theses on religion and theology, but this present work is as touching as it is enlightening. It answers so many questions that I have always held in my heart, but whose answers I have not yet managed to get, despite my efforts at wide reading. My namesake, the late Bishop Meshack Owira, whose religious journey is detailed in this work, would be proud of the research, as it immortalizes the true history of my denomination of Hera, Holy Trinity Church in Africa. I salute the painstaking and groundbreaking research by Bishop Francis Omondi and will be keeping his book next to my Bible for step-by-step study, to understand the history of Christianity in Luo-Nyanza and, specifically, the role Rev. Omulo played in shaping the destiny of Christianity in Luo-Nyanza.

This study sets a new standard of reference for current and future researchers working on the theology and church history of Luoland, as well as the general reader of Luo history. It has changed my perception of the education and church growth in Luo-Nyanza for good!

Meshack Owira Amimo, PhD
Hydrologist and Geophysicist

Shrouded Witness: Unearthing the Mission Praxis of Reuben Omulo is a groundbreaking study of the foundation and spread of Christianity and education in an African community. The study challenges past thinking on mission and evangelization through an encompassing Afro-centric and theoretical framework, detailed research data, and analysis. *Shrouded Witness* reveals, and rightfully credits, the grounding and spread of mission work to the pioneering African converts. Furthermore, it corrects the narrowness and neglect that was evident among some earlier African historians.

This is an excellent and indeed refreshing study of the far-reaching contribution of early Christians to the augmentation of Christianity in a local community. Uncovering Reuben Omulo, the person, cultural context, emerging tensions, spirituality, and wide-ranging work, is a theological and historical adventure. Hopefully, this book will inspire future research and reflections on mission praxis in African situations.

Kabiru Kinyanjui, PhD
Chancellor, Chuka University, Kenya
Former Director, Institute of Development Studies,
University of Nairobi, Kenya

Bishop Omondi's book *Shrouded Witness: Unearthing the Mission Praxis of Reuben Omulo* is a fascinating text that articulates the beautiful story of Padre Omulo and embodies a mission story through encounters. The narrative captures Bishop Omondi's intellectual curiosity on mission while confirming African agency in mission work in Nyanza. The book critically evaluates the work of Omulo among the Luo people and how he was able to educate the missionaries and the Luo people about missions based on the gospel of Jesus Christ. The book shows clearly that Omulo's theological and missional understanding surpassed that of the mission agencies of his time. The book also lays the foundation for the mission themes of indigenization and inculturation in practical ways. This is inclusive of the discourses around theoretical frameworks in mission studies. I commend this book to scholars of mission at all levels as a text worth reading. Mission is about agency and this book is a practical example of the theme of agency.

Esther Mombo, PhD
Senior Lecturer, Faculty of Theology,
St Paul's University, Limuru, Kenya

This well-researched book is a narrative of Christianization in Luo country from the early 1900s to 1970, with a focus on the mission of Padre Omulo, a mission in which Christianity and formal Western education were inextricably bound. The author clearly demonstrates Christianity as a lived experience that although initially alien, gradually found its place in the Luo social structure through a process of syncretism. While forthright about the origins and sometimes not so well-meaning intent of some of the European missionaries, the author convincingly presents the case of Christianity's appeal and enduring message to humankind. Thus, although written primarily for the audience of church historians, the book's religious theme intersects with virtually all aspects of the social, political and economic lives of the Luo through the seven decades that it covers. Of special interest is the deconstruction of what has so far been regarded as the given knowledge about the pioneer of formal Western education in Gem. This is a definite must-read not only for church historians but for social scientists with an interest in this formative period of the history of the Luo nation.

Dickson Mudhune Ombaka, PhD
Senior Lecturer, Department of Sociology,
Kenyatta University, Kenya

This book opens our eyes to the immense contribution the local evangelists gave in enabling Christ to be understood in the context of the local receivers. This is a book to be read by patriotic Kenyans, theologians and historians all over the world.

Enoch Harun Opuka, PhD
Dean, School of Education Arts and Social Sciences,
Africa International University, Kenya

Bishop Francis Omondi, in *Shrouded Witness*, is meticulous in unearthing his family's history. He tells the story of his grandfather, Reuben Omulo, and his pivotal role in indigenizing the Anglican church while navigating the colonial complexities of the Church Missionary Society. To decolonize a metaphor, the guava truly fell right underneath the tree. His grandfather dedicated his life to bridging the chasm between indigenous Luo spirituality and the demands of this new Christian faith. In his story, I saw echoes of my own family: my grandfather, the first convert, and the foundations of my Christian roots.

I saw the sacrifices and choices of those early Christian men and women who faced the onslaught of the colonial system and did not surrender their cultural souls. They consciously wrestled with the contradictions of their new Christian faith, embedding it deep within their indigenous cultural realities, and forging communities where their ancestral spirit was not erased but profoundly reshaped into new ways of being and belonging, laying authentic pathways for generations.

Oyunga Pala
Satirist and Columnist, Kenya

Shrouded Witness

Unearthing the Mission Praxis of Reuben Omulo

Francis Omondi

ACADEMIC

© 2025 Francis Omondi

Published 2025 by Langham Academic
An imprint of Langham Publishing
www.langhampublishing.org

Langham Publishing and its imprints are a ministry of Langham Partnership

Langham Partnership
PO Box 296, Carlisle, Cumbria, CA3 9WZ, UK
www.langham.org

ISBNs:
978-1-78641-009-2 Print
978-1-78641-206-5 ePub
978-1-78641-207-2 PDF
DOI: https://doi.org/10.69811/9781786410092

Francis Omondi has asserted his right under the Copyright, Designs and Patents Act, 1988 to be identified as the Author of this work.

All rights reserved. No part of this publication may be reproduced, stored in a retrieval system or transmitted, in any form or by any means, electronic, mechanical, photocopying, recording or otherwise, without the prior written permission of the publisher or the Copyright Licensing Agency.

Requests to reuse content from Langham Publishing are processed through PLSclear. Please visit www.plsclear.com to complete your request.

Scriptures taken from the Holy Bible, New International Version®, NIV®. Copyright © 1973, 1978, 1984, 2011 by Biblica, Inc.™ Used by permission of Zondervan.

Scripture quotations marked (NJKV) New King James Version (NKJV). Copyright © 1982 by Thomas Nelson, Inc. Used by permission. All rights reserved.

British Library Cataloguing-in-Publication Data
A catalogue record for this book is available from the British Library

ISBN: 978-1-78641-009-2

Cover & Book Design: projectluz.com

Langham Partnership actively supports theological dialogue and an author's right to publish but does not necessarily endorse the views and opinions set forth here or in works referenced within this publication, nor can we guarantee technical and grammatical correctness. Langham Partnership does not accept any responsibility or liability to persons or property as a consequence of the reading, use or interpretation of its published content.

Contents

Acknowledgements xv

Abstract xvii

Abbreviations xix

Foreword xxi

Chapter 1 1
Introduction
   1.1 Background Information 1
   1.1 Research Rationale 2
   1.2 Statement of the Research Question 2
   1.3 Assumptions 3
   1.4 Practical Significance 4
   1.5 Theoretical Framework 4
      1.5.1 Praxis Matrix 4
      1.5.2 Encounterology 7
   1.6 Area and Scope of Study 8
      1.6.1 Chronological scope 8
      1.6.2 Geographical scope 9
      1.6.3 Ecclesial Scope 9
      1.6.4 Broader Encounters 9
   1.7 The Nature and Structure of the Thesis 11
      1.7.1 The shaping function of the praxis matrix 11
      1.7.2 An Overview of the Chapters 12
   1.8 Research Methodology 13
   1.9 Research Approaches 15
      1.9.1 The Historical Background 15
      1.9.2 The Mission Praxes of Reuben Omulo and the CMS ... 15
   1.10 Literature Review 17
   1.11 Conclusion 21

Chapter 2 23
The Broader Context of Encounters in Central Nyanza
   2.1 Introduction 23
      2.1.1 People the Luo Met in Central Nyanza 24
   2.2 Settlement of the Southern Luo 26
      2.2.1 Luo Consciousness 31

2.2.2 Organization of Luo Society 33
2.2.3 Luo Heroes and the Rise of States 34
2.3 The Luo War and Conflicts 37
2.3.1 Inter-Luo Wars 37
2.3.2 Luo – Abaluyia Wars 39
2.4 The Luo-European Encounters 44
2.4.1 Military Expeditions and Collaboration 45
2.4.2 The Gem Collaboration 49
2.5 Establishment of Colonial Administration 50
2.5.1 The Uganda Railway 53
2.6 Conclusion 55

Chapter 3 57
The Inaugural Stage: Tracing Interactions Between Mission Praxes in Central Nyanza from 1906 to 1920
3.1 Introduction 57
3.2 Key Political, Economic, and Cultural Events in Central Nyanza in the Period between 1906 and 1920 58
3.3 Agency 61
3.3.1 Reuben Omulo's Agency 62
3.3.2 CMS's Agency 67
3.3.3 Interaction between the Agency of Reuben Omulo and CMS 72
3.4 Contextual Understanding 75
3.4.1 Reuben Omulo's Contextual Understanding 75
3.4.2 CMS's Contextual Understanding 79
3.4.3 Interaction between Reuben Omulo and CMS Understanding of Context 82
3.5 Ecclesial/Religious Scrutiny 84
3.5.1 Reuben Omulo's Religious Scrutiny 84
3.5.2 CMS's Ecclesial Analysis 90
3.5.3 Interaction between Reuben Omulo and CMS 95
3.6 Interpreting the Tradition 97
3.6.1 Reuben Omulo's Interpretation of Tradition 98
3.6.2 CMS's Interpretation of Tradition 101
3.6.3 Interaction between Reuben Omulo and CMS 104
3.7 Discernment for Action 107
3.7.1 Reuben Omulo's Discernment for Action 107
3.7.2 CMS's Discernment for Action 109
3.7.3 Interaction Between Reuben Omulo and CMS on Their Discernment for Action 112

3.8 Reflexivity 114
   3.8.1 Reuben Omulo's Reflexivity 114
   3.8.2 CMS's Reflexivity 115
   3.8.3 Interaction Between Reuben Omulo and CMS in
      their Discernment for Action 117
3.9 Spirituality 119
   3.9.1 Reuben Omulo's Spirituality 120
   3.9.2 CMS's Spirituality 121
   3.9.3 Interaction Between the Spiritualities of Reuben
      Omulo and CMS 123
3.10 Overview of the Encounters 124

Chapter 4 127
Indigenization Stage: Tracing Interactions of Mission Praxis in Central Nyanza from 1921 to 1945

4.1 Introduction 127
4.2 Central Nyanza from 1921 to 1945: Key Political
   Economic and Cultural Events 128
   4.2.1 Political Context 128
   4.2.2 Devonshire White Paper 129
   4.2.3 Colonial Education 130
   4.2.4 Economic development 132
4.3 Agency 134
   4.3.1 Reuben Omulo's Agency 135
   4.3.2 CMS's Agency 138
   4.3.3 Interaction Between Reuben Omulo and CMS on
      Agency 141
4.4 Contextual Understanding 145
   4.4.1 Reuben Omulo's Contextual Understanding 145
   4.4.2 The CMS's Understanding of the Context 150
   4.4.3 Interaction of Omulo and CMS on Understanding
      Context 154
4.5 Ecclesial and Religious Scrutiny 157
   4.5.1 Reuben Omulo's Ecclesial Analysis 157
   4.5.2 CMS's Ecclesial Analysis 163
   4.5.3 Interaction Between Reuben Omulo and CMS on
      Ecclesial Scrutiny 171
4.6 Interpreting the Tradition 176
   4.6.1 Reuben Omulo's Interpreting of the Bible and Tradition ...176
   4.6.2 CMS's Interpretation of the Bible and Tradition 183
   4.6.3 Interaction Between Omulo and CMS on
      Interpreting the Bible and tradition 186

4.7 Discernment for Action 190
    4.7.1 Reuben Omulo's Discernment for Action 190
    4.7.2 CMS's Discernment for Action 204
    4.7.3 Interactions Between Omulo and the CMS on
        Discernment for Action 213
4.8 Reflexivity 218
    4.8.1 Reuben Omulo's Reflexivity 219
    4.8.2 CMS's Reflexivity 221
    4.8.3 Interaction Between Omulo and CMS on Reflexivity 226
4.9 Spirituality 229
    4.9.1 Reuben Omulo's Spirituality 229
    4.9.2 CMS's Spirituality 233
    4.9.3 Interaction Between Omulo and CMS on Spirituality 235
4.10 Overview on the Encounters in this Period 238

Chapter 5 241
Independence Stage: Tracing Interactions Between the Forms of Mission Praxis in Central Nyanza from 1946 to 1970
    5.1 Introduction 241
    5.2 Key Events: Political, Economic, and Cultural Features of
        the Period 242
        5.2.1 Societal Changes in Politics 242
        5.2.2 Demand for Education 243
    5.3 Agency 247
        5.3.1 Reuben Omulo's Agency 247
        5.3.2 CMS's Agency 249
        5.3.3 Interaction between Omulo and
            CMS/Anglican Church 253
    5.4 Contextual Understanding 254
        5.4.1 Reuben Omulo's Contextual Understanding 255
        5.4.2 CMS's Contextual Understanding 261
        5.4.3 Interaction Between Reuben Omulo and CMS on
            Contextual Understanding 265
    5.5 Ecclesial and Religious Scrutiny 268
        5.5.1 Reuben Omulo Ecclesial Scrutiny 269
        5.5.2 CMS Ecclesial Scrutiny 274
        5.5.3 Interaction Between Reuben Omulo and CMS on
            Ecclesial Scrutiny 277
    5.6 Interpreting the Tradition 280
        5.6.1 Reuben Omulo's Interpreting Bible and Tradition 280
        5.6.2 The CMS's Interpreting Bible and Tradition 291

       5.6.3 Interaction Between Reuben Omulo and CMS on
           Interpreting Tradition 294
   5.7 Discernment for Action 298
       5.7.1 Reuben Omulo's Discernment for Action 298
       5.7.2 CMS's Discernment for Action 303
       5.7.3 Interaction Between Reuben Omulo and the CMS
           on Discernment for Action 306
   5.8 Reflexivity 308
       5.8.1 Reuben Omulo's Reflexivity 308
       5.8.2 CMS's Reflexivity 310
       5.8.3 Interaction Between Reuben Omulo and CMS on
           Reflexivity 314
   5.9 Spirituality 316
       5.9.1 Reuben Omulo's Spirituality 316
       5.9.2 CMS's Spirituality 321
       5.9.3 Interaction Between Reuben Omulo and the CMS
           on Spirituality 323
   5.10 Overview of the Encounters 325

Chapter 6 327
   Theological Reflection
   6.1 Introduction 327
   6.2 African Agency 327
   6.3 Mission Praxis 330
       6.3.1 Evangelism 331
       6.3.2 Translation and Vernacular Liturgy 333
   6.4 The Luo Gospel Message 335
       6.4.1 Gospel of the Hereafter 335
       6.4.2 Response to Colonialism 338
   6.5 Indigenous Church: Theological Link with the Past 341
   6.6 Conclusion 344

Chapter 7 347
   Conclusion
   7.1 General Overview of the Research, Highlighting the Findings 347
       7.1.1 Overview of the Research 347
       7.1.2 Findings of the Research 349
   7.2 Appraising the research objectives 352
   7.3 Evaluation of the Praxis Matrix in the Study of Mission 353
   7.4 Issues this Research Could Not Discuss 354
   7.5 What the Study Has Meant to Me 356
   7.6 Concluding personal remarks 357

Appendix 1 359
    The Luo Migration

Appendix 2 375
    Research Guiding Questions

Appendix 3 379
    The Canon Law of Marriage

Appendix 4 381
    CMS Memorandum 1901

Bibliography 383

List of Figures

Figure 1: Theoretical Framework by Kritzinger & Saayman 5

Figure 2: Encounters Between the Luo, Abaluyia and the Europeans 11

Figure 3: Thesis structure highlighting agencies of Omondi, Omulo and CMA 12

Figure 4: Transformation and Growth in the Luo Pre-literate Society 30

Figure 5: Structure of the Luo Legal Institution 34

Figure 6: Growth of Christians Between 1913 and 1918 108

Figure 7: The Six-fold Typology – Cannon and Foster 119

Figure 8: Translation of "Abide with Me" into Dholuo 200

Figure 9: Translation of "Safe in the Arms" into Dholuo 201

Figure 10: Literal Translation of "When He Cometh" into Dholuo 202

Figure 11: Actual Translation of "When He Cometh" into Dholuo 202

Figure 12: Chart of the Traditional Luo Universe 337

Figure 13: Luo Migration Path from South Sudan to the Lake Victoria Region 363

Figure 14: Luo Migration into Central Nyanza Adopted from Ndeda 365

Figure 15: Abstract of Replies to Report and Constitution Memorandum 381

Acknowledgements

This work would not have been possible without the extensive help and support from numerous people. Primarily I wish to thank my supervisor, Professor Klippies Kritzinger, and Dr. Johannes Malherbe for their patience and encouragement over the last three years. I was very fortunate to find myself studying under people whose knowledge and understanding of mission is so extensive.

Work on this thesis has taken place during the COVID-19 lockdown, while it was a trial to meet people for information. It allowed a quiet moment to focus on writing. Thanks to The Sheepfold Ministry (TSM) for giving time out that allowed time to write this thesis. Thanks to Barnabas Fund for paying my tuition for PhD studies.

The main library for this research was at Birmingham University, and I wish to thank all the staff in the special collections department for their enormous help. Their professionalism, patience and courtesy seem to know no bounds.

I would also like to thank Prof. and Mrs. Aloo Mojola who nudged me to do a PhD, Dr. Johannes Malherbe my MTh. Supervisor introduced me to the South African Theological Seminary (SATS) and for developing my research skills. Thanks to Mari Chevako of University of Wisconsin for helpful textual advice and proofreading. Finally, thanks go to my wife, Dr. Anne Omondi, and sons Daniel, Moses and Jean for their patience and tolerance over the last three years.

I hope that this thesis will be useful to students of history, education, and missiology, particularly those from churches whose story relates to the work of the CMS.

Abstract

This research examined the Anglican Church's history of mission in Central Nyanza, focusing on the formative role played by Reuben Omulo, a Luo mission innovator. It explored the key features of the mission praxis of Omulo and his encounters with the Church Missionary Society (CMS).

It adopted Kritzinger's[1] seven-point "praxis matrix" in an "encounterological" approach to probe the encounters between the mission praxes of Omulo and the CMS. This involved investigating the dynamics of the interaction between those praxes, focusing on each of the seven dimensions in turn. The study used data from personal interviews and discussions with a selected group of respondents from Siaya and Kisumu Counties, among families and places where Omulo worked. It analysed secondary data from relevant published works and other written materials from private archives.

The pre-colonial encounters forged the diverse Luo people into a nation, as this research clarified, and further described those complex relations, which shaped critical features of the Southern Luo world, priming them for their encounters with European colonialists and CMS missionaries.

The CMS's intention for indigenizing the church met resonance in Omulo. As the research illustrated, Christianity met spiritual needs that traditional religion could not. For Omulo and his colleagues, more so, the vernacular Scriptures eliminated ambiguities in the Luo religion, making the transition to Christianity more effortless for them.

The study revealed a creative tension between Omulo and CMS praxes, which for Omulo was an attempt to balance Christianity's demands with traditional responsibilities and integrate the Luo into Christianity. But the

---

1. Kritzinger, "Faith to Faith," 764–790.

CMS sought to interpret the Luo worldview to infuse it with the scriptural message of Christianity.

Omulo and his colleagues proved to be active recipients of the gospel, as the study showed, for protesting colonial injustice, compelled authority to reform, and further stimulated the CMS and the Anglican Church in Kenya to embrace a social justice spirituality.

The challenges facing the Anglican Church of Kenya (ACK) can be traced to how the CMS established the African Anglican Church in Central Nyanza, as this research showed. This research, therefore, suggests that the ACK should focus on empowering the laity as her primary agency for mission and that the church's mission praxis must reaffirm culture to speak to the core needs of the people. It recommends that mission history be studied with the praxis matrix as part of an "encounterology" approach.

Abbreviations

AAC	African Anglican Church
ACMDO	African Christian Marriage and Divorce Ordinance
ACK	Anglican Church of Kenya
APCND	Anglican Padres Central Nyanza Deanery
BCC	Butere Church Council
BFBS	British Foreign Bible Society
CEC	CMS Executive Committee
CMC	CMS Mission Committee
CEN/KAV	Central Kavirondo
CEN/NZA	Central Nyanza
CMS	Church Missionary Society
CMSA	Church Missionary Society Archives
CNO	Chief Native Officer
DCC	District Church Council
DC/KSM	District Commissioner Kisumu
DMN files	Diocese of Maseno North files
EAP	East Africa Protectorate
EARM	East African Revival Movement
EEA	Eastern Equatorial Africa
GCC	Group Congregation Council
IBEA Co.	Imperial British East Africa Company
KANU	Kenya's African National Union
KAU	Kenya African Union
KDCC	Kavirondo District Church Council
KMC	Kavirondo Mission Council

KSM	Kisumu
KRC	Kavirondo Ruri-decanal Council
KTWA	Kavirondo Taxpayers Welfare Association
LEGICO	Legislative Council
NAC	Native Anglican Church
NCC	Native Church Council
NCU	Native Customary Union
NRC	Nyanza Rural Deanery Council
NRC SC	Nyanza Rural Standing Committee
NZA	Nyanza
PC	Parent Committee
PMS	Protestant Missionary Societies
PUR	Provincial Unit of Research
SDAM	Seventh Day Adventist Mission
YKA	Young Kavirondo Association

Foreword

A luminous and necessary remembrance. Bishop Omondi restores African agency to the heart of mission history with grace, rigour, and deep humanity.

Shrouded Witness: Unearthing the Mission Praxis of Reuben Omulo is not simply a book. It is a generous act of remembrance. In these pages, Bishop Francis Omondi invites us to listen carefully to a story that has long lingered in the interstices of history. The result is a profound meditation on the intersections of faith, culture, and colonial entanglement, rendered with the care of a scholar and the tenderness of one who knows these soils and their stories intimately.

This is a book that moves beyond the rigid boundaries of genre. Part memoir, part ecclesiastical history, part theological reflection, *Shrouded Witness* offers a textured narrative that brings to light the life of Reuben Omulo, a Luo Christian leader whose legacy has remained, until now, in the margins of the Anglican Church's grand narrative. Omondi's work is not just recovery; it is a reframing of how mission history can be told when those once considered peripheral are given back their rightful agency.

What unfolds is a portrait of a man poised at the delicate threshold between profound ancestral theological worlds and the imported strictures of an imperially-delivered faith. Omulo's journey from his early formation in Central Nyanza to his leadership within the Anglican Church reveals a life lived in negotiation: between worlds, between powers, between visions of what faith could be when truly incarnated in African soil. His story is one of courage, adaptation, and pushing through resistances without losing his essence.

Omondi writes with a steady, unflinching gaze, that is also tender. He explores the layered complexities that undergird Omulo's rich yet challenging journey: the paternalism and imperial hubris of the missionaries are laid bare, yet so too are their genuine acts of service and the unexpected solidarities that formed. Bishop Omondi invites us to see Christianity in Africa not as a foreign graft, but as a long, unfolding confluence where foundational currents flowing and rich among a people meet new tributaries and better define their direction and meaning. To this goal, the reader finds Omulo's own critical engagement with Christianity as a clarifying thread, a testament to profound African agency reshaping the contours of mission praxis.

There is in this book an attentiveness to history as lived experience, to faith as a field of contested meanings, and to the small, precise acts through which dignity is claimed. Omondi's analytical use of the praxis matrix is not mere academic scaffolding, it is a means of giving theological weight to lived realities, of showing how faith takes root, not in abstraction, but in the thick of life's contradictions. What makes *Shrouded Witness* quietly remarkable is its resonance with the present. Questions of cultural identity, religious hybridity, and the lingering shadows of colonial legacy remain pressing in contemporary discourse. This book does not offer easy answers. Rather than a tale of rupture, Bishop Omondi offers a meditation on the long, bending river of faith, its source deep in the wells of Luo and African memory, its waters flowing towards the vast, longed for sea of eternity. Here, Christianity is not a graft upon alien soil but a living confluence, where enduring traditions and Christian witness meet in sacred continuity. *Shrouded Witness* invites a profound reckoning with how we remember, how we belong, and how every human heart strains towards the ultimate, a quiet yet insistent longing to be gathered into the great story of God. Omondi offers not a story of Christianity 'arriving', but of a river's ongoing journey where African spiritual legacies shape each new bend towards a shared, hoped-for sea. In the end, this is a work of profound generosity. It honours the overlooked, challenges the inherited narratives, and offers a vision of African Christianity that is both critical and hopeful. Bishop Omondi has crafted a vital contribution to the ongoing conversation about faith, history, and the enduring quest for integrity.

A masterful and necessary book, *Shrouded Witness* will leave you challenged, not by spectacle, but by the quiet insistence that every story matters. In recovering the lustrous thread of Reuben Omulo's witness, Bishop Omondi weaves a resonant tapestry of Kenya's becoming. One where faith, memory, and the unrecorded labours of many are revealed as foundations of our shared history.

Yvonne A. Owuor
Author: *Dust, Dragonfly Sea*
Nairobi, May 15, 2025

CHAPTER 1

Introduction

1.1 Background Information

This research examines the mission praxis of Reuben Omulo, a pioneer Luo Christian leader, and his interaction with the praxis of Church Missionary Society (CMS) missionaries, during the years 1905 to 1970 in Central Nyanza.

Scholars such as Omulokoli and Nzioki discussed how CMS established the Anglican Church in Western Kenya, focusing on its historical expansion.[1] Others, such as Richard, Richards, Odwako, Walaba, and Onyango, zeroed in on the CMS's mission activities.[2] But I premised this study on Farrimond's argument that the untold histories of the indigenous churches around the world contributed to the grand historical narrative of the Anglican Communion.[3] These histories are local, with non-Western players at the centre. In this investigation, I explored the stories of these other actors and their missiological contributions.

The CMS mission praxis espoused by various missionaries did not surface in a void. It evolved. This study identified how the encounters the CMS missionaries had elsewhere in their mission fields shaped the organization's mission praxis. It also explored transformative encounters between the Luo people, their neighbours, and Europeans in Central Nyanza from 1905 to

---

1. Omulokoli, "Historical Development"; Nzioki, "Development of the Anglican Church."

2. Richard, *Archdeacon Owen of Kavirondo*; Richards, *Fifty Years in Nyanza*; Odwako, "Church and Education;" Walaba, *Role of Christian Missionaries*; Onyango, *Gender and Development*.

3. Farrimond, "Concerning the Development."

1970. It further examined how these encounters shaped the mission praxes that contributed to the creation of the Anglican Church in Central Nyanza.

My concern, as an Anglican cleric working in missions, a Luo, and a grandson of a pioneer African Anglican priest, Rev. Canon Reuben Omulo, was the dearth of detailed documentation of African pioneer Christians' stories and their contribution. Their innovation or missiological insights remain unnoticed and inaccessible to the present-day church. I am interested in documenting this and making it public.

1.1 Research Rationale

In this study, I explored a series of transformative encounters in Central Nyanza. I correlated the encounters between the mission praxes that gave rise to the Anglican Church among the Luo, to investigate the influence they had on one another between 1906 and 1970. This has relevance to the history of the Anglican Communion as a whole, since the Anglican Church in Central Nyanza, which owes her existence to CMS mission praxis, must now contribute to the church's global mission. The study further clarified:

- Components of the Luo world that were shaped by their encounters with their Abaluyia neighbours, CMS missionaries, and British colonial rule.
- The mission praxes, which developed through reciprocal interaction, that led to the founding of the Anglican Church in Central Nyanza.
- Forms of emerging mission praxis at present that were produced by the earlier encounters.

1.2 Statement of the Research Question

What were the key features of the mission praxis of Reuben Omulo and his encounters with CMS missionaries, which shaped the Anglican Church in Central Nyanza and its ongoing mission?

To address this central research question, the following sub-questions had to be explored:

1. What were the cultural, economic, and political dimensions of the context in Central Nyanza during that period, forming the backdrop against which the encounters need to be understood?
2. What was Reuben Omulo's family background and how did he relate to the Luo community of which he was a part?
3. Who were the CMS missionaries that played a central role in Central Nyanza, and what were the features of their mission praxis?
4. What were the features of Reuben Omulo's ministry praxis and the dynamics of his encounters with the CMS missionaries?
5. What are the theological issues that emerged from this series of encounters?

1.3 Assumptions

I explored the dynamics of these mission encounters in the cultural, economic, and political tensions between the Luo, Abaluyia and colonial (British) communities. This research proceeded with the following fundamental assumptions:

1. Mission endeavours to establish churches do not happen by chance. An interacting set of philosophical and theological ideals, objectives, policies and practices guide them.
2. The term "praxis" is used to describe the interaction between the dimensions of planned activities or projects that are intentionally aimed at transformation.
3. Every form of mission praxis has personal, cultural, economic, political and theological dimensions and therefore the nature of mission must be explored through a model that gives attention to all these factors.
4. When researching the dynamics of mission in a particular context, it is inadequate to study only the praxis of missionaries; the innovative, "receiving" praxis of a community that responds to it positively, as well as the dynamic interaction between the two forms of praxis, should be explored together.

5. The encounters that the mission agents had with various other groups and in communities in the context always influenced the encounters between their different forms of mission praxis.
6. Reuben Omulo's mission praxis between 1908 and 1974 represents the response of the first generation of Luo Christian leaders to the Anglican presence in Central Nyanza.
7. The encounters between the mission praxes of Reuben Omulo and the CMS missionaries contributed to the establishment of the Anglican Church among the Luo people in Central Nyanza.
8. Those encounters had far-reaching consequences for the Luo people; it also shaped the character of the Anglican Church in Central Nyanza and thus has implications for the ongoing mission praxis of the Anglican Church in Kenya.

1.4 Practical Significance

The strategic aim of the study was to help the Anglican Church in Kenya to a clearer understanding of its history of mission, to appreciate and reclaim the formative role played by Luo mission innovators and to reassess its present mission praxis by engaging the praxis matrix.

There were two academic ambitions of this study: to add new missiological insights into the emergence of the Anglican Church among the Luo in Central Nyanza; and to apply a praxis matrix to explore the encounters between CMS mission praxis and the mission praxis of Rev. Reuben Omulo (hereafter referred to as Omulo). I provide the justification for selecting Omulo in §§1.7; 1.11; 3.1; 4.1; and 5.1.

1.5 Theoretical Framework

1.5.1 Praxis matrix

The Anglican Church among the Luo emerged out of the encounters between the mission praxis of the CMS and the mission praxis of pioneer Christians in Central Nyanza, like Omulo. To do in-depth research on the dynamics of those encounters, one first needs to describe each mission praxis in its own right. This thesis uses Kritzinger's seven-point "praxis matrix" to do that.[4] The matrix focuses on the following seven dimensions of mission praxis: Spirituality, Agency, Contextual understanding, Ecclesial scrutiny, Interpreting the tradition, Discernment for action and Reflexivity, as presented in the diagram below:[5]

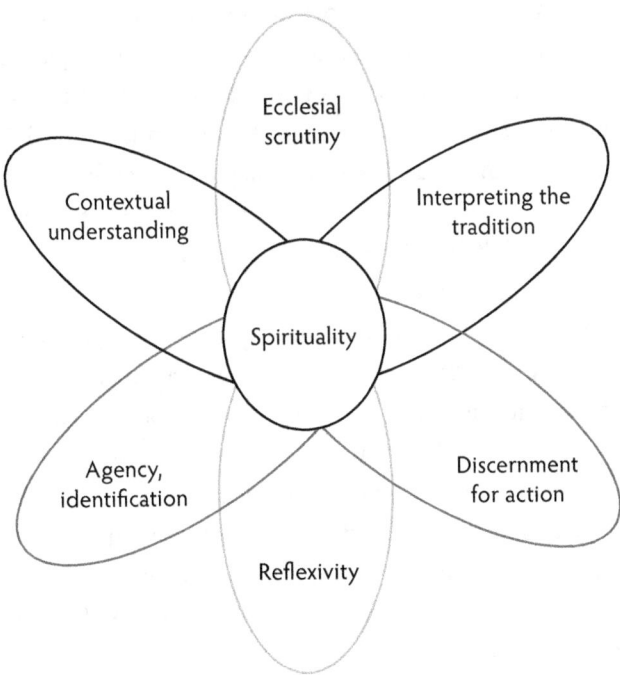

Figure 1: Theoretical Framework by Kritzinger & Saayman

When using the matrix as an analytical instrument, to research transformative attempts (mission praxis) of a person or community, the following questions need to be asked concerning the seven dimensions:

1. Agency (Ag): Who were the innovating adopters (and adapters) of the witness or service they received? Who are their interlocutors? What role did power relations play? How did these factors influence the decision and their ongoing involvement?

---

4. Krintzinger, "Faith to Faith."
5. Kritzinger and Saayman. *David J. Bosch Prophetic*, 4.

2. Contextual understanding (CU): How did the missionaries and recipients of mission analyse their context? Did the change agents' perceptions influence the approach they adopted? How did the adopters "read the signs of the times"? How have these factors influenced their decision to adopt the innovation?
3. Ecclesial analysis (EA):[6] How did the adopters perceive their own "former" religion and culture? What were the push and pull factors involved? How did those factors shape the peoples' decision to adopt the incoming Christian innovation? Did they join the formal churches, or did they form their own Christian communities? Was there a level of privileges that the change agents exploited, such as positions of power and privilege or influential public contacts?
4. Interpreting the tradition (IT): How did the adopters and agents interpret the Bible in relation to traditional religion? Was there a unique formulation of the Christian message arising from this context? How did these theological insights shape their approach?
5. Discernment for action (DA): What concrete steps of faith did the change agents and the recipients take in relation to the community at large? What decision-making structures and patterns were there in the community? What lifestyle or cultural decisions were involved?
6. Reflexivity (R): Did the adopters and change agents reflect on the impact of their decisions on the community? Did the change agents consistently reflect on the impact and results of their work in the community? Did they learn from their experiences? Was there evidence in their praxis of a conscious journey of self-reflection and learning? Did they admit when they had been wrong and change their ways?
7. Spirituality (Spir): What were the characteristics of the spirituality manifested at the heart of a particular mission praxis? What was the dominant spirituality among them? How did this shape the character of the Anglican Church?

---

6. While adopting Kritzinger's praxis matrix, I prefer not to use his term "Ecclesial scrutiny" and use "Ecclesial analysis" instead. This does not imply a change of focus in this dimension of the matrix.

In chapters 3 to 5, I examined the mission praxes of Reuben Omulo and the CMS side by side by asking these seven questions of each praxis.

1.5.2 Encounterology

An exploration of the *encounters* between the praxes of Omulo and the CMS involved more than a side-by-side description of their respective praxes. It required an examination of the dynamics of the interaction between those praxes. In chapters 3 to 5, this study therefore also explored the nature of the encounters between Omulo and the CMS by asking how each dimension in Omulo's matrix related to each dimension in the matrix of CMS missionaries.

Acknowledging the complexity of studying transformative encounters by using a praxis matrix, this research concurred with Kritzinger's conclusion of the necessity to construct the "transforming" praxis of CMS as an agent of change.[7] This was done by tracing the interaction between the seven dimensions of their praxis in each period by means of the matrix.

Alongside the CMS praxis, the study constructed the "receiving" or "adopting" praxis of the community among whom the witness or service was being rendered. The Luo people responded to the CMS mission impulses as active agents, appropriating the ideas, habits, and practices of the Christian mission. Bundy and Leedy Comaroff stressed that African communities "adapted rather than adopted" impulses from missionaries; they never passively received their instruction either about life or religion.[8] This research explored Omulo's praxis as representing the "adopting/adapting" praxis in the Luo community, constructing his praxis in terms of the seven dimensions of the praxis matrix. In chapters 3 to 5, I first discussed the praxis of Omulo, before looking at the CMS praxis and then exploring how they interacted.

To examine the nature of the interactive encounters between Omulo's praxis and CMS's praxis in chapters 3 to 5, I used insights from Robert Schreiter, David Lochhead, and Wim Overdiep, among others.[9] In describing responses to incoming cultural and religious impulses, Schreiter uses the terms "syncretism" and "dual religious systems" to describe the different

---

7. Kritzinger, "Using Archives Missiologically," 18–42.
8. Comaroff and Comaroff, *Of Revelation and Revolution*, 153; Bundy, *Rise and Fall*, 35–36; and Leedy, "History with a Mission," 255–270.
9. Schreiter, *Constructing Local Theologies*; Lochhead, *Dialogical imperative*; Overdiep, *Het gevecht*.

dynamics that unfold in such encounters, which gives a range of options to describe the nature of the interactions, depending on the relative power relationships between the local and the incoming messages and cultures.[10] Lochhead identifies a series of five "ideologies" of encounter, namely isolation, hostility, competition, partnership, and dialogue.[11] Overdiep developed an "emotional distance scale" to distinguish between the emotional aspects of relationships with enemies, opponents, strangers, colleagues, and friends.[12] I showed in chapters 3 to 5 how these three approaches to exploring encounters can illumine the interactions between different forms of mission praxis.

1.6 Area and Scope of Study
1.6.1 Chronological Scope

As indicated already, the chronological focus of the thesis is the period from 1906 to 1970. The reason for these dates is that the CMS began its mission in Central Nyanza in 1906 and "handed over" control of the Anglican Church to local church leaders in 1970. This period therefore encompassed the period of CMS's mission praxis dominance in Central Nyanza. Reuben Omulo's first contacted with CMS was in 1908 and he was among the earliest converts of their mission. He was employed by CMS in 1914 and remained in the mission's service during the whole period of mission described in this study. He passed away in 1974, at the age of 79.

To do an in-depth study of the encounters between Omulo and the CMS and to trace how their mission praxes developed through mutual interaction, it was necessary to divide the historical scope of the study into three periods, each with its distinctive set of characteristics: 1906 to 1920; 1921 to 1945; and 1946 to 1970. Such a division was also necessary because the praxis matrix is primarily a synchronic interpretive instrument. It was used in each specific period to describe the respective mission praxes of Omulo and the CMS and to show how they interacted with each other in that period. In Sections 3.1, 4.1 and 5.1, respectively, I explain and justify the beginning (*terminus a quo*) and ending (*terminus ad quem*) of each of these periods.

---

10. Schreiter, *Constructing Local Theologies*.
11. Lochhead, *Dialogical Imperative*.
12. Overdiep, *Het gevecht*.

1.6.2 Geographical Scope

The geographical focus of this thesis was on Central Nyanza Province in Kenya, in particular the Siaya and Kisumu Counties. The area in Kenya that has been called Kisumu and Siaya Counties since 2010 was previously known as Central Nyanza District. The Colonial administration had initially named the greater Western part of Kenya "Kavirondo" but later called it "Nyanza."[13] The Nyanza region was later divided into three districts, North Nyanza, Central Nyanza, and South Nyanza. Since this research is focused on both Kisumu and Siaya counties it is more convenient to use the old name. Central Nyanza was the name used for that area for the whole period covered in this research.

The reason for this is that these two counties are the main areas where the Luo people reside. I focused on the Luo people because Reuben Omulo was a member of that ethnic community and because it was the space in which he made his unique contribution to the emergence of the Anglican Church in Central Nyanza. In addition to Siaya and Kisumu Counties, I also interviewed people who consider Siaya and Kisumu Countries their home, but presently live in Nairobi or elsewhere in Kenya, when they were of material benefit to the research.

1.6.3 Ecclesial Scope

The ecclesial focus of the study is on the CMS, which is part of the Anglican tradition, even though different Christian missions engaged the Nyanza region to establish churches. The Anglican Church became the dominant Christian church in Central and Northern Nyanza, while the Seventh Day Adventists (SDA) mainly worked in Southern Nyanza. Focusing on Kisumu and Siaya Counties met the conditions of addressing both the Luo community and the Anglican Church, which together constituted the key focus of this study.

1.6.4 Broader Encounters

As stated in assumption 5 (in §1.4 above), the interaction between Omulo and the CMS cannot be isolated from the surrounding cultural, economic and political context. The surrounding context could be conceived as a complex set of encounters between a wider variety of role players, including the

---

13. Ogot, *History of the Southern Luo*.

Europeans (colonial administrators, traders, CMS missionaries), the Luo people and the Abaluyia people. Figure 2 below depicts the complex web of encounters between these role players. It was within this web of interactions that the encounters between Omulo and the CMS took place and that the Anglican Church of Kenya (ACK) among the Luo and Abaluyia emerged. To examine all these interactions in detail would be far beyond the scope of this thesis. Its focus was on the interaction between Omulo and the CMS, even though there are occasional references to those wider encounters, where it is necessary to explain the dynamics of the Omulo-CMS interaction.

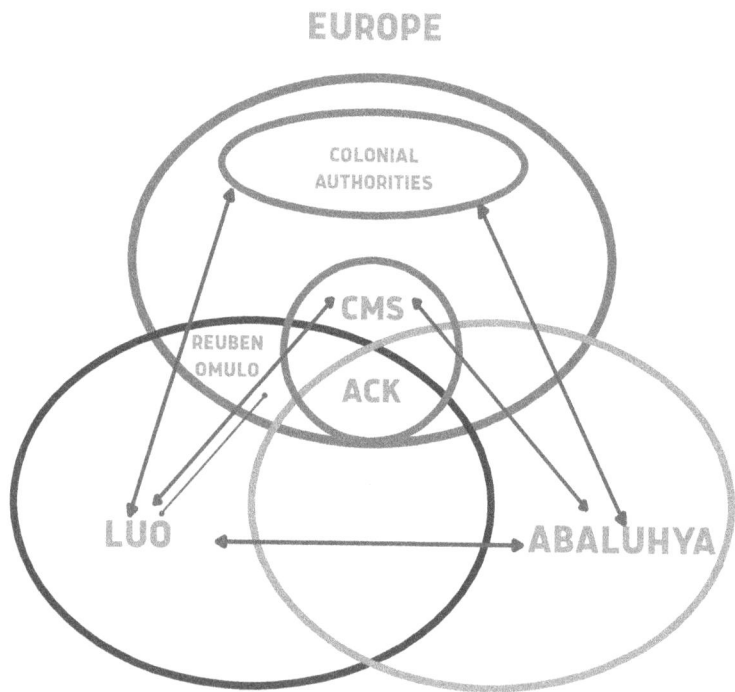

KEY
1. COLONIAL AUTHORITIES
2. COLONIAL AUTHORITIES -> LUO -> ABALUHYA
3. CMS -> LUO -> ABALUHYA -> REUBEN OMULO
4. LUHYA -> ABALUHYA -> COLONIAL AUTHORITIES
5. REUBEN OMULO -> CMS -> LUO -> ACK

Figure 2: Encounters Between the Luo, Abaluyia and the Europeans

1.7 The Nature and Structure of the Thesis
1.7.1 The Shaping Function of the Praxis Matrix

This is a missiological study of the unfolding encounters in Central Nyanza which uses the praxis matrix. As stated before, the focus was on the interaction between the mission praxes of Omulo and the CMS missionaries. It is necessary, however, to admit the existence of a third praxis involved in the research. That is my own. Kritzinger has pointed out that a researcher, especially a missiological researcher, cannot be neutral about the topic they are studying.[14] Hence, we should understand research as praxis. In this thesis, my praxis encounters the praxes of Omulo and CMS, which makes it a three-way encounter. For integrity reasons, I have therefore asked of my mission praxis the same questions I asked of others, by using the praxis matrix. This helped me enter the study without feigning neutral or value-free information, but acknowledging my assumptions, presuppositions, biases, and commitments.

Chapter	My praxis	The praxes of Omulo and CMS						
1	Ag/Spir							
2	CU							
3	EA	Ag	Cu	EA	IT	DA	R	Spir
4		Ag	Cu	EA	IT	DA	R	Spir
5								
6	IT							
7	DA/R							

Figure 3: Thesis Structure Highlighting Agencies of Omondi, Omulo and CMS

The interaction of my mission praxis with those of Omulo and CMS shaped the macrostructure of the thesis. I clarified the nature of my Agency (Ag) in chapter 1, where I explain my reasons for undertaking this project, declare my interests and show the overall intention, entry point, and purpose of the study. The Spirituality (Spir) dimension in my praxis, revealed in chapter 1, permeates through the other dimensions, expressed in an attentive spirituality of listening-observing and respect for neglected voices. I hinged

---

14. Kritzinger, "Using Archives Missiologically," 18–42.

the thesis on my Contextual understanding (CU) (chapter 2) and Ecclesial analysis (EA) (chapters 3 to 5). In chapters 3 to 5, I use the praxis matrix to explore the interaction between the praxes of Omulo and CMS. Chapter 6 has my Interpretation of the tradition (IT). Meanwhile, chapter 7 has my Discernment for future action (DA) and Reflexivity (R). Figure 3 below portrays this structure:

As I have already indicated, there are three praxes at play in this thesis' seven chapters. My praxis is the overarching praxis that interprets and defines the other two. Placing mine adjacent to the other two explains my limitation to fully explain them, hence opening the probability for diverse perspectives of the praxes. I discussed the two praxes from my perspective, exploring them as part of my Ecclesial analysis, thereby analysing the establishment and growth of the Anglican Church in Central Nyanza.

The praxis matrix not only shapes the macro structure of the thesis "vertically," by determining the flow of thought from chapter 1 to chapter 7. It also shapes the internal "micro" structure of chapters 3 to 5 "horizontally," by tracing the seven dimensions of the matrix in the praxes of Omulo and CMS respectively – in each historical period – and how those dimensions interacted.

1.7.2 An Overview of the Chapters

Some additional information about the following chapters will further clarify the thesis structure.

Chapter 2 presents the historical background and setting for the encounters between Omulo and CMS. It discusses the features of the Luo people, shaped by their encounters with their Abaluyia neighbours, the CMS missionaries,[15] and the British colonial authorities. It explores the transformative encounters that occurred in Central Nyanza before 1906, when the CMS missionaries began work there.

The central section of the thesis, chapters 3 to 5, does not only analyse the two praxis matrices of Omulo and the CMS side by side, in isolation from each other – an impression that the above figure could create. Instead, it explores

---

15. Nyanza region was part of Uganda until 1920 when it became part of Kenya and ecclesiastical authority transferred to Mombasa diocese. CMS work began in 1904 with a station established at Vihiga North Nyanza in 1905. But the major work among the Luo in Central Nyanza began in 1906, which is the focus of this study; see §3.3.2.

the dynamics of how they related to, encountered, and mutually influenced each other. It investigates how these two forms of praxis overlapped and intersected, noting the dynamics of their encounters with other communities as well. It highlights the nature and quality of those interactions, and how the different participants were transformed. This research juxtaposes the two mission praxes, revealing fault lines and points of conflict, convergence, and agreement.

Chapter 6 contains my theological reflection ("Interpreting the Tradition"), based on the findings in chapters 2 to 5, from examining the mission praxes of Omulo and the CMS. This interpretation of the Christian tradition emerged as I engaged with the central theological issues arising from the previous chapters. I evaluated the position adopted by both Omulo and the CMS, as well as how they influenced (or didn't influence) each other. I also identified the key theological priorities that need to be addressed for a relevant and transformative future mission praxis. This chapter also notes issues raised by the research that I could not deal with in this study, but that may be important for the understanding of the church and significant for mission studies. The chapter outlines them and makes recommendations for further research.

In chapter 7, I evaluated the research framework and method, to determine the efficacy of the praxis matrix as a method for studying mission. In this section, I appraised the praxis matrix and recommended its use for mission research. I also reflected on what the study has meant to me and described what I discovered about myself, mission and research, having used the praxis matrix.

1.8 Research Methodology

The praxis matrix, with its seven dimensions, provided the overarching framework for this research, but it needed to be complemented by several approaches, especially in understanding the context and ecclesial scrutiny, which are concerned with questions like "How do they [Omulo and the CMS] understand their community? What do they see as good and bad around them? What are the problems that they seek to address? How do they view the prior role of churches and religions in that community? How does that affect their present encounters?" (See §1.6.1 above.) To explore such questions, I used historical, ethnographic and orature approaches.

The research used historical methods, which according to Walliman involves the interpretation of documents and diaries, among other available written materials.[16] Borg and Gall defined historical research methods as "the systematic search for documents and other sources that contain facts relating to the historian's questions about past events and facts."[17] These filled the gaps left out of primary sources, such as eyewitness reports, original interviews and writings, and other original documents. It does this through criticism, by asking and researching to help determine truthfulness, acknowledge bias, include omissions, and prove consistency in data.

An ethnographic approach is evident throughout the study. Depicting a people group requires telling a credible, rigorous, and authentic story.[18] Ethnography gives voice to people in their local context, relying on verbatim quotations and "thick" descriptions of events.[19] This study tells the story through the voice of local people as they pursue their daily lives in their communities. Of particular interest to this research was how the Luo interpreted their behaviour themselves. Fetterman identifies the ethnographer both as a storyteller and a scientist; the closer the reader of an ethnography comes to the local point of view, the better the story and the better the science.[20] The ethnographer is interested in understanding and describing a social and cultural scene from an emic (insider's) perspective.

The adoption of an ethnographic approach was helpful for this study when describing culture, as it expressed both cultural behaviour and cultural knowledge. Each definition offers a starting point and a perspective from which to approach the Luo culture, describing what their existence is and what their symbols mean.

I carried this research out in an orate society. Therefore, I expected to extract data, the preserved knowledge, through orature tradition. African orature is the creative and imaginative art of composition that relies on verbal art for communication, that culminates in a performance and was popularized in the discipline of African literature and performance for the transformation

---

16. Walliman, *Research Methods*, 24–25.
17. Borg and Gall, *Educational Research*, 373.
18. Walliman, *Research Methods*.
19. Fetterman, *Ethnography: Step by Step*, 1.
20. Fetterman, 2.

of the society.[21] Prof. Micere Mugo avers, "Orature partakes in the social production and reproduction process of pre-colonial African communities.[22] The dynamics of composition, subject matter, and performance (distribution) show that orature contributes to the society's perpetuation of itself." Orature was a crucial bridge between written material and oral sources (oral narratives of living members who may recall the past events). Although such oral sources present a challenge because the people recalling don't always remember or interpret the story, because of the time-lapse, the information obtained can be corroborated, which adds value to the research.

1.9 Research Approaches

1.9.1 The Historical Background

The data for writing chapter 2 on the background and development of the Luo community and their settlement in Central Nyanza was obtained mainly from written sources.

1.9.2 The Mission Praxes of Reuben Omulo and the CMS

1.9.2.1 Field Research

I gathered data for chapters 3 to 5 from both primary and secondary sources. Field research made up a key source of information. It comprised personal interviews and discussions with a selected group of respondents from Siaya and Kisumu Counties. I selected the respondents from parishes where Omulo served, who included both clergy and laity of the ACK.

Primary data was collected using personal face-to-face interviews. I used a tape recorder during the interviews, to ensure the accuracy of the information that I gathered during interviews and to allow me to return to the interviews during data analysis. I did not transcribe the interviews for coding purposes, as is often done in qualitative research, since the "codes" that I used to examine and order the data were contained in the seven dimensions of the praxis matrix. In other words, my research was not intended to generate theory, but to apply an existing theoretical approach. The interviews were semi-structured, following the interview guideline attached to the thesis as

---

21. Mugo, *African Orature*.
22. Adéléke, "Theory and Practice," 222–227.

appendix 2, which is based on the matrix. However, in many interviews I allowed participants to speak freely about their memories of Reuben Omulo (if they had met him personally), their knowledge of Omulo and his teachings, and their impression of his role and impact in the establishment of the Anglican Church in Central Nyanza. In some cases, I interviewed a few people together as a family, who shared their memories and experiences as a group.

I interviewed only adults, over eighteen years of age, without regard to their literacy status. I obtained ethical clearance for this empirical investigation, as evidenced by the certificate issued by the South African Theological Seminary (SATS) in this regard (appendix 4).

I gathered data through the participant observation approach.[23] By being in the community as a researcher, I observed encounters of faith and culture and how people are taking part in God's mission.

1.9.2.2 Documentary Research

Secondary data were gathered from relevant published works and other written materials. I got helpful information from the following archives:

- Anglican Church of Kenya archives, Nairobi
- ACK Diocese of Maseno North and Butere's Chadwick's Library archives
- St. Paul's University Library archives, Limuru
- Kenya National Archives, Nairobi
- CMS archives at Birmingham University, Birmingham, UK
- Reuben Omulo's personal archives, Yala, Siaya County

I also drew data from other written sources, such as publications in anthropology, history, literature, theology and missiology from the period under review (1906–1970), and from more recent research data as well. These documents form part of the bibliography. Using multiple methods allowed for verifying the accuracy of the collected data.

---

23. Fetterman, *Ethnography: Step by Step*, 37–40, 100.

1.10 Literature Review

The Anglican Communion's grand history comprises the various histories of individual indigenous churches that emerged from the work of the Anglican mission agencies. The CMS mission praxis did not emerge in a vacuum. Encounters the CMS missionaries had abroad and locally shaped the organization's mission praxis, similar to what Jansen[24] observed in *God on the Border*,[25] which recognizes God's workmanship and orchestration in our human encounters, therefore happening in us, through us, despite us, before us, and after us. The prevailing worldviews also shaped the mission praxis because mission agencies and their missionaries were not immune to the imperial attitudes of the time. Their notion of European superiority, racism, and entitlement made some see Africa as the space for social mobility. They soon became recruits of the European civilization process when they used colonization to bring the Christian gospel to the peoples of the nations.[26]

It is noteworthy that, in the twentieth century, there was growing interagency cooperation, as manifested in the major missionary conferences where ideas and experiences in missions were shared.[27] For instance, the Kikuyu Conference of 1913, which laid the groundwork for interagency cooperation, sought to shape the future of Protestant mission and future church growth in Kenya. Each missionary agency, however, developed its own approach to the task, although most adopted approaches used by bigger missions.

An odd feature in mission practice was a discovery of variance between local approaches and the detailed central expectations of their agencies, including the CMS. Missionaries' relationships to their organizational structures vary. Strayer[28] described the setup of CMS authority structures and how these were manipulated by strongly individualistic, status-seeking missionaries. This made it difficult to tell whether the way CMS missionaries functioned in the local stations was typical of the CMS as a whole or whether individual missionaries were being innovative. A vital connection, therefore, ought to

---

24. Jansen, "God on the Border," 45–62.

25. Abbreviated version of her inaugural lecture delivered in Dutch as, "God op de grens: missiologie als theologische begeleiding bij grensoverschrijding," at the Protestantse Theologische Universiteit, 2008. I used the English version (2010).

26. Neill, *Christian Missions*, 140.

27. Reed, "Denominationalism or Protestantism," 207.

28. Strayer, "Anglicans in Kenya," xi, 174.

be made between the missionary work in the local context and the decisions made by the CMS in London on general matters of missionary policy, which might have had a significant effect on the local situation.

The CMS missionaries were dominant narrators of these stories, largely forming the historical material of the churches' stories. It portrayed the missionaries as responsible for expanding the church worldwide. In the memoir of Archdeacon Owen of Kavirondo, Richard praises Owen, a pioneer missionary in Nyanza who worked there for twenty years, for his courage, his fight for African liberty, his identification with Africans, his progressive ideas, and his social welfare activities.[29] Richards continues in this same vein of praising work by Western missionaries as the sacrificial work that enlightened the region.[30] However, the association of missionaries with the colonial enterprise affected the general impression nationals had of them. By the last half of the twentieth century, in the dying days of the colonial era, Comaroff and Comaroff viewed missionaries as "ideological shock troops for colonial invasion whose zealotry blinded them," besides being colonialism's "agent, scribe and moral alibi."[31] Such varying perceptions pose the danger of obscuring the indigenous church's story in the labyrinth of missionary stories, their negative baggage notwithstanding.

Thus, some national historians like Odwako,[32] Walaba,[33] and Onyango[34] have written to support the work of missionaries, by focusing on the mission projects such as education and healthcare services that benefited Africans. Others, like Ogot, remained critical, highlighting their perceived cultural insensitivity.[35] They argue that cultural conflicts of Western and African origin had formed the basis of the divisions in the general questions of marriage, dressing, naming, polygamy and who could partake of the sacraments. Of significance in their work was the position that the Anglican Church was ill-prepared to deal with the problems and schism that cropped up because of the cultural insensitivity of missionaries. However, Ogutu dismissed such

---

29. Richard, *Archdeacon Owen of Kavirondo*, 15.
30. Richards, *Fifty Years in Nyanza*.
31. Comaroff and Comaroff, "Africa Observed," 52.
32. Odwako, *Church and Education*.
33. Walaba, *Role of Christian Missionaries*.
34. Onyango, *Gender and Development*.
35. Ogot and Welbourn, *Place to Feel*.

reasoning and suggested that the breakaways or schisms stemmed from the manner of initiation and pace of growth of the missionary churches.[36] There is, therefore, a need to appraise Ogot and Welbourn's conclusions to set up the actual causes of the schisms, for they call for readjusting the mythology and the structure of the church in Africa, to accommodate Africans and make them "feel at home."[37]

The work of African religion historians will also inform this study. Such include Omulokoli, who studied the development of the Anglican Church among the Abaluyia (North Nyanza).[38] His research gives a helpful historical setting of the CMS mission work by mapping a chronology of the church's establishment when the entire region was one diocese.

The other is Nzioki, whose work on the development of the Anglican Church in Central Nyanza is another important study for this research.[39] Her work, besides being historical and descriptive, contains some level of analysis that shows how the church affected the Luo culture. She filled a vital information gap through her contribution to the understanding of the origin and growth of this church. This research seeks to make a deeper analysis of how Luo culture encountered the church, analysing the mutual influences rather than merely the influence of the CMS on Luo culture, as in Nzioki.[40]

The criticism of Christian mission, as highlighted by Sanneh,[41] often proceeds "by looking at the motives of individual missionaries and concludes by faulting the entire missionary enterprise as being part of the machinery of Western cultural imperialism." Sanneh calls for a different perspective, arguing that "Missions in the modern era have been far more, and far less than the argument about motives customarily portrayed."[42]

Farrimond's study represents a departure from the norm by examining the mission policy of the CMS, which sought to develop indigenous churches during the first half of the twentieth century. He examined "what

---

36. Ogutu, *Origins and Growth*, 25.
37. Ogot and Welbourn, *Place to Feel*, 132.
38. Omulokoli, "Historical Development."
39. Nzioki, "Development of the Anglican Church."
40. Nzioki.
41. Sanneh, "Christian Mission," 332.
42. Sanneh, 333.

the CMS's actual objectives were, and how it sought to reach these objectives."[43] Farrimond makes a significant observation in his study, namely that the histories of the indigenous churches around the world contribute to the grand historical narrative of the Anglican Communion and include the other local and non-Western players in this grand story. In this point, Farrimond differs from other missionary writers, African nationalist writers, and religious historians' claim that the missionaries established the church. He instead acknowledges the role African nationals played, arguing that Africans across the continent had shown a desire for Westernization at the time of European arrival. To them, Christianity provided access to a civilization and culture pattern. Bediako observes this when he argues that, for Africa, the missionary movements represented the first and most important facet of Western contact.[44] To adopt Christianity also meant acculturation into the world of Western civilization with its ideas and technology, so that with Christianity came Westernization.

Ward and Stanley assert, "one cannot come to adequate understandings of entire areas of the historical experience of many people and cultures . . . without addressing the impact of Christian missionary activity."[45] The environment of establishing the church reveals the complexities of the missionary scene and the varied nature of the African responses, making up the transformative encounters this research seeks to explore. Kritzinger makes a vital observation that mission encounters transform the "missionaries" or witnesses as much as the "missioned" or "receivers."[46] A careful study of these transformative encounters has the potential of opening new areas of knowledge on mission as the crossing of boundaries, which some missiologists have seen as the very nature of mission.[47] This research is interested in studying such transformative encounters (and attempts at transformative encounters) between people at a particular time and place.

Farrimond acknowledges his inability to bring to the fore the voices of the indigenous Christians who were the fruit of CMS policy.[48] In particular,

---

43. Farrimond, "Concerning the Development," 2.
44. Bediako, "Roots of African Theology," 58–65.
45. Ward and Stanley, *Church Mission Society*, 5.
46. Kritzinger, "Using Archives Missiologically," 3.
47. Bosch, *Witness to the World*, 248.
48. Farrimond, "Concerning the Development," 3.

he notes the role that non-Western mission agents, the pioneer generation of indigenous Christians, played and how the church took root in the local context. The converts were trained and recruited to serve in the mission, becoming key mission agents. Omulo is a good example of such a leader and is acknowledged by the Anglican Church to have had "great influence on the development of the Church in Nyanza."[49] Hence he was selected for this study. But the mission praxis of this fascinating and important Luo leader has remained virtually unresearched. This research explores how transformative encounters shaped Omulo's mission praxis.

1.11 Conclusion

In conclusion, to achieve the goals this study sets in this chapter, the research had to answer whether there was anything more in the Christian message itself, distinct from its educational and social aspects, that attracted the Luo people. What did religious innovators like Omulo see in the CMS praxis, which affirmed what he already believed so that he could use it to strengthen Luo identity and resilience in the face of many threats and challenges? Did Christianity meet spiritual needs that the traditional religions were less able to meet?

Having set the scene and explained the logic of the thesis in this opening chapter, the focus now moves to an exploration of the broader context of central Nyanza and the emergence of the Luo nation.

---

49. Provincial Unit of Research, *Rabai to Mumias*, 80.

CHAPTER 2

The Broader Context of Encounters in Central Nyanza

2.1 Introduction

The Luo people's experience, through their movement from their cradle land into Central Nyanza, forged them into the Luo nation[1] that CMS missionaries engaged in 1906.[2] The encounters with their African neighbours shaped aspects of the Luo world, preparing them for the encounter with Europeans, including the CMS missionaries. It was these transformative encounters, before 1905, between the Luo and the communities they encountered in Central Nyanza, that shaped mission praxes in the district. A description of the Luo people, their journey to Central Nyanza, and how they grew into a nation, as argued in this chapter, will provide a concise explanation of the historical experiences that later shaped the mission praxes that established the Anglican Church.

The Luo people of Central Nyanza, also known as the Southern Luo, are a product of both the community encounters and environmental changes in the five centuries of their southward migration from their cradle land in Southern Sudan. Their interactions with communities on that route, and the environmental changes they came across, can be observed in the notable

---

1. The concept of the Luo Nation exists both in academic journals and political discourse. Bible translators have also used it, arguing the notion of *ethne* referred to nations and peoples, not countries in the format we have today.
2. Cohen and Atieno-Odhiambo, "Ayany, Malo and Ogot," 275–279.

similarities to, as well as obvious differences from, their northern kin. During this southward trip, the Luo people gained dominance over the societies they encountered, so that at their eventual settlement in the Lake region, they had created a broad nation from where a group of them still spread to the greater East African region.

2.1.1 People the Luo Met in Central Nyanza

Having encountered the Bantus (see appendix 1) first in eastern Uganda, the Luo groups met other Bantus in Nyanza, making the Bantu, the Abaluiya, Abagusii and Abakuria their enduring neighbours. According to Ochieng', both the Abaluyia and Kisii people were the first migrants into the region.[3] Ndeda argues that since the region had been home to the Bantu people as far back as the Iron Age, it is plausible that the Gusii and Luyia are the descendants of the earlier Bantu groups who introduced iron smelting and iron tools to the region.[4] Ndeda considers the Kisii as related to the Abaluyia groups of the Abanyore and Maragoli, who split from them 600 years ago.[5] According to Were, they originated from the south end of Lake Victoria.[6] As they moved eastwards, they got separated from each other by the Kano plains and the Nandi escapement, the Abaluyia to the north, and the Kisii to the South.

The Abaluyia belong to the Niger-Congo Bantu-speaking linguistic group, found in Western Kenya north of Lake Victoria, where they form the largest concentration in the Western Province.[7] The Abaluyia were part of the great Bantu expansion out of Western-Central Africa around CE 1000. They journeyed into eastern Uganda from where they moved into their present locations between 1598 and 1733. The Abaluyia are a hybrid community founded by people of varied origins and cultures. Were agrees that they came from diverse directions to settle in what became Abaluyia land.[8] The earlier Bantus, Marama, Kisa and Idakho settled in the southern areas. Ndeda observes that the Abaluyia who arrived between CE 1450 and 1550 and settled

---

3. Ochieng', *Pre-colonial History*, 9.
4. Ndeda, "Population movement," 84.
5. Ndeda, 90.
6. Were, *History of the Abaluyia*, 59.
7. Bradley, "Luyia," 203.
8. Were, "Western Bantu Peoples," 190.

in the northern half were of Kalenjin origin.⁹ They were the ancestors of the Tachoni of Ndivisi and North Kabras, the Shieni of Marama, and the Nashieni, Tobe and Mulembwa of Wanga. The Mount Elgon Kalenjin, who kept their language and culture, are the Bongomek, Bok and Kony. Other Abaluyia groups arrived from eastern Uganda between 1598 and 1733, who according to Were are the ancestors of the Tiriki, Wanga, Bukhayo, Samia, Marama, Banyore, parts of Kabras, Busotso, Maragoli and Marachi.¹⁰ They settled in Central Nyanza until the Luo appeared and pushed them further away to the north and south.

These Bantu groups kept their clan identities despite embracing Abaluyia as their defining term. According to Mojola, "The term Abaluyia is a cover term for a cluster of several contiguous dialects found in Western Kenya and parts of eastern Uganda."¹¹ Linguist P. A. N. Itebete suggests the term and its cognates first came into existence in June 1935 as a cover term for the groups in Western Kenya now called by the name.¹² They brought it into popular vogue in the 1930s and 1940s to galvanize these groups into political solidarity, forging a new and singular ethnic identity, as was happening elsewhere in Kenya. A similar period included the creation of the Kalenjin group in the Rift Valley region, the Meru group in Central Kenya, and the Mijikenda on the coast. The cover term Abaluyia did not exist as the name of an ethnic group. What existed was a chain or continuum of mutually intelligible dialects, starting with Lubukusu and Tachoni in the extreme north, continuing to Lunyore and Lulogooli in the extreme south, and ending with Lusamia in the extreme west. Historian John Osogo, in *A History of the Abaluyia*, includes the Abasonga in the Kenyan Abaluyia cluster as neighbours of Abanyala and Abasamia of Busia. Rachel Angogo Kanyoro divides the Luyia into six groups, which she calls a practical grouping for literary purposes.¹³ For Were, the Abaluyia community emerged from fusing the pre-1500 Bantu settlers and the later Bantu migrants, thus concluding the Abaluyia are a cultural community.¹⁴

---

9. Ndeda, "Population movement," 92.
10. Were, "Western Bantu Peoples," 190.
11. Mojola, God *Speaks*, 115.
12. Itebete, "Language standardization," 93.
13. Angogo, Linguistic and attitudinal factors in the maintenance of Luyia group identity.
14. Were, *History of the Abaluyia*, 59.

2.2 Settlement of the Southern Luo

Ogot considers the period between 1500 and 1800 as the time of arrival and consolidation of the Luo in Central Nyanza.[15] It was a period marked with an exponential population rise, with an accompanying need for the acquisition of more land for agriculture, besides establishing territorial authority. These three centuries of settlement were untidy, irregular, unplanned, sometimes unorganized, yet executed with purpose. Each of the arriving groups acted independently of others, responding to their own impulses, often against each other. The settlement was a slow process thus, as Ogot suggests, allowing the Luo to either assimilate, subjugate, or force the Bantus out.[16] The dispersing Bantu groups went east of the lakeshore and the plains (Abaluyia), while others climbed to the higher lands, which they deemed safe (Gusii). The Bantus moved north and south of the Victoria Gulf in search of new homes. In most cases, however, other Bantu families chose peaceful co-existence. They assimilated and became Luo by language and culture. Dholuo became the prevalent language, yet the Bantu speakers had major settlements in Yimbo and Samia as early as the fourteenth century.[17] The population of the Luo increased, making them a majority in the region. Ayany attributes this to the cordial relationships the Luo forged with the Abaluyia.[18] Luo people seldom fought against the Abaluyia. It was likely the Luo groups fought each other, but they were kind and hospitable to outsiders, and the Abaluyia in particular. During famines, Luo people traded with the Abaluyia for food. In return, the Abaluyia often sought the help of Luo rainmakers and medicine-men.

During this period, a curious way of naming settlements occurred. Henceforth they named settlements after the pioneer leaders of their groups. Also, the groups became known by the names of the founders of the territory that they occupied. From the naming pattern, Ocholla-Ayayo observes:

> [W]e can determine when the Luo were still most mobile and when their way of life changed to a more settled way of life. At the time of their arrival in East Africa the groups used "Jo" prefix - Jok-Owiny . . . the prefix denotes people of- then the name of

---

15. Ogot, *History of the Luo*, 485.
16. Ogot, 497.
17. Ochieng', *People Around the Lake*, 2–3.
18. Ayany, *Kar Chakruok Mar Luo*, 32.

their leader. But when settlement began, we find the use of the prefix "Ka" being attached to name of the leader of the group e. g. Karachwonyo (the land of Chuonyo) Kadem (Dem country) or suggesting land ownership of the leader of the group, or the village of the leader.[19]

Thus, land was not just a crucial source of life but became a key part of Luo identity. And since Siaya was the original landing country for the Luo, it became a centre for the diffusion of Luo speakers into Kenya. As Cohen and Atieno-Odhiambo argued:

> Groups and lineages that have maintained settlements in Siaya are the "parents" of an expanding and dispersing Luo population. They spread east and south, across the Winam Gulf into south Nyanza and Tanzania, and more recently into the urban areas of East Africa. It is an ennobled landscape, for groups elsewhere to refer in their histories to sacred or original sites in what is today Siaya.[20]

A section Luo groups (see Appendix 1) were slow in adopting this shift. Cohen and Atieno-Odhiambo note the Owiny, unlike the Omolo groups, maintained a stronger association with fixed sites of settlements, but this attachment to their earlier settlements' sites did not wane, an experience they built in Bukooli and Alego.[21]

The land's ability to support the swelling population diminished with time. This set communities in conflict over the limited resources they required to support them. They desired more territory. The land Abaluyia occupied became the hotbed of many skirmishes involving the Luo against fellow Luo, and Luo against Abaluyia. These clashes did not prevent cultural exchanges or intermarriages between the Luo and their Bantu neighbours.[22] Luo people gained new agricultural skills as they settled in the land, courtesy of the Bantus who were now part of their society. The Luo needed to grow in agriculture, and not abandon their pastoral experience. Animal husbandry, for

---

19. Ocholla-Ayayo, *Traditional Ideology*, 17.
20. Cohen and Atieno-Odhiambo, *Siaya: The Historical*, 16.
21. Cohen and Atieno-Odhiambo, 19.
22. Ndeda, "Population movement," 95.

the Luo, found new meaning in economy and culture. They had large herds of cattle, goats and sheep that each clan brought with them into Nyanza, which allowed them to secure domination of the richest grazing areas, such as the river valleys of southern Nyanza and the Kano plains. Ayany highlights this:

> A mar Luo Bunyoro, no yudo ka gin gi dhok mogwarore chuth. E rawo margi Nyanza dhoudi mathoth ne ni kod dhok kuonde ka kuonde. Kendo ne gin ge jamni mang'eny putu. Jokisii, Maragoli, kod Wanyore ma noyudo osed dar e Nyanza neonge kod dhok ahinya kaka Luo ma ne rawo e pinyin ndalono.[23]

> *Translation:* When the Luo people left Bunyoro, they had large herds of cattle. At the time they arrived in Nyanza, many of the Luo clans had an enormous flock of livestock. The Abagusii, Abalogoli and Abanyore who had moved out of Nyanza in the wake of the Luo arrival did not have cattle.

The Luo groups diverged in their attitude to pastoralism. Cohen and Atieno-Odhiambo, in analysing the Owiny and Omolo groups,[24] recognized the Owiny group's "commitment to pastoralism and a valorization of cattle, particularly in rituals of governance."[25] They swapped pastoralism for agriculture in eastern Busoga. There, they traded the affinity towards cattle, and pastoral mobility, for established sites of settlement and agriculture, thus maintaining their pastoral tradition only for ritual reasons. The Omolo groups, however, developed a domestic economy based on livestock, pasturage and mobility during their sojourn in Western Uganda. This remained during their migration and settlement stage. They were slow to embrace settled communities in exchange for pastoralism while in Busoga and were not hasty to switch from pastoralism to fixed settlement life upon arrival in Alego, where they lived on the fringes, at the pasture, and not affecting the region.

The coming of Luo with cattle in Nyanza enticed cattle-raids from the Maasai Kipsigis and the Nandi. Ayany mentions the Maasai wandering across the land raiding cattle from any people they met, for, according to the Maasai,

---

23. Ayany, *Kar Chakruok Mar*, 29.
24. Cohen and Atieno-Odhiambo, *Siaya: The Historical*, 19–21.
25. Cohen and Atieno-Odhiambo, 19.

all cattle in the entire world belonged to them.[26] They claimed to have loaned cattle to other communities long ago for safe keeping. Thus, when they raided cattle, they were taking back what was theirs. This explains the Maasai raids for the Luo cattle during both day and night. Once more, Ayany observes how the Luo neutralised the day raids with ease, overcoming the raiders in their enormous groups.[27] The night raids were tougher to defend against in the initial periods of settlement. The Luo groups created bigger village clusters and erected defences in preparation for such assaults.

Cohen and Atieno-Odhiambo contend that *ligala*, the initial Luo settlements, were extensive walled homes, with built-up walls and dug out ditches referred to as *gunda bur*.[28] Ayany attributes the development of *gunda bur* to those frequent raids.[29] The *gunda bur* were large villages made up of fifty or more homesteads, thus putting many people together to dispel attacks. They dug trenches that looped around the villages, elevating them as a fortress. Climbing up the walls was difficult, which deterred their enemies from reaching the homes. These trenches were not unique to the Luo, but they used them effectively in preventing Maasai, Nandi and Kipsigis raids. The raids forced divided clans to unite to survive since staying in large groupings, in many villages together, gave them security. Clan unity became an important feature of the Luo, and grounds for nationhood.

When the expansion of the settlements became necessary, they built new homesteads, *dala*, outside the *gunda bur*. Several of those homesteads would then form new communities referred to as *gweng'* (locality). In the initial order, the *gwenge* (pl.) comprised agnatic kinsmen but included the Bantus, with whom they formed pacts for mutual survival. A group of *gwenge* existed as security alliances against invaders and provided the labour required for developing unused lands, done in cooperation and for trade networks. Such locality developed gradually. It began with a single group followed by a neighbourhood group, and then a whole band of people infiltrated the areas the Bantus had occupied.[30] These alliances played a crucial role in helping the

---

26. Ayany, *Kar Chakruok Mar*, 29.
27. Ayany, 30.
28. Cohen, and Atieno-Odhiambo, *Siaya: The Historical*, 14.
29. Ayany, *Kar Chakruok Mar*, 30.
30. Ndeda, "Population movement," 95.

Luo people settle in the unused lands. They learned and benefited from the Bantu speakers' experience of sedentary life where they cultivated grain, rice and bananas. Fishing was central to the Luo customs and economy. The Luo migration introduced pastoralism and new crops like sorghum, groundnuts and *simsim*, brought from eastern Uganda. These became products of trade.

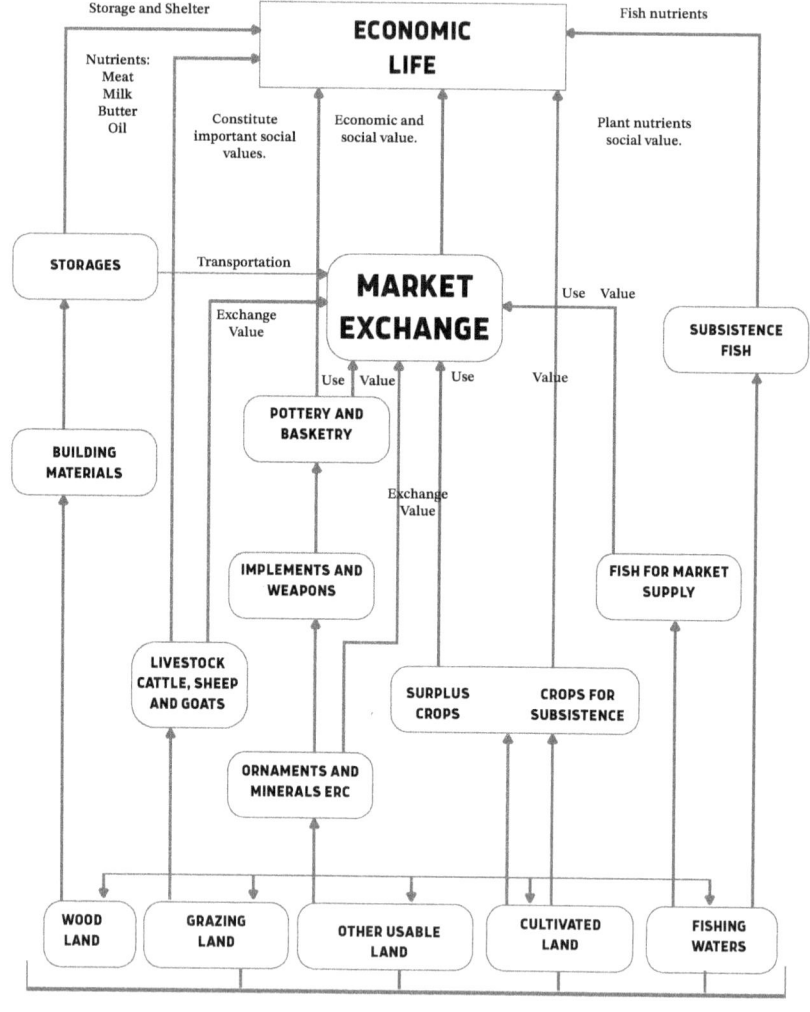

Figure 4: Transformation and Growth in the Luo Pre-literate Society[31]

---

31. Adapted from: Ocholla-Ayayo, *Traditional Ideology and Ethics*, 21.

In figure 4, Ocholla-Ayayo describes the booming economic life of the Luo society in Central Nyanza from the time they settled and throughout the colonial period:[32]

2.2.1 Luo Consciousness

During the eighteenth century, the Luo forged an ethnic consciousness, but not out of the purity of lineage.[33] The Luo had assimilated diverse and sizable peoples in their midst. It became imperative to settle them within the Luo society while keeping the dispersing Luo clans connected. They had to create Luo oral traditions. These stories of their origin are still held sacrosanct despite many years of journeying and extensive interactions with different communities. The Luo historical traditions offer narratives going back to the world's beginning.

They developed elaborate genealogies to prove the common origin of the Luo, thus attaching mythological figures such as Jok, Podho, Sinakuru, and Twaifo to their clan genealogies.

Evans-Pritchard asserts, "all the Luo clans ultimately trace their descent from the same mythological name of Podho and Ramogi, so that it would be possible to place them all on a single chart of Descent."[34] But evidence exists of groups tracing their ancestry to the Bantu, or other Nilotic groups, the progeny of the assimilated groups, to challenge this position. In refuting the notion of the Luo people's common eponym, Jo-Ramogi, Ogot asserts:

> [T]his belief that all the Luo are descended from a single eponym is the product of a later age during which Luo history and Luo nationality had been constructed. A close look at traditional evidence, however, reveals that different clusters of Luo clans arrived separately in Nyanza and at different times. Three major clusters have been discerned: a. Jok'Ojok b. Jok'Owiny c. Jok'Omolo. Then other Luo groups exist such as the Luo-Abasuba, Sakwa, Asembo, Uyoma, and Kano whose histories

---

32. Ocholla-Ayayo, *Traditional Ideology and Ethics*, 21.
33. Ogot, *History of the Luo-speaking*, 520.
34. Evans-Pritchard, "Luo Tribes and Clans," 30–31.

deserve separate treatment. But these Luo cluster groups were not homogeneous: they incorporated many non-Luo elements.[35]

There exist different versions of Luo genesis that emerged around this time. But we have unanimity in the version that affirmed the Luo descended from Podho, who fell from the sky, hence the name Podho. He was dropped at Lamogi or Ramogi hill in northern Uganda. He introduced food crops such as millet, and sorghum as well as cattle, fowls, spears, shields, and fire. After he died, his son Ramogi Ajwang' migrated to Nyanza, settling at Ramogi hill in Yimbo.

Through the creation of a mythical figure in Podho, the Luo formed the society around a belief in a shared beginning of the world and the Luo nationality. The Luo speakers were called Joka Podho, in the Upper Nile region of the Sudan, in their history.[36] We can understand Podho to mean "the land of the people," or "the mother-earth," a term that was later personified into an "Adam of the Luo." Ogot infers:

> If Podho is regarded as the Adam of the Luo, Ramogi features in their traditions as their Abraham . . . The biblical parallel would be that the Podho phase of Luo history corresponds to the first eleven chapters of the book of Genesis, and the Ramogi-Jok phase with the patriarchal stories, as contained in the second section for Genesis from Chapter 12 to the end of the book.[37]

Regarding religion and worship, the Luo also gained a new vocabulary from the Bantu whom they assimilated. While in central Nyanza, they dropped the familiar name for God, *Jok/Juok*, used by their Nilotic kith and kin, for the Bantu name, *Nyasaye*. The Luo groups in Sudan and Northern Uganda called God *Jok/Juok*, but since settling in Nyanza they adopted *Nyasaye*, which they shared with both the Abaluyia and Abagusii. Others among them called God *Were*, the same name used by the Abaluyia.

---

35. Evans-Pritchard, "Luo Tribes and Clans," 30–31.
36. Ogot, *History of the Luo-speaking*, 486.
37. Ogot, 486–487.

2.2.2 Organization of Luo Society

Ndeda acknowledges that the Luo movement into Western Kenya faced political, social, and economic complications.[38] They devised a political society of discontinuous Luo groups out of diverse communities. This chiefdom differed from what they had known during the journey, although it incorporated aspects of their past principles. The Owiny group, for instance, felt entitled to the Luo chiefdom-ship and were sanguine about it. They developed a new centre of authority embodied in the term of *Karuoth*[39] the royal family. Cohen and Atieno-Odhiambo observe, "Owiny groups carried into eastern Busoga and Alego an aura of prestige and particular ideas of domination and subordination that would play crucial roles later in the institutionalisation of political control in later generations."[40] Thus, scholars credit the *Karuoth* concept for the genesis of a centralised authority among the Luo in Central Nyanza in the Alego state.

The *Doho* was the local law court and dealt with matters within its local territory. They heard cases of both a civil and criminal nature. There was a police force, the *ogulmama*, to enforce judgments of the *Doho*.[41]

The *Karuoth* concept led to conflicts with the inheritors of traditional Luo authority manifested in the cradle land. Such included the Omolo groups, who concealed their dominance during their migration period only to manifest it late in the pre-colonial period. Ogot argues that "the emergence of states controlled by Luo-speakers or former Luo speakers as a result of a small, well-organised group successfully imposed its rule over a disorganised majority."[42] The *Oganda* (pl. *Ogendni*) concept articulates this organizing by the Luo, showing how the pre-European Luo society organized its political, judicial, and economic systems. *Ogendni* varied in sizes ranging from 10,000 to 70,000 people, divided into twelve or thirteen groups,[43] thus existing separately but formed from lineages of patrilineal clans, which were further subdivided into smaller patrilineal segments. In this way, they provided the link between the

---

38. Ndeda, "Population movement," 95.
39. The *Karuoth* idea gives emphasis to inherent and hereditary capacity and surrounds all members of a family with an aura of privilege.
40. Cohen and Atieno-Odhiambo, *Siaya: The Historical*, 20.
41. Ocholla-Ayayo, *Traditional Ideology and Ethics*, 90.
42. Ogot, "Kingship and Statelessness among the Nilotes," 298.
43. Ogot, "British Administration," 52.

territory and the lineage groupings. At the apex of the Luo societal stratum was the *Oganda*. Each *Oganda* had its own *Ruoth* (chief), who were prophets in some clans, but they were all jural-political leaders. Ogot explains that the *Ruoth* did not rule alone but through Buch-Piny (tribe council), which comprises clan elders (*jodong dhoot*), the peacemaker (*ogaye*) and the war leaders (*osumba mirwayi*).[44] This made up the *Doho Ruoth*, the highest court of the tribe, which formed the peoples' court of appeal. Below it was the tribal court (*Doho Dhoot*), headed by the tribal head (*jatend dhoot*), helped with heads of *Libembni* as council members. Each head of *Libamba* led a *Doho Libamba*. His council was comprised of heads of *Keche* (a group of villages). Each village head led a *Doho gweng'* (village court), which consisted of *jodong' mier* (head of villages). The head of a village, *jaduong dala* (head of homestead), formed a village forum which was a court at home level, led by the head of each homestead. (See hierarchy of leadership in figure 5.)

2.2.3 Luo Heroes and the Rise of States

The Alego state is one of the two earlier states, other than the Kadimo in Yimbo, established in Central Nyanza. The Kadimo State lacked territorial space for expansion and so focused on containing its internal dissections. While the Alego State strived to consolidate her domestic and regional power against the Omolo groups encroaching on her territory, the Omolo imperial ambition triggered the Omolo-Gem to create a state of their own, which existed into the colonial period. The period 1850–1905 became the age of Luo heroes. It characterised the age of protracted conflicts over land, out of which *thuondi Luo* (eminent warriors and heroes both men and women) emerged, by leading their clans in wars. Such included Nyawade *wuod* Ojak from Ugenya Kager clan, Ogutu *woud* Kipapi from Yimbo, Nyagudi *wuod* Ogambi from Seme, Okore *wuod* Ogonda from Kisumu Kogony and Tawo K'Ogot from Alego Mur. Ayot recognises women heroes, the *nyiri mathuondi* or *mon mathuondi* or *thound mon*, who led female regiments and fought alongside men.[45] There are two most mentioned, Owigo and Odete *nyar* Olonde from Karachuonyo, who fought against the Bantu groups of the Waswa and Kakseru and against Jo-Kagan, a Luo group.[46]

---

44. Ogot, 52.
45. Ayot, *Historical Texts of Lake Region*, 232.
46. Ogot, *History of the Luo-speaking*, 232–237.

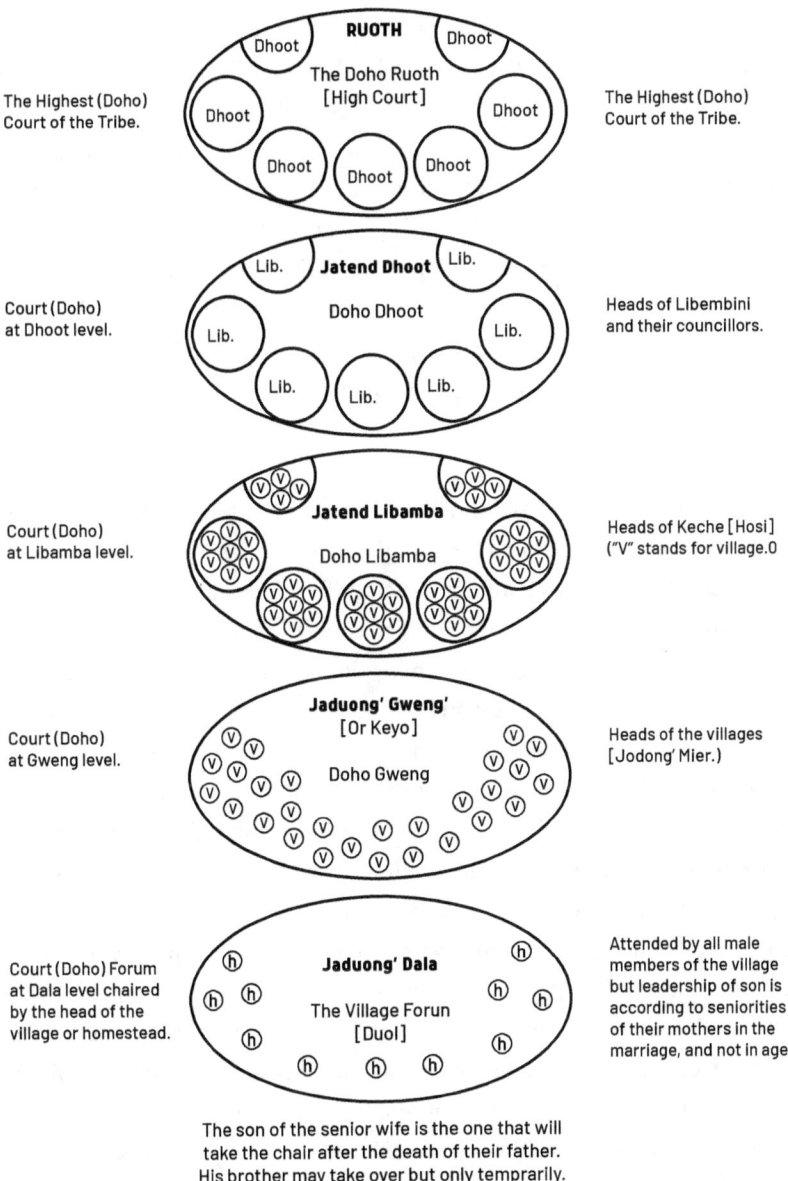

Figure 5: Structure of the Luo Legal Institution[47]

Some earned fame throughout Luo land for their heroics. Lwanda Magere is one such Luo hero. The Nandi often raided people in Nyanza, and later

---

47. Ocholla-Ayayo, *Traditional Ideology and Ethics*, 91.

the Arab slave merchants carried out raids. Baker cites the raids as a reason for Luo's mistrust of strangers and their difficulty in making friends.[48] At the inception of the nineteenth century, a clan of Laibons expelled from the Maasai became chiefs of the Nandi people. They organised the Nandi in a grand raid upon the Luos. But in one raid, the Nandi suffered one of the worst defeats ever noted in stories of African tribal wars. Baker notes, "850 men were slaughtered in this battle, which ended the raids."[49] The Luo hero, Lwanda Magere in Kano, became a Luo legend and a distinguished warrior who subdued the Nandi, but he was murdered by a Nandi woman he married, in an episode like that of Samson and Delilah.

2.2.3.1 The Alego State

Ruoth Onyango emerged as a Jo-Alego hero after the 1820s, after he subdued Jo-Ugenya who had occupied their land between 1650 and 1700.[50] Onyango created an organised government structure for his people. He was in charge as the moral and political leader of Alego country (*piny*). Onyango appointed agents, giving them responsibility in his domain. He instituted and chaired *Buch Piny*, which he ruled by striving to reach consensus on all matters, upon the advice of his council. He had no absolute power, but it was his call to declare war. Since he was the custodian of the country's laws and customs, he had a duty to accord his subjects fair administration of justice. His subjects turned to him as a peacemaker in conflicts. They expected fairness from him, for he was the final mediator in matters affecting his subjects.[51] The Alego people established an elaborate system of selection and installation of the *ruoth* in office. *Joduong Ngaga* (college of electors) elected the *ruoth*. Upon election, the *ruoth*-elect was anointed and presented with a Luo spear, a Luo stool and a shield made from buffalo skin. *Buch Piny* confirmed the *ruoth* into office and conducted an installation ceremony with the *jobilo* and the college of electors. The *ruoth*-elect was given the ceremonial spear (*tong liswa*), the spear of Alego, inherited from his predecessor. Ogot notes: "These objects are symbols of the unity of a sub-nationality, a clan or a lineage, and they

---

48. Baker, *Short History of Nyanza*, 10.
49. Baker, 10.
50. Ogot, *History of the Luo-speaking*, 603.
51. Ogot, 600.

were used in times of war or common calamity, such as drought, famine or Locust invasion."⁵² What kept the *ruoth* in office was his personal charisma and statesmanship, not the elaborate structures and rituals. The state structure empowered the Alego people to build trade and religious contacts with neighbours. These communities sought the services of Alego's rainmakers or medicine men and women. Hence the Alego traders became middlemen in the iron trade (e.g. hoes, spearheads) between Samia (Bantu), and Gem, Yimbo, Asembo, Sakwa, and Usonga (Luo groups).

2.2.3.2 The Gem State

Jo-Gem built their state in the shadows of the Alego state. Between 1820–1830, they began settling in eastern Alego, a united community with institutionalised *ruoth*-ship already developed in Yimbo. Their *Buch Piny* was functional and accommodated the assimilated clans in its leadership. Ogot asserts that they based the leadership on the Gem clan divisions of Joka-Kwenda and Jok-Ojuodhi. *Ruoth* Rading Omolo of the Kojuodhi clan chaired the *Buch Piny* and was deputized by Ayieko of Joka-Kwenda, where they made major decisions affecting the Jo-Gem.⁵³ The Gem group displaced the Umuswa people (Bantu) and established settlements on either side of river Yala in eastern Alego, where they built *gundni buche*, at several sites.⁵⁴ It was a growing state. (See appendix 1.)

2.3 The Luo War and Conflicts

2.3.1 Inter-Luo Wars

With an established territorial state and institutions set by 1800, the Alego state experienced threats from the Omolo groups within their territory in central and north Alego. They wanted to evict Jo-Ugenya, who between 1650 and 1700 had settled in the Alego land, on which they were establishing an alternative state. Under pressure, part of Jo-Ugenya had surrendered to Alego's supremacy. Alego thought Jo-Gem a greater security threat. Jo-Gem settled

---

52. Ogot, 600.
53. Ogot, 621.
54. Bungu Ochilo (Ochilo son of Ndunya). Rakuom Komonge; Ochok (*gunda bur* belonging to Ayieko the son of Oti, Nyadude Ombok son of Olwasi); Ojalo and the *gunda bur* belonging to Rading' Omolo.

in east Alego for a generation without Alego's assent. Following the sleeping sickness epidemic at the outset of the nineteenth century in Malanga, Alego South, the demand to move the populace brought land occupied by Gem into focus. The state resolved to retake the land and settle the Mur and Nyala clans there but had to eject the Gem people first. Alego deployed warriors from Mur, Nyala, Agoro and Kaluo clans for the operation. Of the several battles fought, two were momentous: the one at Nyawara Hill and the other at Gunda Siala. Rabuogi Achieng from Agoro clan forced down the hitherto impregnable walls of Gunda Siala, a well-buttressed base of Jo-Gem and the Mur and Nyala warriors captured Nyawara Hill, a strategic stronghold for Jo-Gem people. Ogot mentions this triumph as having restored peace and security to the Alego country. People started moving from *gundni buche* to build their own homes (*mier*).[55]

Ejected from Alego, Jo-Gem encroached on land already occupied by other Luo groups, which included the land of Jo-Kisumo, Jo-Seme and Jo-Sakwa. These encounters ended in battles. *Ruoth* Rading' Omolo believed that their security would come from an alliance of Luo tribes. He was aware of the security threat posed by the Bantu communities. Rading' reached out to *Ruoth* Otiende, son of Rombo of Jo-Kisumo, proposing an alliance. Otiende dismissed Rading' with disdain, bragging: "Ja Kondo ok wuogi e rot, Rading' mondo otug mana gi Mwache" (One who wears a hut should not exit through a breach in the fence, let Rading' fool around with the Bantus). But Rading' persisted. He sent a second envoy to Otiende, beseeching him to accept his proposal to no avail.[56] Rading' died with the pact un-concluded. His successor, *Ruoth* Odera Rangira, had a different security policy. He concluded that Jo-Kisumo were the greatest impediment to security and attacked them. As a result, Jo-Gem and Jo-Kisumo fought in two battles. They first fought at Lundha, and defeated Jo-Kisumo, thus occupying their area. Here they built new villages, while Ndere remained their main *gunda bur* (Ndere Karading'). The second followed the battle at Regea where the Jo-Gem defeated the AbaMarama. Jo-Gem pushed Jo-Kisumo to *got* Maseno, and further on to Pap Onyoso, bringing cessation of war with Jo-Kisumo.

---

55. Ogot, *History of the Luo-speaking*, 622.
56. The site where Rading' beseeched Otiende in Gem was named *Asayi* (I beseech you).

Having defeated Jo-Kisumo, Jo-Gem opened a new battle frontier with Jo-Seme clan of Jo-Kanyikal. According to Ogot, this encounter led to two wars.[57] In the first battle, Jo-Seme overpowered Jo-Gem, driving them out of their settlements on the southern part of River Yala except in Sipoklo Kaduol. The second battle saw a new Gem hero emerge in Odera Ulalo, son of Omole. He had just succeeded his uncle Odera Rangira as *Ruoth* of Gem and led his troop to success. Jo-Gem subdued Jo-Seme, pushing them southwards towards the lake.

2.3.2 Luo – Abaluyia Wars

2.3.2.1 *Ugenya vs. Wanga*

The Ugenya retreating from the Alego aggression crossed into northern forested banks of the river Nzoia. Owino explains how they entered this county in small unsuspected groups. As a result, the Bantus welcomed and merged with them through marriage.[58] In time new multi-lingual and multicultural communities developed, like the Umugusa, Umuswa, Urinda, Usumunya, Kamrembo. The details of this interaction are noted by Osogo:

> [B]efore the arrival of the Iteso people in 1840s, the Marachi, Samia and Ugenya clans interacted peacefully, trading and intermarrying. Former Samia settlements were Luonized as was former Marachi settlements at Sega, Yenga... The intermarriage was so intensive that the historian John Osogo, himself a Muluyia, had to confess that it is now difficult to ascertain whether the Abafofoyo clan of Marachi was Luo or Luyia in the origin.[59]

Not all Bantus in the region welcomed the Luo groups. Such included the Marachi, Bukhayo, Abakholo (Kakeny), Wanga and Marama. Jo-Ugenya had to contend with them. Led by their Kager clan, they embarked on building a defence army by forging a local alliance with the assimilated Bantus. They soon had to resist the Wanga and the Iteso.

---

57. Ogot, *History of the Luo-speaking*, 629.
58. Owino, "Colonial Neutralization," 94–95.
59. Osogo, *History of the Baluyia*, 36.

The Iteso people, according to Ogot, reached Western Kenya about 1850.[60] Ogot suggests the ancestors of the Teso people came from the area between Mount Elgon, Mount Kadama and the Suk hills of Western Uganda, from where they migrated to Western Kenya by an eastern route.[61] Their arrival disturbed the region's harmony. The Iteso provoked wars by plundering for crops and cattle in the land. But Jo-Ugenya defeated the Iteso and occupied the abandoned territory, building a buffer between them. By 1850, the Ugenya had expanded to the banks of Soi River. Their victory sparked a quest for solidarity among the Abaluyia. Chief Dindi of the Bukhayo appealed to the Iteso, Marachi and later the Wanga to create an alliance as a counterforce against the Luo.[62]

The Jo-Ugenya incursion into the Owiny land on the edge of the Wanga Kingdom, threatened Chief Shiundu, the new Nabongo of the Wanga who had begun his reign in 1840. He thought it urgent to find viable alliances to stop Jo-Ugenya. Tribal alliances, according to Ogot, were for political hegemony and territorial extension.[63] Thus, Were noted the Ugenya-Kager allied with Jo-Gem and the Abakholo against the Wanga alliance of the Marama, Abamumia, Wanga Mukulu and the Maasai.[64] The Wanga brought in the Marimba who aided them three times at Musanda and once at Eshikangu.[65]

In the battles that followed, the victorious Kager clan captured the Wanga territory of Bukaya and Musanda. They occupied Shikalame before being stopped at the Imanga hill. The Kager instead shifted to the out-lying areas of Lukoba, Abamumia, and later Lurego and Ekeru, forcing the Wanga to retreat further inland. Dealing notes, "At the end of Shihundu's lifetime . . . all the Wanga territory up to Imanga and Kusimu river had fallen to the Luo",[66] that is, the land to the south of the Lusimu river, including Ejinja.

The defeat forced Shiundu to move his capital from Lurego to Mwilala, and in surrender sought peace with Jo-Kager. So, in the "*ng'ado guok*"

---

60. Ogot, *History of the Southern Luo*, 116.
61. Ogot, *History of the Luo Speaking*, 453.
62. Osogo, "Reverend Alfayo Odongo Mango," 1.
63. Ogot, *History of the Luo-speaking*, 611.
64. Were, *History of the Abaluyia*, 137. Shiundu gave refuge to the Moitanik Maasai, fleeing the civil turmoil in Uasin Gishu to settle in his kingdom in return for military services.
65. Were, *Western Kenya Historical Texts*, 153.
66. Dealing, "Politics in Wanga," 199.

(peace covenant) rite, Shiundu gave his two daughters in marriage to their Ugenya enemies to ratify peace. His daughter Wasamba married Opondo Ka-Murembo of the Kager clan, while Ademba, his other daughter, married Gero K'Okado of the Puny clan. As Dealing observes, this peace lasted until the Arab-Swahili slave traders appeared. Then the battles erupted anew.[67]

2.3.2.2 Gem versus Abaluyia

The defeat and banishment of the Jo-Gem from Alego transformed them into one of the most powerful warrior-states in the region. Jo-Gem used a wide range of tactics to get victory. They revived old alliances and built new ones with both the Luo and the Abaluyia people. In separate incidents they suggested and secured peace pacts to avoid war. Only when these measures failed did they go to war and pillage their opponents. Having conquered and pushed out the Luo groups Jo-Kisumo and Jo-Seme, they had to confront the Bantu people on whose country they began encroaching. They encountered resistance from Aba-Umani and Aba-Kisa, while Jo-Yiro and Aba-Umsuwa welcomed and backed them.

The persistent cattle raids on Gem settlements compelled them to attack Aba-Umuswa against their intentions. They overwhelmed the Aba-Umuswa and scattered as far out as Kano (Jo-Kamswa in Wang'aya), while chief Waudi led another Umuswa group to the Wanga where they became identified as the Abamasawa. Waudi moved to Ulohowe where he died. Years afterwards, the Gem chief Odera Rangira, mindful of Waudi's and Aba-Umuswa's generous reception, invited them back to north Gem.[68]

Jo-Gem capitalised on intra-Abaluyia animosities to further reduce them. They took sides in the feud between Aba-Kisa and Aba-Umani in the battle of bar Malanga. Gem supported Aba-Kisa to subdue the Aba-Umani, who fled to Udura among the Abatura in North Wanga. Later, the Ojuodhi clan heads of Gem called them back and worked out a blood brotherhood pact with them.

In the conflict against the Marama over Regea Hill, Sathala, and Ugingo, Jo-Gem sought help from Jo-Ugenya. They routed the Marama by pushing them to Siraha. But Ogot[69] notes that the fiercest battle was the one against

---

67. Dealing, 20.
68. Ogot, *History of the Luo-speaking*, 625.
69. Ogot, 625.

Aba-Kisa. It had signs of all the strategies Gem had used. At first, *Ruoth* Oloo Ramoya explored a co-existence path with Aba-Kisa and requested the ritual of *ng'ado guok*. He sent the proposal to the Kisa leaders. Sijwaya favoured this proposal and debated it at the Aba-Kisa leaders' assembly. But the Kisa war leaders Ombonya ali Elwayi and Ombato overruled him. They assumed Jo-Gem were worn out from their battles with Jo-Kisumo and thought it was their chance to break them. It was an arrogant response. According to Ogot, *Ruoth* Ramoya declared war against Aba-Kisa, saying: "*Ero gigochonwa gi thuondi ariyo, wan bende wagochni gi gi thuondi ariyo*" (Since they have thrown down the gauntlet at us, we shall take it up).[70] Jo-Gem, therefore, fought Aba-Kisa at Nyamninia and vanquished them, leaving Ombonya ali Elwayi and Ombato dead. However, the Kisa clan of Ugambri refused to capitulate. In the war against them, the battle at Anyiko was fiercest. During this battle, Jo-Gem lost gallant warriors but crushed the Kisa people. Contrary to Luo ethics the Luo warriors descended on the Kisa villages, looting and killing women. They also carried away many young girls from Kisa.

After the war, Jo-Gem assimilated the Kisa survivors into Luo society, therefore increasing both population and territory. The Gem state turned into an impressive community through building alliances. This tactic would continue until the coming of the Europeans. *Buch Piny* of Gem decided on alliances with other communities, Luo or non-Luos. Ulalo cemented Gem's alliance with Jo-Bunyore (Bantu) and Jo-Asembo (Luo) by marrying into their families. Odera married Ayieko, the daughter of Nganyi, an influential leader of the Abanyore and a famous rainmaker. Ayieko was the mother of Mathayo Onduso, a founding student at CMS Maseno in 1906. He afterwards became Chief of Gem between 1914 and 1917.[71] Sometimes Jo-Gem gave military backing to their allies. For instance, chief Nganyi sought Ulalo's service against the Umuri and Uyalo (Embuyalu), two Bunyore clans challenging his authority. The Gem-Bunyore forces crushed Aba-Umuri. While some retreated into Seme, others took sanctuary in Gem as *jomotur* (refugees). But they failed to crush the Uyalu people. Fearing the repercussions, Nganyi's people fled, some to Seme, others to Kisumo, and a larger group moved to Gem. After

---

70. Ogot, 627.
71. Ogot, 630.

these wars the Banyore and Kisa people living north of River Yala became Ulalo's subjects.

Jo-Gem society comprised *jodak* (clients allowed to farm and live in Gem). They included Jo-Umoya, Jo-Usula and Jo-Ndagaria who had joined Gem much earlier in Alego. The *jomotur* (refugees) and assimilated people, both Luo and non-Luo, included Bantu groups like Jo-Umswa, Jo-Umani, Aba-Kisa and Abanyore, some of whom they fought and defeated.

2.3.2.3 *The Slave Raiders*

The slave merchants' raids had a considerable effect on how Central Nyanza people accepted the Europeans. For some Luo groups, the raids created a need for cooperating with a more formidable power, while for others, resisting the slave traders exposed and marked them as targets of imperial aggression. Slave raids occurred in both South and Central Nyanza. In South Nyanza, Ochieng' states that traders based on Mageta Island sailed south to Uyoma, Rusinga, Mfangano Island and South Nyanza where they ambushed women, men and even elders.[72] They sold most of their slaves to the Baganda, who would then sell them to the Arabs. But they kept some slaves to work on Mageta banana plantations. Hartwig[73] recounts the activity of Songoro, the slave trader in the region who acted as an agent for the Ganda. He transported Ivory from Kageyi to Unyanyembe and in the process gained many slaves.

The most consequential slave raids in Nyanza were by the Arab and Swahili traders coming through the Wanga. Sayyid Said's decision to transfer his capital from Oman to Zanzibar in 1840 spurred the Arab-Swahili ventures into the interior of East Africa.[74] They traded in guns, ivory, exotic animal skins, ghee, honey, and other trade goods. By 1875 the Arab merchants had appeared in the Wanga kingdom. Salim states that visitors to the region noticed the presence and fraternity of the Arabs in and with Mumias people.[75] Carl Peters, according to Dealing, arriving in Mumias in 1890, found an Islamic demeanour exhibited in the dress and language of the local people.[76] In the

---

72. Ochieng', *History of Kadimo Chiefdoms*, 48.
73. Hartwig, *Art of Survival*, 125–126.
74. Salim, *East Africa in the Nineteenth Century*, 220.
75. Salim, *Swahili-Speaking Peoples*, 32.
76. Dealing, "Politics in Wanga," 280.

same year, Frederick Lugard met Mumia and noted that Mumia was fluent in good Swahili.[77] John Ainsworth, the Provincial Commissioner of Nyanza (1902 to 1907), attests to the Arabs and Swahili joining Mumia in his courts.[78]

As claimed by Were, Mumia used the Arabs and Swahili in an expedition against their enemies.[79] He not only asked the Arab-Swahili for guns, but their direct participation in the wars. Dealing notes that Mumia trashed peace deals he had reached with neighbours, like Jo-Ugenya.[80] It was against this background that the Arabs-Swahili began incursions into Luo land, raiding slaves and cattle. The result was a direct confrontation of the Arab Swahili and the Wangas with the Luo people. Owino narrates how the Ugenya leaders were at first hesitant to retaliate on account of the peace deal with Shiundu, chief of the Wanga.[81] They sent Opondo ka Murembo and a famous *jabilo* Omoro K'Omolo to request a halt of the Arab-Swahili and Wanga slave raids on Ugenya, but he ignored their plea. It was then that the Ugenya people attacked to protect against the now frequent slave raids. Jo-Ugenya defeated the Wanga and his allies, who lost many lives and properties. But in the subsequent battle, Jo-Ugenya got crushed and pushed back from Musanda to Sigomre, and their people were scattered into Gem and Alego. But in the 1885 war, with the support of Jo-Gem, Jo-Ugenya gallant warriors crushed the Wanga Arab-Swahili alliance, despite the latter having guns and ammunition, and occupied more of the Wanga's land. Were notes that Jo-Ugenya occupied the gates of Lurego (Mumias).[82] Lonsdale confirms that the Luo of Ugenya reached the walls of Mumias.[83]

2.4 The Luo-European Encounters

The coming of the Europeans into Nyanza upset the Luo world. As the colonial regime dominated the region with force and propped up the Wanga Kingdom, they stopped the continued Luo incursion into the Abaluyia land.

---

77. John Osogo, *Nabongo Mumia*, 9.
78. Provincial Commissioner Nyanza, Report 1904, 109.
79. Were, *History of the Abaluyia*, 125.
80. Dealing, "Politics in Wanga," 278.
81. Owino, Colonial Neutralization of Indigenous," 132–133.
82. Were, *History of the Abaluyia*, 127.
83. Dealing, "Politics in Wanga," 255.

The Europeans used both force and pacts to win Central Nyanza. This was the platform the CMS used to set up their mission movement among the Luo. The Luo people were ready for the missionary experience, which prepared them for the eventual establishment of the Kenya Nation and the Anglican Church in Kenya. With the Imperial British East Africa Company (IBEA Co.) going bankrupt, the British Government declared a protectorate over the Buganda Kingdom on 1 June 1894, transferring the country between the Indian Ocean coast and Baganda from the IBEA Co. to the British government. This affected Nyanza. Henceforth, Ogot noted that the purpose adduced by the British for administering that area was to protect the supply route to Uganda against "wild tribes."[84] To enforce this policy, the British government appointed C. W. Hobley, a former servant of the IBEA Co.[85] He arrived at Mumias in Nyanza in February 1895 as a Sub Commissioner, tasked to occupy, pacify, and open up the Kavirondo. Between 1895 and 1900, he made peace treaties with friendly African rulers and organised punitive expeditions against those who resisted, forcing them into capitulation.

2.4.1 Military Expeditions and Collaboration

Even though the Luo offered no armed resistance to the Europeans, the British used military expeditions to compel submission to colonial rule. Hobley gave the Wanga Kingdom the power they craved. The Wanga, with Hobley's help, eliminated the threat posed by her neighbours, including Jo-Ugenya. Hobley bombarded Jo-Alego to force their submission to the British Crown. But Hobley needed an ally among the Luo. He needed to find a strong and friendly chief. He met this in Ulalo. With Ulalo's help the people of Uyoma, Sakwa and Seme came under British fire to force their submission. Thus, the British established their hegemony with ease in Central Nyanza.

2.4.1.1 *Ugenya Expedition*

Had Jo-Ugenya not been triumphant over the Wanga, and had the Europeans not found in chief Mumia a useful imperial agent, the military expedition against the Ugenya-Kager would not have occurred. The Ugenya's occupation of Wanga land bothered chief Mumia. Ernest Gedge of IBEA Co. noted the

---

84. Ogot, "British Administration," 249.
85. The Luo called him Obilo.

vicious Ugenya attacks at the confluence of Rivers Nzoia and Lusimu.[86] In desperation, Mumia appealed to Frederick Lugard and other Europeans for guns and other types of military help. Lugard recorded that Mumia wanted to buy guns from him in exchange for ivory.[87] Ernest Gedge noted that Kwa Sundu (Mumias) wanted Europeans to join him in attacking Jo-Ugenya.[88] Ogot observes that Mumia asked Carl Peters for help against his enemies after giving him an extravagant reception.[89]

The British found in Mumia an amiable and eager ally. But Fredrick Spire, appointed as the new British representative at Mumias, was reluctant to offer the military help Mumia demanded against Jo-Ugenya, stating:

> I have not assisted Mumia yet with the Wanyifwa (Jo-Ugenya) as from all I have heard Mumia is to blame. The bottom of it is slave raiding.[90]

Later, the British resolved to give Mumia military backing in line with British policy. Osogo remarks that the British:

> [R]equired the formation of alliances with strong chiefs and bolstering of weak, but friendly ones like Mumia. If he was to be useful to the British his powers had to be enhanced, an empire created for him, and history distorted to sustain them. It is therefore not surprising that G. F. Archer, the District Commissioner (DC) of Mumias from 1907 to 1909 and his successor K. R. Dundas, could unashamedly claim that Mumia's position "resembled that of kingdoms of Buganda." his influence extended across the Uganda border to the people of the slopes of Mt. Elgon.[91]

The British carried out punitive expeditions against Jo-Ugenya in two battles: one in 1896 and the other in 1897. Ogot points out how, at Manga in 1896, Mumia held a peace meeting with the Ugenya elders and warriors to

---

86. Were, *History of the Abaluyia*, 128.
87. Perham, *Diaries of Lord Lugard*, 402.
88. Dealing, "Politics in Wanga," 281.
89. Ogot, *History of the Luo-speaking*, 615.
90. Dealing, "Politics in Wanga," 309.
91. Osogo, *History of the Baluyia*, 25–6.

disguise an attack.[92] Mumia deceived Hobley, claiming that Jo-Ugenya had besieged him. In defence, Hobley ordered his soldiers to shoot the Ugenya elders, killing nine warriors including Obanda Kanyamginya, their military commander, and Konya Ojanja.[93]

To avenge the death of their leaders, Jo-Ugenya regrouped, attacked and defeated the Wanga, forcing the British forces to intervene to save Mumia. Hobley accused Jo-Ugenya of "raiding and murdering."[94] He justifies the assembling of a force to prove to Jo-Ugenya "the futility of their hostile attitude."[95] Sensing danger, Jo-Ugenya abandoned their homes and gathered at Anyiko at the home of Gero K'Okado, the husband of Ademba, Mumias' sister. Osolo K'Otekra, the military commander, overruled Gero (who had advised surrender) and vowed to fight to the death. They permitted those opposed to military confrontation to leave, but the brave warriors secured the fortified village.

During this war, Jo-Ugenya defied Hobley's order to surrender. As a result, Hobley bombarded the walls of the village, destroying the home of Osolo K'Otekra, killing 200 Ugenya warriors and confiscating their properties.[96] Hobley found Gero K'Okado seated outside his houses, surrounded by his followers.[97] In Fazan's words, "Gero sat outside his house, alone, with his bracelets and ornaments, and waited like a Roman Senator for death."[98] Hobley arrested Gero and his family and took them to Mumias. Upon learning that chief Odipo Miyoyo had fled to Bunyala. He ordered his soldiers accompanied by Ogingo K'Okado, the brother of Gero who knew Odipo, to bring him to Mumias. When Odipo arrived at Mumias, Hobley forced him to accept the British flag, which he did. Hobley directed Odipo and his people to go back to their homes, this time under British protection. In accepting British authority, Gero, Opondo Ka'Murembo and Odipo brought Jo-Ugenya

---

92. Ogot, *History of the Luo-speaking*, 617.
93. District Commissioner North Nyanza, 10/1/1, 1926–40.
94. Hobley, *Kenya: From Chartered Company*, 87–88.
95. Dealing, "Politics in Wanga," 321.
96. Were, *History of the Abaluyia*, 233.
97. Hobley, *From Chartered Company*, 87–88.
98. District Commissioner, Central Nyanza 3/1, 1900–1916; Were, *History of the Abaluyia*, 141.

under British protection and became their headmen. Thus, Hobley ended the heroic era of Jo-Ugenya.

2.4.1.2 Alego Expedition

Owira became chief of Alego towards the end of the nineteenth century and guided her through a turbulent era. A period prone to various natural calamities, including rinderpest (*aremo*) in 1887, and trypanosomiasis (*tho-nindo*) in 1892, resulting in widespread depopulation, displacement and suffering in Alego. Owira established the first pre-colonial market at his new court in Boro. *Ruoth* Owira refused the British request to bring Alego under colonial rule. So, on a framed charge that he had ordered the death of *janawi* (a witch), Hobley charged him with murder and dispatched a punitive expedition from Mumias to arrest Owira.[99] Hobley's forces overwhelmed the Alego warriors and captured him. They released the old and ailing Owira six months later from Mumias, where they had imprisoned him. Owira died early in 1887, a bitter man.

2.4.1.3 Seme, Uyoma and Sakwa Expedition

The Imperial agents assumed that to set up British authority in Kenya, the use of force was inevitable. This thinking prompted the Special Commissioner, Sir Harry H. Johnson, to authorise a punitive expedition against the people of Sakwa, Uyoma and Seme in December 1899. Two British officers, Captain Charles E. Collard of the Uganda Rifles as a military commander and Hobley, the officer in charge of Kisumu, and Nandi as the civilian chief, led the expedition.

The government accused Jo-Sakwa of killing an askari sent to recruit porters, and Jo-Uyoma for attacking a party of CMS missionaries and an Indian officer whose boats entered the Winam Gulf. They blamed Jo-Seme for attacking and killing a group of Baganda traders travelling by canoe. Further, Jo-Seme attacked a British official travelling with a boatload of spices from Kisumu to Port Alice. Hobley relied on Odera Ulalo whom he appointed Paramount Chief over the locations south of the river Yala, including Seme, Alego, Sakwa, Asembo and Uyoma. This expedition was, according to Johnson, "to protect our water communication (between Port Alice

---

99. Ogot, *History of the Luo-speaking*, 653.

and Kisumu) from undue risks."[100] The Luo saw this as an excuse to impose colonial rule. Apart from subjugating them by force, the British wanted to confiscate their livestock and to secure their future compliance with the demands of colonial rule. Hobley believed that once they learned the power of the administration, they would not forget.

As a result, from 12 December 1899, the expedition overran Sakwa and Uyoma. Collard forces were brutal, killing many and confiscating cattle. They reached Seme on 23 December and destroyed homes, burnt crops and confiscated livestock. The British crushed the Kadipir clan, who attempted to resist by fighting at Nyagito hills. Collard estimates that "250 were killed and wounded" in Seme and Uyoma since there was little fighting in Sakwa. But this report suppressed the number of people killed from the expedition.[101] Hay argues that the defeat of the Luo at Got Nyagito extended beyond the numbers of the captured stock (six hundred cattle, eight thousand sheep and goats).[102] It marked the end of another heroic era. The operation delighted Hobley. Through the peace pact that followed, the Jo-Seme, Jo-Uyoma, and Jo-Sakwa came under British authority. In the peace pact, they agreed to pay Hut Tax, supply labour and allow traders and travellers free and safe passage.

2.4.2 The Gem Collaboration

Having won over North Kavirondo by propping up Mumia and vanquishing the Jo-Ugenya, Hobley needed a powerful chief in central Nyanza to succeed there too. This he found in Odera Ulalo, the Gem chief, who had two reasons for seeking an alliance with the Europeans. First, the Gem diviners (*jobilo*) had warned them against resisting the "red strangers," who had been foretold to come from the sea. Showing hostility to them would incur the wrath of the ancestors. That prophecy was pivotal in their cooperation with the Europeans. Second, the Wanga alliance with the Arabs gave them an edge over other groups in the region. But being allies of the Europeans would restore the balance of power. Ulalo seized that chance and allied Gem with the British. The British found in Ulalo a useful ally. Ulalo was the son of

---

100. District Commissioner Central Nyanza Kisumu, *Annual Report 1899*, 86.
101. Hobley, "Report on Uyoma Expedition."
102. Hay, "Economic Changes in Luoland," 81.

Omole and grandson of the revered Gem chief Rading' Omolo. Ulalo ruled over a large yet diverse population and had extensive territorial influence.[103]

British expeditions to crush Jo-Gem's perennial enemies, like Jo-Seme and Jo-Alego, helped set up Ulalo as the main chief in central Nyanza. The British administration reported the invaluable support they got from him, acknowledging that Odera Ulalo gave Hobley unflinching support in his efforts to subjugate the Nandi.[104] Ogot notes that Ulalo profited off the booty from the expeditions given to him as a service reward and shared with his people the enormous gifts of captured cattle.[105] At his administrative centre in Kusa (Luanda K'Odera), he built a large walled village with eight gates, guarded by Nubian soldiers. He had bodyguards of elite marine soldiers. This centre became a transit hub for caravans bound from Uganda to Mombasa. As the new administration was being established, Ulalo supplied the needed labour for the buildings and the Uganda Railway network.

2.5 Establishment of Colonial Administration

A monumental challenge to the British in building a colonial administration was the absence of explicit traditional kingdoms in Nyanza, which is why direct rule became necessary. In Uganda, the British proffered indirect rule through traditional kingdoms, but Kenya lacked such native authorities. How could they then exploit the region without instituting an effective "law and order" machinery? This exploitation did not start until after the 1905 Nandi subjugation, as Matson comments:

> Administrative and military efforts had been concentrated in the first place on securing the caravan routes and later on making roads, organising, and protecting the transport services across the Province, trying to give some protection to these tribes who had accepted Hobley's regime, and finally pushing through the telegraph and railway with the least possible interference from neighbouring tribes. With all this on their hands, it is not surprising that the few officers found little time to organize their

---

103. Ogot, *History of the Luo-speaking*, 632.
104. Hobley, *Kenya: From Chartered Company*, 109–124.
105. Ogot, *History of the Luo-speaking*, 636.

districts, to get to know the people, their customs and language or to extend the area of effective jurisdiction.[106]

To maintain security, the administration required large numbers of personnel to quell potential security challenges to the provision of services. They needed collectors and sub-collectors in charge of the districts under a sub-commissioner resident in their assigned areas. Besides being administrators and tax-collectors, they were builders, judges, policemen, engineers, doctors, etc. In theory, Sir Charles Eliot wrote,

> Their chief duties are to collect revenue and administer justice. An inexperienced man of between 25 and 30 often finds himself in sole charge of a district as large as several English counties and in a position, which partly resembles that of an emperor and partly of a general servant.[107]

The administrators who were sent out to East Africa in those days – excluding the former servants of IBEA Co., most of whom were first-rate people, and a few top people in the service – were below standard. As Col. Meinertzhagen stated:

> Few of the (administrators) have had any education, and many of them do not pretend to be members of the educated class. One can neither read nor write. This is not surprising when one realises that they require no examination to enter the local Civil Service. Sir Clement Hill, who visited the colony on behalf of the Foreign Office, remarked that "so long as Civil Servants were enlisted from the 'gutter' we could not expect a high standard of administration." When such men are given ultimate power over uneducated and simple-minded natives, it is not extraordinary that they should abuse their powers, suffer from megalomania, and regard themselves as little tin gods.[108]

So, the under-manned administration, often staffed with the wrong personnel, led to the misuse of power by a section of the officers. Thus, the

---

106. Matson, "Uganda's Old Eastern Province," 48.
107. Eliot, *East African Protectorate*, 186.
108. Meinertzhagen, *Kenya Diary 1902–06*, 132.

original friendliness towards the Europeans changed into suspicion and distrust by the Africans. Their questioning of the "white man's" motives soon turned into open hostility. It was this lack of qualified personnel that forced the British to use any indigenous authority to exercise power. In Uganda, the British recruited Baganda Agents to fill administrative positions, but a similar choice was not available in Kenya.

Eliot and his ilk did not believe that Kenyans had any experience in administration.[109] That is why they trusted inexperienced British Officers with the task. Had Eliot been discerning, he would have appreciated that by the nineteenth century, Luo society had developed a contextual governmental system suited to their way of life. This ignorance made administration work harder. Later, the British government had to adapt the Luo segmentary system of governance, which the Luo developed as a semi-pastoral community during their migration.[110] They changed it in their settlement by superimposing it on a centralised and settled agricultural population. The administration noticed, in the former *ogendni* boundaries, a workable model to set up locational boundaries, which they did. The change was further noted in recruiting colonial chiefs to work under a District Officer. Appointing those chiefs from dominant clans, or in other cases from chiefly lineage, reinforced the pre-colonial order, for there was no significant difference now (colonial era) from then (pre-colonial era) in the way the chiefs worked. The chiefs continued to hear both criminal and civil cases in their locations. Scoffing at the administration, Hailey noted: "Thus the Government, in introducing a direct system of ruling, decided somewhat unwittingly to base it on indigenous institutions."[111] The regime, therefore, created a new crop of leaders who owed their authority to the colonial regime, thereby subverting the old order. The new leaders had no obligation to keep tribal customs or laws, because they were civil servants appointed by the Provincial Commissioner. And by enacting the college Headman Ordinance in 1902, the authority appointed headmen, briefed to maintain law and order in their locality. Besides, new chiefs had to collect taxes and supply labour for public works, hence becoming as hostile as the colonial officials to the subjects. As the traditional belief in

---

109. Eliot, *East Africa Protectorate*, 3.
110. Ogot, "British Administration," 247.
111. Hailey, "Native Administration," 13.

fate, the authority of elders and Luo worldview – which had restrained the old rulers from excesses – disintegrated, no guardrail remained to shield the new chiefs from the abuse of power.

Colonial rule ushered in a different tranquillity in Nyanza. Hitherto communities gained land through vicious and sometimes fatal wars. Clans demarcated boundaries through feuds and occupation by families. The new peace would create a fresh problem over land subdivisions. Before colonial rule, the need for land was solved through secession or migration, but the marked and fixed boundaries presented a threat, which Watts explained:

> The administration has had a long experience of Luo segmentary units within the Native Authority. Forever multiplying, forever jealous of each other, each and every unit has been in dispute quick to demand at the cost of a rival the promotion of their own interests. Successive generations of administrative officers from the earliest days have complained bitterly of the clan jealousies of the tribe and their disruptive effects on social life.[112]

The new dispensation prohibited war for settling land or boundary disputes. People had to report land disputes to the government, who affirmed the locational boundaries and resolved land cases through tribunals.

2.5.1 The Uganda Railway

Central Nyanza was revolutionized by the coming of the Uganda Railway. Mumias lost its place as the imperial regional headquarters to Kisumu. Earlier, Mr. R. J. D. Macalister had earmarked Port Victoria as the railhead and opened a substation in 1896, but due to poor facilities there, he turned to Port Ugowe (the present Kisumu). In anticipation of the Uganda Railway's completion, the acting Commissioner for Uganda, Colonel Ternan, ordered the headquarters of the province to be moved to Kisumu towards the end of 1899. When the line reached Kisumu in 1901, the caravan route shifted and so did the headquarters. Henceforth, the Luo became the focal point of the British administration in Nyanza.

Bringing the Uganda line under one administration required transferring the region between Naivasha and Kisumu from Uganda to Kenya. They did

---

112. Watts, Comments on "The Luo Customary Law."

it in 1902 when they changed the name from Uganda Protectorate to East African Protectorate (EAP). The change coincided with Sir Charles Eliot's appointment as the Commissioner for the EAP (1901–1904). Eliot introduced white settlements as a way of making the protectorate viable and recouping the cost of the Uganda Railway. The settler policy structured relationships between the Imperial regime and its subjects and drew the contours of the economic topography of the country for the future. During Sir Eliot's tenure, there was an influx of European settlers, who were audacious to demand that Kenya become a "white man's country." The administration alienated African land, thereby mobilising labour for exploitation by European settlers. This economy excluded Africans from participating except to supply labour. That led to enacting cruel labour laws to force the supply of African labour for public works and on European farms. Through harsh tax policies, Africans supplied cheap labour wherever demanded. Central Nyanza became a major source of labour conscripted through the camps erected by the District Officers, chiefs, and headmen for Hut Tax collection.

The Asian problem remained unresolved. Hill noted that, of the 32,000 indentured Asian railway labourers, 6,724 opted to settle in East Africa at the expiry of their contracts.[113] That group demanded the same agricultural land that the European settlers got and proposed to bring their families from India. So, in April 1903, Eliot declared Kibos, ten kilometres outside Kisumu town, an Asian Settlement area. This allotted agricultural land along the Kenya-Uganda railway line between Kibos and East of Muhoroni, Miwani, Songhor areas, to Asians. Those were settlements in the lowland areas considered to have an unsuitable climate for white settlement.[114] But the Luo leaders dreaded the impending alienation of their land. In 1903, the colonial regime ejected the Jokano and Jokajulu in Kisumu County from the land between Kibos and Muhoroni. They destroyed five African *bomas* (homesteads) of twenty-three huts in the land north of the railway line, west of Kibigori, to make room for the Asian settlers.[115] In response, the Luo sought guarantees that there would be no further interference with their dwellings.

---

113. Hill, *Permanent Way*, 254.
114. Sorrenson, *Origins of European Settlement*, 65–66.
115. Provincial Commissioner Nyanza Provincial Report 1922.

The Uganda Railway linked the Kenyan Coast and Kisumu, and via steamer service, joined Kenya with Uganda. As a result, Kisumu developed into a major trading hub. A cash economy replaced the old barter trade. The British levied a Hut Tax, thereby compelling people to work for cash. Kisumu attracted an immense influx of traders and merchants, interpreters, and clerks to serve the colonial authority, sailors for the township, and workers for the railway and the port. It introduced people of different faiths to the region, including Christians, Hindus and Muslims.[116] Kisumu, according to Omulokoli, "had about 20 Europeans, a great number of Indians and people from the Kenyan coast, thousands of the indigenous people on Nyanza, and about 350 Baganda with about 50 of the latter being baptised Anglicans."[117] Indians and Swahili performed skilled work, the Baganda were porters, but the Luo and the other residents cashed in on the invading cultures and their unique relationship. Mr. Maclellan, the colonial administrator in Kisumu, spoke in wonderment of their enterprise:

> There is a crowded market and all the forenoon the place is very busy. They say all Kavirondo people are born traders, and most business-like in all their bargaining . . . it is surprising to hear that these Kavirondo, who cannot boast a shred of clothing, manage to bring in annually the sum of £700 in cash in hut tax.[118]

2.6 Conclusion

The Luo world was sculpted through their encounters with their neighbours. Their migration contributed to a population surge in the East African territory. As a result, there erupted inter-clan and tribal conflicts and land acquisitions which culminated in securing an abiding settlement in Nyanza.

This movement disintegrated some societies and built up new integrated ones that adjusted to the environmental changes. The period marked the start of oral traditions designed to spell out the origins of the people of Western Kenya. Because of the continued and enormous intermixture in the region,

---

116. Richards, *Fifty Years in Nyanza*, 9.
117. Omulokoli, "Historical Development," 54.
118. Omulokoli, 54.

the continuity of the Luo came to depend less on its single-origin purity, and more on its strength to integrate and assimilate its diverse population segments. So, one observes the paradoxes in the Luo society: First, it created elaborate genealogies to prove the common origin of the Luo, yet proof exists of the assimilated Bantu and other Nilotic groups within it. Second, the Luo cling to the purity of their religious traditions from their cradle land, while incorporating new concepts at the centre of their new faith, such as the name of God (*Nyasaye*), which they shared with their Bantu hosts.

The Luo in central Nyanza developed their identity through the land. So, Siaya became significant to the Luo, transcending the important value of territory into how the Luo constructed their identities and organised their lives. The *gunda bur*, built to offer defence, shaped the ordering of the Luo society in the *ogendni* concepts. The Luo society did not have political systems such as federation or confederations, but in *ogendni* concepts they developed the rudimentary kernel for the Luo state. That prepared the Luo for their next encounter, with the European colonialists, who further shaped the Luo world.

A conspicuous feature of the Luo world mentioned in this chapter is the Luo segmentary units. The units were forever multiplying out of jealousy of each other, thus affecting the colonial era administration, with the potential of influencing the mission. In yet another paradox, segmentary units aided the entrenchment of colonial administrative units of locations and chiefs, while laying the foundation for multiplication and divisions of churches and schools because of clan competition.

The complex relations described in the encounters of this chapter shaped key features of the Southern Luo world and their impact on the theme of this research. The description of the initial phases of the encounters provides key pointers to the study theme. Its later influence on the study will be addressed at the relevant points in chapters 3, 4, 5, and 6, especially on how the encounters shaped the mission praxes in central Nyanza.

CHAPTER 3

The Inaugural Stage: Tracing Interactions Between Mission Praxes in Central Nyanza from 1906 to 1920

3.1 Introduction

This chapter explores mission praxes in Central Nyanza from 1906 to 1920. It constructs the "innovative" praxis of Reuben Omulo (representing the Luo people among whom witness was rendered) and the "transforming" praxis of CMS as the mission or change agent. In constructing each praxis, we trace the interaction between the seven dimensions of their intentionally transformative ideas and actions, in terms of the praxis matrix explained in §1.6.1: agency, contextual understanding, ecclesial analysis, interpreting tradition, discernment for action, reflexivity, and spirituality. This chapter brings the two sets of seven responses into dialogue with each other to analyse the encounters between Omulo and the CMS. To achieve that, it does not complete the exploration of Omulo's praxis (all seven dimensions) and then move to a complete exploration of CMS praxis. Instead, it explores one dimension at a time to trace how that dimension features in both praxes and what the nature of their encounter was in terms of that specific dimension.

In §3.3.3 (and the equivalent sub-sections) the nature of the interaction is explored by using various analytical perspectives, such as theories developed by Schreiter, Lochhead and Overdiep (see §1.6.2). This allows the character of the mission encounters between them to emerge (§1.6.2; repeated in §§4.3.3 and 5.3.3), by exploring major fault lines and identifying points of confrontation, positive contact and agreements, to explain transformative mission encounters in Central Nyanza during the 1906 to 1920 period. However, to situate those encounters in the real-life context of Nyanza at that time, it is necessary first to survey the most important factors shaping the surrounding context (§3.2).

3.2 Key Political, Economic, and Cultural Events in Central Nyanza in the Period between 1906 and 1920

This era brought a rapid transformation to Central Nyanza. The colonial regime took firm control of the region after making the Luo people cooperate, either through political pacts or by force. The promised benefits of accepting colonial rule became a nightmare by 1920 when Kenya became a colony. The bias against Africans was explicit. Their burden was heavier because of the officials' vicious and punitive policies, hence confrontation between the authorities and the people became inevitable. This outcome threatened to dim the momentum CMS had gained, that needed mitigation to allow for a constructive engagement. For this, John Ainsworth (1864–1946), the Provincial Commissioner of Nyanza from 1907 to 1913, stands out among administrators in Kenya. Nyanza was fortunate to have had him, for he supported the Africans' cause, despite the atrocious colonial policies. Ainsworth undermined the policies meant to exclude the Africans from agricultural development, the backbone of the economy.

CMS conceived the Nyanza mission as early as 1892, during Bishop Alfred Tucker's episcopal visit to Nyanza. On that visit, Tucker made two journeys on foot. The first was to the southwestern shores of Lake Victoria, from where he sailed to Buganda. The second was by the new eastern route that brought him to Mumias' court. As he journeyed, he pondered:

> Can nothing be done for Kavirondo? If only Christians at home could see us surrounded by swarms of these poor ignorant people, and unable even to promise them teachers, they would

pity us and them and provide the men and the means for this vast field and this most blessed.[1]

In response, CMS executives sent Rev. William Arthur Crabtree and Rev. Frank Rowling to negotiate with the Mumias chief for land to set up a CMS mission station, arriving at Mumias in April 1894.

The CMS made fresh attempts in 1904. Bishop Tucker, accompanied by Rev. John Jamieson Willis and Rev. John B. Purvis (the missionary in charge of Masaba) returned to Nyanza and set up a mission station for Nyanza in Maragoli among the Abaluyia in 1904. Mr. Willis headed this first station. In February 1905, Mr. Hugh Osborn Saville joined him. But later that year, CMS decided to move the station to Maseno, marking the beginning of outreach to the Luo people in 1906. At the 1907 Missionary Conference the mission societies, through a comity arrangement, apportioned Nyanza as the CMS's sphere of influence.

The Luo people considered Europeans, missionaries, settlers and British administrators as one. Thus, some found it hard to accept missionaries, due to the experience of the punitive expeditions. In one such area, Rev. Omollo narrates:

> The missionaries taught for some time about Jesus Christ to some Africans who came to listen. When told to close their eyes so that they could all pray, the Africans ran away in different directions, thinking that the missionaries would shoot them with their eyes closed.[2]

Evangelising the Luo was a priority for CMS, which used education, medical and industrial work to achieve the goal. They used church buildings for both worship and school. As schools grew, churches grew also, and baptism classes bulged. 30 January 1910 was historic for CMS in Central Nyanza. On this day, they baptised fifteen Maseno School pupils, who became the first Christians from Central Nyanza to be accepted into the Anglican Church.

The Maseno students were trained to evangelise their own people. Some students built schools and churches in their home areas, thus winning many of their folk to Christianity, a success that solicited varied reactions across

---

1. Tucker, *Eighteen Years in Uganda*, 219.
2. Nzioki, "Development of the Anglican Church," 48.

the region. The students, starting schools in their villages, proliferated the districts with schools, which CMS brought into their network. This led to the rapid growth of the church as well and made it imperative to offer Scriptures that were used in the Luo language, Dholuo. The CMS cooperated with other missions, and the British and Foreign Bible Society (BFBS) undertook this translation project. Willis and A. E. Pleydell of CMS translated and published Mark's gospel in 1911, and Luke and John in 1912.[3] But the rigid demands for becoming Christians, and the criminalisation of aspects of African religious practices and customs by the government, caused concern. In 1913 Onyango Donde from Alego formed the Mumbo cult in Central and South Nyanza, which called for a total rejection of Christian mission and the European administration.

In 1919, the East Africa Protectorate convened an Education Commission to discuss African grievances in education. The commission noted that, between 1846 and 1911, missions managed schools with little or no help from the government. It also acknowledged the role of missionaries in providing education and urged the government to subsidize mission schools with technical students according to the policy of technical education for Africans. The implicit reason for insisting on technical education was to train labour for the settler economy. But the cranial study, purporting that the natives were not educable, remained the explicit reason.[4] Hence, technical education based on trades in building and carpentry formed a big part of education for Africans instead of purely academic content. But since the CMS educational goal was to produce catechists for pastoral ministry, an academic component was grafted in alongside the industrial part.

The eruption of the First World War impacted the CMS's work in the region. The British sought Africans' help with the war against the Germans in Tanganyika. Communities in Central Nyanza fought in, and made huge sacrifices for, a war alien to them. In 1917 and 1918, a total of 9,000 Luo men

---

3. Mojola, *God Speaks*, 217.

4. In the 1830s and 1840s, American craniologist Samuel Morton collected and measured hundreds of human skulls in what he described as an attempt to compare the brain size of five human racial groups. Across the world, German anatomist Friedrich Tiedemann was conducting similar research. They found Caucasians had the largest skull size and therefore, the highest intelligence and that Africans had the smallest skull size and lowest intelligence. They also point to the importance of scientific interpretation.

enlisted in the Carrier Corps from Central Nyanza district.[5] They donated over 2,000 cattle and 3,000 goats to sustain the British forces in the war.[6] The critical contribution of the Luo on the battlefield was pointed out by Mr. Ainsworth.[7]

> As the campaign progressed, the civil administration was very employed in finding porters for transport . . . a very large portion of the responsibility in producing porters fell on the Nyanza Province. It can be said with truth that they helped to win the war. The Kavirondo porter became a well-known feature in "German East Africa" during the war. He was usually referred to as Omera.[8]

WWI exposed the Europeans' brutish nature, which the Luo had not known before. The Africans' main complaint was how they were treated. Of the 165,000 African porters employed during the war, over 50,000 died. They died in great numbers because of the poor treatment, medical and otherwise, they received during the campaign.[9] To the Luo, the government was ungrateful and unsympathetic to the veterans, a situation made worse by insensitive post-war policies.

Although the colonial regime laid the groundwork for transformation in Nyanza, it was the coming of Western missions, among them CMS, that speeded up social change through educating the masses. The Africans who embraced those impulses became part of the church and gave unflinching support to the administration, thus affirming their place in the new Kenya.

3.3 Agency

Omulo was among the early believers and innovating adopters of Christianity. He became one of the most influential Africans in the development of the

---

5. District Commissioner Central Nyanza Kisumu, *Annual Report 1917*.
6. Proceedings of the CMS, for Africa and the East, 1922–1923.
7. Goldsmith, *John Ainsworth, Pioneer Kenya*, 94.
8. A Luo word meaning "brother."
9. After the formation of the Carrier Corps in East Africa protectorate a total of 162,578 men were recruited, of these 23,311 or nearly 15 percent were known to have died while a further 23,695 were returned as deserted or missing of whom half might be presumed to have died. Groves, *Planting of Christianity*, 72.

Anglican Church and education in Nyanza. This segment discusses who Omulo was, his crucial breakthroughs, and the role power relations played in his journey (§3.3.1). This section further identifies the agents of transformation among the CMS missionaries engaged in witnessing in Central Nyanza, besides explaining their relationship to the people they served (§3.3.2). Furthermore, it examines the extent to which their social, economic, gender and class position, in relationship to the "others," influenced their approach. The final part of this section (§3.3.3) explores the key relationship between Omulo and CMS to explain the length to which their encounters affected the Christian witness in Central Nyanza.

3.3.1 Reuben Omulo's Agency

The question this section seeks to answer is, who is this man Reuben Omulo Owiti who got involved with the CMS missionaries, and what were the crucial turning points in his journey? It also examines why he got involved and explores the role that power relations played to influence his decision.

Omulo was born in 1895 to Owiti K'Oburu and Orem *nyar* Aganda from Boro, Ugenya at *got* Regea. *Got* Regea[10] belonged to the Luyia, who still call it *Eshikulu shia Aberecheya* or *Irecheya*, but the Luo people of Ojuodhi clan dislodged them. Omulo, also called *Ja-Regea* since Regea remained *gunda Jo'Kojuodhi*, grew up in Marenyo. Marenyo is near the confluence of the rivers Yala and Edhawa, where Owiti established his kraal. Part of Owiti's family settled among his K'Agola kin in Ulumbi, opposite Marenyo, separated by the River Edhawa. Jo-Gem occupied the area upon subjugating Jo-Kisa, around the time of European arrival in Western Kenya.

Owiti, Omulo's father, was a polygamous man, having married six wives during his lifetime. He owned large tracts of land and had an enormous family. Orem was Owiti's *mikaye* (principal wife), who was vital in matters of protocol at home. She settled disputes in Owiti's homestead and was the first to clear fields for planting, weeding, and harvesting. To act before her was to

---

10. It was named in honour of Kusesechere father's Recheya. Recheya's descendants, the Aberecheya, called it Irecheya Hill, which provided a watchtower for its security. Regea area flowed with many springs and the Isika, Mulutonyi, and Emakhuli Rivers. River Isika is on the south with the Abamukhula people to the North. The Abaamolia and Bashieni to the east, where some Luo people also live to the west. All these are in Kakamega county. Some Aberecheya live in Ebuloma and Mundobole which is across River Isika on the other side of Siaya county.

breach the village's discipline. Owiti's home had many households (*udi*), where each of his wives built their house around the homestead according to their seniority in marriage, while Owiti built his *abila*, head of the home's house, at the centre.[11] Orem had four other children after Omulo: Pricilla Odera, twins Doris Nyando Apiyo and Bethsheba Akoth Adongo, and James Aweyo. Being the firstborn, Omulo shared his mother's influence within Owiti's homestead, and much more fame derived from his father's position in the clan.

Orem brought her younger sister Aduol to be Omulo's nanny (*japidi*). According to the Luo custom, women brought along their relatives, especially younger sisters (of fourteen years and older), to help care for their newborn babies. The *japidi* living with the family as a sister-in-law, would in years perform the role of a wife. In this way, Aduol became *Nyar-ot*[12] in Owiti's home, for she shared Orem's interests.[13] Owiti later married Aduol. With Aduol, Owiti fathered Jason Wahore, Denge who died young, Asenath Ngalo, and Sibia Rogo. She gave birth to Joseph Owiti Otieno, through Owala K'Oburu.

Owiti's first wife died before Omulo's birth, leaving a son called Handa K'Owiti, nicknamed *Otenga*. Handa was a prolific wrestler and a gallant warrior like Owiti.[14] Handa through his wife *Nyar Kanyibuop* had Charles Owala, and his sister married in Gem Uriiri. Through Maritha Obinda from Asembo, he fathered Lavinia Owala, Clementine Owade, Handa Okidhi, and Richard Omolo (through Omole K'Owala after his death). Abigail Wanga *nyar* Ndagaria, Bwayi, was Owiti's wife. She bore him Adhiambo, Gladys Mangia, Ateng' and Gilbert Owiti. Amisi from Kisa was Owiti's youngest wife. At the time of Owiti's death, she had had no child with him. So, after Owiti's death in 1916, Nyando K'Oburu married her under a levirate marriage arrangement. Nyando, Owiti's younger brother with his own family, was the father of Oburu Ragwanda, Agoro, Hosea Ateng' and Jecton Mangia. Owala Oburu became the father of Omole and Joram Ateng'.

Omulo came from the Ojuodhi lineage of Gem. His father Owiti was the son of Oburu, the son of Mijeni, the son of Jeje, the son of Adhaya, the son of Ojuodhi, the son of Ra'Gem, the son of Ochielo, the son of Omolo, who

---

11. Ocholla-Ayayo, *Luo culture: A reconstruction*, 34.
12. Often a close relative to a wife in a polygamous home who supports the interest of her relative.
13. Ocholla-Ayayo, *Traditional Ideology and Ethics*, 145.
14. Owiti, Personal interview.

was the son of Ramogi Ajwang. Jo-Gem, through its K'Ojuodhi clan, kept the Luo *ruoth*-ship into the nineteenth century. Ogot maintains that their kin Jo-Kwenda and Jo-Kanyanga affirmed the legitimacy of Ojuodhi's authority, vested in a bracelet and three pairs of pots containing medicine to control rain, wind, and army worms.[15] Yet it was the assimilation of Jo-Kanyanga, the custodianship of the sacred spear of leadership, that enhanced Ojuodhi's leadership status in the succeeding generations. Besides, several of Ojoudhi's descendants became *jobilo* during the reign of Rading Omolo (1830–1850) and they soon fused the hereditary *ruoth* on rainmaker and *jobilo*.[16] Further, Ogot claims that their skills gave the Gem people the ability to peer into the future and so developed indigenous cosmologies.[17]

Adhaya, Ojuodhi's firstborn, had three wives, Agola, Mugande (Akwany) and Dingwa. Customarily, Luo sub-clans derived names from their matriarch, hence, Omulo belonged to the K'Agola sub-clan. Adhaya's firstborn Jeje understood the privileges and responsibilities of being the heir of Adhaya's chieftainship. And of Jeje's three sons, Opiyo Raduk, Mijeni and Sasia, Raduk as his eldest son would inherit his chieftainship. One responsibility Jeje assumed was to be a levirate husband to Dingwa, Adhaya's youngest wife. This he did, and she gave birth to Ochola. After Ochola, Dingwa had other sons, including Chiedo. Dingwa was a shrewd and conniving woman, seeking to shift the chieftainship to her son. She wielded much power to block the release of cattle to pay Raduk's dowry. With support from a group of elders, she did not allow any cows out, for if Raduk's marriage occurred, Rading' would never have inherited the *liswa*. The elders supporting Raduk countered the plan. They breached the fence and abducted the cows for Raduk's dowry. A deep division arose in Adhaya's home, forcing Raduk and his brothers, Mijeni and Siasia, to leave. They came to Regea, where they were called Jo-Kagola *ma bar*, following what happened in "*baro chiel*" (breaching the fence to take cows for Raduk's dowry). But Dingwa remained in Jeje's home, retaining her wealth and influence. She had more children, and her progeny Jo'Karading wielded influence in Gem also.[18]

---

15. Ogot, *History of the Luo-speaking*, 661.
16. Ogot, 622.
17. Ogot, 665.
18. Okero, Personal interviews, 10 September and 3 December 2020.

Omulo's family belonged to *"Jokagola ma bar"* (Kagola people who breached), who became prosperous leaders within Gem. The three main family heads that formed *Jokagola ma bar* were the family of Raduk son of Jeje, who fathered Ochola, Madao and Were. Ochola became father to Otiang'a, who was father to James Omolo: Madao *wuod* Raduk through Otigo, fathered Ibrahim Okero, who by Abia fathered Clement Odeny, and through Jokabedi fathered Adiambo and by Flora fathered Rev. Odera Okero and Hon. Omolo Okero: Were *woud* Raduk was the father of Saola, the father to Mariko Otambo, the father of Shem Ambayo and Agoro. Mijeni *woud* Jeje was the father of Oburu, the father of Owiti, the father of Omulo. Owiti, the firstborn of Oburu Ka'Mijeni through his wife Mangia, had two brothers, Nyando and Owala. Siasia was the father of Ogoye, the father of Aruwa, the father of Joseph Simeon Nyende.[19] Aware of his privileged heritage, Omulo conducted himself with honour. With dignity, he bore the responsibility his K'Agola clan bestowed on him.[20]

In 1907, Omulo was initiated into the Luo community through the *nak* ceremony (where six lower teeth were extracted). Both men and women went through *nak*. The agemates or the in-laws scolded the cowards who shied away from this.[21] Omulo was connected to his people through this nominal formation, which began at the cradle, reaching a critical peak after *nak*. Hence, he was bonded to his people and his people to him.[22] Ancestral secrets are introduced to the initiates at the *nak* stage, and include learning sexual matters, marriage life, procreation, and family responsibility.[23] In enduring the pain, the youth proved their bravery and signalled their readiness for the responsibilities of adult life. To face the adult world, Omulo underwent this physical training to overcome the difficulties of pain and to cultivate courage, endurance, perseverance, and obedience. It equipped him mentally, bodily, emotionally and morally for adulthood.[24]

As a responsible man, Omulo was available for any of his society's duties, for after initiation, the adult entered a state of responsibility, gaining new

---

19. Okero.
20. Amoth, Personal interview.
21. Ogutu, "Historical Analysis," 89.
22. Ogutu, 44.
23. Nzioki, "Development of the Anglican Church," 74.
24. Mbiti, *Introduction to African Religion*, 94.

rights and obligations.²⁵ After Omulo's *nak* at age thirteen, his father sent him to Maseno to gain knowledge, paying for his schooling and upkeep. At Maseno, Willis and Pleydell taught Omulo, leading to his conversion to Christianity. Willis baptized him on Easter Day, 16 April 1911, in the last baptisms Willis conducted before his furlough that year.²⁶ That was another turning point for Omulo, for in making public confession, he declared his determination to renounce Luo customs and embrace Christianity. A year later, on 6 October 1912, Willis confirmed him. In the meantime, Willis had become the bishop of Uganda, replacing Bishop Tucker. Omulo preached in the villages around Maseno along with other students as part of their training. The boys were sent out into the villages for a week at a time to teach and preach. In school, Omulo excelled at mastering the skills he was taught, which included the Christian faith and doctrine. He qualified in masonry. In 1913, CMS hired him as a pupil-teacher, in a program where Africans supplemented the European instructors. That was the beginning of an approach, argues Omulokoli, which gave "such success of these beginnings that the perfect system was to become a hallmark of the Maseno School for decades to come."²⁷ With more responsibility, the students shaped indigenous leadership, leading to the initial quick success of Christian mission work in Central Nyanza. The increasing need for teaching staff during WWI made the diocese appoint Omulo in 1914 as a teacher because missionaries were being conscripted for war, while fewer joined the mission, hence creating openings in the school for teachers. According to Owen, Omulo was later "given responsibility of being the head native teacher in our Maseno School."²⁸

Omulo's parents died in the 1916 outbreak of smallpox at their kraal in Marenyo. This tragedy pushed Omulo to become his father's heir according to Luo customs. But he turned to his father's brother, Owala, to take care of the kraal, freeing him to continue his appointment in the mission as a teacher.²⁹

In 1919, Omulo married Leah Odiembo *nyar* Obare at a Christian wedding in Maseno. Marriage among the Luo was a social affair, whose arrangement

---

25. Nzioki, "Development of the Anglican Church," 74.
26. Albert E, Pleydell, Annual Letter, 13 November 1911.
27. Omulokoli, "Historical Development," 121.
28. Owen, "Letter to Heywood," 27 June 1927.
29. Omulo, "Statement taken by Archdeacon."

involved not only the bride and the bridegroom, but their two families. Both his Christian and biological families were involved in planning the wedding. Jo-Gem fulfilled the customary requirements to satisfy Jo-Alego. This included giving a dowry preceding the Christian wedding at Maseno. Leah was the daughter of Obare K'Apindi, an Alego Mur clan resident in Ng'iya. Her brother Mathias Yinda became a colonial-era sub-chief of the Alego region. Her other siblings included Mathayo Oyugi, Robert Obwogo, Adala and Chief Aggrey Aloo. Ng'iya had received Christianity through a relative, Apindi Odondo. Apindi contacted Christians as a freed slave in Mombasa and went to school at Frere Town. Upon his return, he taught his people, inspiring them to embrace Western education and religion.[30]

The Luo society's decision to accept European ways, education and faith made the Gem people ready when CMS reached out to the Luo people. And Omulo's studies in Maseno brought the light of Christianity to his family while the support of his father made his mission possible as a minister to his people. His ability, hunger and prowess, which were discovered and acknowledged by the CMS, led to his recruitment for mission work. He showed his innovation in adapting to his new faith and working with both the mission and his people.

3.3.2 CMS's Agency

We credit European missionaries and other CMS staff for the rapid transformation in Central Nyanza. They each made unique and significant contributions to the success, since they represented an array of social, economic, gender, and class positions. The missionaries include two bishops, three archdeacons, four canons, priests, teachers, doctors, and nurses. How their exposure influenced their approach to mission will be the interest of this section.

Alfred Tucker was the bishop of Uganda from 1890 to 1911. He was one of the few missionaries (17 percent) with a university degree. Omulokoli notes that he was a Quaker who became an ardent evangelical in the Anglican Church while at Oxford (1880–1882).[31] He volunteered with CMS after a stint as an assistant curate in St. Andrew's Clifton (1882–1885) and St. Nicholas, Durham (1885–1890). Tucker was nominated to replace Bishop Henry Perrott Parker in the Diocese of Eastern Equatorial Africa (EEA) and was consecrated

---

30. Omachar, "Contribution of the Church," 69.
31. Omulokoli, "Historical Development," 221.

on 25 April 1890.³² For the duration of his service in EEA, his wife and son remained in England. This appointment placed him in a double role as bishop of EEA and mission director of CMS at the time imperial rule was being established in East Africa. His insights, innovation, and courage permeated the strategies he employed. He had a passion for the conversion of souls, and his iron will, sense of justice, allegiance to the constitution and bias for the lowly, rubbed off on missionaries who served under him. The Africans welcomed him in crowds during his episcopal visits, expressing their acceptance. Mattia remarks that "he had an imperial mind, and his grasp of native politics was marked."³³ Tucker retired in 1912, ending his tenure in the Uganda Diocese with over 100,000 Christians, to become a canon in Durham.

Born in about 1872, Rev. John Jamieson Willis studied at Pembroke College and Ridley Hall, Cambridge, where he received a BA in 1894 and an MA in 1898. He was made a deacon in 1895, and the Bishop of Norwich ordained him as a priest in 1896, before he joined CMS. He was a curate at Great Yarmouth until 19 December 1899 when he became a CMS missionary.³⁴ He sailed for Uganda with a group of missionaries on 30 August 1900. Willis was posted to pioneer work in Ankole, but in 1902 Bishop Tucker appointed him chaplain to the European community at Entebbe, along with "missionary work among the natives of the district."³⁵ In 1904 he volunteered for pioneer work in Nyanza, a move sanctioned by the Executive Committee. Arthur Crabtree and Willis were sent to Nyanza, with Willis based in Vihiga, "but as he finds opportunity will itinerate among the Nilotic as well as among the Bantus."³⁶

In 1905 Bishop Tucker appointed Willis the archdeacon of the Nyanza region. He was to focus on the Luo, although the region included the Bantu, the Nandi and the Kipsigis peoples.³⁷ Ogot noted how Nyanza was lucky to have Willis, a man of remarkable personality, a man who "was strongly opposed to the paternalistic attitude of most of the Europeans missionaries

---

32. Equitorial East Africa diocese had a vast territory covering roughly modern-day Kenya, Uganda, Tanzania and Eastern Congo.
33. Mattia, "Walking the Rift," 248.
34. Omulokoli, "Historical Development," 67.
35. *Uganda Report*, December 1906, 189.
36. Tucker, "Letter to Crabtree."
37. Oliver, *Missionary Factor*, 169.

working in Kenya. He was a firm believer in Venn policy."[38] In 1912, Willis became Bishop of Uganda, which included Nyanza, where he served until 1934 when he retired to England.

When Mr. and Mrs. Huge O. Savile arrived in Vihiga in 1905, the number of CMS missionaries in Nyanza rose to three. Mr. Savile desired to develop industrial work. Omulokoli notes that Mrs. Savile, trained as a nurse, made her unique contribution to medical care and work among women.[39] Savile, who had "little medical training at Islington and a lot of practice in Uganda, was helpful in the work in Nyanza."[40] Mrs. Savile was successful, for one Sunday afternoon thirty or forty women and girls attended a service to which she had invited them, while on another fully one hundred were present.[41] The girls mimicked the activities of the missionaries, as Mrs. Savile commented:

> In the morning, while we were at breakfast, a great din was heard outside, and a line of men in single file came prancing along, shouting at the top of their voices the chorus of one of the hymns translated by Mr. Willis, "Isa, Isa akulanga" ("Jesus, Jesus calls us") arriving in front of the house they ran round and round in a circle, and finally broke up amid yells of laughter, being hugely delighted with themselves.[42]

Savile found help in 1910 with the arrival of an industrial specialist, Mr. Frank H. White, boosting the technical section of the school. In the mission establishment there was: "Mr. Savile, for Industrial Work, Mrs. Savile doing useful work among women and girls, and medical. Mr. Willis, itineration and language work and school organization."[43]

In 1907, the Rev. Albert Edward Pleydell was transferred from Patiko in Acholi to Maseno.[44] Pleydell came to Uganda in 1904, and to Maseno in 1907, where he was put in charge of the station in 1912, when Willis became

---

38. Ogot, *History of the Luo-speaking*, 685. The Venn policy describes "indigenous" churches in terms of church policies rather than in terms of culture itself.
39. Omulokoli, "Historical Development," 77.
40. Savile, "Letter to F. Baylis."
41. Savile, "Proceedings of the CMS," 99.
42. Savile, 99.
43. Tucker and Willis, "Memorandum of Interview."
44. Pirouet, *Black Evangelists*, 157.

bishop. He served in Ng'iya from 1921 until his retirement in 1934. In 1931 he was named Honorary Canon of Mombasa Cathedral. His translation work was not affected by the supervisory responsibility in the pastorate and the school during the war period.[45] Pleydell, according to Osawe, was "a gentle, lovable, self-effacing person who believed in personal contact with people so that he always found time to meet and converse with them and visited them in their homes in times of joy and sorrow."[46] He remembered names, even after a long absence, irrespective of the people's family status, polygamous and extended family notwithstanding. They nicknamed him *bwana Orengo*, in English Mr. Fly Whisk, following his characteristic gesture of swinging his arm. The Luo gave him the *nying pak* (praise name) *apala wuod Olaya* (Son of Europe, or the West). No missionary matched Pleydell's mastery, knowledge and understanding of the Luo language, customs, and beliefs. He preached and composed church songs in Dholuo.[47] In 1919, Ng'iya became the second mission station for the Luo, with Pleydell becoming the first resident missionary. The Luo celebrated him as one of the key translators of the first Luo Bible. He served the Luo people for thirty years, until deafness compelled him to retire to England in 1934.

Archdeacon Walter Chadwick was born in Armagh, Ireland, in 1874, to the Rt. Rev. Alexander Chadwick, bishop of Derry and Raphoe. He studied at Trinity College, Dublin, where he graduated with a BA in 1898 and was ordained a deacon the same year. In 1899, the Bishop of London priested him. His calling to foreign missions came while doing his curate services at St. Matthew's, Fulham. The CMS admitted him as a missionary on 15 May 1900 and sent him for training at the Church Missionary College, Islington. After completion, he started his missionary service in Uganda on 9 June 1901. Despite his ill health, he persevered with courage while serving in Bugisu, Budaka, Singo, and Mityana in Uganda. During WWI, he was conscripted, like other missionaries in British territories, and joined the African people of Western Kenya already on the battlefield. The monthly drafting for recruits troubled him, "a few recruits in the army, but most of them as carriers,"[48]

---

45. Richards, *Fifty Years in Nyanza*, 40.

46. Omachar, "Contribution of the Church," 67.

47. Omachar, 67.

48. Chadwick, *Early Years*, Chapter 10. By the beginning of 1917, it seemed as if there were about 4,000 men from western Kenya at the war front. Then in April of the same year,

judging it would affect the CMS work in Western Kenya. Chadwick died in the war in 1917 while serving in Tanzania.

Rev. and Mrs. Fredrick Henry Wright came to Maseno in mid-1909 when CMS closed down work in their previous mission station of Nassa on the southern shores of Lake Victoria in German East Africa. They transferred that field to the African Inland Mission.[49] The Wrights left Nassa with the other CMS missionary, Alfred J. Leech, who was transferred to Nabumali in Masaba, while they were posted to work among the Luo people of Nyanza. They were sorry to say farewell to the people of Nasa, whom they had learned to love for over thirteen years. Wright found it challenging to grasp the Luo language. He blamed not learning Dholuo on the fact that "natives take out six of their lower teeth and this affects their pronunciation, so I doubt whether we shall ever be able to 'speak like a native.'"[50] During his years of service, he was also the chaplain of the European community in the Western Kenya region. He retired in 1923.

Rev. Walter Edwin Owen (1878–1945), who was Irish, served in Uganda from 1904 and began his service in Kenya in 1918. He was born in Birmingham on 7 June 1878, but grew up and worked in Belfast, Northern Ireland. Owen educated himself through night school while working at the Belfast Free Library. His interest in CMS work made him quit the library to serve as CMS assistant secretary in Belfast. He trained for missions at Islington College in 1901 and passed the Oxford and Cambridge Preliminary Theological Examinations in 1904. In that same year, on 19 April, Owen got accepted as a CMS missionary; on 29 May 29 he was made a deacon by the Bishop of London and on 17 September 17 he departed for Uganda. Bishop Tucker ordained him as priest in 1905 in Uganda, where he worked in Bunyoro, Ankole, Toro, and Buganda. In 1916 Owen served as chaplain to General Crewe's forces in Tabora and Mwanza.[51] He had married in 1907, but his wife died in 1910, with no children. He remarried in 1912 and had

---

there was an intensive and widespread draft in which many young men were called up. In what was the period of greatest involvement, the year 1917 saw at least seven missionaries from the Uganda Mission "engaged at the Front, either as chaplains or in other capacities." CMS Report: 1917–1918.

49. Wright, "Letter to Baylis."
50. Wright, "Letter to Baylis."
51. Richard, *Archdeacon Owen of Kavirondo*, 3–7.

three children when he moved to Nyanza in 1918. His elder brother, John Simpson Owen, served with CMS in Nigeria from 1899. But Owen mastered Dholuo so that his contribution, alongside Pleydell and Clark from SDAM, was acknowledged at the publishing of the final Luo Old Testament translation in 1953 by BFBS. Hewitt notes that Owen was an enthusiastic archaeologist and geologist, a skilful administrator, and a formidable champion of the oppressed.[52] He was an independent-minded "forceful man of original ideas."[53] He was tough in his dealings with the powerful, but he supported the powerless. His service began at the outbreak of the great plague of 1919. In three months of the pandemic, he inoculated 11,000 people and won their hearts. The Luo leaders noticed his sacrificial love when he shuttled on his motorcycle between Kisumu and the villages to pick up serum to help the dying women and children.[54]

3.3.3 Interaction between the Agency of Reuben Omulo and CMS

The interaction between Omulo and the CMS started when he entered Maseno Mission School. Omulo was the kind of ideal student the missionaries wanted at the boarding school. He was at an impressionable age, ripe for training in a Christian atmosphere, ready as a young Luo to receive his first lessons in Christianity.[55] Coupled with this, the coming of Pleydell provided the intimacy and sympathy the young Omulo needed in navigating the mission context, as Willis attested: "He [Pleydell] was particularly useful among smaller boys, whose affection and confidence he completely won." Omulo was helpful in return, assisting Pleydell in his translation work "in giving to the Luo people a large part of the Bible in their own tongue."[56]

The rapid expansion of mission fields and CMS's need for resources occasioned a crisis, leading to the recall and reassignment of missionaries from engaged fields of Uganda to new fields in Western Kenya. This resulted in the closure of some fields. For instance, the Patiko station in Acholi was closed

---

52. Hewitt, *Problems of Success*.
53. Millar, Letter to Manley.
54. Richards, *Fifty Years in Nyanza*, 13–14.
55. Willis, "Reflection in 1949: Uganda Revisited," 59.
56. Willis, 59.

in 1907, when CMS transferred Pleydell to join Willis in Maseno.[57] CMS also turned to African agents such as Omulo to fill the gap. Ogot notes that "the few European missionary teachers at the school were assisted initially by Baganda teachers, and soon afterwards by some of the old boys."[58] As a result, the European missionaries laid the foundation for the mission work in existing stations, leaving the outlying fields for Luo agents. In 1913, Kenyon observed, "teachers are coming from amongst themselves. Each of our missionaries is more of a Rural Dean than a parish clergyman. If more men come out, the immediate result will be to prepare more teachers and to push further into the pioneer districts."[59] Evangelists from Buganda kingdom had served every part of Uganda diocese, but Willis noted:

> Nilotic Kavirondo alone has depended on its own resources. With two or three exceptions the entire work of evangelization and education, so far as it has gone, has been the work of native teachers, Kavirondo born. In this matter, Kavirondo independence has asserted itself.[60]

This was a collaboration between Omulo and CMS, who started in 1913 to serve in the Maseno mission alongside the European missionaries and continued serving his people in the villages.

The ease with which the missionaries switched roles – from mission to colonial service or a settlers' farm – reinforced the notion Africans held of European common purpose. The Luo did not notice the change when Mr. Savile resigned from CMS Maseno to manage the adjacent East Africa Industries estate and continued to aid the CMS. When missionaries welcomed European settlers, they assumed that the settlers would have a Christianising and civilising influence upon the Africans, according to the 1919 policy document of the Alliance of Protestant Missions in the Colony:

> The settler can help the missionary. As a fellow European, he can make friends with him. As one concerned in the development of the country, he can show an interest in the work of one of the

---

57. Pirouet, *Black Evangelists*, 157
58. Ogot, *Religion of the Central Luo*, 94.
59. Kenyon, "Letter to Manley GT."
60. Ogot and Welbourn, *Place to Feel*, 24.

greatest factors in that development, Christian education. He can act as a father, and not merely as a critic, of the Christian boys who have passed beyond the care of the mission and are now in his employment . . . He can, by example if not by word, help a young convert to keep straight.[61]

But Willis was concerned that the influx of European settlers, rather than missionaries, was harming the mission work: "As settlers are flocking into East Africa, every year the effort to win the Natives is becoming more difficult."[62] This was due to incongruence between the gospel the missionaries preached and the greed and injustice of the settlers. The missionaries' major concern was that settlers had little interest in maintaining Christian principles. As Hastings observed, the settlers were known for drunkenness, prostitution, and other vices.[63]

Then there were Christian colonial administrators such as John Ainsworth, who supported mission work. Ainsworth helped the missionaries by providing the aid needed for their work. As an experienced administrator, he had learned the value of paying attention to the cultural beliefs and practices of the Africans, and admonished those who sought to work among them:

All persons who have dealings with the natives of this country [are] to investigate their customs and beliefs before attempting to govern them, to proselyte them, to trade with them, or to live amongst them and employ them as labourers, for it is only by understanding and appreciating their superstitions and habits that one can hope to win their sympathy and affection.[64]

Ainsworth's disposition sought fairness for Africans, but it is significant to note that their prosperity aggravated fellow Europeans, who feared African competitors and dreaded the truncation of their labour source.

---

61. See note 4, "The Policy of the Alliance"; Thompson, "British Missionary Policy," 19–20.
62. Willis, *Uganda Notes*, 100.
63. Hastings, *History of African Christianity*, 19.
64. Provincial Commissioner Nyanza 2/3. 1908–1915.

3.4 Contextual Understanding

The recipients and the change agent had different understandings of the context in Central Nyanza. The understanding of Omulo (and his community) of the social, political, economic, and cultural factors that shaped society is discussed first in this section, along with how they "read the signs of the times." Would those factors have influenced their decision to adopt the innovation? Second, how did CMS analyse the social, political, economic, cultural context of Nyanza within which they were working and witnessing? How did their perception of those factors shape their approach? Third, what was the nature of the interaction between Reuben Omulo and the CMS on how they each understood the context?

3.4.1 Reuben Omulo's Contextual Understanding

Through his father's understanding, Omulo comprehended the world around him and the changing times. His father, Owiti, sat in the *Buch Piny* (governing council) of *Ruoth* (chief) Odera Ulalo, who supported and urged him to cooperate with the Europeans. Owiti shaped his son's view of the Westerners, positioning Omulo to jump ahead of the queue by sending him to Maseno.[65] When the Gem chief Ulalo (d. 1901) embraced the British, his people would enjoy benefits accruing from this alliance. Ulalo had worked with Hobley in establishing the colonial administration by subduing Jo-Alego, Jo-Uyoma, Jo-Sakwa and Jo-Seme.[66] Gem people became the first to experience changes that came with colonialism in Central Nyanza. Working with Mr. Ainsworth, they embraced the changes he introduced, including new crops, which aided African economic development. They grew the new crops which included cotton, groundnuts, *simsim* and a new variety of corn or maize. Growing maize was transformative in Luo food habits. They shifted from millet to maize, making *ugali* (a dish made of flour, maize or millet cooked with water to a dough-like consistency) as their staple food. The government incentivised growing maize as a cash crop to improve African agriculture. Unlike millet, farmers could plant it twice a year in certain areas, hence its popularity. As a result, it stimulated trade in the region, creating a need for access to markets. In the place of old clan villages, new villages and urban centres (like Kisumu

---

65. Amoth, Personal interview.
66. Ogot, *History of the Luo-speaking*, 632–637.

emerged, along with improved roads, market centres and schools. The chiefs seized the opportunity to build roads. Nyanza, which "in 1908 supplied no export traffic to the railways, was by 1913, their best customer."[67]

Implementing the settler-based economy had deep social ramifications in Nyanza. The settlers' demand in 1907 for a Legislative Council, which they got that same year, was to enhance their powerful economic position. They firmed up their grip in politics in 1911, by forming a settlers' parliament, or the *Convention of Associations*, to champion the settler's demands and autonomy to rule themselves. The settlers pressured the administrators to discourage African agriculture, which they claimed would undermine the protectorate's economy, by decreasing the African labour available for settler farms. To secure African labour, the settlers demanded a further reduction of the African reserves and an increase in taxes. Ainsworth, as the Nyanza PC, opposed that pressure on Africans, which led to a tacit war against him manifested in the notion of European superiority. These nuances are captured in editorial comments of the journal *Leader of British East Africa*:

> If a choice is to be taken between assisting the European farmer to flourish and assisting the Kavirondo to live in independence, then for progress' sake – for the sake of our boasted civilization – let the Kavirondo be dependent upon the white man for ages to come at least.[68]

Since the concept of work for a wage was new to most Africans, Ainsworth argued for incentivising African labour and against coercing it, which diminished the economic force. In his view, boosting African labour was possible if employers afforded their workers satisfactory accommodation, a balanced diet and better wages. He warned that coercing Africans for their labour, by further reducing the sizes of the reserves and increasing tax, was immoral and would trigger a revolt.[69] Ainsworth insisted that the prosperity in the African reserves, through better agricultural methods and implements, would create surplus labour available for hire. He comments in his report:

---

67. District Commissioner Central Nyanza, *Annual Report 1913*.
68. Ainsworth, "On Native Treatment," 8.
69. Ainsworth, "Memo Re: Native Labour," 8.

> Unless, however, the incentive for actual work comes to him from the desire to get means to produce for his increased wants, he will regard all attempts to force him to work as some kind of punishment. The result of any kind of force to go out to work for wages would therefore be that such work should be avoided in the same way as a man would endeavour to avoid punishment, and so the means employed would defeat the object.[70]

Through both incentives and coercion, Nyanza produced the largest number of manual skilled and professional labourers in all East Africa, so that by March 1912, over 35,000 men had gone out of Nyanza as waged workers. But while the settler economy relied on their labour, Nyanza stagnated in the tangle of peasant economies, robbed of its most valuable resource, labour.

As indicated before, the Luo did not distinguish between the various European groups: The settlers' demands were the government's demands, and accepting the mission was submitting to the colonial administration. Hence, as Hewitt pointed out, there was a readiness to accept what the missionaries proffered.[71] The chiefs gave in to missionaries' requests since they considered them to be the bridge into the new order. So, when CMS came to Maseno in 1906, Luo leaders considered them to be representatives of the British, since it was the government that enforced leasing of Maseno land to CMS.[72]

With the mission societies' help, European education began eclipsing the Luo educational system, as the age-old normative programs soon became inadequate for preparing the youth for life. The dwindling in the importance of Luo learning institutions – such as *siwindhe* (a house where girls slept), *Simba* (a hut for unmarried boys in the homestead), or *abila* (a hut for the head of the homestead), where the youth acquired beliefs, customs, traditions, norms, rights, and obligations, corresponded with the rising in the importance of Western education. The learning mediums soon changed from proverbs, short stories, riddles and songs to schoolbooks, vernacular primers and other European materials. European education as sanctioned by the government became the key to the future for the youth. The Government wanted

---

70. Provincial Commissioner Nyanza Province, *Annual Report 1912–1913*, 3.
71. Hewitt, *Problems of Success*, 142.
72. Owen, "Outline of the History," 2.

educated chiefs. The acting Governor told the Kenya Legislative Council (LEGICO) on 11 August 1925:

> The number of Headmen fit for admission to such a service [Native Administration Service] is, at present, limited, though as education spreads throughout the Reserves, the number will certainly increase. It is likely that this Colony will then be faced with a problem in its Native Administration as to whether the Headmen should be drawn from the class of Chief with territorial influence, whose claim to office will be based on his authority over the natives in his reserve and on his inherited position, or from the young men who have received an education at the Mission School, and who have acquired a knowledge of Swahili and possibly of English. It should be our object to utilise both classes and find employment for them in Government.[73]

So, education became significant in ascension to leadership, forcing changes in Luo society. CMS took advantage of this and envisaged using Maseno School to train chiefs' sons to transform society.[74] At first, the Luo leaders were cautious. But in order not to disregard the sages' admonition, and to honour their commitment to the government, they sent older boys. The chiefs, as Omulokoli observed, "did not give their own sons, but rather their relatives, or even simply some boys who happened to reside with them in their homesteads."[75] As a result, boys who were not in the chiefly lineage gained education, leaving behind the actual sons of chiefs. When *Ruoth* Ndeda, the custodian and successor of Odera Ulalo, sent Mathayo Onduso to Maseno, Odera's chieftainship was bound to slip away from its legitimate heir. Onduso, though Odera's son, was far down in the line of chieftainship, which should fall to Odera's first son or any sons of his *mikaye*. His mother was Ayieko, the daughter of Nganyi, the Bunyore rainmaker chief. Onduso's case is illustrative of the shift in society. As the son of a prominent chief, he was one of the first mission-educated aristocrats to be in government appointment as chief. He became a prototype of the new order, in which educated chiefs lead,

---

73. Buell, *Native Problem in Africa*, 363–364.
74. Willis, "Reflection in 1949 Uganda," 51.
75. Omulokoli, "Historical Development," 111.

irrespective of their heritage. So other educated sons of chiefs led in their respective homes (Onduso was chief of Gem between 1914 and 1917). Soon, the new ideas and skills gained by the young aristocrats opened to them many vistas hitherto not accessible to others and now lay open to ordinary folk also. Thus, these educated folks had a path to leadership, about which Ogot commented: "the spread of education and the egalitarian doctrine preached by the missionaries soon rendered the situation intolerable."[76] Besides, the government could no longer show favour to the aristocrats when making administrative posts appointments in rural areas. Basing appointments on birthright instead of education and merit could only be continued at the expense of alienating a large section of the population – the emerging young and educated. Such was the new world that Omulo's father was preparing him for. Omulo took advantage of his father's foresight to be among the first to gain education and assume a leadership role in Nyanza, although this was in the church.

3.4.2 CMS's Contextual Understanding

The CMS missionaries were Victorian in their worldview, and that shaped how they approached ministry in Nyanza. But they understood that a correct analysis of the social, political, economic, and cultural factors would aid their perception of the Luo and influence their approach to ministry. After the 1850s abolitionists, among them missionaries, suggested replacing the slave trade with legitimate trade and industry.

In East Africa, they depended on the colonialists to effect those changes. The Africans were ready for that impetus. Nyanza, for instance, had encountered the Arab and Swahili slave traders by the mid-nineteenth century. In that feisty encounter, the people either fought off the slave raids or sought trading links with the Arabs. But the Arab alliance with Chief Mumia of Wanga sent the Luo scampering for a protective alliance, which they saw in the Europeans, an alliance that was achieved through the IBEA Co. and the missionary enterprise. Missionaries flooded into East Africa from many societies, including CMS, with the mantra "Christianity, Commerce and Civilisation."[77] That idealism included a wide spectrum of beliefs shared by

---

76. Ogot, "British Administration," 255.
77. Hastings, *Church in Africa*, 446.

the government and CMS. But the missionaries soon discovered that Western civilisation was sometimes at odds with Christianity. The clash was explicit in the tension that sustained debate among the CMS missionaries, questioning whether Christianity brings "civilisation" or whether "civilisation" (Western structures) prepares the way for Christianity to take root. Such collusion between the ideals of empire and Christianity came to the fore in Bishop Tucker's dilemma of walking between the two influences or simultaneously adhering to both. Tucker exposed his imperial leanings when advocating for continued IBEA Co. administration in Uganda, although he later became critical of their forced labour policy on the cotton plantations, arguing that it hindered the indigenous economy.

European missionaries, as noticed by Lonsdale, "looked forward to the country of their own kind. They saw settler farms as centres of enlightenment, analogous to mission estates, providing a model for industrious husbandry which they might emulate."[78] Such a vision tacitly backed building the settler economy instead of promoting an indigenous economy, which affected missions in Nyanza as well. For when missions downplayed the cruel imposition of imperialism, it tainted the mission with its atrocious policies, which included further annexation of African land, coercion or exploitation of African labour on the settlers' farms, taxation and forced labour practices, all of which betrayed Christian ideals.

Nyanza's multi-religious milieu of the early twentieth century presented competition to CMS missionaries. Early into the work, Willis acknowledged Islam's arrival in the region earlier than Christianity, through the Arab and Swahili traders, and recognized Islam's attractiveness to the Africans, which raised his concern.[79] The Arab traders blazed the trail, developing roads and centres that the Europeans would later improve on. The construction of the railway to Kisumu brought in more Muslims from Mombasa and Buganda, thereby introducing other religions to the region. Willis remarked:

> It is inevitable with the railway should come a gush of Swahili . . . It was clear that with the coming of the line the simple and untaught Natives through whose land it passes should become increasingly more difficult to reach and influence for good as

---

78. Lonsdale, "Mission Christianity," 12.
79. Willis, "Reflection in 1949," 43.

they become more and more under the influence of unprincipled strangers from the coast and India.[80]

To Willis, Islam posed the most formidable obstacle to reaching the Luo people with the gospel. Willis thought that Islam's claim to be the final and complete revelation of God, a revelation superseding all earlier ones, would persuade the African listener.[81] He acknowledged Islamic dominance in the past, the way Islam swept away the Christian churches of North Africa, conquering Catholics in Spain and advancing into France. Islam backed this with a long tradition of culture, achievements, and civilization while Europe lay in barbarism. He noted how Islam irresistibly spread over the pagan tribes of Africa because of its appeal to the African mind, arguing that "it comes to him in African dress, bringing with it a sacred book, a definite and simple creed, a moral standard which is not beyond his power, and tolerates much of his former life and animal instincts."[82] Islamic tenets rhymed with the African lifestyle requiring no radical adjustments upon conversion. Islam, because of its cultural appeal, gave a quick choice to Africans seeking to exit traditional religion. For Willis, the notion that Islam would bring Africans into the Umma, the universal brotherhood where in theory all men are equal, was much more attractive than a European Christianity enmeshed in racial segregation, since Islam offered to elevate Africans to a higher level of culture than they had known before. Willis feared that once hooked on those attractions, and the African allegiance secured, any later approach by the mission would be ploughing on a rocky field.[83]

Despite that pull, Islam had a crippling handicap in the region, due to its past association with the slave trade and slavery, the effect of which undermined its advantage over Christianity. While the Luo resented Islam for its traditional slave raids, they also found in the Arabs and Swahili a superiority complex over the Africans, expressed in their aloofness, as well as discrimination against Africans whenever they came together. To them, Africans were former slaves.

---

80. Willis, 43.
81. Willis, 36.
82. Willis, 36.
83. Willis, 36.

By comparison, the first attraction to Christianity for the African seemed handicapped. It was crippled by the European desire for prestige and their assumption of "the weight of an obviously higher form of civilization of the governing race."[84] To the African, Christianity was introduced as a foreign religion, wrapped "in a European dress."[85] Christianity struck a complicated pose, "with its Trinitarian belief which is theologically more difficult to understand. It demands a much higher moral standard, particularly in the matter of marriage, a standard as clearly above native competence as the Moslem standard (recognizing and allowing polygamy) is within it."[86] Unlike Islam or traditional African religion, it was more intellectual than practical.

3.4.3 Interaction between Reuben Omulo and CMS Understanding of Context

The First World War period was the backdrop of the interaction between Reuben Omulo and the CMS, for it birthed and buried opportunities. As much as the war disrupted the social order, Nyanza saw tremendous progress.

Omulo and CMS agreed on the provision of education. CMS wanted education to evangelize Africans; hence it was heavily religious in content, while Omulo and his people saw education as an opportunity to align themselves with the regime. The demand for schooling to open job opportunities drove it a notch higher. The African's demand for education outpaced the supply by the missionaries. Besides, Africans were dissatisfied with services at mission schools. Meanwhile, the white settlers demanded a separate education system for their children. As a result, the colonial administration's 1908 Fraser Commission proposed a segregated education system based on race: European, Asian, and African. It proffered industrial education for Africans, which was enacted in 1909 and became a guiding principle for African education in the British colonies. This change forced CMS to adapt the syllabus to fit with the new government requirements. While the schools produced trained labourers, whom the settlers characterized as unfaithful servants, education in the mission schools undermined as much as it aided the settler economy. This is because Africans from mission schools irritated the settlers by joining the

---

84. Willis, 37.
85. Willis, 37.
86. Willis, 37.

missionaries in lobbying British public opinion in defence of their interests.[87] The war trimmed European personnel in mission services, and education in particular, while it gave Africans the opportunity to serve in the mission and government. It revealed the value and reliability of the Africans to both the mission and the administration. CMS thrust Omulo into mission service early as the war ended the career of missionaries like Chadwick. In 1914, he was appointed to teach at Maseno. In this respect, he shared with the missionaries the success accruing from the mission school program.

WWI exposed the underbelly of the tenets propounded by the missionaries and colonial administrators. They had judged the intertribal wars as evil, sinful, and uncivilised. The Africans noted the deafening silence of missionaries on the war question, and the administrators' ditching civility. They lost the bragging rights of moral superiority, as one missionary lamented:

> Our consistent and universal teaching has been that it is sinful to fight. Any transgression of this law by the native has been almost universally followed by punitive measures on our part. Casting this teaching to the winds, and without any reason apparent to him, we have suddenly called upon the native not only to kill his fellow native, but to kill the white man . . . The sudden and, to the native reasonless reversion from our teaching has without question weakened the white man's prestige, while at the same time the native has gained – and justifiably so – the knowledge of his own indispensability to us and his prowess generally as a soldier.[88]

The transforming experience of the 1914 to 1918 war awakened the Luo people from the sleep of centuries.[89] During the war, the Africans discovered that "the white man" was human too. The mystic perception of invincibility projected by the Europeans waned in the battle's heat. The European and African soldiers ate, washed, slept and fought together. Sometimes the warrant and non-commissioned African officers instructed European volunteers in the techniques of modern warfare. The Africans had something to teach the

---

87. Githige, "Mission State Relationship," 112.
88. Groves, *Planting of Christianity*, 74–75.
89. Philp, *New Day in Kenya*, 32–33.

Europeans. As a volunteer under African instruction, Philip Michel concedes: "No one, in those days would say bluntly that these African warrant-officers were our superiors, but that was the fact; and they dealt with us, while they taught us our business, tactfully and sensibly, so that they were respected and obeyed."[90]

After the war, however, despite their abilities, the demobilised African soldiers were folded back into oblivion. The government wronged them by not compensating them, which made them bitter. The ingratitude of the regime for the kindness and sacrifices during the war became obvious when it sided with the settlers and increased the Hut and Poll Tax in 1916, without regard for the Africans' hardships occasioned by the war. CMS missionaries sympathised with Omulo's people, leading them to question colonial policies, which became more stringent. Thus, the collaboration of the missionaries and Omulo against the government became more explicit, as we will discuss in the next chapter.

3.5 Ecclesial/Religious Scrutiny

This section explores how the adopters perceived their "former" religion and culture, to explain what drew them to Christianity. It also explores how the change agents perceived churches prior to their actions in the community of witness. Beginning with Omulo's perception of the Luo religion and culture in the light of Christianity, the section explains both push and pull factors involved in Omulo's and the Luo peoples' decision to adopt Christianity, and how they joined the mission church. The other part of the section will explain how CMS perceived the churches before their activities in Nyanza. It discusses the churches' influential public contacts and asks whether these factors shaped the CMS approach. This segment concludes with the interaction between Omulo and CMS ecclesial analysis to show the points in which they agreed, where they cooperated or where they took differing positions.

3.5.1 Reuben Omulo's Religious Scrutiny

Luo leaders, including Omulo's father, pursued European ways in adherence to the Luo seers' admonition. Specific injunctions were issued by their diviners

---

90. Philp, 46.

(*jobilo*), who wielded considerable influence in pre-European days against such resistance. According to Ogot, they foretold the coming of marvellous red strangers, who would emerge from the sea, and advised the people against showing hostility to the intruders lest they incur the wrath of their ancestors.[91] Hence, the Luo people welcomed the Europeans, cooperated with the administration and expected great things of the white newcomers. They welcomed Christian mission because it offered them the path to Westernization. Baptism of the fifteen Maseno students in 1910 cleared the way for many more Luo people to accept Christianity. Although the demands for being a catechumen were stringent, people came in droves. Omulo's baptism and confirmation occurred after affirming the six catechumen's questions:

1. Do you agree to be taught the words of Christ and to serve Him?
2. Do you consent to pray to God daily, either alone or with others?
3. Will you abandon all customs contrary to God's word, fornication, evil speaking, heathen sacrifices, quarrelling, stealing, and lying?
4. Will you remain with one wife (or husband) all the days of your life?
5. Do you agree to bring your wealth, as far as you are able, towards the spread of God's word?
6. Do you agree to teach the people of your household the Word of God?[92]

The six questions were crafted to remove impediments to a Luo enquirer's mind and focused on: God (Questions 1 and 2) whom they must be ready to learn about and pray to: God's word (Questions 3 and 4) which they were to study and believe as new authority for ethical norms; the God whose Word they would henceforth propagate (Questions 5 and 6), using their resources and beginning in their households.

The readiness with which Omulo embraced Christianity can be attributed to the understanding that the God whom the missionaries proclaimed was the same he had learned to revere from his parents, and who now spoke in vernacular Scriptures. While laying the groundwork of the concept of God, Willis like Rescoe before him began with a methodical inquiry into the

---

91. Ogot, "British Administration," 249.
92. Wright, General Letter, 30 August 1910.

understanding of the concept of God among the Luo.[93] They discovered that the Luo had a deep sense of the reality of God, believing in the existence of a supreme being, Nyasaye, and a supernatural force or power, *Juok*. Ocholla-Ayayo builds the notion of Nyasaye on the following premises:

> The entire universe was created by and continues to be sustained by the Supreme Being.
>
> Everything that happens does so because it was willed to be so by the Supreme Being.
>
> Man is the centre of all creation, and things were given to him by the creator.

In adopting the term *Nyasaye* for God, Omulo was convinced that missionaries did not proclaim a strange God, since Nyasaye as God permeated the Luo orature, religious ceremonies, daily life and rituals.[94] The Nyasaye notion was transferable with ease to God in Christianity, which strengthened the idea of belief in the same God. The Luo understanding of Nyasaye had many parallels with the Christian view of God. For instance, Nyasaye, as *Were* (*Wele* in Luhya), represented God as gracious, merciful and kind, while Nyasaye, as *Nyakalaga*, referred to God as an omnipresent guardian. Then there is the notion of Nyasaye as a universal parent, referred to as *Wuoro* or Father, which gave credence to the supernatural paternalism, from which Ocholla-Ayayo inferred patrilineal dominance,[95] the source of ownership, leadership and inheritance, which were all linked to male roles.[96] However, in the Luo religious context, using ordinary workers' language to describe activities of Nyasaye strengthened the notion of God, which, according to Ocholla-Ayayo, portrays "strong bisexual connotations."[97] This differed from the way Christians referred to God with the pronoun "He" and in the idiom of parenthood, such as father (*wuoro*). For instance, about creation, they refer to Nyasaye as *jachuech* (moulder or maker), a metaphor derived from pottery or basketry, which are both female activities among the Luo. Nyasaye

---

93. Willis, "Reflection in 1949," 48.
94. Roscoe, *Uhuru's Fire*, 9; Auger, *Anthem Dictionary*, 210.
95. Ocholla-Ayayo, *Traditional Ideology and Ethics*, 168.
96. Mboya, *Luo Kitgi gi Timbegi*, 24; and Ogutu, "Historical Analysis," 73.
97. Ocholla-Ayayo, *Traditional Ideology and Ethics*, 167.

was also referred to as *jakwath* (herder or shepherd), a metaphor which has the connotations of a guardian, derived from cattle herding, which is a male activity among the Luo.

Omulo and his compatriots received a translated faith premised on the missionary preaching of God as sustainer, judge and redeemer, which Sanneh explains: "The specific Christian understanding of this is expressed in the understanding of Jesus Christ as the historical and personal manifestation of God's power."[98] For Omulo and the early converts in Maseno, there was enough common ground between the missionary message and their Luo beliefs that shifting to Christianity was more or less seamless.

With their newly enhanced understanding of God, the Luo catechumen made prayers in response to the catechumen's question 2: "Do you consent to pray to God daily, either alone or with others?" Prayers were not new to Omulo, who had frequently joined his father in prayers, but it was now reformulated. Previously, to offer prayers the Luo needed the mediation of the spirits, their forefathers and ancestors. It was seldom that an individual would make a direct sacrifice, although they could make direct prayer. God, although the Supreme Being over all, was believed to be personal, for each individual had his or her god who along with the ancestors cared for their safety. So, in instances when someone escaped danger, people would comment: "Nyasache ni kode" ("his god is with him").[99] It was also the purview of the family to intercede for their families or people. The old men would meet the setting sun by spitting gently towards the sun, praying: "Thou hast given me a good day. Give my village a good night."[100] Now in Christianity, all individuals or groups shared the responsibility of making prayers to Nyasaye, alone or in groups, either in the morning or evening, and directly or through intercession. Omulo made incessant intercessory prayers for his family and people, which he had learned in the monastic environment at Maseno.

There is no evidence to suggest that Omulo imagined exiting Luo religion since in his view, as articulated by Sanneh, they assimilated the ancestral God into the Yahweh of ancient Israel and the God and Father of our Lord

---

98. Sanneh, "Christian Mission," 158.
99. Odaga, "Education values," 23.
100. Ocholla-Ayayo, *Traditional Ideology and Ethics*, 170.

Jesus Christ, albeit with some differences.[101] By adopting the vernacular name of God, the missionaries affirmed the indigenous religion, ushering in the popular participation of Africans in spreading the faith. They invited the catechumens in questions 5 and 6 to get involved in propagating God's word with their own resources, beginning in their own households. Their zeal in propagation forced CMS to speed up the training of Luo evangelists. As Omulokoli observes:

> The indigenous Christian adherents, as soon as they mastered the barest fundamentals of the Christian faith, they were engaged as purveyors of these same truths to their fellow countrymen. Apart from the question of deliberate policy, the involvement of the two later categories of personnel was made imperative by the smallness in the number of European missionaries in the region.[102]

Through translation, Christianity was indigenized, giving the pioneer catechumens like Omulo the Christian faith as an improvement of the old, which they could present to their kin.

On another front, the Luo people had to learn from CMS missionaries' the scientific knowledge to address some things as physical, which they had believed to be spiritual. The period up to 1920 saw an intensification of plagues in Nyanza. There were three outbreaks of smallpox – in 1899/1901, 1909/1910 and 1915/1916. Omulo's parents died in the 1916 outbreak. The Luo people knew about smallpox, which they called *nundu*. They regarded it as the worst epidemic instigated by ghosts (*Jochiende*), an understanding Omulo shared. Those affected explained it thus, according to Ocholla-Ayayo:

> They were heard talking as they came to a village or as they passed to neighbouring villages. Some people maintain they could sing as they pass. (The stories told by my grandmother are compared with those I later got from one of my chief informants, Rabet wuon Oliech. He strongly maintained that nundu did in fact talk and sing, when [going] to other villages. All the informants confirmed that nundu travelled by night at dawn and by

---

101. Sanneh, "Christian Mission," 159–160.
102. Omulokoli, "Historical Development," 105.

twilight (Ang'ich welo and Kogwen). The belief that ghosts can cook was maintained with nundu. It was believed that nundu are cooking and their food could be smelled, and that the path they follow could be observed.[103]

Ocholla-Ayayo further explained the Luo understanding of smallpox: When smallpox appears on a patient as a visible sore, that person will survive, but when the sores are internal, they would die.[104] The patient would die from a high fever, generated by heat in the body. The *nundu* who spread it were viewed as nocturnal travellers, often talking and moving in bands. Hence keeping silence at night would keep people safe. The people deceived *nundu* by drawing misdirecting marks away from the village at road junctions by using ashes. But during those outbreaks none of the traditional actions helped, leading people to believe that *nundu* were "shadows" from the underworld who invaded the upper world. Ocholla-Ayayo classifies *nundu* as *jochiende* (ghost).[105]

The European medicine introduced by the missionaries afforded an alternative understanding of infectious diseases such as smallpox. The efficacy of Western medicines against the dreaded mysterious diseases that the Luo associated with ghosts, coupled with the sacrifice and dedication of the missionaries during the plagues, drew many to the Christian faith. As stated already in §3.3.2, the Christian love and care shown by Owen made a lasting impression.

In the view of Omulo and the pioneer converts, the missionaries did not proclaim a strange God to them. The Scriptures in the vernacular gave voice to God's words, replacing taboos and norms by Christian doctrines as sources of ethics in society. Ambiguity in the Luo religion was in the new vision of God and Christianity, enabling converts to proclaim Christianity. Supported by the care and potency of missionary education and health care, coupled with the awareness that accepting the mission was signing up to support the government, the Luo people embraced Christianity with less difficulty during this period.

---

103. Ocholla-Ayayo, *Traditional Ideology and Ethics*, 177, 191.
104. Ocholla-Ayayo, 177–178.
105. Ocholla-Ayayo, 172.

3.5.2 CMS's Ecclesial Analysis

The imperial background of CMS missionaries coming to Nyanza influenced their view of the context of their work. This understanding also shaped their perception of the church they established. Their association with the imperial regime afforded them privilege and power, which they shared with the national church. Thus, the church gained positions of power and privilege in society, shaping their approach in mission.

The ecclesial thinking of the CMS was fluid before 1901, other than Venn's ideals of the indigenous church. Williams admits this was "increasingly removed from reality," although the CMS had to "wrestle sufficiently with the ecclesiological implications within itself."[106] But the 1901 memorandum gave a pragmatic guide in lieu of a theological position for a period, which Williams describes was marked by "theological shallowness, ecclesiological unimaginativeness, and cultural arrogance."[107] The 1901 memorandum drew the ecclesial map for CMS, setting its overall aim and tasking CMS to produce self-governing yet Anglican, indigenous yet racially inclusive, churches.[108] However, it did not specify how to achieve this objective, since CMS Missions still controlled the churches they had begun. This tension is explicit in Tucker's sermon at the division of the Uganda diocese:

> I come now to the question of Control. Naturally, the European missionary thinks that he can do things much better than any native. He therefore attempts to do everything himself. In this (in my opinion) he commits a grievous blunder, and unless turned from his purpose will mar the development of any Native Church with which he may have to do. The fact is, the native can do many things much better than the European, and should be used from the very beginning. The missionary should do nothing that the native can do.[109]

Tucker's support for the Africans was manifest when he wrote the Uganda Church Constitution and ordained forty-seven African clergy. His action put missionaries in a bind of either upholding the ideal of racial equality or

---

106. Williams, *Ideal of the Self-Governing*, 259–260.
107. Kevin and Stanley, *Church Mission Society*, 147.
108. Farrimond, "Concerning the Development," 79.
109. Mattia, *Walking the Rift*, 258.

remaining tethered to the power of an empire.[110] Many missionaries resisted the attempt to integrate natives into the national church. George Baskerville, archdeacon of Uganda from 1912, protested: "To me the greatest objection seems to be in the proposed equality of European and native workers – thereby in some cases placing Europeans under native converts."[111] Thus, racial discrimination crept into the church, a setback to the evangelical hope. But Tucker, in addition to integrating staff, provided both the structure and personnel for advancing the indigenous church. Hence by 1913, the Uganda Diocese, to which Nyanza belonged, had a formal constitution that ruled that missionaries and African clergy were equal members of the synod and its committees. Meanwhile, in Willis's view, no self-governing "native" church existed in Kenya, despite having a bishop and "native" clergy, the first of whom were ordained already in 1885.

The CMS missionaries who came to Nyanza were part of the Anglican Church's global mission of the eighteenth and nineteenth centuries, whose perception of the church was tainted by two prevailing moods in Europe: On the one hand, the secular Enlightenment, which sparked a suspicious rational reaction to the Christian message and, on the other hand, the Pietist movement, which affirmed positive spiritual commitment and passionate evangelism. According to Stanley, the missionaries were influenced by "the Church as a fellowship of renewed believers with God-given responsibility within the vision of Christendom."[112] Stanley described the five features of their mission theology as:

- Non-Western peoples were "heathen"
- Other religions were "idolatrous" or "superstitious"
- Western "civilization" was superior
- Christian "rationality" could be regenerative
- Individual and personal "conversion" was essential.[113]

These missionaries simultaneously displayed their imperial and pietistic leanings in their local engagements. Trapped in their urge to civilize, educate, heal and evangelize, they found it difficult to break from hooking the native

---

110. Jeffrey, *Imperial Fault Lines*, 6, 13.
111. Williams, *Ideal of the Self-Governing*, 43–44.
112. Stanley, *Christian Missions*, 8.
113. Stanley, 14.

on the "superior race" narrative. Venn acknowledged the value of civilization as a consequence of Christianity, but not as integral to it, since he has "never been able to detect inferiority of natural ability in natives."[114]

Emulating Venn, Bishop Tucker used the image of a cell with two nuclei, which was "destined to divide opinions into two separate camps."[115] The first nucleus is that of civilization, with the perceived destiny of Britain to liberate and tutor the world. The second nucleus is that of Christian idealism, deriving its force from the teachings of Paul: "There is neither Jew nor Greek, there is neither slave nor free, there is neither male nor female; for you are all one in Christ Jesus" (Gal 3:28 NKJV). But for as long as the missionaries embraced the theory of social Darwinism as the basis for making distinctions between different peoples, they would not cease viewing certain clans, tribes, and nations as more advanced than others. Such a perception would be a subtle threat to Venn's three basic convictions that:

- The evangelical and biblical message is that under God there is one common humanity.
- The gospel message of salvation prioritizes evangelization over civilization.
- The evangelical egalitarian intuition is that one race is not superior to another.[116]

These three convictions held ongoing importance for the CMS missionaries, but they were often overshadowed and eclipsed by their imperial loyalties and commitments.

To Venn, the "purpose of missionaries was church planting and to be available to do the same elsewhere."[117] Hence, he deployed missionaries as evangelists, reserving the pastor's role for converts. To actualize an indigenous church, national customs or "the English form of Christianity" should not be put in front of indigenous cultures.[118] Venn grappled with cultural distinctiveness and the yearning to develop a biblical missionary strategy. Williams maintains that Venn believed "culture and context matter and that

---

114. Williams, *Ideal of the Self-Governing*, 38.
115. Mattia, *Walking the Rift*, 253.
116. Williams, *Ideal of the Self-Governing*, 38.
117. Williams, 38.
118. Ward and Stanley, *Church Mission Society*, 148.

paternalism is the enemy of the effective church,"[119] more so in establishing leadership in the local church from the beginning. In Central Nyanza, the early engagement of converts hastened to indigenize the church, but the challenge lay in the assimilation of certain aspects of Luo culture.

Following the 1913 Kikuyu conference, Archbishop of Canterbury Randall Davidson ruled on the character of the church in East Africa, directing Bishops Willis, Heywood, and Weston that it must incarnate the gospel into the very fabric of society. Davidson stated:

> It is the paramount duty and privilege of those who are already Christians to promote the upbuilding of the Church of Christ among all nations and kindreds and peoples and tongues. The Church so up built must, in every land be, or become, what we call for shortness' sake a Native Church, a Church, that is, into whose structure the characteristics of the people of that land are for the common good of the whole Church of Christ taken up and interwoven.[120]

Here, Davidson criticised mission agencies who imposed their "home" culture, and of the Anglican Church for reproducing an English church in the mission fields. It was with this understanding that Willis endeavoured to develop an indigenous church that was both true to the gospel and sensitive to Luo society.

The success of this mission demanded of CMS and other missions an answer to whether it was best to have a united Protestant church with no organic connections to outside bodies or to exist as distinct denominations. The comity arrangements of 1907 created a problem for the converts.[121] As Christians moved, upon finding employment outside their home areas, they found different denominations from the one that nurtured them. Locating worship places became a problem. To find a solution, the Protestant Missionary Societies convened the 17 June 1913 conference in Kikuyu, Kenya

---

119. Ward and Stanley, 148.

120. Davidson, "Archbishop of Canterbury Statement," 425.

121. From 1907, to maximize the use of their slender resources, the Protestant missionary agencies had come to a "comity agreement" by which the different missions, denominational and nondenominational, worked in different geographic areas.

where they agreed on a federation of churches.[122] In the agreement, Christians would take part in church life wherever they lived under the principle of "common membership" when in another denomination and would have "all the privileges of membership as visitors" except voting rights.

However, the CMS's dilemma with that agreement was how to administer holy communion. Would non-Anglicans receive communion in Anglican churches? To support the *Federation Agreement*, Willis argued that such Christian converts should be admitted to the Anglican service: "The responsibility of agreeing to this practice was great, but the responsibility of refusing the sacrament to a Christian was greater."[123] But he ruled out a non-Episcopal ordained minister offering the sacrament in an Anglican church, for that would violate the Lambeth Quadrilateral agreements.[124] The church praxis envisaged in the proposed federation had a stillbirth. The paralyzing differences that occasioned the failure persisted to the second Kikuyu Conference of 1918, chaired by Bishop Willis. During that conference, Bishop Weston outlined his principles for unity, which he insisted must be predicated on acceptance of episcopacy and Episcopal ordination.[125] For him, the "existence of the Catholic Church of Christ, which he intended to be one universal brotherhood, must be acknowledged by all . . . and Episcopal ministry was the only form of ministry that can be historically justified."[126] When the conference failed to reach agreement on the ordination issue, Bishops Willis and Heywood prepared a proposal for the formation of an ecumenical body, a council of churches, to allow for common representation to the government and through which missions would unite on activities such as providing educational and health services.

Since CMS was a church society, it had to operate within church structures. They were inclined to set up a church in the image of the Anglican Church in the United Kingdom, abandoning the federation idea. CMS, however,

---

122. Fisher, *On the Borders*, 7.

123. Willis, "Proposed Scheme of Federation," 34.

124. The four guiding principles of the Lambeth Quadrilateral can be found at www.anglican.ca/about/beliefs/lambeth-quadrilateral. See also "Lambeth Quadrilateral," Encyclopaedia Britannica.

125. Frank Weston, the Anglican bishop of Zanzibar, in response to news of the conference lit the fire. Weston was a missionary of the Universities Mission to Central Africa (UMCA), a "Catholic" Anglican Society.

126. Blood, *History of the Universities' Mission*, 75.

remained open to a future united (Protestant) indigenous church although "no self-governing native Church exists," according to Willis's report to CMS.[127] He referred to the ideal of establishing a self-governing, self-supporting, and self-extending church, which had been a fundamental aim of the society all along and need not be either a typical Anglican church or an indigenous one.[128]

3.5.3 Interaction between Reuben Omulo and CMS

One area of interaction between Omulo and CMS regarding the nature of the church during this inaugural period was the early involvement of African agents in the school projects. If CMS was to establish an indigenous church, it would have to integrate Africans as missionaries from the beginning. Willis put indigenous leadership in place by transforming the senior student leadership in Maseno School, which included Omulo, into a "Native Church Council," in line with the CMS policy. Justifying the policy after leaving Nyanza, Willis stated:

> The methods adopted in the work of evangelization and Christianization. The key to these methods lies, in a word, in the establishment of an indigenous Church. As the consummation of the best British rule, whether in Asia or in Africa, is ultimately self-determination and self-government, so the euthanasia of the Christian mission is the birth of the native Church. It has been the policy of the C.M.S. Uganda Mission, becoming, as the years passed, more explicit and more articulate, to build up a self-governing, self-supporting, and self-extending native Church.[129]

On African ability, Willis believed that "not only must Africa be evangelized by the African but that every native Church must be built up by its own sons. This is fundamental . . . That mission will do best in any country which

---

127. Willis, "Proposed Scheme of Federation," 30.

128. Thompson discusses this attitude in English evangelicals but seems to confuse a unified Anglican Church, such as that advocated by Stock, and a more general ecumenism. He is correct in seeing evangelical Anglicans using the established nature of the church as a defence against ritualism, but it seems in the mission field, keeping a degree of independence from the generally high church English missionary bishops was an alternative form of defence, See Thompson, "British Missionary Policy," 19–20.

129. John J. Willis, "African Church in Building," 5–6.

is most successful in developing the resources of the Christian community of the country itself."[130]

Despite this stated policy, when establishing the church in Kisumu, the CMS walked the segregated road. In Maseno, the segregation challenge was not huge, for the missionaries entered the African community. Yet in Kisumu, the colonial polity which created the three-tier segregation – Europeans at the top, then Asians and Africans at the base – was in full play. Mixing service to Europeans and Africans would be problematic, since white settlers demanded separate schools and churches from Africans on account of their perceived superiority to other races. Could CMS integrate races in Kisumu, a segregated city?

The test came in the first church established in the town's white section. That was a specialized work influencing the larger population. According to Omulokoli the CMS worked first among Baganda and then among the Europeans.[131] The work among the indigenous Luo population came much later. There were two categories of ministry to the Baganda. First, there was a small number who had settled in Kisumu. Second, there was the larger section made up of temporary residents in transit. The transient nature of this latter category meant that CMS could not rely on them to establish a stable Christian community, given that the service attendance was quite small because only a small number had settled in Kisumu.[132] The mission did not give it much attention. The work among the Europeans in Kisumu got regular attention and required resources, so they were the first group to get a church building for worship services. They built a church in memory of a young British official, Mr. E. M. Boughton-Knight, who died of blackwater fever in February 1904 while on duty in southern Nyanza.[133] Boughton-Knight's parents, who pledged to build a church and a chaplain's house for the European community in Kisumu, funded it.

Fredrick H. Wright was the first resident missionary posted to Kisumu in 1909. His primary task was to shepherd the European congregation and help the Baganda Christians. He was also to guide mission work among the

---

130. Willis, 37.
131. Omulokoli, "Historical Development," 145.
132. Willis, "Annual Letter," 24 November 1910.
133. Ochieng', *Outline History of Nyanza*, 232.

indigenous people, the growing numbers of local adherents of the Anglican Church. Apart from the Sunday worship service, three sections of the town stood out as the focus of the day-to-day activities during the weekdays. Wright discovered that his work consisted of supervising "the teaching by the native teachers who are able, by their intimate knowledge of the language, to teach the enquirers in the town better than I am too presentable to do."[134] Work among the Africans in Kisumu was spontaneous and happened within the African sector of the town. A Mr. Owino, a government interpreter, invited Willis to speak to this African congregation in March 1909.[135] Out of this meeting the mission work began. Willis deployed the Maseno students with outstanding ability in church and class. Omulo was among those who were sent. The Provincial Commissioner, Mr. Ainsworth, one of the churchwardens in Kisumu, aided in allocating land for the African church at the edge of the white section in 1910, near the African quarters, for the construction of an African church. The Africans built this church in Kisumu, with their own resources, sweat and tears.

3.6 Interpreting the Tradition

In the light of the questions raised in the earlier three dimensions of agency, contextual understanding and ecclesial scrutiny, this section discusses how both Omulo and the CMS interpreted tradition and Scripture. It begins with how Omulo understood Christianity in relation to the Luo cultural tradition and examines the explanation of the Christian message he developed. This is followed by how these same dimensions influenced CMS's way of (re)interpreting the Bible and their theological tradition. It also explains a special formulation of the Christian message and how these theological insights shaped CMS's approach. It concludes with a correlating interpretation of tradition between CMS and Omulo on areas in which they agreed, disagreed, or collaborated.

---

134. Wright, "Report" in *Uganda Notes*, November 1910, 172.
135. Willis, General Letter, 26 May 1909, 219.

3.6.1 Reuben Omulo's Interpretation of Tradition

What did Omulo do with his father's faith? His father inducted him into Luo's religious beliefs before sending him to Maseno. Having been baptised in 1911 and confirmed into the Christian faith in 1912, Omulo was in a bind between his new faith and his traditional past. How would he balance or integrate biblical guidance with Luo customs?

According to Ocholla-Ayayo, Luo beliefs, common to other African people, were centred on two sets of questions about the origin and destiny of humankind.[136] First, where did mankind come from and what will become of humanity after death? Second, what are the causes of man's sufferings and the remedies for those sufferings? The answers to these questions shaped the Luo religious beliefs and worldview.

The Nyasaye notion of God as creator explains the creation and origin of humankind but, as Ocholla-Ayayo observes, "the destiny of man never appears in the beliefs related to the creator."[137] Rather, for the Luo, the destiny of man is best explained in the thought of *Juok*, which deals with spirits, their world, and their contribution to human activities. While some researchers, including Hauge, noted the diminishing significance of the *Juok* concept in Luo understandings of God,[138] several others, such as Ogot, Okot p'Bitek, Lienhardt and Mbiti, emphasized its pivotal position among the following Luo groups in Uganda and the Sudan: the Acholi, Anuak, Lango, Dinka, Shilluk, Mao and Kunama.[139] But among the Southern Luo who adopted Nyasaye, according to Ocholla-Ayayo, *Juok* was relegated to a supreme spiritual power or a being of supernatural power.[140] Ocholla-Ayayo holds three basic premises for the concept *Juok* as:

1. All living creatures as well as non-living material objects contain some forms of power.
2. Man, and animal possess spirits, soul and shadow beside their physical forms.

---

136. Ocholla-Ayayo, *Traditional Ideology and Ethics*, 166.
137. Ocholla-Ayayo, 170.
138. Hauge, *Luo religion and folklore*, 18, 98.
139. Ogot, "Concept of Jok," 123–30; Okot, "Oral Literature," 15–29; Lienhardt, "Shilluk of the Upper Nile," 155; Mbiti, *Concepts of God*, 332–372.
140. Ocholla-Ayayo, *Traditional Ideology and Ethics*, 171.

3. The spiritual attributes of man and of animals continue to exist after the decomposition of their physical shapes.[141]

Humankind, in this case, ought to establish a peculiar relationship with animals, plants and various natural phenomena and objects, making up the environment in which they live and by which they are sustained. For although animals also possess their own spirit and power, humankind is endowed with more spiritual powers. But some humans possess special knowledge and the ability to accumulate and or manipulate and use powers: "the magico-medical experts, that is *Ajuoga, jo-juogi, jo-bilo* and others."[142] For the Luo, humans exist both as spirit beings and in bodily form. They exhibit dualism with varying degrees. For instance, the upper world is the abode of the living, and the underworld is where the natural spirits of the dead, *juok* of heroes and mythological personalities dwell. That is also where *juogi* conduct their activities.[143] Living beings possess a dual composition of a physical body and a spirit. Since "All that possesses life in some way or another have their own *Juogi* (spirits). And that is why we were able to notice that people in the underworld have cattle, goats and even places for hunting and fishing."[144]

There is an interface for the Luo between the destiny of humans and their present life, hence, the joy or suffering experienced here affects the next life, and they tie that to Nyasaye. This is Ocholla-Ayayo's argument why the Luo do not ask God to revive the dead, because they do not preoccupy themselves with where God takes the dead, for they are resigned to fate when death occurs, saying: *ekaka, nose wacho* (it is how He decided) or *ekaka nose kor* (as predicted).[145] To the Luo, Ocholla-Ayayo asserts, one's death is determined at birth.[146] The Luo limit Nyasaye operations to the creation of life and death only, leaving humans to innovate or find help from other forces during the in-between life. Hence, the proverbs: a man is not complete without *bilo* (magical power) and *wuoyi imedo gi ariyo* (a man adds extras).

---

141. Ocholla-Ayayo, 171.
142. Ocholla-Ayayo, 171.
143. Ocholla-Ayayo, 173.
144. Ocholla-Ayayo, 173–174.
145. Ocholla-Ayayo, 169.
146. Ocholla-Ayayo.

Furthermore, when calamities such as epidemics, locust invasions, drought, defeats in war, floods and plagues occur, the Luo regard these as punishment for individuals' or communities' crimes. At first, they would blame a particular human agent, but soon shift the responsibility for tragedies to Nyasaye. The notion in the Luo religion that allowed worshippers to find help whenever it was available, freed Omulo to find help in Christianity, without a sense of contradiction. So, the Luo had no hesitation in seeking help for malignant diseases like smallpox. It is therefore arguable that the Luo understanding of approaching God via multiple mediations allowed them to try Christianity as a possible way.

When Omulo and colleagues embraced Christianity, they excavated the old faith and filled it with the Christian teaching of God, so the origin and destiny of humans became clearer to them through reading the Scriptures. That is the background that shaped Omulo's interpretation of the Bible. In the absence of concrete writing or speeches that Omulo made, Bevans's creation-centred approach would best describe Omulo's theological inclination, which sees the world as sacramental and "the place where God reveals Godself" and therefore causes one to approach life with an analogical imagination of seeing "a continuity between human existence and divine reality."[147]

Another area where we see Omulo responding to his father's faith is the area of marriage. Growing up in a polygamous home, Omulo's sympathy was with this institution's value in stabilising society. This was evident in his loyalty to his father. As a committed Christian, who upon baptism consented (*Ayie*) to catechumen Question 4: "Will you remain with one wife (or husband) all the days of your life?" Omulo yearned to reconcile the Luo customs, expressed in polygamy and levirate marriages as his family responsibility, with the teachings of his new faith, which prohibited them.

At the end of 1916, when his father died, Omulo became his father's heir. Thus, he had to ensure the after-death customs were adhered to. His stepmothers needed to be taken care of through levirate marriages and, according to the Luo custom, he had to inherit Amisi, his father's wife. But he would not, for he reasoned, "Had I not been a Christian, I should have kept Amisi."[148] Since the custom allowed brothers of the deceased to take care of the widows

---

147. Bevans, *Models of Contextual Theology*, 16.
148. Omulo, "Statement taken by Archdeacon."

in a levirate marriage, Omulo arranged that his father's brothers, Owala and Nyando, play that role. So, in 1917, he arranged for Owala to move to their kraal and take Aduol and Wanga, two of Owiti's wives, in a levirate marriage. The arrangement worked for both parties. Omulo states, "Owala's wife had died while my father was alive; it was convenient for everyone that he should take them as wives."[149] They bore children to Owala, both named Owiti after his late brother: Gilbert to Wanga and Joseph to Aduol. Meanwhile, Nyando "took" Amisi, with whom he raised a family besides his own. The arrangement freed Omulo, still a bachelor, to remain in mission service at Maseno. He remained their head and provided for his father's family as the home stayed intact.

Even though the missionaries taught against both polygamous and levirate marriages, and gave harsh sanctions to discourage them, Omulo's family experience restrained him from condemning the practices. To him they were reminiscent of the narrative of Ruth. Since Omulo did not write his thoughts on this challenge, we may deduce, from his actions, his departure from the mission's harsh treatment of people from a polygamous home. He affirmed the place of levirate marriage in the stability of society at that stage. He rejected the stigmatizing of children of polygamous marriage, being one himself. Because of his action, members of his wider family believed in Christianity. His status at the mission and the action he took also led missionaries to moderate their attitude.[150] On this point, Omulo agreed with Johana Owalo, his onetime teacher who had been expelled from Maseno for challenging the missionary teaching on polygamy and levirate marriage (§3.8.3).

3.6.2 CMS's Interpretation of Tradition

The Luo people's reaction to the missionaries' impulses were as varied as the missionaries' approaches, due to their backgrounds, education, skills, and mission experience. The tenets of CMS, as an evangelical Anglican mission, and the prevalent mood in the church's global mission at the time, affected how the CMS missionaries interpreted the Bible. There was also a dynamic contextual role that Nyanza played in reformatting their approach to Scriptures, the people and tradition. This section seeks to find any unique

---

149. Omulo.
150. See the description of Pleydell's attitude in §3.3.2.

formulation of the Christian message arising from that context and any theological insights that shaped their approach to mission.

Willis's approach to the Luo is best illustrated by Bevans's redemption-centred approach, which views culture and human experience as "either in need of a radical transformation or of total replacement,"[151] and therefore approaches culture with suspicion, and with a "dialectical imagination."[152] Bevans recognizes salvation as God's recreation of the fallen cosmos. He notices tension between creation and recreation, which does not always remain creative in his imagination. For in the first Adam, we have all sinned. Again, in the second Adam we are all reconciled, renewed, and incorporated into a new community, where there is neither Jew nor Greek, neither Black nor White, but all are one in Christ.[153]

As the CMS leader in Nyanza, Willis's interpretation of the Bible and tradition epitomised the change agent's position. He laid the foundation that other missionaries built on. Understanding the African mind before developing ministry among the Luo was vital for missionaries. Willis, therefore, embarked on Bible translation, convinced that: "The most powerful weapon the missionary holds in his armoury is the Bible in vernacular, and the sooner some portion of it, in his own tongue can be put in the hands of the hearer the quicker and the more rewarding will be the results."[154] But his Maragoli experience shifted his position, for coming to Maseno, he realized that ministry was "more than a knowledge of the language, something more than preaching is needed, if the words spoken are to be understood, and to bear any practical fruit."[155] Willis, aware of the dissonance between what hearers heard and missionaries preached, insisted that the orientation of the African mind be understood. He argued, "The familiar religious terms which we habitually employ – God, prayer, Heaven, Spirit – will convey to the primitive African mind something startlingly different from anything which we have in our own minds when we use the words."[156] Hence, Willis sought to penetrate the

---

151. Bevans, *Models of Contextual Theology*, 16.
152. Bevans, 17.
153. Bevans, *Models of Contextual Theology*, 158.
154. Willis, "Reflection in 1949," 59.
155. Willis, 46.
156. Willis, 46.

Luo mind and understand their worldview to tailor the message around it by "exploring the labyrinth so tenaciously guarded against all outside intruders."[157]

So, seeing little children with clusters of charms on their necks revealed to Willis the fear, the faith and the love with which caring mothers navigated their dangerous world.[158] The Luo, Willis observed, lived in a shadow world that was very real to them, in which the spirits of the departed enter. This belief rendered them "intensely psychic; to him the unseen is more real and vivid than the seen."[159] In his general observation, all Africans believed in and accepted the ghost story. They had an absolute conviction of the veracity of the spirit world. The African understood "that all diseases, all suffering is the direct work of malignant spirits, and that no one can afford to ignore them or hope to escape their vengeance."[160]

The Luo found relief and protection as remedies against the spirits. Help would come from the ancestral spirits of the dead who live to make intercession for the living, Willis observed:

> They still act. The chief still guards his old Kraal: the father still watches over his child. The spirits depend on human help and the supply of food. Yet they are more powerful than the living. Still, they move around their old haunts, the place in which they lived, the grave in which they lie buried. They still form part of the clan, blessing or cursing its living members as occasion demands, but always to be remembered, honoured, feared, and propitiated.[161]

When this did not work, they would seek help from the "witch doctors," believed to have intimate access to that mysterious spirit world. Such witch doctors with the skills to tackle emergencies were rare and, when available, too dear to afford. As a result, amulets and charms were the alternatives available to the poor. They were popular and convenient as they provided constant protection against any attack from the underworld.

---

157. Willis, 49.
158. Willis, 50.
159. Willis, 49.
160. Willis, 50.
161. Willis, 49

While he worked at the translation of vernacular Scriptures to place it in the hands of the Luo, it was imperative for Willis to "penetrate into the secret of an African mind to understand and to sympathize, before he can really influence."[162] This approach convinced him that no African tribe, who had not had contact with the industrial West or Islam, would resist the gospel.[163] Such a mysterious underworld remained impenetrable and unknown to the Western world. The Westerners lived in a different world, a world in which the light of reason and faith have shone for long. To Willis, the African had no understanding of the Christian hope of "the life of the world to come."[164] In this challenge, Willis saw the possibility for introducing the gospel: "the idea of a mediator, of sacrifice, of prayer in its crudest form, and above all of life after death have been familiar thoughts to the African long before he ever hears the message of the Christian Gospel."[165]

3.6.3 Interaction between Reuben Omulo and CMS

The interaction between Omulo and CMS placed the Luo tradition and Christianity in creative tension. Omulo's interpretation attempted to balance Christianity's demands with the traditions, therefore, to accommodate the Luo within Christianity. CMS missionaries, Willis in particular, attempted to understand the Luo worldview and to infuse it during translation by using Luo idioms, proverbs and thought patterns before proclaiming Christianity. This was akin to Bevans's synthetic model, which he described as dialectical, dialogical, or analogical.[166] Bevans developed from it a set of five "models" of contextual theology: translation, anthropological, praxis, synthetic, and transcendental. His synthetic model in the Hegelian sense is "attempting not just to put things together in a kind of compromise, but of developing, in a creative dialectic, something that is acceptable to all standpoints."[167] The process by which Omulo received Christianity and the CMS missionaries undertook the vernacular translation of Christianity triggered a "creative and dynamic

---

162. Willis, 46.
163. Willis, 58.
164. Willis, 49.
165. Willis, 49–50.
166. Bevans, *Models of Contextual Theology*.
167. Bevans, 83.

relationship between the Christian message and a culture or cultures."[168] Such dynamic relationships occur, according to Bevans, since when "cultures are in dialogue that we have true human growth. Each culture has something to give to the other, and each culture has something from which it needs to be exorcised."[169] Bevans's synthetic approach describes the interaction between Omulo with Willis and the emerging dialogue between Christianity and Luo customs, where "Truth, in this scheme of things, is understood not so much as something "out there," but as a reality that emerges in true conversation between authentic women and men when they 'allow questions to take over.'"[170] Thus, the synthetic approach illuminates the need that the Luo felt to embrace Christianity and "Perhaps more than any other model, the synthetic model witnesses to the true universality of Christian faith."[171]

A curious act from this pioneer period remains the Luo translation of God: Why did the translators choose *Nyasaye* instead of *Juok*? The use of Nyasaye for God by the Luo predates the missionaries, who might have begun using it between 1500 and 1800.[172] Whisson suggests that *Nyasaye* was borrowed from the Bantu.[173] While Wagner notes how both the Bantu groups (Kisii, Nyole, Kisa, Tiriki and Idakho) and the Southern Luo used this term for God, it is unknown in this sense among the Northern and Central Luo in Uganda and South Sudan.[174]

A context of multiple languages like Nyanza presented difficulties when choosing the vernacular name of God:

> The multiplicity of languages in Africa meant a corresponding multiplicity in the terms by which God was addressed. And since each language carried differing connotations in the concept of God, missionaries could not be sure what precise implications might come to attach to usage. It thus came about that in the religious and theological sphere, missionaries became ultimately

---

168. Bevans, 83.
169. Bevans, 84.
170. Bevans, 87.
171. Bevans, 87.
172. Ogot, *History of the Luo-speaking*, 486–487.
173. Whisson, *Some aspects of functional*, 3.
174. Wagner, *Bantu of North Kavirondo*, 175.

helpless in the face of the overwhelming contextual repercussions of translation.[175]

The choice of Nyasaye was convenient for the missionaries who, recognizing the divide between Luyia and Luo, did not wish to introduce a new name of God for the Luo. This was a way of using a word that more tribes already used, underscoring the universality of God, and pointing to the ideal of Christian unity. Perhaps the Luo kept the name *Juok* a secret, due to their animist worldview which keeps strangers from their sacrosanct issues.

While Christianity, as proclaimed by the missionaries, was exclusive, Omulo and colleagues embarking on translation with the missionaries, brought with them the inclusive nature of African religions, which as Sanneh contends, helped deepen the pluralist ethos of the gospel: "The missionaries stimulated this ethos, thus helping to lay the foundation for a remarkable stage in the religious evolution of African communities."[176] Unlike Christianity, African religions' accommodation of other religions could lead to a plurality of religion. Such plurality is acceptable, argues Turaki because truth flows from God and not from humans.[177] Hence, Opoku acknowledges the difficulty of restricting understanding of divine truth to one's religious tradition, since "the divine truth is beyond the reach of a single religious tradition."[178] The new faith restricted them to the Christian God alone, and as Sanneh concludes, "The 'God' of missionary preaching was a jealous God who forbade the worship of other gods."[179]

Willis's concession was that the Westerner could not comprehend the underworld, for their Enlightenment worldview inhibited them from comprehending the spirit world so well grasped by Africans.[180] He worked with Omulo and other converts to develop teachings in vernacular for addressing questions of faith raised by the Africans. They found the vernacular Scriptures to have far greater power in communication to create a dynamic religious encounter than versions in a "lingua franca." Barrett explains that "vernacular

---

175. Sanneh, "Christian Mission," 158.
176. Sanneh, 160.
177. Turaki, "Human Dignity and Identity," 29.
178. Opoku, "African Traditional Religion," 67.
179. Sanneh, "Christian Mission," 160.
180. Willis, "Reflection in 1949," 48.

translation enables the ethnic group concerned to grasp the inner meanings of . . . profound and intricate biblical doctrines."[181] Omulo, worked with Willis and other converts to bridge the gap between indigenous beliefs and the Christian faith. Together they wrote a small book, a step-by-step guide to the gospel (§3.7.3). This introduced certain cardinal Christian truths in Dholuo and in their own thought patterns, using Luo idioms and proverbs.

Using the term *Nyasaye* for God, though rich in many aspects, still left a gaping chasm between this life and the spiritual world of the Luo. Omulo brought to the table a deep awareness of the spirit world of Luo religion, thus aiding the interpretation and translation of Scripture and Christianity.

3.7 Discernment for Action

This section focuses on the concrete steps of faith taken by both CMS and Omulo in serving the Luo community. We explore the lifestyle and cultural decisions involved in Omulo's world and the decision-making structures and patterns that existed for him. This section also explains the concrete faith projects and organizations that the CMS missionaries initiated, attending to the plans they made to embody their theological insights in the community. It is important to note that both Omulo and the CMS mission developed a holistic view of mission, which included a wide spectrum of activities. As was expressed many years later by Bosch: "Mission is a multifaceted ministry, in respect of witness, service, justice, healing, reconciliation, liberation, peace, evangelism, fellowship, church planting, contextualization, and much more."[182] In its conclusion, this section discusses the relation between Omulo's and CMS's discernment for action: what they agreed on, where they disagreed and their points of collaboration.

3.7.1 Reuben Omulo's Discernment for Action

What programs and projects did Omulo engage in? How did he take part in God's mission in Nyanza? How did he discern the actions in which he got involved and the movements he supported? In this period under examination, Omulo's actions can be divided between the period of 1906 to 1913, when

---

181. Barrett, *Schism and Renewal*, 133.
182. Bosch, *Witness to the World*, 512.

he was a CMS student at Maseno mission, and 1914 to 1920, when he was a mission-appointed teacher in Maseno. This section highlights what he did, his motivation and planning.

During his pupillage in the mission, Omulo adopted the approaches he learned, although his contexts and personality influenced his output. As a student, Omulo, like all other Maseno boys, proclaimed the good news in villages around Maseno. After his baptism in 1911 and confirmation in 1912, Omulo preached in Ulumbi, his home village. This centre became the foundation upon which his clan established Ulumbi school and church. He applied the mission approach of teaching literacy by using Christian primers to communicate the Christian faith, which offered an immense boost to the work for literacy and above all else drew people to the mission.

As a teacher at Maseno, from 1914 to 1920, Omulo wielded significant influence over his students. He taught literacy by using Christian religious texts, thus exposing the learners to the Christian religion in the most basic way. Many Maseno students went to their own villages and gathered people, teaching them as they were taught, thereby continuing Omulo's impact. This model spurred a spontaneous growth of schools and multiplied numbers of Christian catechumens to such an extent that, by 1918, Nyanza registered about half of all catechumens in the Diocese of Uganda, numbering 5,706 out of 11,534.[183] Most of them got their preparation for the catechumenate at Maseno, which involved a special weekend of instruction and examination where over two hundred a day would join.[184] The tabulations for the years 1913–1918 shown by Pleydell are:

Year	Catechumens	Baptisms	Teachers
1913	466	102	40
1915	1284	526	100
1916	1688	938	102
1917	4537	1706	150
1918	6438	2650	205

Figure 6: Growth of Christians Between 1913 and 1918[185]

---

183. CMS Gleaner, 1 October 1918, 138.
184. Pleydell, "Mass Movement in Kavirondo," 133.
185. Pleydell, 132.

These figures show a phenomenal increase in the number of Christians, but the full extent of the expansion is not captured by numbers. As Omulokoli[186] contends, they "give little idea of the scope of such movements, recording as they do only those actually baptized or under definite instruction as catechumens. They necessarily leave out of account the tens of thousands who are under more or less direct influence."[187]

In 1916 Omulo's family in Gem thrust him into the leadership of his father's home. He determined to establish the home on Christian principles, even though there were visible Luo customs lingering. Also, as Onyango observed, in areas where people accepted the Christian message, people developed Christian homes and not churches, which she called Christian villages *dala* or homesteads.[188] Here, both the Bible and the Luo ideals formed sources of authority. Since they founded the homes on Christian practices, they discontinued some Luo customs while accommodating others. The inclusion of certain Luo cultural values was clear in the setting up of such homes.[189] Onyango marvels at the effectiveness of this model, indicating that by 1910 early evangelists like Ezekiel Apindi, Samuel Okoth and Alfayo Odongo Mango had all set up Christian villages in Central Nyanza.[190] Omulo established a Christian home of his father's by eliminating certain aspects of a traditional Luo home, like *abila* and *siwindhe*, and developed large houses able to accommodate the whole family. Most notable was the conduct of morning and evening Christian prayers.[191]

3.7.2 CMS's Discernment for Action

In approaching ministry to the Luo, CMS had to choose between the industrial mission approach (focusing on farming) and evangelistic mission (through mission schools). Missionaries within CMS held differing opinions on the best way the mission would succeed. While CMS policy favoured a method that would yield fast evangelistic results, Savile argued for an industrial mission.

---

186. Omulokoli, "Historical Development," 225.
187. Willis, "Buganda Teachers," 304–305.
188. Onyango, *Gender and Development*, 102.
189. Spear and Kimambo, *East Africa Expression*, 12.
190. Indalo, "Critical Study"; confirmed in interviews of Nyende, Omulo and Okwiri with Crispin Onyango in 1967, St. Paul's University Archives.
191. Otieno, Personal interview, 21 and 23 September 2020.

Savile thought that the CMS erred in Uganda for not taking an industrial mission approach. He contended that aligning the mission's agriculture-based program with the settler-based economy in Kenya would achieve development rapidly.[192] Although he agreed to provide basic elementary education, his preference was an industrial program. His position was at variance with the majority of CMS missionaries, who were apprehensive to aid the cause of settlers and traders.[193] Savile's approach proffered advancing economic prospects for the Africans before accepting Christianity, thus making the entire community the focal point of mission. However, his community empowerment vision via industrial mission would slow the CMS vision of an indigenous Church.[194]

While Savile had support from mission leaders on the ground, with both Willis and Bishop Tucker recognizing the projects' value, London dictated the approach that CMS adopted. The Parent Committee (PC) in London, therefore, instructed Willis on the approach to employ.[195] In 1906, Willis and Bishop Tucker jointly appeared before the Society's Group No. III Committee, where it was determined that evangelism was the ministry approach that CMS would pursue at Maseno and in Western Kenya.[196] CMS had to achieve evangelization of the people, with urgency, as Warren noted:

> [M]eans must always be subordinated to the ends they serve. The end for which the Society exists is the preaching of the Gospel, the conversion of those who hear, and their baptism into the Church. Educational work, Industrial Missions, Medical work, these, and all other activities are means to the supreme end. They are nowhere to be considered as ends in themselves.[197]

Willis[198] conceived of a boy's boarding school as a means of evangelism, and argued: "A central school for boys, say two from each chief would probably

---

192. Savile, Letter to the CMS Committee.
193. Walker, "Appeal for Kavirondo," 118–119.
194. Strayer, "Anglicans in Kenya," 22.
195. Willis, Letter to Baylis.
196. Tucker and Willis, Memorandum of Interview.
197. Warren, *Unfolding Purpose*, 9–10.
198. Willis, in *Uganda Notes*, 118–119.

be the quickest and most efficient way of sending the gospel throughout the country." He explained this later:

> The case for such a boarding school in a heathen country such as this is very clear. It secures what the old monasteries secured in the Middle Ages and in its measure, its effects what they effected. It affords a shelter amid a sea of temptation; it makes Christian teaching practicable and Christian living a possibility. It is significant that God Himself does not attempt the practically impossible. He does not attempt to give Israel the Law in Egypt; He first brought them out and then taught them. John the Baptist drew his masses away from their own surroundings, into the wilderness: then he taught them. The greatest of all sermons was preached on the Mount, to those who would take the trouble to go there. And so, repeatedly when our Lord would teach His disciples, He withdrew Himself.[199]

With the success of the Iona monastic model in evangelizing the northern parts of Britain, a Maseno School as a version of Iona appealed to Willis for a similar country where Christian faith had no roots.[200] CMS adopted a boarding school model which guaranteed a controlled Christian environment for leadership training and Christian formation. The CMS Maseno Boys' Boarding School began at the end of 1906.

CMS also embarked on Bible translation. By 1908 Willis had mastered Dholuo, with the aid of his students, to begin translating the Scriptures. His Dholuo translation of Mark's gospel was a typewritten copy,[201] which he planned to give to each Maseno student as their own "as soon as he had enough paper to use on the duplicator which had just been put in working condition."[202] Weatherhead saw this copy in use during worship, along with several hymns, when visiting Maseno in 1909, but there was a need to improve it as their knowledge of Dholuo deepened.[203] Pleydell, therefore, revised the Gospel of St. Mark by the end of 1910, began translating St. John's, and began

---

199. Willis, Annual Letter, 24 November 1910.
200. Richards, *Fifty Years in Nyanza*, 17.
201. Report of Uganda Bible Committee, 1908.
202. Willis, "Willis Papers," 111.
203. Weatherhead, "Pioneer Missionary Work," 47.

revising St. Luke's. The British and Foreign Bible Society published St. Mark's gospel in 1914. Pleydell also translated "the Holy Communion Office, Litany, an outline of St. Mark for teaching, and a new First Catechism."[204]

The situation regarding Christian Literature in 1918 was such that "the gospels printed by the British and Foreign Bible Society (BFBS) sell rapidly at sixpence per copy."[205] This Luo eagerness for Christian literature was observed by Pleydell:

> When the mass movement began after 1914 the demand for books was so great that editions of five or ten thousand were quickly swallowed up and, when the new edition arrived, my office was besieged with readers eager to buy gospels and Luo primers. In 1915 Mrs. Pleydell sold 2125 gospels, in 1917 she sold 7215. People often walked thirty to forty miles for the Book that was now so precious to them . . . They read it so often that they could recite whole passages by heart.[206]

Wright voiced concern for the need for literature: "Until quite recently we have been badly hindered in our teaching by lack of books, the first edition of primers and Gospels being speedily exhausted, and great delay having arisen in getting new ones."[207] It placed a potent tool for evangelization in the hands of the converts.

3.7.3 Interaction Between Reuben Omulo and CMS on Their Discernment for Action

Establishing schools was the most significant action CMS and Omulo undertook together to reach the people in Nyanza, as mentioned above (§§3.7.2, 3.3, 3.4 and 3.5.3).

During this inaugural period, CMS succeeded in engaging young Luo converts in their model of mission by involving them in preaching in their villages. At the end of the school session, they were sent back to their villages to preach. In tandem with this vision, Willis wrote: "I look for the time when in all parts of the country we shall have little groups of Christian boys who

---

204. CMS Report, 1912, 55.
205. CMS Gleaner, 1 October 1918.
206. Pleydell, Annual Letter, 13 November 1911, 132–133.
207. Wright, General Letter, 4 February 1914, 3.

shall in their villages, be witnesses of Christ."[208] Maseno students and other converts set up a range of schools that required inspection for standardisation. CMS missionaries took to carrying this out. Although Archdeacon Chadwick, Mr. White, and Pleydell itinerated as much as they could to inspect and affirm the schools, "the movement had gathered such impetus that it was impossible to inspect all schools. Only central schools could be visited, and there, tremendous crowds would assemble for service."[209]

In mid-1910, Willis paid for the printing of 1,000 copies of the "Introduction to the Gospels."[210] With that evangelistic tool, the evangelist had a basis of presenting the gospel to the Luo people, in an apologetic approach, which Willis described as follows:

> We begin with the basis on which our belief in God, common to us and them, rests; we show what is good in native religious life, in creed and practice: where, as in sacrifice, it suggests higher truths: where it comes short, and where it fails: then give in suitable outline the main facts on which our own faith rests, especially the life of Christ: show on the basis of these facts, who he was and what He came to do: and finally take up common heathen objections to Christianity and answer them.[211]

Even after the change in mind through an elaborate evangelistic approach, Willis aimed at inner transformation and conversion to Jesus Christ in his hearers, a change that "can only come in one way, by the Spirit of God making a radical change in their hearts. God grant indeed that this, and nothing less may be done, and that soon."[212]

In severing ties with Savile, CMS not only avoided spreading its meagre resources thinly on community projects but also avoided blurring its focus. CMS had hoped to free itself from the accusations of aiding settlers or being part of the conspiracy to annex African land, but the blame stuck. Omulokoli observes that CMS not only got eighty acres of land at Maseno for the mission station, but that Savile's company, which hung on the coattails of the Society,

---

208. Willis, "Willis Papers," 197.
209. Pleydell, "Mass Movement in Kavirondo," 133.
210. Pleydell, 133.
211. Willis, Annual Letter, 24 November 1910.
212. Willis, "Willis Papers," 214.

also acquired about 1,000 acres.[213] The local populace could not distinguish between the Company and the Mission since Savile started both. The people were therefore justified to blame CMS for their displacement and the expropriation of their land.

Omulo and the CMS missionaries also cooperated to develop and advance literacy in Nyanza. The Bible translation necessitated developing Luo grammar, dictionary, and orthography, resulting in unintended positive consequences, as it preserved the Luo culture and language by the transcription of oral material. It thus propelled a literary revolution marked by a hunger for literacy among the common people. Besides, it met the intention of CMS and Omulo to achieve the goal of evangelising the Luo. Through their linguistic and ethnographic efforts, Omulo and fellow converts had an effect like that of Crowther, who (in Sanneh's observation), "planned terms for Christianity as an African religion, with the use of African languages in Scripture, prayer, worship, and study to promote it."[214]

3.8 Reflexivity

In this section, we seek to answer whether the adopters and the change agents reflected on the impact of their decisions on the community. We explore whether Omulo and CMS reflected on the results of their work in this period. Did CMS and Omulo learn from their experiences, and did the experiences shape their ministry approach? The section ends with exploring the interaction between Omulo's and CMS's reflexivity, pointing out the areas where they agreed, disagreed, or collaborated.

3.8.1 Reuben Omulo's Reflexivity

In this dimension we ask two sets of questions:

1. Is there evidence in Reuben Omulo's praxis of a conscious journey of self-reflection and learning? Were there turning points that he identified as defining moments in his pilgrimage of faith? Did he admit when he had been wrong and change his ways?

---

213. Omulokoli, "Historical Development," 104.
214. Ward and Stanley, *Church Mission Society*, 184.

2. Is there evidence that Omulo consciously and intentionally held together the different dimensions of praxis? Was there wholeness in his life – between theory and practice, faith and action, prayer, and planning?

Omulo did not speak or record his personal experiences in that early stage of his life, making it difficult to gauge whether he sensed mistakes that needed correction. But we can describe Omulo's faith journey as a series of conversions through which he progressively realized aspects of his life that he had to abandon to inch closer to God's will.

Since the decisions and actions taken in the community were not his own, his impact on community development was not explicit. The missionary approach was effective and transferable. The Maseno students stood out, having gained the coveted skill of reading and writing, and transferred their knowledge with others who never attended Maseno. The students established schools that also served as churches, but since they had no adequate instruction in the Christian faith the risk of syncretistic churches emerging was high, which would undermine the mission church.

The stringent and indiscriminate condemnation of African customs was an issue of concern for Omulo. He did not write to challenge the missionary teaching, but he worked to accommodate the victims in finding an agreeable blend between the old customs and the new teaching in Christianity. As mentioned above (§3.6.1), he worked around sanctions on polygamous families and families in levirate marriage, forcing their acceptance and helping missionaries to appreciate the role they play in stabilising society. As a result, missionaries changed their attitudes, and more of the previously excluded people believed.

3.8.2 CMS's Reflexivity

Willis and the CMS missionaries initially planned to spread Christianity through the chiefs. He argued that if chiefs embraced Christianity, not only would it improve their service to the people, but their examples would attract the rest to Christianity. With Christian chiefs, the flow of the gospel would be from the centre of power to the peripheries, from the aristocracy to the commoners. In the same way that the colonial administration enabled the mission, the chiefs would enable the converts in their area to do mission.

Richards observes that Willis started with four sons of Luo chiefs, Onduso, Orao, Owiti and Odindo as the first pupils, who had begun their learning at the Friends' Mission at Kaimosi, but Willis transferred them to Maseno.[215]

In fact, however, the people who spread the gospel among the Luo were not the sons of chiefs, but students coming out of Maseno School, in their unrecognized informal schools. They mimicked the missionaries by building their own schools, where they became teachers, and which also acted as churches. Onyango[216] noted that those African teacher-evangelists built two hundred and twenty-five school-churches in their home areas for their clans, creating Christian educational centres deep into the hinterland, thus allowing both for numerical increase and a spiralling extension of the gospel.[217]

Once this began after 1910, the subsequent spread was both spontaneous and indigenous. The converts convened meetings on their own on Sundays and also met on other days to learn to read, since as Leech pointed out from his Butere experience, given "a constant increasing number of catechumens, many of whom live some forty or forty-five miles off . . . we have so few teachers qualified to help them and so few books as yet from which they may learn."[218] Pleydell recorded that

> many of the young men who joined the catechumenate in the early days were fired with evangelistic zeal and became voluntary unpaid teachers in their districts, so keen were they and their disciples that congregations existed in places of which we had no cognizance. These teachers did "yeomen" service.[219]

The Luo became eager purveyors of the message they received, which was evidenced by three unique aspects noted by Wright[220] and Matthews.[221] They pointed out, first, that the young Luo agents made those efforts despite the opposition they faced from their older folk in the reserves, as far as twenty or thirty miles away. Second, they did it without payment: "These recent converts

---

215. Richards, *Fifty Years in Nyanza*, 34.
216. Onyango, *Gender and Development*, 97–98.
217. Pleydell, "Mass Movement in Kavirondo," 132.
218. Willis, "Buganda Teachers and Mass Movements."
219. Pleydell, "Mass Movement in Kavirondo," 132.
220. Wright, General Letter, 4 February 1914.
221. Matthews, *CMS Gleaner*.

from heathenism are gathering the men and women and children together, and without payment, are teaching them to read the Gospels in their own language."[222] Third, they were full of zeal: "Their natural independence is a useful factor in spreading the gospel. As each one gets to know it, he wishes to pass on the news. In fact, they wish to evangelize their own people."[223]

3.8.3 Interaction Between Reuben Omulo and CMS in their Discernment for Action

In hindsight, CMS should not have hired Johana Owalo, following the effect he had on Maseno students and African staff. Willis's decision to hire Owalo as a Maseno teacher in October 1910 provides a case for reflexivity analysis, since Owalo was Omulo's teacher for a couple of years. Willis likely met Owalo during the Nairobi conferences, and only later realized Owalo's doctrinal position, following communication with Dr. Scott of the Scottish Mission in Kikuyu and Canon Burns, the CMS missionary in Nairobi. Willis knew that Owalo's position contradicted the mission's teachings, yet he hired him anyway, hoping to harness his potential to develop the church in Nyanza. Besides, Willis counted on the environment in Maseno to mould him. Owalo taught reading, writing and Kiswahili, although the missionaries soon noted Owalo's refusal to join together with others in worship at Maseno.[224] He further began propagating his controversial beliefs against the Christian faith taught by the mission.[225] Ndeda shows that Owalo's main points of disagreement with missionaries were his belief that Jesus was not of the same substance as God and his rejection of monogamy as a European, not a biblical ideal.[226] On the account of his vision, Owalo rejected the doctrine of the Trinity and the deity of Jesus Christ. He defended his beliefs before the Maseno Council, which included staff and students, but in 1912 CMS expelled him from his teaching position and membership.

The paradox is that while this challenge shook the core of Christian teaching on Christ, it also strengthened it, by forcing a clarification and adopting

---

222. Wright, General Letter, 4 February 1914, 2.
223. Matthews, *CMS Gleaner*, 138.
224. Ogot, *History of the Luo-speaking*, 692.
225. Willis, "Appeal to the African."
226. Ndeda, "Nomiya Luo church," 19.

the doctrine to the context. Willis, working with Omulo and others in Maseno, developed material on the doctrine of God that became a guide for enquirers.

One difference between Omulo and CMS, as noted, was in the treatment of people in polygamous families. While Omulo also affirmed the missionary position on polygamists, he did not agree with the demands made to discard extra wives and their children. It was a point on which he agreed with Owalo, and he advocated against stigmatizing and rejecting women and children in polygamous homes. Owalo stopped Daudi Migot, a CMS staff member in Maseno, from divorcing his second wife. Conversely, many Anglican adherents, such as Samuel Otieno of Manyatta and Nickodemu Tambo of Nyakach, joined Owalo's movement because of its teaching on polygamy.[227]

The mission's tough stance on aspects of Luo customs, coupled with the government's atrocities in colonial policy, triggered one of the most ardent religious oppositions to Westernisation in Nyanza. The rise of the Mumbo cult in 1914 presented a serious political challenge to the colonial administration from within the Luo community. Its leader, Onyango Dunde, claimed that an enormous serpent from Lake Victoria had swallowed him and addressed him as follows:

> I am God Mumbo whose two homes are in the Sun and in the Lake. I have chosen you to be my mouthpiece. Go out and tell all Africans . . . that from henceforth I am their God. Those whom I chose personally and also those who acknowledge me will live forever in plenty . . . The Christian religion is rotten and so is its practice of making its believers wear clothes. My followers must let their hair grow, never cutting it. Their clothes shall be the skins of goats and cattle and they must never wash. All Europeans are your enemies, but the time is shortly coming when they will all disappear from our country.[228]

Mumboism adjured the Luo to return to African traditions and worship. It forbade European wares and worship, claiming that if the Luo rediscovered their lost traditions, they would come into a golden age and a peaceful society. Between 1914 and 1918, Mumboism gained a large following in Alego

---

227. Ndeda, 5.
228. Nyangweso, "Cult of Mumbo," 13–17.

and its neighbourhood. It spread across the Winam Gulf into Kabondo in South Nyanza, championed by Mosi Auma, and later to Kisii. Frightened of Mumboism, the colonial government moved to suppress it. This was one more distraction the government could not tolerate while being involved in an ongoing war in German East Africa (Tanganyika). In 1919, the government stamped out Mumboism, exiling its leader to Lamu island.[229] It is probable that Pleydell was posted to Ng'iya, Alego in 1921 to deal with the effects of this movement.

3.9 Spirituality

At the heart of the praxis matrix is the spirituality of the agents. To analyse the spirituality of CMS and Reuben Omulo, this research uses a six-fold typology developed by Dale Cannon[230] and Richard Foster,[231] which constructs a spectrum of Christian spiritualities (see figure 7 below). While Cannon called his sixfold typology "ways" of praying, marking a Christian's experience of God, Richard Foster called his similar typology "streams" of spirituality:

Dale H. Cannon	Richard J. Foster
Sacramental liturgy	Incarnational tradition (The sacramental life)
Faith seeking understanding	Evangelical tradition (The Word-centered life)
Meditative contemplation	Contemplative tradition (The prayer-filled life)
Spiritual empowerment	Charismatic tradition (The Spirit-empowered life)
Devotional surrender	Holiness tradition (The virtuous life)
Deeds of justice	Social justice tradition (The compassionate life)

Figure 7: The Six-fold Typology – Cannon and Foster

For both Cannon and Foster, these streams were not mutually exclusive, for most believers experience their faith in terms of more than one of them. This section explores the types of spirituality that adopters displayed and the dominant spirituality that moved them to adopt the Christian innovation.

---

229. Mumboism continued to be a force until the late 1930s, opposing such things as inoculation against smallpox. Bethwell Ogot, "British Administration in Central", noted that at least 500 members of the cult are scattered across Central and Southern Nyanza.
230. Cannon, "Different ways of Christian prayer," 309–334.
231. Foster, *Streams of Living Water*.

This section also describes the spirituality of the change agents, examining the types of spirituality practised by the CMS missionaries. What was the dominant spirituality among them? And how did those factors shape their mission approach?

3.9.1 Reuben Omulo's Spirituality

As Omulo embarked on his studies in Maseno, the rational tradition of theologizing that characterizes the Anglican tradition started influencing him. It was in studying Scripture that Omulo most experienced the presence and guidance of God and discerned the word of God for his life and for the Luo. In discussing the basic spiritual experience and the work of the Holy Spirit that motivated Omulo to participate in God's mission, this section will seek to accurately describe his spirituality.

Omulo's earlier experience in Maseno shaped his spirituality. At a young age, he entered the spiritual crucible engineered to mould his thinking, which Willis described as a "Christian environment" where they prayed, studied the Scriptures and sang spiritual songs, in line with the liturgical prescriptions of the CMS.[232] Even though Omulo had observed his father and community pray, there was no formal and organized worship such as he learned as a Christian in Maseno. He taught it to his students, who emulated it in Maseno, Kisumu and Ulumbi, the places where he served. The Maseno boys exhibited a noticeable character change, prompting Luo workers in Kisumu to request CMS to send the boys to teach them what they had learned, for they said: "Something had happened to them, and they were changed manifestly for the better."[233] This "better" was the holiness tradition that characterised their lives. Besides sharing in this tradition, Omulo was a teacher whose life the boys emulated.

A virtuous life, characterized by "devotional surrender" was another dimension of spirituality noted in Omulo's life, in terms of the typology above. His devotion to Christ, which exemplified his surrender was evident when his parents died in 1916. He remained faithful to Christ by remaining in the mission to teach, rather than assume a role in his father's family and live among his people.

---

232. Willis, "Reflection in 1949," 51.
233. Willis, 50.

At this early stage, Omulo's spirituality in the social justice tradition (the compassionate life) was yet to blossom, but it showed itself already in his compassion for the children and women in polygamous marriages. He manifested a desire to include them and invite them to Christ. This feature of Omulo's spirituality developed gradually, as the struggle against colonialism intensified during the late 1920s and the 1940s and the polarization between Blacks and Whites exploded (see chapters 4 and 5).

3.9.2 CMS's Spirituality

CMS represented multiple spiritualities because its various members expressed multiple spiritualities. Each of these CMS missionaries played a spiritual role in mission field, hence contributing to the mission's spirituality.

Maseno became the crucible that forged CMS's spirituality. The manifest CMS spirituality was the Anglican liturgical tradition driven by Willis and Pleydell. They not only led in liturgical worship but also translated the liturgy into the vernacular for the students' usage. So Maseno had the Book of Common Prayer, hymns and liturgical tradition in Dholuo, which enabled the Christians to dramatize and live in God's presence in their worship. At each gathering, the church became a constant reminder and demonstration of God's presence with His people in his world. As Ratzinger has said, "Liturgy in the proper sense, is part of this worship, but so too is life according to God's will."[234] Their actions were a participation in God's work in the world, which translated into service to God. The Maseno environment was set up according to a monastic model, creating "a Christian environment and a Christian atmosphere,"[235] with communal prayers conducted every morning and evening. This created a spirituality of sacramental life through prayers modelled in Anglican prayer service using the Book of Common Prayer.

The pioneering work demanded prayer of the CMS missionaries, who developed a contemplative spirituality. Willis, reflecting from his apparent abortive experience at Maragoli, was led into contemplation by asking whether he had wasted the eight months working there. Aggravating it was

---

234. Ratzinger, *Spirit of Liturgy*, 5.
235. Willis, "Reflection in 1949," 51.

the sympathetic lady's question, "and do you think, Willis, that you are doing any good?"[236] He thus pondered:

> At such a time, almost inevitably, such questions suggest themselves. . . . In England one had been doing a worthwhile job, every hour of the day usefully occupied; here one might work, but without a knowledge of the language, without a school or a church, without scholars or congregation, what good was one really doing? How different it all was from the days of the apostles, when they went forth armed with supernatural powers, backing their words by impressive miracles? How different from the days of St. Augustine, when he landed in Kent, supported by a body of forty monks, and welcomed by a king whose queen was already Christian? How different from the beginning of the mission in Uganda, when the first pioneer, C. T. Wilson, stood alone but was there by the initiation and as a guest of the Kabaka himself? And how different were the people themselves? People on an immeasurably lower social and intellectual level than the Baganda, completely uninterested and completely indifferent.[237]

Willis and his CMS colleagues exemplified a contemplative spirituality since in this experience they learned to absolutely depend on God, and to live with a deeper consciousness of God's presence near them in the hour of disappointment and dependence. Thus, they ploughed in hope, anchored in the scriptural text of knowing that since "the labour is not in vain in the Lord, those months were not wasted."[238]

Because of the nature of genuine pioneer work, the CMS missionaries' spirituality was visible in their devotional surrender as they sacrificed more in the field than they did in Britain. For Willis, the scriptural verse undergirding their devotion was: "Cast your bread upon the waters and thou shalt find it after many days."[239] His horrifying physical experience, amplified by an unbearable fever, personal family loss (the death of his father) during his stay in Kenya, caused him to lament, "as very opportune as I felt I had

---

236. Willis, 42.
237. Willis, 42.
238. Willis, 50.
239. Willis, 43.

reached the end of my tether"[240] He could not have borne those difficulties without divine help.

Walter Owen showed the spiritual dimension of deeds of justice better than any of the CMS missionaries. He acted in compassion to save the lives of the sick, risking his own health by inoculating about 11,000 people. Owen's actions stood out, mirroring the sacrificial love of Christ. This social justice spirituality would be amplified in the succeeding years,[241] and is addressed in chapters 4 and 5.

3.9.3 Interaction Between the Spiritualities of Reuben Omulo and CMS

By choosing the Iona model and creating, in the words of Willis, a Christian environment where the African can learn Christian faith with no undue influence from tradition, both Omulo and CMS missionaries prayed together in the morning and evening, used the liturgical worship established in the Book of Common Prayer translated into the vernacular, and sang hymns, psalms and spiritual songs to express their spirituality. The Luo religion did not have a structured liturgical order in worship that Christianity had; therefore, Omulo imbibed what Christianity taught him in terms of sacramental spirituality. By adopting the Anglican liturgy also in their household prayers, they ordered their worship in the church's liturgical calendar whose liturgy pointed, in the words of Watts in two directions: "both to God and Humanity."[242] Such congregational worship gave glory to God in obeying the divine command and upheld the Spirit-filled tradition. The worship also demanded that they lift people towards God, and thus they contributed to human transformation.

Omulo practised an integrated spirituality that rejected the "separation of spiritual salvation from earthly welfare."[243] CMS focused on developing a spiritual religion of salvation but, in the evangelical tradition, integrated it into society. The interaction between his inclusive spirituality and the CMS's evangelical spirituality continued to play an important role throughout Omulo's period of service and life.

---

240. Willis, "Reflection in 1949," 43.
241. Richards, *Fifty Years in Nyanza*, 13–14.
242. Watts, "Experiencing Liturgy."
243. Gollwitzer, "Why Black Theology," 54.

3.10 Overview of the Encounters

In this chapter we discussed the praxes of Reuben Omulo and the CMS during the period from 1906 to 1920, using a praxis matrix. By exploring the role of each dimension in the matrix, the chapter brought out insights from that period and helped identify the mission praxes that led to the establishment of the Anglican Church in Nyanza. The extent and depth of the "overlap" between these two praxes and the nature of the interaction in each dimension determined the unique dynamics of the encounter.

CMS mission expected to proclaim the gospel in Nyanza through the Europeans. But CMS, inhibited by the numbers, the expanse of the task and the cost of missionary sustenance, looked to African agents instead. Nyanza depended on its own resources. The entire work of evangelization and education was the toil of African teachers, among them Omulo.

Omulo's people of Gem had decided to accept the Europeans before they arrived in Nyanza. To embrace the mission, therefore, signalled an acceptance of the imperial regime. For the Luo, CMS was the means to that goal, while the embrace motivated missionaries to engage the Luo as "civilizing" agents. To offer education was a mutual interest of Omulo and CMS, and together they used education for evangelism. But for Omulo and his people it was a means to new opportunities proffered by the new order. The spiralling demand for schooling led to a literary revolution and the quick spread of Christianity among the Luo.

CMS's goal for indigenizing the church found resonance and help in Omulo and the Luo people. This implied an integrated church, connected to the global Anglican Church while under indigenous leadership, presenting a message sensitive to the cultural context. To Omulo and his fellow converts, the missionaries did not proclaim a strange God. This made the transition to Christianity easier, and with the vernacular Scriptures as God's words, removed the ambiguity in the Luo religion.

The interplay between Omulo's and CMS's interpretation of tradition revealed a creative tension between the Luo tradition and Christianity. It also showed how religious and non-religious outliers in their societies shaped the interaction with the Christian message in significant ways. For Omulo, it was an attempt to balance Christianity's demands with traditional responsibilities and so integrate the Luo into Christianity. For Willis of CMS, it was an attempt to understand the Luo worldview in order to infuse it with the scriptural message and to proclaim the faith through translation.

Education remained the hallmark of significant CMS activity in Nyanza and was made successful by both the mission and Omulo. Omulo played a part in the CMS's translation work, which spurred a literary revolution among the Luo. This commitment to translation diminished the dominant role of missionaries as evangelists and elevated the local agents.

Although Omulo affirmed the missionary teaching on polygamists, they disagreed on how the church should treat polygamous families. CMS demanded that polygamous men should discard extra wives and their children. The paradox is that while this disagreement shook the Christian position, it led to a re-evaluation, which granted the victims latitude and hence strengthened Christianity.

The Luo religion lacked structured liturgical worship. That was an innovation Christianity provided to the converts. Omulo imbibed what Christianity taught him of sacramental spirituality and passed it on to his students and people, as a service to both God and humanity. But colonial experiences nudged both Omulo and the CMS to realize the need for Christian involvement in matters of justice as an integral dimension of discipleship. The next chapter will discuss how justice spirituality bloomed.

By investigating in this chapter how the praxes of CMS and Omulo overlapped and intersected between 1906 and 1920, we discerned the patterns of encounter between them. Our interest has been the nature and quality of those interactions and the transformations they exerted on both parties as they interacted in Central Nyanza.

CHAPTER 4

Indigenization Stage: Tracing Interactions of Mission Praxis in Central Nyanza from 1921 to 1945

4.1 Introduction

The people of Central Nyanza experienced existential angst when they became part of the Kenya Colony. Between 1921 and 1945, as explained in this chapter, the colonial regime introduced inhibiting changes that unsettled their society. This is the context against which the chapter interrogates mission praxis by first constructing the "innovating" mission praxis of Reuben Omulo (as internal change agent) by using the praxis matrix. The chapter then constructs the "transforming" praxis of CMS as an external change agent, by using the same matrix. It concludes by tracing the interaction between those two praxes, examining how each of the seven dimensions of the matrix, representing their intentional transformative ideas and actions, responded to or corresponded with each other. Each of the seven sections brings the two sets of responses into dialogue.

During this period CMS attempted to indigenize the Anglican Church it established, as the archival sources on mission work have shown, which was vital in formulating the CMS's agency. Omulo and fellow African Christians built the church during this era, thus asserting their faith. Narratives and records of events about Luo Christians during this stage offer information with which to locate Omulo's agency. In this study, the agency is both personal and corporate.

This chapter continues to analyse the encounters between Omulo and CMS, using the approach described in §1.6 and §3.1. As a result, the emergent dialogue displays the character of the mission encounters between them.

4.2 Central Nyanza from 1921 to 1945: Key Political Economic and Cultural Events

As in Chapter 3, this chapter also surveys key aspects of the surrounding society before focusing on the praxes of Omulo and CMS. During this period, the colonial government enacted rafts of societal changes in Central Nyanza, starting with changing the country's name in June 1920. The government re-named the British East Africa Protectorate to Kenya and declared it a Crown Colony. This move had such far-reaching consequences for the people of Nyanza and the CMS that I chose this event as the *terminus* to mark the second period of this research.

After 1920 there followed a series of overbearing policies introduced to exploit Africans. However, the irony of the period was that the white settlers' greed gave birth to the 1923 Devonshire White Paper, which actually trimmed their interests. The Paper established African interests as the Colony's priority, thus setting the stage for Kenya's independence struggles.

4.2.1 Political Context

In the re-organisation that followed, Nyanza ceased to be a Ugandan protectorate. The government implemented changes which included reducing Africans' wages by a third, introduced the *kipande* system,[1] increased direct tax to 16 shillings per head and adopted forced labour. Forced labour for public works was upsetting and most unpopular among Africans:

> District Commissioner issued labour quotas to chiefs and headmen, and the chiefs were turned into labour recruiters. Chiefs were subject to pressure and bribery to exact more and more

---

1. "Registration certificate recording work periods, wages, comments by employers, and other employment-related matters; from 1920, they required all adult males to carry the Kipande under penalty of heavy fines." Sicherman, *Ngugi wa Thiong'o*, 210.

labour from their areas, and recruiting methods became a major grievance among the people. Chiefs or sub-chiefs, issued with an order for labour, arbitrarily picked batches of forty men at a time from a location, and had them signed up for six months work contract under which it was a penal offence to decline.[2]

The people protested the government's actions. First, African teachers in Maseno called for a boycott by both students and staff at Maseno, demanding that Nyanza revert to the pre-colonial state. Then those teachers mobilised the Luo people through the chiefs to agitate for changes. They convened a general meeting at Lundha, Gem, in 1921, during which they articulated their grievances, and created a political organisation, the Young Kavirondo Association (YKA), to negotiate with the government (§4.7.1).

The state's worry was an imminent countrywide revolt, for political agility in Nyanza was rising to Central Kenya's level. Aware of the regime's capacity for violence and eagerness to crush any revolt, the people chose a different approach (§§4.7.1 and 4.7.2.5). Working with Archdeacon Owen, Nyanza leaders in 1923 transformed the YKA into the Kavirondo Taxpayers Welfare Association (KTWA). They engaged the government through cooperation and avoided overt politics. Because its primary concern was the welfare of the people, the association got the government's support.

4.2.2 Devonshire White Paper

European settlers were determined to turn Kenya into a "Whiteman's Country," but African and Indian grievances bothered both the missionaries and the Colonial Office in London. That led to meetings in Devonshire, England in 1923.[3] The Devonshire conference resolved the Colonial Office's dilemma by balancing the conflicting interests of European settlers, Africans and Indians. The Indians demanded land in the White highlands and permission to bring their families from India. However, the White Paper declared African interest paramount and made a clever compromise of "a longstanding controversy surrounding Indian claims for equality with European settlers in Kenya."[4] The paper reserved the Kenyan Highlands for exclusive use

---

2. Ochieng', "Colonial Famines in Luoland," 26.
3. Maxon, *Struggle for Kenya*, 270–279.
4. Maxon, "Devonshire Declaration," 268.

by European settlers but lifted the cap on the Asian migration quota into Kenya. It established a Legislative Council (LEGICO) with the following representation: eleven Europeans, five Asians, one Arab, and one missionary (to represent African interests). To the latter post, the government nominated Dr. Arthur. Even though the settlers dominated the legislation, they could not make any attempts towards self-rule in Kenya, for the paper ruled out any constitutional changes to favour the White land. This kept Africans out of national politics, although it allowed their participation in the country's administration at the local council level. The paper envisioned African involvement in the native councils to continue until 1931 when they would be allowed to have representatives in the LEGICO. Meanwhile, the Colonial Office became the guarantor of African interests, for the White paper was unequivocal that Kenya was an African territory. It urged the racial groups to work towards gradual African self-rule. Hence, the colonial government had to balance safeguarding the settlers' interests with training and educating Africans to prepare them for responsibilities and future independence.

The Paper affirmed Kenya as a settler economy, which intensified the influx of European settlers after the Great War. That in turn increased the demand for labour on settlers' farms, which caused cracks to appear in the colonial design, since the alleged "prioritizing of African interests" excluded the key issues of land and labour. That exclusion aroused African political consciousness, laying the foundation for future political resistance. Importantly, it coalesced Africans and Asians into an opposition group of those affected. So, in clarifying the priority of African interests in the Colony, the Devonshire White Paper became one of the most consequential edicts in Kenya's political history. This edict also shaped education policies, which affected CMS's work.

4.2.3 Colonial Education

The Devonshire White Paper recommended the improvement of African education to prepare them for leadership. In pursuit of that goal, the Phelps Stokes Commission for East, Central and South Africa was appointed in 1924 to produce an official formulation and design of education for Africans. The commission recommended Booker T. Washington's Hampton and Tuskegee Institutes in the United States as a model for African education. In response to the recommendations of the Commission, the government instituted the Education Ordinance of 1924. The British Colonial Office issued "The 1925

Memorandum," a paper on Education Policy in British Tropical Africa, which became the basis of education policy in Kenya for 1920–1945. In 1926, it established thirteen broad principles that guided education policies, in which missions assumed major responsibilities for primary and secondary education. It recommended four tiers in African education. The first of these was sub-elementary schools run by missions and manned by untrained teachers. They were unaided and teaching had heavy religious content, with literacy, arithmetic, hygiene, and gardening taught as well. The second was elementary schools, whose course ran for five years on a prescribed syllabus. The third was primary schools, which were boarding schools but admitted a few day pupils. These ran for three years between classes six and eight, majoring in literacy and practical work. They instructed students in Kiswahili and English unless sanctioned by the director of education. The fourth was secondary schools, which were at the apex of the system. Those included Alliance High School, started in 1926 by the Protestant missions for African boys. The Catholics established Kabaa secondary school in 1928. The number increased such that by 1939 Alliance had one hundred and six pupils, Maseno fifty-eight and St. Mary's Yala, seventeen. In 1940, Alliance and Kabaa students attempted the Cambridge School Certificate for the first time.

The government established Jean's School at Kabete in 1924, tasking it to train school supervisors, who would train teachers for vocational schools. As a result, the Local Native Councils during 1925 instituted a tax of two shillings per adult to expand educational institutions. As a result, the government could build similar schools in Narok in 1922, Kericho in 1925, Kajiado in 1926, Tambach in 1928, Loitoktok in 1929, Kakamega in 1932 and Kagumo in 1934.[5]

Important changes in Kenya's education policies occurred between 1920 and 1945. In 1922, the Department of Education established a grants-in-aid system, where schools deemed to meet certain standards received financial aid. But the need for a policy paper for effectively running education remained. As a result, the administration developed the 1927 White Paper,[6] which invited the Europeans as co-agents to safeguard African educational interests yet without discussing African grievances. The neglect of these

---

5. Furley and Watson, *History of Education*.
6. Maxon, *Struggle for Kenya*, 279.

grievances led to the Black Paper of 1930. Its unique counsel was to promote African participation through education in affairs of the local areas. That gave grounds for the establishment of independent schools in Kenya after 1930.

4.2.4 Economic development

By the end of 1920, Nyanza had outlived the effects of the *Kanga* famine[7] of 1917–1919, which was so named after the soldiers returning from the First World War. The Provincial Commissioner reported a "magnificent crop in Native Reserves." But the colonial economic policies still considered settler agriculture the backbone of the Kenyan economy, implying that Africans would remain mere suppliers of labour. Since the African population had increased by the mid-1920s, using force to recruit their labour was no longer necessary, for population pressure on land and taxation guaranteed enough labour on European farms. Ochieng'[8] estimated that, by 1928, more than half of the able-bodied men in the two largest African nationalities (the Kikuyu and Luo) worked for the Europeans. Meanwhile, the authorities continued to harvest labour, neglecting peasant agriculture, which was the food mainstay in Nyanza. Hence, Ochieng'[9] argues that colonial economic and labour policies created a crisis in Nyanza's peasant agriculture, by draining crucial labour and ending the traditional *mondo* (surplus) storage system.

Lack of roads exacerbated the early colonial famines in Luoland in areas around the Lake, rendering the areas inaccessible. Although African tax contributions increased, the colonial government expenditure on services in the African areas was appallingly lacking. During his visit to the district in 1932, Lord Moyne found the district spent merely a sixth of the revenue collected from Africans on the Native services of the district.[10] Insufficient transportation meant that food shortages remained a chronic problem.[11] Many in the rural areas suffered, unlike the urban dwellers, because of a lack of food market access. For instance, since there was no direct road between Yimbo

---

7. Ochieng', "Colonial Famines in Luoland," 27.
8. Ochieng', 33.
9. Ochieng', 31.
10. District Commissioner Central Nyanza, District Annual Report 1932.
11. Maddox, "*Njaa*: Food Shortages," 17–33.

and Kisumu town, people's only option was to walk more than sixty miles to Samia or Luanda (Kamang'ong'o) to buy grain.

Nyanza again experienced famine in 1928. Ochieng' mentions the *Nyagweso* famine of 1928 and 1929, in which a few poor people died around the lake.[12] The famine was occasioned by the desert locusts. To mitigate the problem, the government set up a Famine Relief and Food Control Board, capitalized to the tune of £200,000, and distributed maize to affected areas. But in 1931 the locusts returned to Nyanza, destroyed crops and precipitated the *Bonyo* famine of that year. From 1931 to 1934, there was a disastrous drought in Kenya. The drought led to several crop failures in Luoland, which led to the *Otwoma* famine in 1933. Again, the Luo locations around the lake were most affected.

To support the population, the government distributed maize flour free to people in those affected areas. Meanwhile, in Alego, Lolwe and North Ugenya and other parts of Central Nyanza, the government promoted the growing of cassava and potatoes to support the population. The government facilitated Indian and European traders to import and stock food for sale in the province. As a result, Ochieng' notes, "More Indian-manned trading centres, such as Asembo Bay, Kadimo Bay, Rangwe and Ndere were established."[13] The administrators encouraged the peasants to plant famine crops, such as cassava and sweet potatoes, in the swampy areas: "A considerable amount of hybrid seed was introduced and distributed during this period. For example, in the Western Province (then part of Nyanza), which was equally affected by this famine, 800 loads of maize seed, 850 loads of bean seed, and 50 loads of rice seed were sold to the natives."[14]

The period addressed in the chapter ends with World War II (1939 to 1945), during which the government called on Africans' involvement. It was urgent because the British needed to defend Kenya against an Italian invasion around 1943. The Colonial administration made it a priority in 1943, and they conscripted soldiers and collected supplies for the war. Africans responded with a sense of duty. Many enlisted under the King's African Rifles, the Pioneers, the police, and other unit formations. Those who remained

---

12. Ochieng', "Colonial Famines in Luoland," 30.
13. Ochieng', 29.
14. Leys, *Underdevelopment in Kenya*, 31.

supported the war with great sacrifice. To avoid being conscripted, many Luo men left the province for wage employment. Nyanza had 91,218 men working outside the province by the end of 1941, besides the 5,131 men conscripted for the war. That same year, 553,771 bags of maize, 27,126 bags of finger-millet, 65,000 bags of sorghum and 12,679 cattle went from Nyanza to support the war.[15] By 1942, 95,000 men worked outside the province. The government bought from Nyanza 544,446 bags of finger millet and 483 tons of fish that year. That precipitated the *Otonglo* Famine, which lasted from 1943 until 1945. The famine was ostensibly caused by the short-rains failure at the end of 1942, but Ochieng' blames it on the government's depleting both labour and food surpluses from Nyanza while ignoring the provinces' food needs.[16] His views comport with Hunter's (Nyanza Commissioner) conclusion that it was because of the administration's "inability to estimate accurately the already vastly increased rate of food consumption in the province."[17] They should have focused on forestalling food shortages rather than disposing of surpluses.

This brief survey of the political, economic, and social context of Central Nyanza between 1921 and 1945 provides an adequate background against which this study explores the mission praxes of Omulo and the CMS, and the interaction between them, in this period. As in previous chapters, the analysis of their praxes starts with the dimension of agency.

4.3 Agency

This section explores the agency of Omulo and the CMS missionaries for the period between 1921 and 1945. The period marked Omulo's work as an "innovating" agent of Christianity as he played a crucial role in crystallising the work that began on education and the church. The section further discusses changes in Omulo's life and the crucial turning points in his journey. It then discusses selected agents of change among the CMS missionaries, those continuing in service and those newly deployed. It explains their relation to the people they served, and the measure to which their social, economic, gender, and class position in relationship to the "others" influenced their

---

15. Ochieng', "Colonial Famines in Luoland," 30.
16. Ochieng', 30.
17. Ochieng', 31.

approach. Finally, the agency section explores the nature of the relationship between Omulo and CMS to explain the extent to which their encounters shaped Christian witness in Central Nyanza.

4.3.1 Reuben Omulo's Agency

The agency section in chapter 3 discussed how Omulo got involved with the CMS from 1908 to 1920. It further described how that involvement transformed his life and his society. On that foundation, this section discusses Omulo's agency from 1921 to 1945 by explaining changes in his life and exploring the innovations he adopted in his service as a Christian witness. It pays attention to crucial turning points in Omulo's life, identifying the role power relations played and how these factors influenced his decision for ongoing involvement.

4.3.1.1 Omulo's Family

By 1921 Omulo held a significant teaching position at Maseno mission. Having been a teacher since 1914, Omulo rose to what Owen called "Head Native Teacher in our Maseno School."[18] That was a very responsible position, one of influence with the missionaries, with the African staff and in Luo society at large. His marriage in 1919 to Leah Odiembo further enhanced his societal status among the Luo, paving the way for his siblings to be married. Pricilla Odera married Jairo Mbeya of Alego Ka'Ruoth Malele. Doris Nyando Apiyo, the mother to Baker Otieno of Bar Kalare, Naphtali Oyanda, and her twin, Bethsheba Akoth Adongo, married Naaman Dulo in Umani (Abamani) and later moved to South Nyanza. His last-born brother James Aweyo married Stela Aweyo. Asenath Ngalo, Omulo's half-sister, married Silfano Ayayo in Umani. Akoth's marriage to Dulo, the stepbrother of Ayayo, made Ngalo's marriage to Ayayo possible. Omulo presided over their wedding in 1925 at the Ulumbi Anglican Church.[19] Ngalo's brother, Jason Wahore, married Felesia Adwar from Alego and worked in Mombasa. Joseph Owiti married Wilkister *nyar* Kisumo and worked in Nairobi. She had one sister, Sibia Rogo.

His siblings, stepmothers and uncles looked up to him and Leah to offer leadership at their homestead. Besides, Omulo had to raise his own

---

18. Owen, Letter to Heywood 27 June 1927.
19. Wanyanga, *Triumph Through Faith*, 25.

family. Two of their sons were born at Maseno. Towards the end of 1920 Habakkuk Walter Owiti (d. 1937) was born (see §3.3.1) and in December 1922 Humphrey Malaki Otieno (d. 1983). While in Kisumu, they had their other four children.[20] Their third was Gilbert Hezron Oduor in 1925, and Christine Jesika Anyango (d. 1997) in 1927, breaking the pattern of boys to the delight of the family, who in jubilation called out *Leah okelo wendo* (Leah brought us a visitor), giving her the nickname Wendo. Then they had Janet Agnes Awuor in 1930 and Alfreda Edwina Athieno Odera in 1933 (d. 1969). While at Kisumu, Omulo's family experienced many challenges. Malaki Otieno suffered a polio attack in 1926 that left him paralysed on the right side. But a severe tragedy struck them in 1937 when Walter Owiti died at school, following a fatal head strike by his teacher, Clement Odeny.[21] Omulo buried his son, embraced Mr. Odeny and carried on with the mission (§4.9.1.3).

4.3.1.2 Reuben Omulo the Padre

The Nyanza Archdeaconry came under the jurisdiction of the Mombasa diocese after 1920. An archdeaconry is an authorised division of a diocese for administrative purposes within which the archdeacon, a senior priest, exercises jurisdiction.[22] Many deaneries combine to form an archdeaconry. The Uganda diocese had a reasonable number of ordained Africans, unlike Mombasa, for it took over fifteen years from the first baptism in Nyanza before Africans were ordained.[23] The majority of the teacher-evangelists were self-appointed volunteers, whose inner conviction inspired their informal work. Their success earned them recognition by the missionaries who gave them official sanction and appointment for work they had been doing, like what happened in Uganda in 1891 under Bishop Tucker.[24]

In 1924, CMS selected four African teachers from Maseno for diaconate training. These were Reuben Omulo, George Samuel Okoth, Musa Auma, and Yeremiah Musungu Awori.[25] CMS did not expect every teacher and pioneer

---

20. Alice Otieno, Personal interview, 22 and 25 September 2020.
21. Okero, Personal interview, 16 November 2019.
22. Ravenscroft, *Role of the Archdeacon*.
23. Omulokoli, "Historical Development," 288.
24. Alfred Tucker, *Eighteen Years in Uganda*, 111–115.
25. Omulokoli, "Historical Development," 290.

Christian to transition into the ordained ministry.[26] Omulokoli[27] notes that the discussions on the ministerial needs of the region took centre stage at the committee meeting in early 1923. Bishop Heywood's presence gave urgency to the meeting, which resolved that "a class for training candidates for deacons' orders be started at once, the Archdeacon and Mr. Pleydell to confer with the bishop as to details."[28]

For two years, Omulo and his three colleagues trained for ministry. They trained for the first year (1923) under Pleydell at Ng'iya. Pleydell had been Omulo's teacher in 1908 and was his colleague at Maseno. The second year (1924) he trained under Owen, whom he had come to know and worked with.[29] On completing his training, Omulo was ordained as a deacon by Bishop Heywood on 21 December 1924 in Nairobi, making history as one of the first four indigenous clergy in Nyanza. CMS posted him to Kisumu in February 1925, giving him a responsible position as "leader of the Native Church in Kisumu."[30] He developed the school in Kisumu mission as an integral part of the mission.

When CMS re-opened the Divinity School at Frere Town, Mombasa in 1928,[31] Omulo and other deacons returned for studies. They trained under Rev. Butcher, who arrived at Frere Town from the Alliance High School, Kikuyu. On 8 September 1928, they began their Divinity class, a course that lasted for one term, preparing them for priesthood. During this time, the friendship between Omulo and Jeremiah Awori became firm, as they connected with fellow deacons Levi Gachanja and Samuel Nguru from central Kenya. Bishop Heywood ordained as priest Omulo and his cohort on 28 December 1929 in Mombasa.[32] The CMS posted Omulo to Kisumu,[33] where he ministered as the padre, a teacher, and a missionary in charge. He was

---

26. Butcher, "Kenya's Native Ministry", 202; Kavirondo Ruri-decanal Council Minutes, 3 June 1922.
27. Omulokoli, "Historical Development," 289.
28. Kavirondo Ruri-decanal Council Minutes, 8 February 1923.
29. Omulokoli, "Historical Development," 290.
30. Owen, Letter to Heywood, 27 June 1927.
31. CMS Executive Committee Minutes, 17–18 June 1928.
32. Cole, "Theological Training," 10.
33. Provincial Unit of Research, *Rabai to Mumias*, 22.

transferred in the 1940s to rural pastorates beginning at Ndiru (discussed in chapter 5).[34]

4.3.2 CMS's Agency

During the period between 1921 and 1945, two kinds of missionaries characterised the CMS agency in Nyanza. The first were the carry-over missionaries from the earlier period, who were discussed in the previous chapter. They had served in the Diocese of Uganda's Nyanza archdeaconry and were transferred to the Diocese of Mombasa after 1920. These included Pleydell, Wright and Owen, who had deep ministry connections in Nyanza, having been pioneer missionaries there. It became a transition period for those missionaries as well. Wright retired in 1923,[35] while Pleydell retired in 1934 due to deafness and went back to England.[36] Owen retired in 1944 and died in 1945.[37] The second category of missionaries arrived in the 1920s, bringing specific skills and qualifications the mission needed. These missionaries included schoolmasters, medical staff and churchmen required to set up the embryonic mission institutions.

Two bishops served the diocese of Mombasa during the period which is the focus of this chapter. First was the Rt. Rev. Richard Stanley Heywood, who was born on 27 October 1867, and educated at Windlesham House School, Wellington College and Trinity Cambridge. He was ordained in 1892 and served as a curate in Walcot, Bath.[38] He then became principal of the CMS Divinity School in Poona and later served in Bombay in a similar position. Heywood became Bishop of Mombasa in 1918, where he served until 1936. Upon his retirement, Heywood became an Assistant Bishop of Coventry, at Kenilworth, until 1952. He died on 16 December 1955.

The Rt. Rev. Reginald Percy Crabbe succeeded Bishop Heywood as the Anglican Bishop of Mombasa in 1936. Bishop Crabbe was born on 15 July

---

34. A pastorate is one or more congregations which form the "sphere of a pastor" (Regulations 1905 G/AH 1/6, 4). Each congregation would elect delegates for a Pastorate Committee, which would meet monthly and be chaired by the pastor who normally had an effective power of veto. Each Pastorate Committee would in turn send delegates to the District Church Council (DCC).

35. Hewitt, *Problems of Success*, 142.

36. Mojola, *God Speaks in Our Languages*, 216.

37. Murray, "Archdeacon W. E. Owen," 644.

38. Wilson, *Windlesham House School*.

1883 to a clergyman father. He was a gifted athlete who represented Great Britain at the 1906 Olympic games in the 800m and 1500m. Crabbe was educated at Trent College and Corpus Christi College, Cambridge and was ordained in 1907. After a curacy at St. George's, Newcastle-under-Lyme, he became Chaplain of the Bishop of Sierra Leone. Then he held incumbencies at St. Mary's Peckham, and St. Mary's, Sheffield.[39] Crabbe served as the Rural Dean of Greenwich, then Dulwich from 1924 to 1936, before he became Bishop of Mombasa. He returned to England in 1953.[40]

Edward Carey Francis was born at Hampstead on 13 September 1897, and educated at William Ellis School, Hampstead. There he showed extraordinary promise, both at work and at games. Francis was the head boy of the school, and the captain of football, cricket, tennis and athletics. He served during World War I as a commissioned officer of the Honorable Artillery Company. After the war, Francis picked up the scholarship to which they had elected him at Trinity College, Cambridge. His mathematical interests were in analysis, and he was much influenced by three Trinity mathematicians, Hardy, Littlewood and Pollard. In 1923, he won the Rayleigh Prize award for a substantial essay on the Denjoy-Stieltjes Integral, and two papers on "Differentiation regarding a function" and "The Lebesque-Stieltjes Integral."[41]

In 1928 Carey Francis left Cambridge for Kenya to serve as a lay teaching missionary under CMS. He often yearned to serve in missions. Hence, he left a promising academic career in England to teach in Maseno School, where CMS assigned him the administrator's role. He became the sixth principal of the school (1928–1940). His transformative ideas in education improved services there. Under his leadership, Maseno became one of the best schools in East Africa, but for Francis, Maseno was the training ground for his most significant work, the headmastership of the Alliance High School from 1940 to 1962. His Maseno students called him *Achuma*, the man of steel. He died in Nairobi on 27 July 1966.

In 1921 Miss Fanny Moller, from Australia, joined the staff at Maseno as a teacher. She served as a mentor to young African girls. Moller learned the Luo language and ran women's and girls' classes at Maseno. She helped Dr.

---

39. *The Times*, "Bishop of Mombasa," 27 February 1953, 8.
40. *The Times*, "Rt. Rev. R. P. Crabbe," 10.
41. Pars, "Edward Carey Francis," 8.

Stones at the Maseno hospital as well. In 1922 she stood in for the recovering Miss Downer at the Butere school, and Omachar[42] noted that other times she helped in Mrs. Hirsute's school, which was held in the afternoons to educate local herd boys and girls. CMS appointed Miss Moller the first principal of Ng'iya Girls in 1923 and she served until 1952.[43] She was a social person, and had gained vast mission experience from her work in Butere and Maseno. She was proficient in Luo and had dealt with African students.[44]

Handley D. Hooper was the son of Douglas Hooper, a missionary in Kenya. He was born in Jilore, Kenya, but following his mother's death, an aunt (his mother's sister) in England raised him. Handley was educated at Queen's College in Cambridge where he got a BA in 1912. He trained for ordination at Bishop's Hostel and Bishop's Auckland. In 1916, a year after his marriage to Margaret Cicely Winterbotham, Hooper came to Kenya with the Kenyan Mission Volunteers during World War I. Hooper continued his father's work at Kahuhia after his death until 1926, then returned to London and served as the CMS Africa Secretary until 1949.

Hooper became Canon of Mombasa Cathedral and has been depicted "as one of the newer post-war breeds of CMS recruits, Oxbridge educated and liberal-minded."[45] Hooper's family was staunchly evangelical, but with an independent streak,[46] which may account for Hooper seeing ecclesiastical organization as of lesser importance. Hooper had "an acceptance of the colonial distribution of power in Kenya combined with a moral earnestness about the ideal of trusteeship."[47] His perception of the missionary role as parallel to the British Government's in aiding development was manifest in his involvement in education as a missionary in the 1940s.[48] Though paternalistic, Hooper believed that the African race would in time develop to adulthood,

---

42. Omachar, "Contribution of the Church," 69.
43. Omachar, 69.
44. Omachar, 57.
45. Casson, "Plant a Garden City," 398.
46. Hewitt, *Problems of Success*, 136.
47. Casson, "Plant a Garden City," 398.
48. Handley D. Hooper, Letter to Cash, 377–381.

a perception that eluded many missionaries of his time.[49] Hence, he believed in the spiritual, intellectual, and political development of Africa.[50]

Missionaries assigned to Nyanza during this period bent more towards the much-needed technical work of service than pastoral work. This chapter discusses a selection of CMS missionaries whose work affected the lives of the Luo people.

4.3.3 Interaction Between Reuben Omulo and CMS on Agency

This section explores the interaction between Reuben Omulo and CMS by applying Kritzinger's three categories of encounter: shoulder-to-shoulder, face-to-face, back-to-back, and a fourth as front and behind.[51]

4.3.3.1 Relating Shoulder-to-shoulder

This posture in a relationship implies that partners look in the same direction and share the same goals, values, hope and vision. The interaction between CMS and Omulo began and continued in jointly serving the Luo people in the villages and Maseno. Having begun his teaching in 1914 at Maseno, Omulo proved to be very helpful in plugging the teacher gaps. He taught with great zeal and brought into Maseno many people from Gem, who became Christians at the school. The CMS lost considerable support in England because of economic hardship following World War I, causing its budget to be reduced by 25 percent in 1922. But it was a further reduction in 1927 that dealt a deadly blow to its operations, for it hindered CMS's capacity to deploy missionaries. Recruiting Africans into substantive missionary tasks thereby became inevitable. Indeed, Omulo and his colleagues changed roles from teaching to ordained ministry. Owen recognised their immense contribution and admitted CMS's indebtedness to them.[52] Omulo recognised this to be a deeper way of serving his people and the Lord. Hence, CMS devised a plan for selecting and training teacher-evangelists for the ordained ministry.

---

49. Casson, "Plant a Garden City," 403.
50. Hooper, *Africa in the Making*, 19–20.
51. Kritzinger, "Interreligious dialogue," 47–62.
52. Owen, "Memorandum on Native Education."

4.3.3.2 Face-to-face

In a face-to-face relationship, partners enjoy each other's company but can also experience conflict. Here partners embrace and celebrate each other. How did the CMS missionaries enjoy Omulo's company? And did Omulo enjoy closeness and support with CMS, in the face of challenges? Two letters written in the 1930s reveal the kind of relationship Omulo had with CMS missionaries. News of Omulo's illness in the 1930s circulated around the CMS world, prompting Bishop Willis' letter from Leicestershire. The tone of the letter, written in Dholuo, expresses their enduring embrace of brotherhood:

> Mar Owadwa, Reuben Omulo, amosi ng'ang. Rachna ng'ang' kawinjo kaka ituwo kamano ndalo mang'eng, kendo ka podi-tuwo. Ka chon nibedo gi teko moloyo. To kaka ringruok otuwo kamano to aparo ka chunyi podi otek go Nyasaye, kendo ka en ok oweyi ng'ang. Wach Luo koro otekna, ka ndalo okadho akiya kata podi ogik kare, to chunya oyom kodi kuom tuwo ni, kendo asayo Nyasaye Wuonwa mondo obe kodi okoyi. Ok anyal konyi maber kaka ahero, ni kech rupiya koro otek ka e Bulaya, to ahero miyi matin kaka anyalo mondo okonyigo gi tuwoni. Oriti. Chiega bende omosi go joodu . . . An Osiepni. J. J. Willis.[53]

> Translation: Dear Brother Reuben Omulo, Greetings. It saddens me to hear you have been sick now for a long time and are still sick. Previously you were a vigorous man. But though your body is sick, your spirit is well with God, because God cannot desert you at all. I find Luo language difficult for me now because many days have passed since I spoke it. I sympathize with you on your sickness and I beseech God, our father, that he may help you. I cannot help you as I wish because I find it difficult to get money in England, but I would like to give you the little I can afford to help you with your sickness. Goodbye. My wife and all my family send you greetings. I am your Friend. J. J. Willis.

Willis maintained a close relationship with Omulo, although he was retired, and had left Nyanza twenty years earlier. Despite Omulo being fluent in English, he communicated with Willis in Dholuo. Willis sympathised with

---

53. Willis, Letter to Omulo, 18 August 1938.

Omulo's malady and sent him financial support, besides praying for his recovery. They discussed family issues which showed how vulnerable they had become with each other. Omulo also maintained closeness to Pleydell, who wrote to him from Brighton in 1934:

Mar Padre R. Omulo.[54]

Amosi Ahinya. Ingima Koso? An angima ma moromo, kod jooda bende . . . Piny gi cham ber gilala ka eri, bende adenda duogo makere. Jemsi wuoda opuonjore e skul mar Doctor, ose louo penj mokwuongo. Wuoda tiyo e office, ogoyo Typewriter gi tich moko. To agombo winjo wach ma Kisumo gi odi. Leya ongima koso, kod nyithindo?

Kanisa? erokamano ngang'. Tiatiya, kik iol. Mosna jopuonj, Yonathan, Klement, gi jaduong' Kanisa, mon gi nyimine bende. Nyocha bwana Rawnadha okadho ka, mawamor ahinya, manyisa weche mag Luo mondo oland ni jokanisa e piny Ireland ku motiyoe. Mano Kende. Oriti maken.

An mogeni.

A. E. Pleydell.

Translation: Many greetings. Trust you are well. My wife and I are fairly well . . . The crops are wonderful here and I am gaining health. James, my son, is in medical school, where he has done his first exams. My other son is working at the office, typewriting and other office duties. But I long to hear from Kisumu and about your household. Is Leah well, how about your children? What about the church? Thank you so much. Keep on working and don't give up. Convey my greetings to Clement, and the church elders, women, and sisters as well. Mr. Rawnadha (nickname of a mutual friend) passed through here, we rejoiced to hear Luo news which he will share in the Church in Ireland where he works. That's all. Goodbye.

Yours faithfully

A. E. Pleydell.

---

54. Pleydell, Letter to Omulo, 32.

These letters indicate that Omulo and the CMS missionaries remained close long after leaving Nyanza. They show a continued strong family connection, prompting Pleydell to enquire about Omulo's children's welfare and to share about the progress of his children as well. They talked of crops, which is a Luo way of greeting close friends. Pleydell communicated news about the ministry and spoke about other missionaries who served in Nyanza. These were examples of the relationships Omulo had with CMS during his service.

4.3.3.3 Back-to-back

This dimension stresses the loyalty that binds partners in a relationship of faithfulness, assessing whether they really trust one another or not. The true measure of a relationship is in what partners do behind each other's back. So, the question is, did Omulo trust CMS enough to direct his people to them? And could the CMS trust Omulo? Although the Luo viewed CMS and Owen as one with the government, Omulo and his colleagues still trusted him to guide them. Cognizant of the peril of direct confrontation with the colonial administration, Owen saw the urgent necessity of speaking with one voice on social justice issues. He held that working with the government would allow them to avoid being crushed and, as a result, the good would outweigh the atrocious policies. Omulo accepted the advice of Owen and became vulnerable to the process. Henceforth, they worked with the government officials, including the chiefs and the DCs, as ex officio members and the Senior Commissioner as the vice-president of the association. However, they would not give the government a pass in cases of injustice against the people. In return, Owen risked his reputation, and he braved threats and rejection to expose and amplify injustices done against the Luo people (§4.7.2).

4.3.3.4 Walk in Front or Behind

In a relationship, hard decisions can force partners to oppose each other until one of them leads in decision-making and the other agrees to follow. The impression in the relationship between Omulo and the CMS is that missionaries gave leadership while Omulo and his colleagues followed. But evidence suggests rather a relationship between opponents marked with both confrontation and respect.[55]

---

55. Overdiep, *Het gevecht om de vijand*, 54.

In 1925, after his ordination as deacon, CMS posted Rev. Reuben Omulo to Kisumu to replace Fredrick Wright. He brought into that position ten years of experience teaching at Maseno and leadership as the schoolmaster. Omulo's commitment to Christianity and his ability to communicate the faith among his people influenced his posting. CMS entrusted Omulo as padre in Kisumu to lead an African Anglican congregation, where he previously served as a teacher under Wright. Building on Pleydell's translated Scriptures and liturgy, Omulo enhanced those tools of worship among African congregations, building on that foundation to create a more contextual worship program (§4.7.1.4). Hewitt attests to CMS's praise of Omulo's work in Kisumu: "After Wright's departure an African pastor, Reuben Omulo, had pastoral charge of the church in Kisumu and the CMS annual reports in the late 1920s frequently praised his work and by the later 1930s the Anglican Church in Nyanza had grown."[56] The interaction between Omulo and CMS led to success in leading the Luo people to Christianity.

4.4 Contextual Understanding

This section explores how the interacting agents understood their context in that period. It begins with Omulo's and his Luo people's understanding of social, political, economic, cultural factors shaping the society discussed in section 4.2 above. It shows the peculiar analysis the recipients made of their context. Hence, it explains how they "read the signs of the times" and what factors influenced their decision to adopt certain changes. The second part discusses how CMS analysed Nyanza's social, political, economic, and cultural context at the time, and how those factors shaped their perception and approach. The last part of this section explores the nature of the interaction between Reuben Omulo and the CMS.

4.4.1 Reuben Omulo's Contextual Understanding

This segment discusses Omulo's understanding and perception of social, political, economic, and cultural factors. It also examines how these factors influenced his society between 1920 and 1945. Thus, it explicates how

---

56. Hewitt, *Problems of Success*, 142.

Omulo and the Luo people reacted to colonial rule and the reactions to the contextual changes.

4.4.1.1 *Response to the Colonial Regime*

Kenya's switch from Protectorate to Colony in 1920 and the immediate policies to implement the changes aggrieved Omulo and the people of Nyanza.[57] Odinga[58] and Ogot[59] have enumerated their main grievances as follows:

1. The state increased Hut and Poll Taxes, an enormous and cruel burden to a people coming out of famine. Even though famine had receded as people harvested more crops by 1921, the effects of *Chew kode* (endure with it) famine left the region vulnerable and open to frequent famines, diseases and plagues. While famine killed many people in Nyanza,[60] Ochieng' observed, many more died because of the accompanying calamities and diseases, which included sleeping sickness, pleuropneumonia, jiggers, small-pox and malaria. The occurrence of cases in Kisumu was because of the proximity of North Nyanza. Also, South Nyanza was a well-known endemic zone.

2. It was, however, the colonial official's highhandedness that aggravated the situation, for their approach was ruthless and arbitrary. Where was the fairness in taxing all huts in the kraal, including *duol* and *abila*?[61] Tax defaulters suffered at the hands of the colonial administration. Those given charge to collect taxes, such as chiefs and tax clerks, resorted to brutal methods, ordering police officers and sub-chiefs to raid villages, set houses on fire, or confiscate property and foodstuffs such as grains, bananas, and cassava.[62]

3. They objected to coercing their people to public works. The regime forced women and children to work building roads and

---

57. Owen, Letter to Heywood, 1922.
58. Odinga, *Not Yet Uhuru*, 27.
59. Ogot, "British Administration," 228; Ogot, *History of the Luo-speaking*, 712.
60. Ochieng', "Colonial Famines in Luoland," 23.
61. Owen, Letter to Heywood, 1922; see also §3.4.1.
62. Owen, Letter to Heywood, 1922.

huts for chiefs, sub-chiefs and administration officials. Besides, they made them fetch firewood and water for the chief's wives, practices that are against Luo customs (§4.7.1.1).

Omulo shared these objections with his colleagues, for Ogot names him among the teachers who organized resistance meetings in Maseno and Lundha in Central Nyanza.[63] Okaro-Ojwang' recorded Omulo as one of the participants of the Lundha meeting of 1921.[64] His leadership position, as "head native teacher" at Maseno, and his active involvement to plan and take part in the resistance, reveal Omulo's stand on those colonial excesses. Although this was political action, it occurred in the context of Christian mission. Omulo and his colleagues did not stay in their expected role as mission agents but ventured into social-political issues affecting their people. They formed "the early opposition to colonial rule," according to Ogot, thus forming YKA through which they attacked increased taxation, government labour camps, and the *kipande* system (§4.7.1.2).[65]

4.4.1.2 Reading the Signs

The YKA leaders sought to avoid combat in their engagement with the colonial regime. They were aware of the state's reaction to the March 1922 uprising by the Young Kikuyu Association (YKA) in Nairobi, the proscribing of the organization and exiling of its leader, Harry Thuku to Kismayu.[66] Knowing that agitation in Nyanza would lead to a brutal confrontation, they agreed to change tack. On Archdeacon Owen's advice, YKA officials created the Kavirondo Taxpayers Welfare Association (KTWA, §4.7.1.2), which avoided overt politics, proposing to cooperate with the government for the welfare of its members. So, when establishing the Local Native Council (LNC) in 1924, it was a straightforward decision for authorities to appoint the KTWA leaders to represent the community. Although Omulo was one of those appointed to the LNC, he, like most of the people, preferred to voice grievances and agitate for change through KTWA, which the Luo called *Piny Owacho*, aligning it with YKA (§4.7.1.2). The Africans regarded the LNC as the DC's mouthpiece

---

63. Ogot, *History of the Luo-speaking*, 713.
64. Okaro-Kojwang, "Origins and Establishment," 111–128.
65. Ogot, British Administration, 216.
66. Lonsdale, "Political Associations," 33.

on local problems, and hence got their direction on government policies from *Piny Owacho*. Omulo and his people opted to create a political pressure group while dealing with the colonial administration in the KTWA *Piny Owacho* leaders' forum. By the 1930s it had gained a reputation as their legitimate mouthpiece on social, political and development issues.

Land acquisition for settlers gained political, not only economic, significance. From 1903, when the government annexed land east of Kisumu for the Asians, *Piny Owacho* and the 1930s Kakamega gold rush, demanded individual titles on land. They regarded land titles as the most secure method to protect the land. In 1932 at a meeting in Kisumu, the Governor assured the KTWA that nobody in Central Nyanza would be evicted from his land without compensation, as had occurred during the Kakamega gold rush.

For the KTWA, healthcare was an integral part of members' welfare for which they needed government cooperation. They urged members to follow simple hygiene rules, to wear proper clothing, not to get drunk and to kill rats. Rats transmitted the bubonic plague of the late 1920s from which many people died.[67] KTWA worked with the government to eradicate rats. The regime incentivized people to kill rats, thus people earned tax credits of up to 20 percent. By bringing twenty rat tails to Panya Company (rat company), the special government collection offices, for example, implied twenty rats were dead. So, people killed thousands of rats in a short while, which dissipated the plague.

Omulo's concern was how people would manage their tax burden. Two approaches emerged within KTWA: They empowered people economically by improving agriculture in the reserves and by encouraging wage employment outside the province.

First, regarding agriculture, the demarcation of boundaries fixing the reserves impinged on African agriculture since demographic pressure within the reserves and poor agricultural methods led to dwindling yields. The efforts to transform African agriculture came in the late 1920s, when the government introduced cotton as a cash crop and provided agricultural support for African peasants. But low cotton prices inhibited successful agriculture. Reed observed that CMS at Maseno urged teachers to sow new cash crops to

---

67. Wanyanga, *Triumph Through Faith*, 20.

ease their burden in the light of taxes.[68] While Omulo preferred cereals and food, others ventured into cash crops. For instance, Rev. Simeon Nyende of Gem, Regea, persuaded to grow cotton, was enraged at receiving only twenty shillings for his crop. Hence, he led the Gem people of Central Nyanza to boycott cotton planting the following season.[69] The boycott was partial, as the people remained divided for fear of government reprisals for challenging the Local Native Council.

Those who promoted cereals and food crop farming in the reserves proved wise, for while the Depression hit the settler economy and Asian traders, Africans in the reserves were insulated from the capitalist economy, and experienced minimal disruptions.[70] Instead, they produced more cereals and vegetables, expanding their farms during the Depression years. Coinciding with the Depression was the locust invasion of 1930, causing the *Osodo* (locust) famine and the 1932 *Nyangweso* famine, making food security a priority for the Africans. Thus, Nyanza had a shortfall of maize supplies to the government purchasing board, because African growers withheld their supplies from the government, safeguarding against the famine.[71] Africans stopped supplying maize during drought in Nyanza from September 1942 to February 1943 for the first time since 1918.[72] Not even higher prices could attract them to sell off their produce, for they thought primarily of food security.

Second, the opportunity for wage labour remained the most certain source of revenue, following the failure of cotton as a cash crop in Nyanza. Alila concluded that the people's real economic security was in wage employment outside the home, a prospect improved by primary education.[73] Omulo's contribution to education during this period was marked when he taught at Maseno School between 1914 and 1925. At Maseno, education was faith-based and afforded the students literacy and life skills. Their education resulted in employment as clerks in stores and in the administration, and on large farms. This gave students mobility, allowing a large population to move out of the province. But after 1925, the implementation of the Phelps-Stoke

---

68. Reed, "Cotton Growing," 48.
69. Reed, 48.
70. Kitching, *Class and Economic Change*, 282.
71. Anderson and Throup, "Africans and Agricultural Production," 399.
72. Killick, "Notes for the enquiry, 1943"; Oates, Letter to A. B. Killick, 8 March 1943.
73. Patrick O. Alila, "Kenyan agricultural policy," 28.

Commission in Maseno changed the trajectory of African education. There was now a government Education Department, which opened more opportunities for African education. So, at K'Omulo, apart from preparing catechumens, Omulo provided government-approved education for Africans as well.

4.4.2 The CMS's Understanding of the Context

This section discusses the CMS's understanding of the context, based on the responses of its missionaries to Kenya becoming a colony and to the impact colonization had on the people of Nyanza. It explores the social, political, economic, and cultural factors that influenced the society within which they had to witness and discusses the CMS's response to these new challenges.

4.4.2.1 The CMS's Response to Colonialism

The 1920 declaration of Kenya as a Colony induced significant social change in Nyanza. The striking African staff turned their fury on the CMS Mission, forcing Owen to draw a line between the CMS and the colonial government.[74] Owen sympathised with African agitation, but his colleagues, such as Wright, considered the grievances to be exaggerated and imaginary.[75] While Owen and the missionaries espoused CMS's "civilizing mission," they were wary of the colonial regime's excesses, which were expressed in the state's policies on forced labour and taxation. They considered that the government betrayed its imperial trust by promoting international and local agents to exploit Africans. This they feared might cause the government to lose the social control essential to colonial rule.[76] Despite that, Owen held that British standards existed, and he reported and combatted any lapse he discovered.[77] Owen was aggressive in engaging the government, bringing along his

---

74. Ogot, *History of the Luo-speaking*, 218.
75. Wright, Letter to Senior Commissioners, 8 February 1922.
76. Owen, "Relationship of Missionary," 254.
77. Letters to the East African *Standard* claimed that he was engendering sedition when there were "two natives" in the church to hear his treacherous words! He replied that he too was shocked to see Africans in the church: not because he should not have spoken as he did in front of them, but because he should have been clearer. Owen, Sermon, "Christianity and the Subject Races."

colleagues.[78] Owen believed Christians had a duty not only to show loyalty to the administration but also to amplify voices of criticism against it.[79]

4.4.2.2 Reading the Signs

The explicit European racial domination in Kenya, promoted by colonial authority, bothered CMS missionaries. For Owen, the Empire required ethical principles, but not physical distinctions of race and colour, to survive. Besides, any views subordinating ethical and spiritual considerations to physical differences were incompatible with Christian teachings, which CMS rejected as a matter of policy. Owen wrote:

> It therefore seems to me of the first importance that the missionary societies should not take up any position which would give the slightest colour to the supposition that they were influenced by racial sympathies rather than by those principles of universal brotherhood which are basic in the Christian view of life.
>
> Understandably, we should put ourselves in a position where it might appear that as missionary societies, we were more concerned about the protection of our own interests in the narrower sense than about justice which is, in the long run, the most important Christian interest of all . . . while it is legitimate for us to state quite frankly, when called upon to do so, our conviction that the continuance of British rule is in the interests . . . of the native population of East Africa. We should do this independently and should refrain from taking any public part in the existing controversy in East Africa.[80]

Hence, joining with the Alliance of Mission in Kenya, CMS championed African interests. While the Alliance got credit for influencing the outcomes of the Devonshire White Paper, Maxon dismisses the claim as a myth. To Maxon, the British missionary J. H. Oldham and church officials Archbishop

---

78. For the way African production was subordinated to that of Europeans, and its consequences, see Van Zwanenberg, "Colonial Capitalism and Labour"; van Zwanenberg, "Economic Response of Kenya."
79. Owen, Letter to Heywood, 1922.
80. Owen, 1922.

of Canterbury, Randall Davidson, only provided to the Colonial Office the provisions on the doctrine of African paramountcy.[81] And Maxon argues:

> The Colonial Office did not need Oldham and Davidson to devise a settlement for it; officials there had decided the fundamental principles that they would use in making a policy statement long before Oldham entered the Indian question in May 1923.[82]

What the Colonial Office officials got from the missionary leader, besides useful phraseology, was the vital support they needed to sell the policy announced in the White Paper to influential public opinion in both Britain and India.

Ratifying the Devonshire Paper remains the CMS's most significant achievement, which is even acknowledged by their critics.[83] To the missionaries, it stopped the European takeover, allowing for a gradual transfer of authority (§4.1.6). Murray notes that Owen wanted a protracted colonial tutelage for Africans until the "choice spirits" emerged in their leaders.[84] Even then, he saw the role of Europeans as senior partners in government.

To realize the colony's economic potential, the mission's practice of offering their own curriculum for African education had to change. In their education vision, the government and the settlers preferred technical training to literary education for Africans. But the administration lacked the labour force to control the entire educational structure. While the CMS resented government intervention in education, they needed government funding to realize their plans of extending Christianity and development through education.

Missions in Kenya derived their influence from education, through providing the three basic tools for African education, i.e. schools, staff, and equipment. The government did not set up schools for Africans in Kenya until 1913 or later,[85] and they did that by channelling most aid for African education to mission schools as grants-in-aid. The government found that to be the cheapest and least burdensome way for the government to "fulfil"

---

81. Maxon, "Devonshire Declaration," 268.
82. Maxon, 268.
83. Maxon, 269.
84. Murray, "Archdeacon W. E. Owen," 669.
85. Schilling, "Dynamics of Educational Policy," 55.

its obligation to give educational opportunities for Africans. By 1938 there were fifty government schools with 4,720 pupils; 404 mission schools (assisted by grants-in-aid) with 49,995 pupils; and 1,388 mission schools (unassisted) with 73,309 pupils.[86]

Schilling observed a complicated educational decision-making process within the Kenya government and the Colonial Office.[87] Yet groups outside the governmental apparatus also sought to affect African educational policy. Of those decision participants, the missionary societies were the most important, for they controlled much of the educational delivery system. Mission education played a vital role in evangelism, in creating an African church and in preparing African Christians for life in colonial society. It is not surprising that the missions wished to maximize their involvement in the policy-making process, once the government assumed more responsibility for this area.[88]

During the Great Depression of the 1930s, the settler project, as the backbone of the colonial economy, faced an imminent collapse.[89] The financial hardships confronting the settler farmers inhibited their capacity to service their mortgages or capitalize on their farms. This crisis eroded the settlers' political dominance as breaches emerged in their ranks. The more efficient producers refused the prospect of subsidizing their challenged counterparts[90] and were hence forced out of business because of lower commodity prices of agricultural produce, rendering their production uneconomical. Given this situation, the state had to revive African production. It became a choice between a) easing the plight of African commercial producers and b) fostering the survival of the colonial state through protecting inefficient settler farmers and propping up a quarter of Kenya's European community.

---

86. Education Department, Annual Report, 1938.

87. Schilling, "Dynamics of Educational Policy," 54.

88. For more specific examination of the mission-education linkage, see Strayer, *Making of Mission Communities*.

89. John M. Lonsdale has developed this idea comprehensively in: "The growth and transformation of the colonial state in Kenya, 1929–52." Lonsdale's paper "The Second World War and the Colonial State in Kenya," presented to the conference on "Africa and the Second World War" held at the School of Oriental and African Studies in May 1984, elaborates the argument, and sets our work on African production in its wider context.

90. Anderson and Throup, "Africans and Agricultural Production," 328.

4.4.3 Interaction of Omulo and CMS on Understanding Context

The interaction between Omulo and the CMS during this period was based on continued evangelism among the Luo. The CMS approach spurred a dynamic and complex set of interactions, which drew in the government. The interactions included different levels of colonial administration and the white settlers, whom they had to face together. Selectively using Lochhead's relational ideologies[91] classified as hostility, isolation, competition, partnership and dialogue, this section assesses the interaction between CMS and Omulo on areas where they agreed, differed, or cooperated. It makes this assessment on how they responded to colonialism and social ordering.

4.4.3.1 Responses to Colonialism

The interaction between Omulo and CMS developed from isolation to dialogue ideology. According to Lochhead, the ideology of isolation is clear where a group regards itself as superior to others, assuming a duty to enlighten them.[92] Besides Christian instruction, CMS missionaries such as Owen taught Omulo and his colleagues the colonial system's benefits for the colonized, if it operated properly.[93] Omulo and his colleagues at Maseno questioned the Europeans' humanity and the teachings of CMS against the background of the colonial oppression which they associated with CMS as well. Lochhead describes such interaction as a fractured relationship in his hostility ideology. To delink CMS from the state, Owen invited a government official to explain what the establishment of Kenya Colony would portend. He openly disagreed with the officer who stated that the colony applied only to the "white highland" and not to Nyanza. Owen clarified that all of Kenya was a colony.

Owen's brave act convinced Omulo and the African staff that CMS was not supporting the colonial policies. Hence, Omulo and CMS missionaries became vulnerable to each other, committing themselves to a relationship of dialogue.[94] Dialogue pervaded their conversations, relationships and

---

91. Lochhead, *The Dialogical Imperative*.
92. Lochhead, 8.
93. Owen, "Relationship of Missionary and African."
94. Lochhead, *Dialogical Imperative*, 93.

activities, manifested in how they trusted Owen's advice to transform their movement into KTWA, as the instrument through which to engage the state.

The relationship between Omulo and CMS developed into Lochhead's partnership ideology, where groups embrace one another on identifying a common interest and forging meaningful cooperation.[95] Ross observed, "Archdeacon Owen, through the Association, has done much to restrain political agitation and the administration owes him a debt of gratitude."[96] But their continued agitation against the policies and practices of the officials became a challenge for the administration. Blaming the missionaries for it, the Chief Native Commissioner noted in the 1927 report:

> The Association is undoubtedly capable of much good if carefully directed, but its activities appear to be chiefly political and of a nature likely to damage the reputation of the Association, for natives use these meetings for airing grievances, often imaginary, instead of going to their administrative officers. This is especially unfortunate in an Association which is directly connected with a missionary society.[97]

So, through KTWA, Omulo and CMS challenged the colonial regime in law and development, over the economic capacity of the people (§4.7.1.2). Hence, through this dialogue, Omulo and CMS grew a deeper spiritual relationship, as they contended together for social justice issues affecting the people of Nyanza.

4.4.3.2 Social Order and Inequality

In the interaction between CMS and Omulo, described in Lochhead's ideology of isolation, CMS assumed superiority and the duty to "enlighten" the Luo people.[98] The CMS missionaries espoused a Victorian worldview, through which they assumed the role of "civilizing" the Luo through church and schools. The establishment of the church created a privileged class, spurring inequality. In his attempt to suppress the emerging class formation, Owen propagated an unrealistic concern for "tribal cohesion," by championing the

---

95. Lochhead, 24.
96. Ross, "1922: Kenya from Within," 87.
97. Ogot, "British Administration," 264–265.
98. Lochhead, *Dialogical Imperative*, 8.

upliftment of the "entire race." The education approach CMS adopted would create success, but as education elevated the low, it created classes in its wake, an educated elite and the masses without education.

CMS missionaries differed on the type of education they preferred. While Francis preferred to raise a pool of elites, who Murray suggested could be co-opted by any administration seeking higher skills among Africans,[99] Owen thought it would ferment future trouble and was not worth the cost.[100] He argued that such an approach would stimulate rampant materialism and trigger disruptive class distinctions. Instead, Owen rooted for Booker T. Washington's Tuskegee-style education of the "whole man," and urged the CMS to develop curricula better suited to life in the rural areas.[101] He anticipated Africans "becoming an ever more important factor as a producer of the raw materials which Europe needs . . . and by a hundred years of intensive culture producing at last some choice spirits able to share with Europeans in the government of their land."[102] Owen wanted the system to last and believed the creation of a new social order was not the work of a day. He resisted swift economic and social change.

The paradox is that Owen supported class formation among races yet worked against class in Nyanza society. Class divisions were already in African societies like the Luo, but strong family bonds mitigated their impact on the poor. Evaluating the two approaches, Murray noted that Owen's application of the "Tuskegee" principles in KTWA didn't meet social differentiation.[103] Meanwhile, at Alliance, Francis taught entrepreneurship and accumulation to an increasing number of students, as he had done in Maseno. The reward of enterprise inspired Omulo and many Christians in Nyanza. Omulo went along with Owen's practical model during his time at Maseno between 1914 and 1924, but this changed when he took leadership in Kisumu, where the focus was more structured academic schooling (§4.5.1.3).

---

99. Murray, "Archdeacon W. E. Owen," 669.
100. Owen, Letter to Cash, 6 August 1940.
101. Murray, Archdeacon W. E. Owen," 669.
102. Owen, "Empire and Church," 26.
103. Murray, "Archdeacon W. E. Owen," 644.

4.5 Ecclesial and Religious Scrutiny

The ecclesial or religious scrutiny dimension of this study discusses how the adopters perceived their former religion and how the change agents perceived churches before their actions. It begins with a discussion on the push and pull factors involved in the decision to adopt Christianity by examining Omulo's ecclesial position. This segment then explains CMS's perception of the churches before their mission activities in Nyanza. It discusses the CMS's influential public contacts and the factors that shaped the CMS approach. This section concludes with the interaction between Omulo's and CMS's ecclesial analyses, exploring their encounters.

4.5.1 Reuben Omulo's Ecclesial Analysis

This segment explains how Omulo, as an adopter, perceived his former religion and culture as a Christian. Further, it discusses factors shaping the Luo people's decision to adopt Christianity by marking out the push and pull factors. Of significance is how Omulo performed in the role he assumed in the formal church and the mission.

4.5.1.1 Kisumu K'Omulo

Kisumu was in the purview of CMS from the beginning, for after Maseno it opened a centre in Kisumu.[104] By the 1920s, CMS was on the cusp of fulfilling the two foci of Willis' 1904 vision, which was to have mission headquarters in Kisumu as well, led by indigenous Christians. Willis wrote:

> If any place wants a teacher and a European Missionary, this place does, the whole country round just swarms with natives; they come in by the thousand, yet we have not a single teacher here. If anyone else can be found for Entebbe, I would gladly come here: it is high time someone came.[105]

---

104. The 1903 ordinance which created eleven townships established Kisumu, and the number grew to seventy-seven by 1930, their boundaries set by gazette notice. Robert Home notes that "the boundary of the Kisumu township was defined as a 2.5-mile radius of the collector's office, and with beacons, distances and bearings is delineated, edged red, on Land Surveys Plan No. 15135." Home, "Colonial Township Laws," 18.

105. Omulokoli, "Historical Development," 141.

In Kisumu, CMS focused on chaplaincy at first, working only among the Europeans and the Baganda.[106] CMS gave the care of this congregation to Rev. Fredrick Wright (§3.5.3). Hence, Wright had to develop a program to achieve the task.[107]

Omulo came to care for this African flock to succeed Rev. Wright. He had to build on that foundation, expanding the space to bring the church to blossom. He first reformed the church and then expanded the school in a way sensitive to the Africans. In the end, the Luo people renamed Kisumu station K'Omulo, meaning the place of Reuben Omulo, the teacher and padre.

4.5.1.2 *African Anglican Church*

Two mission concepts of the time converged at Kisumu station. First, a European mission station was developed, associated with a White missionary and characterised by a church, a school and sometimes a clinic. Second was a Christian *dala*. It was a common practice for missions to name stations after the leaders, whether a European or an African. The message the individual missionary brought determined the mission's name. For instance, Olang' searched for "Bwana Wright's School," which he found at the Anglican Church.[108] Maseno mission station, built by Willis, came to be known as *K'Ogore*, "the place of Ogore,"[109] and converts referred to Anglicanism as *dini* K'Ogore (religion practiced at K'Ogore), implying their adherence to the teachings of that homestead. Similarly, the Roman Catholic converts were *Jo-K'Opere* after Dutch Father (*Pere*) Bouma, because this pioneer Catholic priest in Kisumu arrived in 1904 and was nicknamed *Opere*.[110]

So, when the local people renamed Kisumu mission station (with its church and school) K'Omulo, it signalled a major shift not only in name from "Bwana Wright's School" to K'Omulo, but in substance as well.[111] The change in substance involved an alternative approach to the church, given

---

106. Omulokoli, 145.
107. Wright, Report in *Uganda Notes*, 173.
108. Olang', *Festo Olang' An Autobiography*, 2.
109. Ogore (Oyawre "good morning"), was the nickname given to Willis because of his frequent use of the word.
110. Nundu, *Nyuolruok dhoudi Mag Ugenya*, 24.
111. Olang', *Festo Olang' An Autobiography*, 2.

the context and ownership. The Luo owned the church, giving them a sense of coming to their home.

Africans could not fit in the Kisumu church built in 1907 and led by Wright, for two primary reasons.[112] First, CMS built the church for Europeans.[113] Second, CMS built the church in the European zone in Milimani, an area reserved for Europeans, with stone-built bungalows in spacious compounds. This, Williams considered, was "the best in the country."[114] With African police housed in nearby huts, the government developed Kisumu township on racial grounds.[115] According to the Kisumu Township Rules,[116] the five thousand to six thousand Africans, thirty Europeans and six hundred Indians, lived in their respective areas of the town. Africans had to breach the law to access church, for the enacted colonial laws barred Africans from accessing worship in the European area. Of these laws, Home considers the *kipande* system, combined with tighter enforcement of the Vagrancy Ordinance of 1920, to have reduced the influx of Africans into the townships.[117] Besides, enthusiastic local authorities enforced the laws to "compel all natives living in the municipality, except as are employed in domestic service or exempted by the Governor, to reside within such locations."[118]

K'Omulo addressed these two challenges. Situated on the edge of the African zone, anyone interested could access and space did not matter. This station embodied African aspirations and pride.

Apart from providing access, the medium of the centre was crucial. That Omulo oversaw such an important station, where Dholuo was the lingua franca,[119] attracted the Luo people to explore Christianity. This made K'Omulo a strategic evangelism centre as envisaged by Wright:

---

112. Wright, "General Letter," 4 February 1914.
113. Wright, in *Uganda Notes*, September 1905, 131.
114. Williams, *Report on the Sanitation*, 11.
115. According to its first surveyed layout, together with a report on sanitary conditions in 1907 done by a visiting consultant civil engineer, G. Bransby Williams. See Williams, *Report on the Sanitation*.
116. First issued in 1904 and revised not fewer than thirty-seven times up to 1926.
117. Home, "Colonial Township Laws," 187–188.
118. Section 43 of the Municipal Corporations Ordinance 1922.
119. Olang', *Festo Olang' An Autobiography*, 3.

> From time to time the Provincial Commissioner calls in all the Kavirondo Chiefs to a public baraza to explain to them some new regulation or decision of the Administration. At these times the town is full of natives from all around and they see and hear morning and evening, Christians of their own tribe together with their households, meeting together for prayer and worship, and the effect must be to make some of them enquire, and to give them some idea of the message of salvation from sin through Jesus Christ, which we have come to preach.[120]

Wright made two important points that Omulo implemented in Kisumu. First, Kisumu took advantage of having a captive audience for the gospel, whose influence was weighty and far-reaching. Kisumu was the administrative headquarters of Nyanza. African chiefs often gathered there on government business. Such gatherings made Kisumu an important centre whose influence reached the entire region. Jairo Owino (§3.5.3) became a firm supporter of K'Omulo.[121] Owino hosted chiefs from all over Nyanza, with whom he attended church. In 1932, Wasawo noted:

> Most of the big chiefs in Western Kenya used to come there. I was thus able to meet the old Chief Mumia . . . Then there was Chief Gideon Magak Odeka from Kasipul-Kabondo . . . Chief Ojungo Kotumba from Uyoma struck me with his red eyes. His son, Adam Midega was staying with us, and went to school with me at K'Omulo . . . Chief Paul Mboya, and Chief Musa Nyandusi from Kisii[122]

Through these encounters, it is plausible that the visiting chiefs and their entourage engaged Omulo at K'Omulo.

Second, Omulo used the vernacular for instructions and worship. He spoke not only in Dholuo but was himself a Luo. He asserted himself in improving the Anglican Luo liturgy in the prayer book and in hymns. He enriched the earlier liturgy developed by CMS by completing the translation

---

120. Wright, General letter, May 1912, 2.

121. The African government official who persuaded Willis to begin the Kisumu mission. Willis, 26 May 1909, "Willis Papers", 219.

122. Wasawo, "We Understand but Darkly," 104.

and introducing hymns and songs fitting the context (§4.7.1.4). This is how Omulo developed an inclusive Christian community at K'Omulo out of aspects of Luo traditions. He gave himself to remodelling the school that until then had been part of the church.

4.5.1.3 K'Omulo School

The school Rev. Wright operated at Kisumu, like others carried on by missionary societies, was classified as "General Education," which in Urch's words,[123] "was to be primarily concerned with reading and writing to proselytize and to train African teachers." But upon assuming leadership in 1925, Omulo embarked on developing the school for African children. He remodelled the rudimentary school he found into the first Protestant school in Kisumu, adhering to the requirements based on the Phelps-Stokes Commission.[124] He started with the first stage, the sub-elementary school, which was run by untrained teachers. Then he established the elementary school (§4.5.1), which allowed for a five-year course according to the government-prescribed syllabus. The syllabus, though heavy religious, emphasised literacy, arithmetic, hygiene, and gardening as well. Teachers instructed in the vernacular and taught English in the last two classes. These changes were complete by 1930, as attested by Professor David Wasawo, a former student, in 1935 or 1936:

> In the 1930s, one started schooling at Sector School, in Sub-standard A. Then after a year, one graduated to Sub-standard B. A year later they went to standard one, then standards two and three in the subsequent two years if their progress was uninterrupted. It was at the end of these five years that one attempted the Maseno School Entrance Examination.[125]

Since these levels were unaided, Omulo recruited volunteers who were later employed by the CMS or government. Omulo's genius was in his staff recruitment, seen when he brought in Johnathan Okwiri Nyakinya as his assistant in charge of the school. Okwiri was born in 1884, in Uyoma Kobong' in Central Nyanza.[126] During World War I the government conscripted his two

---

123. Urch, "Education and Colonialism," 254.
124. Jones, *Education in East Africa*, 18; see also §4.4.1.
125. Wasawo, "We Understand but Darkly," 100.
126. Ogot, *History of the Luo-speaking*, 717.

older brothers, under the compulsory service order, and they were deployed to Lela Depo for the carrier corps. The Luo men had proven reliable in the terrain of southern Tanzania, where the British fought the Germans.[127] Their conscription plunged Okwiri's family into a crisis. The chilling prospect of dying in war, thus truncating the family lineage, was frightening. Okwiri offered to be conscripted instead of his elder brother, arguing that their lineage was best preserved through him.[128] They accepted his proposal and deployed him at Mombasa, where he became a superior headman in the labour department. He gained little education during his time in the war, which stirred his desire for more instruction.

When he returned after the war, Okwiri worked with Chief Ojungo to teach literacy at Chianda Uyoma. His desire to gain more education took him to Ojola, in Kisumu. But this was not what he expected. At Ojola, the Catholics memorised and sang more than they were learning. He left Ojola for Maseno CMS because of what he deemed better education. Okwiri attended Maseno School from 1918 to 1920 and became the best student in English at Maseno. In 1921 CMS recruited Okwiri to teach at Maseno School, where he remained until 1925 when Omulo recruited him to K'Omulo, where he taught until 1940.[129] Archbishop Festo Olang' was one of Okwiri's students at K'Omulo, whom he taught English. Another student of his, Professor David Wasawo, remembers him as a real disciplinarian headmaster and mentions his other teachers as Mr. Gordon Rogo and Mr. Benjamin Olao, qualified from Maseno.[130] Okwiri's interest was more in education than the conversion of students. That was Omulo's task.[131]

Established in the urban context of Kisumu, K'Omulo attracted students from diverse tribes and the entire Nyanza region. For instance, Festo Olang', a Muluyia settled in Nyamasaria Kisumu, discovered the school by himself at age eight or nine.[132] Kisumu Municipal Corporation had hired his father to sweep the pathways around the municipal offices, but his father sent

---

127. Iliffe, *Modern History of Tanganyika*, 205.
128. Okwiri, Personal interview, 23 September 2020.
129. Ogot, *History of the Luo-speaking*, 717.
130. Wasawo, "We Understand but Darkly," 101.
131. Okwiri, Personal interview.
132. Olang', *Festo Olang' An Autobiography*, 2.

him to sweep in his place. So, he swept while his father collected the wages. Olang' narrates:

> As I swept the paths, I noticed inside the offices some cool looking African people shuffling papers and writing on typewriters and asked, "how much do they earn," I was staggered by the fact that they had a much easier, cooler job than myself and yet the salaries my father was drawing was far smaller than that of these clerks in the offices... I was told that the gateway to that cool job was called education. So, from that moment I was consumed with the desire to be educated.[133]

Olang' was accepted at K'Omulo, where he began his education and was baptized with the names Festo Habakkuk "by my teacher Reuben Omulo."[134]

So, what Kisumu town was to Willis in 1910,[135] as Omulokoli noted, a source of majority catechumens for baptism to Maseno, K'Omulo became for Maseno School,[136] for by 1930 the school was a dependable route for young Africans to Maseno School, as both Olang' and later Wasawo attested.[137] At K'Omulo, "we were prepared for the Maseno Entrance Examination, which we were to sit at the end of that year. We even learnt a bit of English in that class."[138]

4.5.2 CMS's Ecclesial Analysis

This segment explains how CMS perceived the church emerging from its work. Of significance is how CMS implemented its indigenous church policy and tethered the church to the Anglican Communion. Further, it discusses the churches' positions of power and privilege or public influence and how those factors shaped CMS's approach among the Luo.

---

133. Olang', 2.
134. Olang', 5.
135. A total of one hundred and sixty-two were baptized at the end of 1910 in Maseno; sixty were from Kisumu town, edging out the fifty-six from the Maseno school. Willis' Annual Letter, 24 November 1910.
136. Omulokoli, "Historical Development," 137.
137. Olang', *Festo Olang' An Autobiography*, 5.
138. Wasawo, "We Understand but Darkly," 101.

4.5.2.1 *The Journey to an Indigenous Anglican Church*

Given that the 1901 Memorandum had not prescribed a formula for arriving at an indigenous church, the CMS in London left the regions to devise their own approaches. Unlike Kenya, Uganda's (including Nyanza's) attempt to indigenize began when in 1909 the Synod adopted a diocesanization policy by accepting Bishop Tucker's constitution.[139] That constitution rested the diocesan authority with the synod and bishop, even though the missionaries still wielded control through the Missionary Committee. The missionaries' reluctance to cede control slowed the implementation of the findings of the Section IV Meeting reported in 1902.[140]

The meeting discussed the working methods of the CMS to identify the training needs of missionaries and concluded that "natives" would gradually take over the evangelistic and pastoral work. But in areas such as higher education and "quasi-episcopal" supervision, they needed more missionaries for an indefinite period.[141]

CMS missionaries in Kenya sided with Hooper, their one-time colleague. As CMS Africa Secretary, he did not favour the diocesanization policy. According to Hooper, Africans could not take a wide role in directing their church. In 1932, he raised various objections to diocesanization but could not persuade the two Group Secretaries. His concern was that diocesanization would focus on clerical organisation and male leadership, to the detriment of women's training.[142] Hooper was much more reticent because he found the policy unpopular and cautioned against taking it "as a final pronouncement." The report, according to Hooper, was to "strengthen our understanding of one another, and to confirm our faith in the common responsibility

---

139. This was a CMS policy aimed at handing control to a diocese, out of the churches formed in their mission, while remaining under Canterbury. It comprised little more than giving control to the missionaries, as officeholders in the church. It involved integrating Africans into the new administrative machinery.

140. The CMS General Centenary Committee in March 1896 appointed committees to deal with various emerging issues. The Section IV Committee was appointed to focus on the communities of Native Christians: as to discipline and measures to promote spiritual life; and as to self-government, self-support, and self-extension among them; particular attention being given to the relations of the Society with the bodies of native Christians who have attained to more or less of independence. See Farrimond, "Concerning the Development," 53.

141. Memorandum on the Constitution of Churches; Stoke, *History of the CMS*, 402–408.

142. Hooper, in a paper prepared by Cash, 28 October 1932, 6.

committed to us."[143] Hence, when Cash visited East Africa in 1937, he found that African opinion was against the idea of a church province,[144] for fear of dominant Europeans, and that non-missionary European opinion in Kenya was in favour, for the same reason.[145] Farrimond observed that, during David Cash's tenure as CMS General Secretary, the attempts to form African CMS dioceses into provinces were abortive, until the 1950s.[146] But a significant development of church government in Kenya came in September 1944, when CMS submitted a constitution to the Archbishop of Canterbury, by which CMS no longer controlled the Anglican Church in Kenya. The church became the African Anglican Church and was granted a governance structure in a Synod.

During the period under review in this chapter (1921–1945), two significant groups emerged from within the Anglican Church. These were expressions of indigenous Christianity, led by Africans who received the gospel from CMS. The first was the Roho movement, a charismatic expression of faith among Africans. This was followed by the Revival movement which focused on evangelical conversion which involved both missionaries and African converts.

4.5.2.2 Roho Movement

The Roho movement first emerged from within the Anglican congregations in southern Wanga. What began as a spontaneous Holy Spirit manifestation among converts from 1912 had become a movement within the Anglican Church by 1933, in both North and Central Nyanza, which mutated into an independent Roho denomination after 1934. Anna Inondi[147] narrates the origins of the movement, when the Holy Spirit manifested in Musanda, South Wanga from 1912. Then, according to Inondi, the Holy Spirit appeared as a voice heard in the eaves of homes of the Musanda Anglican congregation,

---

143. Farrimond, "Concerning the Development," 231.

144. This is used in the study to refer to a federation of all Anglican dioceses in Kenya, which are autonomous under the leadership of the Archbishop of the ACK, but at the same time, maintain full spiritual kinship and doctrinal identity with the other provinces and dioceses in the Anglican Communion.

145. Report by General Secretary on his Visit, 4, 10.

146. Farrimond, "Concerning the Development," 231.

147. Hoehler-Fatton, *Women of Fire*, 12.

under the Anglican catechist Jeremiah Otang'a.[148] Hoehler-Fatton writes that "they were gathering outside, under the trees on a knoll where an unfinished cinder block church belonging to the CPK (Anglican Church) now stands."[149] As Otang'a led the service, several congregants fell down as they confessed their sins before joining others in singing hymns. The tongues of those on the ground grew longer as they cried, "Ouch my mouth, my mouth." Yet as Inondi states, their tongues shrank to normal size as Jeremiah Otang'a prayed for them.[150] This was a charismatic expression within Anglican Christianity.

Recipients of the Holy Spirit began taking over services. For instance, after receiving the Holy Spirit, Ibrahim Osodo of Musanda frequented Christian gatherings and prophesied, interrupting service programs. Inondi observed that Osodo and his followers used to gather on the same knoll where Otang'a held worship services, where they would march and sing hymns with great vigour.[151] The catechist, Otang'a, ordered Osodo to go pester people elsewhere with that spirit of his, urging him to find other schools or churches where he could teach issues on the Holy Spirit.[152] Osodo heeded the sanction and moved away. People across Central Nyanza received the Holy Spirit and joined the movement, becoming known as *Joroho* (people of the Spirit). During the 1920s, the movement coalesced around leaders from among their ranks. Nyanza CMS leaders considered Silvano Nyamogo and Lawi Obonyo of Musanda as leaders of the Roho movement and responsible for introducing the movement to Alego in Central Nyanza. But to Owen, Lawi was "characterised by the most extravagant forms of hysteria."[153] At pains to explain the Roho movement, Owen, in a letter to Pitts, discussed what he saw at a Roho meeting in 1933:

> Lawi was holding forth. He (Canon Pleydell) could not hear what he said . . . but in a short time Lawi stopped dead and fixed his eyes on a decent-looking woman seated on the floor (as were all of them) in front of him. He kept his eyes fixed on the woman,

---

148. Hoehler-Fatton, 12.
149. Hoehler-Fatton, 12.
150. Hoehler-Fatton, 12.
151. Hoehler-Fatton, 13.
152. Hoehler-Fatton, 13.
153. Owen, Letter to Pitt Pitts, 25 October 1933.

without saying a word for about three minutes when the woman began to tremble and shake all over and set up a hysterical yelling. At this juncture, Miss Moller and I arrived. I heard yells rising in the night air, and boldly pushed the door and went in. The hut was packed to suffocation with people about 80, the vast majority of women and girls, though there were children too. As soon as I entered, and they had realised who I was in the dim light of the hurricane lamp which provided illumination, Lawi motioned the people to rise, whereupon a woman who had been trembling and shaking . . . put her baby on the floor and executed a mad hysterical dance in front of me, raising her arms to heaven and behaving in a most embarrassing way.[154]

One of the most prominent leaders of the Roho movement was Rev. Alfayo Odongo Mango, who received the Holy Spirit in 1916. As an ordained Anglican Church deacon, Mango gave Lawi and the movement credence. He baptised Roho members, drifting away from obeying orders by Owen, which became the ground upon which Owen sanctioned him. Owen wrote:

> Alfayo Odongo has broken away from the Anglican Church, repudiated the authority of myself and the bishop, refuses to have any communication with us thus, incidentally, breaking No. 4 of the terms of agreement came to before you on April 10th, 1933, with the Bantu authorities.[155]

It baffled and repulsed Owen that a deacon under his charge, Rev. Mango, would increasingly commit himself to "a strange form of religion."[156] Barrett explains that Mango, after receiving the Holy Spirit, was commissioned by the Spirit "to begin the Roho (Holy Ghost) movement which remained inside the church for 18 years until after his death in 1934, whereupon his followers seceded to set up a distinct church."[157] There is no evidence to suggest that

---

154. Owen.

155. In a letter to Col. Anderson, in January 1934, Owen refers to a document Mango signed promising "to confine himself entirely to Church and other work connected with his calling as given him by Archdeacon Owen and the bishop" and abide by the Wanga authority. One-page agreement. 10 April 1933. Thus, the rule which Owen cites is no. 3, not no. 4. District Commissioner, Letter to Col. Anderson.

156. Owen, Letter to Pitt Pitts, 25 October 1933.

157. Barrett, *Schism and Renewal in Africa*, 258.

Mango declared secession himself.[158] Hoehler-Fatton notes that, even after the massacre (§4.7.3.2), the *Roho* continued for several months to consider themselves Anglicans.[159]

4.5.2.3 Revival Movement

Gehman observed that the Revival, which began in Rwanda in the late 1920s, was one of the remarkable movements of the Holy Spirit in the Christian Church.[160] It is the most consequential group to emerge from the CMS churches. The CMS was evangelical in foundation and rooted in the nineteenth century Great Awakening in Britain.

Wasawo, who was a Maseno student at the time, described the visit of two CMS missionaries, Dr. Joe Church of Rwanda and Dr. Noeman Green, who were also revival movement leaders, to Maseno School in 1938.[161] They preached to Christians whose lives were unchanged after baptism and called on them to attest to their sin and make restitution. If they did, the gospel would rescue them from the grip of sin. Those who heeded that call entered what Taylor described as "a mutual fellowship . . . which appeared to supersede all the older solidarities of family and clan."[162] The Revival preachers demanded the Christians attending their meetings to examine themselves by using the following questions:

1. Do you know salvation through the Cross of Christ?
2. Are you growing in the power of the Holy Spirit, in prayer, meditation and the knowledge of God?
3. Is there a great desire to spread the Kingdom of God by example, and by preaching and teaching?
4. Are you bringing others to Christ by individual searching, by visiting, and by public witness?[163]

Their preaching so impressed Wasawo that years later, he recollects: "They preached to us for about a week, introducing to us a new category

---

158. Barrett, 10.
159. Hoehler-Fatton, *Women of Fire*, 69.
160. Gehman, "East African Revival," 36.
161. Wasawo, "We Understand but Darkly," 65.
162. Taylor, *Process of Growth*, 15.
163. Gehman, "East African Revival," 44.

of Protestant Christians referred to as the 'saved ones.'"[164] This one song he remembers, "Spirit of the Living God" was sung over and over.[165]

Not many people in Maseno joined the movement, for Wasawo wrote:

> We felt that our faith, as it was, made more sense to us. The public declaration of sins committed or imagined was something difficult for us to carry through. Another aspect of the "saved ones," was their tendency to regard themselves as a cut above other Christians.[166]

The Revival won converts in and beyond Maseno. Nzioki observed that among those converts were teachers and medical staff.[167] Wasawo mentions that a few of his fellow students got "saved" as well.[168] The movement appealed to the ordinary members of the Anglican Church in Maseno, which became the centre from where it spread to the whole of Western Kenya. One of the Revival's famous converts was Ishmael Noo from Sakwa Location, who emerged as the leader of the movement in 1938. A gifted orator, Noo preached the new message with zeal, attracting a large number of adherents. The revivalists travelled around Central Nyanza, preaching in open markets and during funeral ceremonies, using a *tung'* (a horn-like metallic speaker); hence they were called *jolendo*, or *Balokole* (proclaimers). An adept leader for the movement, Noo maintained the fellowship and kept together converts to the movement.[169]

A missionary observer noted three characteristics that marked these early revivalists. First, they exhibited spontaneous and unaffected joy, often punctuated in their constant reiterations of the *tukutenderesa Yesu* chorus and a couple of verses of the hymn. They were earnest in their deep experience of Jesus Christ. Second, they loved the fellowship of the movement, where neither class, position, tribe, or race mattered. They exhibited a deeper and

---

164. Wasawo, "We Understand but Darkly," 65.
165. See the following website for the lyrics and a brief history of the song: https://www.praise.org.uk/hymns/spirit-of-the-living-god-fall-afresh-on-me.
166. Wasawo, "We Understand but Darkly," 65.
167. Nzioki, "Development of the Anglican Church," 155.
168. Wasawo, "We Understand but Darkly," 65.
169. Nzioki, "Development of the Anglican Church,"156.

fuller ideal of fellowship, a true practice of *koinonia*. Third, they displayed an urgency to save others (and their church) from the imminent danger of hell.[170]

Indifferent to the movement were the African priests and the missionaries. Hence, CMS did not sanction the movement in Kenya until after 1943. Until then, the revivalists could never hold their meetings within the church buildings, nor take part in the normal church activities. However, they remained within the churches and was always "a movement which has continued to spread with renewed vigour . . . should not have become a separate sect."[171] Besides the clergy, Gehman notes, the revivalists branded Christians not in their company as "lost."[172] Wasawo recounts an incident where one of the *jolendo* saw him smoking cigarettes in his car and remarked, "Look at that devil sitting there smoking."[173] Wasawo continues:

> The "saved ones," for they always seemed to be clear in their minds what belonged to the devil, and what fell under God's grace. I have never been able to quite understand what really moves the "saved ones", why some of them claim and declare such horrendous sins committed before they became saved. It always reminds me of: "Here, but for the Grace of God, I am."[174]

Although they were laypersons, the revivalists' attitude of spiritual superiority often conflicted with clergy, who perceived *jolendo* as a threat to their authority (§5.5.1.1). Activities of the revivalists running parallel meetings during regular church services exacerbated that threat. But often the revivalists would attend the Sunday worship, hold an after-service fellowship and then go to marketplaces or other public places with loud-speakers, witnessing for Christ. The clergy (and others in the community who opposed them) resented their zeal, but they remained within the Anglican Church.

These two movements expressed a spirituality and fellowship that was lacking in the formal church planted by the CMS. They were a response to the Holy Spirit breathing life into a church, like the wind blowing life into dry bones in Ezekiel Chapter 37. However, the Roho movement was an African

---

170. Warren, *Revival, An inquiry*, 50–51.
171. Taylor, *Process of Growth*, 99.
172. Gehman, "East African Revival," 46.
173. Wasawo, "We Understand but Darkly," 66.
174. Wasawo, 66.

initiative, while the Revival had European links, so while the CMS pushed the Roho movement out of the Anglican fellowship, it incubated the Revival within the church.

4.5.3 Interaction Between Reuben Omulo and CMS on Ecclesial Scrutiny

To understand the dynamics in the interaction between Omulo and the CMS, this section will use Schreiter's model to understand syncretism.[175] The model explores the response to an incoming religion or culture and discusses the emerging dynamics from the interaction between Omulo and the CMS showing points where they agreed, cooperated, or differed. Viewed from the vantage point of the receiving religion or culture, Schreiter defines syncretism as an incomplete transfer of the sign system of an arriving religion or culture into an adopting culture.[176] He then identifies four types of syncretistic response or incomplete transfer of the sign system: finding similarities, filling gaps, indiscriminate mixing and domination. These types appear when a receiving culture fails to fully "incorporate the datum into its life, integrating it into the sign systems of the culture, so as to maintain the authority and credibility of its own culture."

4.5.3.1 Syncretism as Domination

Schreiter's *domination* response explains one aspect of how the Luo culture incorporated Christianity.[177] Domination occurs when the sign system of a local culture is so weakened that the sign system of the invading culture "takes over completely, replacing the local sign system."[178] In some ways, in their encounter, the CMS (the invading culture) subsumed the Luo religious institutions, which yielded to a dominant CMS Christianity. The Luo espoused a popular religion, which according to Schreiter was a way of being within and living as part of a culture, for living outside it would be impossible.[179] This aided the notion that becoming Christian was not a taboo but

---

175. Schreiter, *Constructing Local Theologies*, 165–180.
176. Schreiter, 174.
177. Schreiter, *Constructing Local Theologies*, 176.
178. Schreiter, 174.
179. Schreiter, 171.

improved one's connection with God. For the Luo did not know the notion of "religion." So, a domination response is evident in the shift where schools and churches replaced *Siwindhe* and *Abila* institutions as centres of culture and religious instruction.[180]

The mission to evangelise the Luo bound Omulo to the CMS. He agreed with the CMS's use of education and church, as is clear when they established K'Omulo and other mission centres. Omulo and the CMS cooperated to create alternative religious institutions that subsumed Luo popular religion. They developed new instruments of religion by producing vernacular Scriptures, hymn books and holy orders. The holy orders provided by the group of CMS ministers first involved African evangelists, then the padres like Omulo. These examples point to cooperation between Omulo and CMS.

The domination response gave rise to a Christianity that eclipsed Luo popular religion, which always had a unifying effect, giving rise to divisions between faith and religion. Schreiter considers the faith-religion distinction a cultural feature of the West, and a form of Protestant Christianity.[181] With different churches emerging, the Luo were divided into Roman Catholic and Protestant Luos, which sparked antagonism. The missionaries' denominational conflicts spilled over to their adherents.

Ogot attributed the split in KTWA to religious and ethnic animosities.[182] In 1924, the Catholics left KTWA to form the Native Catholic Union, with the same goals as the faction under the auspices of the CMS and Archdeacon Owen.[183] The tension between Roman Catholic and CMS students is another example. Wasawo narrates:

> They banteringly called us in Luo language as Oporo Saitan kuon ochiek mi Wang'i (protestant ugali (food) is ready close your eyes). This was in derogatory reference to Protestant Christians closing their eyes in thankful prayer before partaking of a meal, whereas the Roman Catholics did not close their eyes when praying. But the real reason for the derogatory statement lay in

---

180. Nzioki, "Development of the Anglican Church," 88; Cohen, *Combing of History*, 118; Onyango, *Gender and Development*, 25–28.
181. Schreiter, *Constructing Local Theologies*, 165.
182. Ogot, *History of the Luo-speaking*, 723.
183. Provincial Commissioner Nyanza Provincial Report 1926.

the misreading of the word Protestant. Most Luo names tend to begin with the letter "O"; so, Protestant was broken down into two words: Oporo for "Pro" and Saitan for "testant"! Now Saitan in Luo language means "Devil" or "Satan."[184]

The CMS held their adherents within Anglican schools and churches. They did not receive Catholics into their schools unless they converted. Omulo was aware of the denominational divide and was under pressure to promote CMS's mission and teachings at K'Omulo. However, he declined to espouse sectarian religious impulses. Given that sectarianism among Africans manifested along ethnic rather than religious lines, Omulo opened K'Omulo to students who needed school or church, irrespective of their background. For instance, Wanyanga notes that Omulo admitted Jo-Umani students who had become Adventists (§4.9.1.4).[185] Further, Omulo cultivated the spirit of unity with all religious groups in Kisumu through sports. K'Omulo students interacted with other schools, as Wasawo affirms; "I remember our football team going to Maseno to play a match against some other schools."[186] So, weaving faith and sports, Omulo undermined the existing sectarian divides, to present a united Christian front in Kisumu. He personally appealed for public support for such efforts:

> It has been arranged by a few native Christians to hold sports for all native Christian boys and girls of all Missions on Monday the 26th. December 1932, beginning at 2 or 3 pm. at or near football grounds in Kisumu. I should be grateful to all those who are willing to give helping hands if they would send me anything.[187]

He directed this letter to different Christian missions, some Kisumu business firms owned by other faiths, and European government officials, seeking their support for the event. Omulo thereby displayed an inclusive approach to religious engagement, which was different from that of the CMS. His African orientation probably influenced that approach. In that sense Schreiter's domination response does not fully describe Omulo's approach.

---

184. Wasawo, "We Understand but Darkly," 68.
185. Wanyanga, *Triumph Through Faith*, 41.
186. Wasawo, "We Understand but Darkly," 102.
187. Omulo, General Letter, 16 December 1932.

4.5.3.2 Syncretism as Indiscriminate Mixing

The nature of conversion to Christianity, and the time it takes, often causes indiscriminate mixing between the incoming and adopting sign systems. This is another type of syncretism identified by Schreiter,[188] as pointed out above. The "incomplete transfer" of the sign system in this case refers to the adoption of the surface level signs of the arriving religion or culture, without an adoption of its underlying codes or worldview, thus resulting in contradictions and a superficial identification with the new faith. This type of incomplete adoption is particularly common in situations of fast church growth, as was the case in Central Nyanza between 1921 and 1945.

The number of enquirers pressured CMS to speed up baptism for catechumens, such that between 1921 and 1939, there were 28,431 baptisms and 21,972 confirmations.[189] The numerical success beguiled the quality of Christian life of the converts. The converts, teachers and evangelists were not different from those around them, for they got drunk, were immoral, and practised witchcraft. Baptism, however significant, did not reflect the professed change, hence syncretism occurred because of a partial reception of Christianity. But what baptism achieved for believers divided opinions among CMS missionaries and Omulo with his people. According to Gehman, the CMS preachers often used Mark 16:16: "He who believes and is baptised will be saved."[190] Hence, they equated baptism to salvation. Katarikawe acknowledged this: "No matter how one lived so long as they baptised him, was a ticket to heaven. This was the gospel they often heard from the pulpits."[191]

Omulo agreed with CMS's teaching, which equated new birth with baptism.[192] People received a new birth through baptism, he wrote: "*Kwom batiso nyithindo, kodi kwom jodiko, nitie wach mowacho ka ose nyuologi diriyo kwom batiso*"[193] (Translation: Regarding baptizing children, writers, gospel writers, say they are born again at baptism). To Omulo, one must trust God about their born-again status, for there was no way of knowing it, hence he admonished: "*To wageno Nyasaye, Nyasaye nowacho kwauru to nunwang' eka kwom batiso*

---

188. Schreiter, *Constructing Local Theologies*, 176.
189. CMS Report, 1940.
190. Gehman, "East African Revival," 37.
191. Katarikawe and Wilson, "East African Revival Movement," 24.
192. Omulo, Omulo Notes, 1924, 83.
193. Omulo, 83.

Nyasaye miyogi nyuol diriyo eka wagene" (Translation: But we trust God, God said ask and you shall receive, so in baptism God gives second birth, hence we trust Him).

What the converts could not mark was their point of conversion. New "name," "clothes" and "knowledge" attracted people to Christianity at this early period. Wangulu claims, "One of my counterparts at Maseno School gave away his Testament as soon as he was baptised. He had received his 'name' of what more use was the book?"[194]

Carey Francis lamented this state of affairs, according to Greaves:

> It seems we have evolved an immense baptising machine, giving teaching which is little but parrot repetition, the Prayer Book and even parts of the Bible, translated from difficult English word into an African Vernacular, encourage unreality, which shouts at you when a torrent "Amen" booms in the wrong place. Sermons, not about Christ, but about Trinity and the wickedness of the Roman Catholic Church and the Seventh-day Adventists. No questions, please, except perhaps unreal ones like, "where is heaven"! Do we go there the day we die?[195]

Yona Omolo's case demonstrates Francis's complaint. Omolo spent seven years in Maseno School, where he got a complete Christian teaching. But he did not comprehend Christianity. However, CMS posted him as head of Anglican Church in Yimbo, Central Nyanza. How was he going to convince Yimbo people to follow Christianity, a religion he did not adhere to himself?[196] Many boys attending Maseno came out as Christian converts, but without believing. Being a Christian for them meant knowing the Bible, preaching like the missionaries, behaving as prescribed, singing Christian hymns, having one wife, reading, not drinking beer or working on Sundays.

This segment explained the interaction between Omulo and CMS in the mission among the Luo. It revealed their basic agreement and cooperation in evangelising the Luo people through school and church, which amounted to syncretism as domination (subsuming Luo popular religion). Due to the fast

---

194. Nzioki, "Development of the Anglican Church," 168.
195. Greaves, *Carey Francis of Kenya*, 77.
196. Ochieng', "Biography of Yona Omolo," 79.

growth of the church, the CMS and Omulo also allowed syncretism as indiscriminate mixing and superficial conversion to take place. That was against their will and intention, but perhaps the inevitable result of the powerful attraction of the incoming culture and the credibility of leaders like Omulo. In one aspect, however, Omulo and the CMS did not agree, and that was in Omulo's greater openness to other denominations, while the CMS saw them mainly as competition or as a threat.

4.6 Interpreting the Tradition

In the light of the questions raised in the earlier three dimensions of agency, contextual understanding and ecclesial scrutiny, this section discusses how Omulo and the CMS interpreted tradition and the Scriptures. It begins with how Omulo understood Christianity in relation to the Luo cultural tradition and explains the Christian message he developed. The section next explains how those same dimensions influenced the CMS's way of re-interpreting the Bible and their theological tradition. It explains a special formulation of the Christian message and how those theological insights shaped the CMS's approach. It concludes by examining the interaction between the interpretations of the CMS and Omulo, to explain the nature of their encounter.

4.6.1 Reuben Omulo's Interpreting of the Bible and Tradition

This segment explains how Omulo interpreted tradition in the light of Scriptures during this period. Then we must pay attention to the question at the core of Luo customs. In his biblical interpretation, he needed to consider the traditional Luo beliefs. He had to reconcile these two traditions to which he belonged. Thus, he explored ways through which his people could understand God, away from the traditional ways, through the Scriptures.

4.6.1.1 Omulo's Interpretation of the Bible

Omulo's approach to interpreting tradition can be compared to Turaki's theological position, which uses any scientific, anthropological, sociological and philosophical studies of religions and cultures to illuminate the understanding of God.[197] This is evident in Omulo's teaching on prayer.[198]

Lamo Wuonwa man e Polo:

Jopuonjre mag Yesu nosaye ni mondo opuonjgi lamo kaka Yohana no puonjo jopuonjre mage. Ok negisaye opuonjgi tiende lamo duto to negi saye miyogi weche mowinjore lamo moomiyo nomiyogi lamo Wuonwa manie polo (:50). Tim lamo en tim maduong' e dini marwa onge wach moro maloyo giduong' wachni. Kawadwaro ngeyo gima ne Yesu opuonjo kuom Lamo onego wanon Injili 4 duto.

Yesu no puonjowa wecheni.

1. Kik uchung' ka Jofarisai mondo ji onenu, to lamuru ling' ling' . . .
2. Kik uwach weche mangeny kaka joma poya kagiparo ni Nyasaye biro neno kata winjogi.
3. Wakwa e nyinge.
4. Kik chunyu aa kuom kwayo.[199]

Yesu noyisowa kaka Nyasaye ongeyo gimidwaro ka wan podi kwa kwaye kawalamo.

Singruok ma ne Yesu nosingore kwomwa lamo.

1. Yohana 14:14 kanukwaya gimoro gi nyinga natim.
2. Yohana 15:7 Kubet kuoma kendo wachna obet kuomu eka nukwa gi mudwaro duto kendo notimnu
3. Yohana 16:23 To kanu kwa kwom wuora nomiu kuom nyinga.

Ok wanyal pogo maber, gima ne Yesu osingore kodi joote giwegi, kodi gima ne Yesu osingore kodi ji duto.

---

197. Turaki, "Human Dignity and Identity," 36–51.
198. Omulo, Omulo Notes, 50.
199. Omulo, 51.

Kuom Injili Mat 21:22 Jesu nowacho,²⁰⁰ bende gik moko duto mukwayo kulemo kata kugeno ununwang'. Yesu nowacho kodi joote kama, kose nyisogi kagiyie ginyalo duto . . . Nitie weche moko mane Yesu okoro kuom joote giwegi, kaka nonyisogi ni ibiro makogi terogi e bura kendo negogi. Magi ok ochopo kuom jomoyie duto.

Chalo bende weche moko mane Yesu osingore ok ochopo kwom jomo yie duto. Yesu no wacho ni kwauru kendo ununwang', wan jokristo wadwaro ng'eyo weche mwadwaro geno kwom kwayo Nyasaye. Ngato makwayo Nyasaye miye chiemo to Kodagi jouru ok anyal nuang'o nikech oketho rieko mane Nyasaye omiye, rieko marwa korem wanyalo kwayo Nyasaye konywa.²⁰¹

Jomoko yie margi onyosore nikech okginwango gima gikwayo Nyasaye.

Jomoko gigombaka, ka giwacho onge ohala kwom kwayo Nyasaye. Gi wacho kwayo Nyasaye ok nyal miye timo gima odwaro timo. Eka giwacho nigima Nyasaye odwaro, obiro timo ka wa kwayo onge kata kwayo nitie.

Nitie Ohala kuom kwayo. Yesu owuon ne en Nyasaye en bende, no chikuwa no miwa lamo Wuonwa manie polo, eka en bende no langa. Ka onge kwayo, ka onge lamo, wiji wil gi Nyasaye. Ka wigi wil gi Nyasaye luoro duto mar mudho mar kia opong'o chunygi.²⁰²

Kwayo anyiso kaka ji gigeno Nyasaye eka ng'ato mogeno Nyasaye edwaro nyiso genruok mare e nyim Nyasaye onge ngato e pinje duto kata manyalo golo kia duto kwom tiende mar kwayo. Eka Yesu owuon ok nodwako wach kwom jomawacho onge ohala kwom kwayo. Ohala nitie kwom kwayo Nyasaye, to ng'ato mongeyo Nyasaye. Nyasaye chutho onego kata odagi miye gimokwaye ng'ato mogeno Nyasaye oknyalo sin kode nikech okomiye

---

200. Omulo, 52.
201. Omulo, 53.
202. Omulo, 54.

gimo kwaye. Yesu nolamo nokwayo e ka onego wan Jokristo onego waluwe.[203]

Translation:

Praying to our Father in heaven:

Jesus' disciples asked him to teach them to pray like John taught his disciples. They did not (p. 50) ask him to teach them the meaning of all forms of prayers; their plea was for how to pray rightly. Jesus gave them the Lord's prayer.

The act of prayer is central in our religion, there is no other function as important as this. If we want to know what Jesus taught about prayers, we need to examine the four gospels. Jesus taught us these:

1. Don't stand like the Pharisees to be seen but pray in secret.
2. Don't use many words like the ignorant thinking that God will see or hear you.
3. Ask in his name.
4. Don't give up asking.

Jesus taught us that God knows our needs before we ask in prayer.

There were promises Jesus made for us when we pray:

1. John 14:14 whatever you ask in my name I will give you.
2. John 15:7 If you abide in me and my word abides in you, whatever you ask I will give you.
3. John 16:23 If you ask the Father in my name, I will give it to you.

We cannot distinguish promises Jesus made to his disciples from ones he made to all who follow him. In Matthew's gospel 21:22, Jesus said, also, whatever you ask in prayer if you have

---

203. Omulo, 55.

faith you will receive. Jesus said this after telling his disciples, if they had faith, all things would be possible.

Jesus predicted things that will happen to his disciples. He told them that they would be arrested and be brought before judges, and they would be killed. Not all these were fulfilled in all of them. It appears also some of the promises Jesus made were not fulfilled on all the disciples. Jesus said ask and you will receive, we Christians want to know things we want by faith in asking God.

Anyone who asks God to give him food and refuses to farm, cannot receive, because he wasted the wisdom God gave him. If we lack wisdom, we can ask God to help us. Some people's faith is weak because they did not get what they asked God. Some people argue that prayer has no value. On asking God, they say we cannot make God do what he doesn't want to do. They say God's will be done whether we pray or not.

There is value in prayer. Jesus being God himself, also directed us and gave us the Lord's prayer which he prayed also. If there is no asking, if there are no prayers, people will forget God. If people forget God all fear of darkness and ignorance will fill their hearts. Asking shows our dependence on God, so anyone who trusts God wants to show their faith before God. No one in all the earth can erase all ignorance for asking.

So, Jesus himself did not seek the opinion of those who claim prayer has no value.

There is value in asking God. But one who has complete faith in God, even when he is not granted what he asks, one with faith in God will not be annoyed with God because he did not get whatever he asked.

Jesus prayed and asked, that is what we Christians should emulate.

This teaching on prayer draws out Omulo's profound understanding of the gospels,[204] his trust in God and his determination to follow the example

---

204. Omulo used translated separate Gospel portions available to him in Dholuo. The Luo New Testament was published in 1926 by BFBS. Mojola, *God Speaks our Language*, 216.

of Jesus. He read and applied the gospel texts critically, comparing one text with another to draw lessons of relevance to both him and his audience.[205] He believes Jesus existed and the records of the gospels as his words which are instructions to us today as they were to his disciples. Jesus' commands and promises gave him the confidence that all our problems can be solved through prayer, a lesson he shared with his people. He acknowledged the importance of prayer as a feature of religion, which John taught his disciples, and Jesus as well. We ought also to pray.

Omulo's interpretation of Scripture aims at inspiring faith in God through building confidence in prayers. He argues for the value of prayers in unleashing God's power on behalf of believers that prayers helped in their transition from the animistic world into Christianity.[206] The notion of power encounter, in the supernatural realms of powers and spirit beings, is common to both Christianity and traditional religion.[207] Having experienced God's power in Christ Jesus, he invited his people to share faith in God through Jesus.

4.6.1.2 Omulo's Application of the Bible to the Spirit World of Luo Tradition

In the 1940s Omulo intervened to wed Mr. Fredrick Onyango when no Anglican priest in Maseno would agree. The Maseno community knew that Mr. Onyango, a teacher at Maseno had *sepe* (spirits), despite being a Christian.[208] He argued that Onyango was a legitimate Christian who needed support against such oppressive forces. Even though there still existed a Luo solution to the *sepe* problem in what Ocholla-Ayayo termed *Ajuok Sepe (sepe* traditional healers), Omulo opted to deal with the problem through prayer in Jesus' name, for he did not deny that the spirits existed.[209] He anchored this awareness on his interpretation of the Scriptures:

> Waneno kwom sura Luka 11.14: Ka johaudi negi wacho niya ka Yesu no riembo jochiende e nyig Belzebul. Yesu ne ok ogoyo mbaka kowacho ni Belzebul onge, moko towacho nikeck Yesu

---

205. Omulo, Omulo Notes, 55.
206. Omulo, 55.
207. Steyne, *Gods of Power*, 210.
208. Warambo, Personal interview, August 2019.
209. Ocholla, *Traditional Ideology and Ethics*, 163–164.

ok ogoyo mbaka kodgi . . . emomiyo wawacho ni Belzebul ne en tie chutho.[210]

Translation: We see in Luke 11:14, that when the Jews accused Jesus of casting out demons in the name of Beelzebub, Jesus did not argue that Beelzebub was not real, as others indicated because Jesus did not discuss with the demons . . . that is why we say Beelzebub exists indeed.

Omulo was alert to the spirit world that the CMS's teaching did not discuss. It was not only from his animistic background, but from the gospels as well that Omulo developed a biblical concept of spiritual powers and principalities. This understanding enabled him to minister without fear to Christians like Onyango. Omulo thus incarnated the gospel among his own people, akin to Steyne's position,[211] that the biblical perspective must be embodied in the old belief if it is to replace the old weakness with new strength. Hence, Omulo found the point of contact in animism which the Bible does not reject.

Given the reverence Luo people give to their ancestors or departed parents, how did Omulo venerate his father, who did not become a Christian, without offending Christianity? Owiti's social position, as the head of family *Wuoro* and *Jaduong Dhoot*, and his warrior status among Jo-Gem, demanded respect.[212] Omulo had a duty to honour the *Juok* (departed spirit) of his father, which according to Ocholla-Ayayo, is a religious ethic of keeping the "*juogi* happy."[213] So, those regarded as guardians still struggle to keep happiness in their afterlife, aided by their living kin. He reiterates that the goal of Luo ethics is love, honour and respect for one's own kin.[214]

Since there was no Christian way of venerating such an ancestor, Omulo reverted to the Luo way to honour his father. He named his first child Owiti and christened him Walter Habakkuk.[215] In assuming his grandfathers' name, *nying juok maka kwaro* (ancestral spirit name) the young Owiti is believed to have received ancestral spirits as well. These *juogi* (spirits), Ocholla-Ayayo

---

210. Omulo, Omulo Notes, 57.
211. Steyne, *Gods of Power*, 207.
212. Joseph Otieno, Personal interview.
213. Ocholla, *Traditional Ideology and Ethics*, 188.
214. Ocholla, 189.
215. Alice Otieno, Personal interview.

claims, exist beyond the immediate presence of life on earth.[216] In the notion of *Chieng'* (sun) and *nying juogi/ juok*, the Luos made the sun an object of religion. Ocholla-Ayayo points out the Luo belief that *Juok*[217] (§§3.5 and 3.6.1) dwelt in the sun and that *Jouk* looks on the earth through the sun, which is his eye.[218] Hence, they developed sayings like *Juok ok ne wang'e* (never look into God's eye). Here is a connection with the sun that has eluded most scholars. Ocholla-Ayayo contends that the link with *Chieng'* (sun) is perhaps the most complex relationship, where spirits from the sun dwell in man through the Luo "solar system" of naming of children.[219] He argues that in acquiring *nying jougi* (spirit's name), the Luo children gained spirits' names,[220] which occurred through the basic principle in the day position of *chieng'* (sun) during the day or its corresponding positions by night.[221] Omulo did not jettison this tradition but paired it with his new faith when he applied this principle in naming his children. For instance, he named his second born Otieno (male), and last child Athieno (female) for both were born after sunset. Their third and fifth children, born at midnight, were named Oduor (male) and Awuor (female). While their fourth child born between 7:00 a.m. and 10:00 a.m. was named Anyango, since she was a girl. In Ocholla-Ayayo's estimation, Omulo's children, although baptized, must have received their spirit's name from Chieng', the *Juogi* spirits living beyond the outer world.[222] Through this naming, Omulo maintained continuity between his Luo religious heritage and Christianity. He affirms this tradition, carving a space for it within Christianity.

4.6.2 CMS's Interpretation of the Bible and Tradition

This section explains how CMS re-interpreted the Bible and their theological tradition in the light of the questions raised by the earlier three dimensions. It explores the unique formulation of the Christian message arising in this context, and how those theological insights shaped CMS's approach among

---

216. Ocholla, *Traditional Ideology and Ethics*, 181.
217. The Luo believe in the existence of a supreme being, *Nyasaye*, and a Supernatural force or power, *Juok*.
218. Ocholla, 185.
219. Ocholla, *Traditional Ideology and Ethics*, 180–181.
220. Ocholla, 182.
221. Ocholla, 185.
222. Ocholla, 185.

the Luo. While CMS missionaries espoused a fresh approach to interpreting the Bible, the dominant approach emerged in the light of increased colonial injustice. CMS had to re-evaluate its commitment to creating an Anglican Church intent on a just society in Nyanza. This section explains how Owen's understanding influenced CMS's approach to mission in Central Nyanza.

Owen's theological thinking comports with Bishop Colenso's "broad church" approach, which Guy explains to differentiate between narrow evangelicalism and high church authoritarianism.[223] Colenso was responding to a liberal universalism of the industrialized British society of the 1840s which affected his interpretation of the Bible in two ways. The first was to approach the Bible narrative with scepticism, and the second was to develop a faith defined by the demonstration of divine presence.

Colenso found it hard to accept the literal truth of Old Testament narratives, hence of the Bible as a whole.[224] His doubts were aroused by science (geology) and stimulated by the questions of his Zulu assistant while translating the Bible.[225] Following his enquiry, he affirmed his doubts in "the soundness of the ordinary view of Scripture Inspiration . . . [but] it is rather secretly felt, than openly expressed."[226] It is plausible that Colenso's position influenced Owen's stand on the Old Testament translation. Owen explained, "I have long felt reluctant to put the Old Testament into the hands of converts until they had attained a more enlightened background for it."[227] His concern was that it would tempt the Luo to draw parallels between the Old Testament and Luo customs. Even pro-revival CMS missionaries disliked Owen for his irksome habit of criticizing parts of the Bible.[228] Since he did not apply the Bible literally, he would not allow his flock to do so.

---

223. Guy, "Class, Imperialism and Literary," 223.

224. Colenso, *Pentateuch and Book*, 5.

225. "While translating the story of the Flood, I have had a simple-minded, but intelligent, native, - one with the docility of a child, but the reasoning powers of mature age, - look up, and ask, 'Is all that true? Do you really believe that all this happened thus, - that all the beasts, and birds, and creeping things, upon the earth, large and small, from hot countries and cold, came thus by pairs, and entered into the ark with Noah? And did Noah gather food for them all, for the beasts and birds of prey, as well as the rest?' My heart answered in the words of the Prophet, 'Shall a man speak lies in the Name of the Lord?' Zech. xiii. 3. I dared not do so." Colenso, Pentateuch and Book, Vol. 1, vii.

226. Colenso, xxiii, xxvi.

227. Owen, Letter to the Secretary, 9 August 1943.

228. Murray, "Archdeacon W. E. Owen," 644.

Shards of Owen's theological declarations scattered in his extensive campaigns reveal the prism through which he interpreted the Bible. This includes his words: "I would be failing in my duty if I did not try to show how some features of our rule in Kenya estrange Africans and erect barriers between them and the Christ we preach."[229] Owen hoped CMS would express Jesus in their preaching on behalf of the wronged. To him, "the teachings of our Saviour have a community as well as an individual application,"[230] demanding a broader application of moral protest beyond individual cases. He also sensed that a system of government could, despite the goodwill of its participants, perpetuate injustice. The imperial regime, for Owen, had a propensity for exploitation, hence the unjust colonial infrastructure needed political redress.[231] His political investment articulates the depth of his theological perception.[232]

Industrialization, in Colenso's era, produced in its wake vast political, social, and intellectual casualties, allowing Christians in that era to perceive God's presence in the nature, character and activities of all humanity. Such a perspective justified Christian intervention in the lives of the poor, the destitute and the oppressed. Colonialism had a similar ill effect in Nyanza for Owen; thus, it is understandable that Owen focused his ecclesiastical attention on practical matters aimed at maturing the indigenous African church. Archbishop Festo Olang' stressed Owen's practical, outspoken streak, and his unique dedication and commitment among CMS missionaries to the African cause.[233]

Owen's theological thinking, like Colenso's, developed in response to radical social change. Both worked to forestall violence and disruption by urging continuity and conservation during the change.[234] Meanwhile, Guy's evaluation of Colenso highlights his sympathy for colonialism, which was influenced by the mood of his times.[235] Hence Colenso viewed colonialism as "his God-given duty to subordinate the lives of Africans to the demands made by his perception of the world." Although Guy acknowledges Colenso's

---

229. Owen, Memo, "Salaries."
230. Spencer, "Christianity and Colonial Protest, 54.
231. Richards, *Fifty Years in Nyanza*, 20.
232. Spencer, "Christianity and Colonial Protest," 57.
233. Murray, "Archdeacon W. E. Owen," 644.
234. Guy, "Class, Imperialism," 224.
235. Guy, *Heretic. A Study*.

inclination to paternalism, as Africans called him *Sobantu* (father of the people), which insulated him from seeing that injustice was the essence of imperialism, he highlights Colenso's "struggle against the duplicity, the brutality and the violence of racial oppression."[236] Owen shares this position with Colenso, as Murray calls out Owen's desire for a prolonged colonial tutelage until Africans emerged as able to govern.[237] Besides, Owen considered the European colonialists' role as guardians and senior partners in government both important and vital, and it convinced him that Christianity was valuable in cementing loyalty, even though it bred criticism as well.

Owen's foci were on the administration of justice, forced labour, African political participation and a variety of cultural practices that seemed to violate individual freedom.[238] For example, he focused on administering justice related to abuses in local tribunals coming out of interpretation problems, which impinged on African political participation.[239] On labour, Owen's concern was for the unpaid labour demanded for public works, which were described as "essential undertakings." He demanded effective political organization and was a one-man campaign for translation of laws into the vernacular.[240] And while Owen did not attack African societies regarding African cultural practices, he focused on the forced marriage of young women.

During this period, Owen defined CMS's duty towards the powerless Africans under an unjust colonial regime. CMS embraced social justice as a prism for interpreting the Bible. This guided their approach to mission work in Nyanza.

4.6.3 Interaction Between Omulo and CMS on Interpreting the Bible and tradition

To explain the interaction between Omulo and CMS, this segment uses Schreiter's "dual religious systems" model. It describes the receiving culture's responses to the incoming cultural and religious impulses and discusses the different dynamics emerging in their interaction, showing where they agree,

---

236. Guy, 174.
237. Murray, "Archdeacon W. E. Owen," 669.
238. Spencer, "Christianity and Colonial Protest," 47.
239. Spencer, 47.
240. Spencer, 48.

cooperate, or differ. According to Schreiter, a dual system emerges by developing a parallel model which grows from contact with cultures.[241] This model emphasizes a conflictual aspect of cultures coming into contact.

CMS, as the invading culture, did not penetrate the Luo people's worldview to make meaningful contact. Meanwhile, the receiving culture, the Luo, built an impenetrable ring against the new system. There is no evidence that the CMS missionaries fathomed the Luo animistic worldview, which believed in the reality of the spiritual world. Thus, the Luo allowed Christianity into the culture and tolerated it, but it never replaced that aspect of the culture. Omulo and CMS fused the two religious signs together, but the CMS failed to de-code the Luo sign system, which resulted in a dual religious system.

Schreiter shows the invading culture enhancing the value of the sign system of the local culture.[242] It occurs when the receiving culture, the Luo for instance, sees themselves as inferior to the arriving culture such as the CMS. The Luo kept their societal code while giving due obeisance to the invading culture's code. There are two examples of how this occurred among the Luo.

First, the Luo adopted European names, which became significant for progress and a sign of becoming Christians. CMS also accepted Luo names on the sign level as consistent with local customs. But unbeknownst to CMS, naming children consistent with Luo customs had a spiritual import. The naming had a different connotation to CMS and the converts. Thus, a dual religious system developed, where both naming systems thrived together.

Second, CMS and Omulo cooperated in acts of justice among the Luo people in Central Nyanza. Both based their actions against the regime on their faith. Since Ogot acknowledges that African teachers trained by CMS missionaries formed a political vehicle to agitate for justice, it is plausible that the impetus to seek justice came from their new faith (§4.7.1).[243] Omulo and his people felt let down by the government policies but adjusted by complying instead of revolting. Owen, supported by his CMS colleagues, agreed on the grievances that Omulo and his people raised, leading to their cooperation in the KTWA when the more militant YKA was dissolved (§4.7.1.2). Omulo's tax case provided Owen and CMS with a classic case he wanted for his justice

---

241. Schreiter, *Constructing Local Theologies*, 178.
242. Schreiter, 178.
243. Ogot, "British Administration," 261.

campaign. Through that case, Owen developed an approach to fighting for justice (§4.7.2.5). Meanwhile, CMS, led by Archdeacon Owen, grounded their orientation to justice on Owen's approach to scriptural interpretation (§4.6.2). Murray associates this to Owen's Anglican interpretation of Christian doctrine, which gave him and his colleagues latitude to integrate broad discoveries of modern science, and the bias to affirm justice for humanity from biblical texts.[244]

In Schreiter's third perspective, the invading culture offers alternative sign systems, which are inadequate, although the local culture accepts the new sign system. Here the receiving culture keeps the old sign system to deal with those issues as they emerge. For example, while both Christianity and the Luo customs did not tolerate the pregnancy of unmarried girls, they differed on resolving the moral dilemma it produces. So, when they informed Carey Francis, the Principal of Maseno School, that his student had made a girl pregnant, he considered it a heinous crime against all morals and Christian tenets. Francis then flogged the student before the entire school body as a lesson for the other students.

Omulo and his people were nonplussed at the extreme punishment CMS meted out for what the Luo considered a minor wrong. Besides, getting pregnant out of wedlock was rare among the Luo. Luo families expected girls to be virgins, with the hymen intact, upon marriage. Wasawo notes:

> Indeed, during the first nuptial night woman's relatives would keep vigil outside the bridegroom's hut, and wait to hear the bride's cry of pain, after the consummation of marriage. The following day, they would carry a spot check out to find out that some bleeding had indeed taken place. Then there would be joy all round.[245]

Grandmothers trained girls on ways of avoiding penetration in the *siwindhe*, so that they could remain virgins until marriage was possible. They phased out *siwindhe* when Luos adopted mission education. But, if a pregnancy occurred because of carelessness on the girl's part, or by force, or by overwhelming persuasion by the boy, Wasawo notes, "the boy's extended

---

244. Murray, "Archdeacon W. E. Owen," 644.
245. Wasawo, "We Understand but Darkly," 66.

family would take responsibility and plan for their son to marry the girl."[246] The Maseno students questioned the logic of Christian morals, for to them, the goal for a girl is marriage. A difference between CMS and Omulo was exposed in dealing with such moral conflation. By punishing the young man, both the offender of morals and the pregnant girl were ostracized, but punishment didn't offer the solution that marriage would have. So, during this period, a dual religious system developed, where Christians practised the traditional moral code, by allowing couples to *loso* (amend their ways by fulfilling the customary requirements) and then commit again to the church's need for a wedding.

In Schreiter's fourth perspective, the invading sign system and the local sign system are dealing with two different things. And thus, no real encounter between the two cultures takes place. It may be the key to addressing the question of double belonging. For example, Christianity did not proffer ways to venerate an ancestor who was not Christian. Instead, the CMS considered ancestor veneration paganism, which ought to be discarded on becoming a Christian. But to Omulo, honouring his father was central to his identity. For as Ocholla-Ayayo argues, "the obligation to one's own family, the lineage of a nation becomes an imperative 'duty' for one's actions."[247] Hence, ancestor veneration forms an important aspect of the Luo psyche.

Was there a Luo way of being Christian? The Luo traditions accommodated Christianity, but Christianity could not accommodate them. This ability to accommodate shows their superiority, since dealing with something by excluding it can appear as a sign of weakness. With no stipulated way for reverencing his dead father, Omulo resorted to the Luo way of naming a dead relative. Hence he got a name of honour, *wuon* Owiti (father of Owiti) from *wuod* Owiti (son of Owiti). They assumed in the family that the departed father still watched over them to protect and unite them in the clan. The missionaries were ambivalent about the Luo maintaining such traditional customs, thus allowing a dual system to arise from the perception that CMS viewed Luo names as not only alien, but as inferior, inadequate and unable to offer authentic identity to Luo Christians.

---

246. Wasawo, 66.
247. Ocholla-Ayayo, *Traditional Ideology and Ethics*, 224.

4.7 Discernment for Action

The concrete steps of faith taken by both CMS and Omulo in relation to the community are the focus of this section. It explains the cultural decisions involved in Omulo's world and the decision-making structures and patterns that existed for him. This section also explains the concrete faith projects or organisations that CMS missionaries got involved with in Nyanza. The section attends to the plans they made to embody their theological insights in the community. It is important to reiterate that both Omulo and the CMS mission developed a holistic view of mission, which included a wide spectrum of activities in mission as a multifaceted ministry.[248] This section concludes with a discussion of Omulo's and CMS's encounters regarding discernment for action.

4.7.1 Reuben Omulo's Discernment for Action

This section explains what motivated Omulo in his planning and strategizing, as well as what he did in those areas of mission. It answers questions regarding the concrete steps of faith that Omulo took on injustice, in relation to the community at large, and the decision-making patterns existing in the community. The notions of compassion, inclusivity and vulnerability were central to his practical involvement in social justice campaigns and the development of Luo hymnody and liturgy.

4.7.1.1 Quest for Justice

Omulo's response to the societal changes by the colonial regime beginning in 1921 appears in two broad categories. First was an overt political resistance movement to challenge the colonial authorities. Second was a forging of cooperation without dropping agitation for justice. He cooperated with others and the government, and he agitated for better terms of engagement.

4.7.1.2 Open Resistance

Although Ogot[249] credits Benjamin Owuor Gumba, the administrative clerk at Maseno Sisal Estate, for convening the Maseno meetings for planning protest, it does not seem plausible that one outside the Maseno School would

---

248. Bosch, *Transforming Mission*, 512.
249. Ogot, *History of the Luo-speaking*, 713.

have mobilised the teachers. The impetus for such a sensitive meeting could have only come from Maseno teaching staff. As the "Native" head of Maseno School,[250] Reuben Omulo, joined fellow teachers – including Simeon Nyende, Johnathan Okwiri, Ezekiel Apindi, George Samuel Okoth, Mathayo Otieno, Jeremiah Awori, Micheal Were, and Joel Meshak Omino – to organise the protest. Their first act was the boycott at Maseno by the staff and students to protest the government actions. To mobilise support, they recruited the missionaries who were discontented with the transfer of the Nyanza Archdeaconry from Uganda Diocese to Mombasa Diocese, since they started showing empathy for the Africans' plight.

The group held several secret meetings and consulted widely with different categories of Nyanza leaders on their grievances and on problems that were bound to arise following the transformation of Kenya from a protectorate to a colony. The teachers represented the educated elite in Nyanza and had to develop their own means to be heard, without relying on the missionaries. They found a model in Harry Thuku's Young Kikuyu Association in Central Kenya. Okero narrates that Thuku came to Nyanza, seeking Omulo's support for the Young Kikuyu Association and encouraged them to form their own association.[251] Wright confirmed Thuku's visit and mission, writing to the Senior Commissioner in Nyanza about the origins of the Young Kavirondo Association (YKA): "The Association came into being as far as my information goes as a result of propaganda brought from Kikuyu by a mission boy last November."

In mobilising Nyanza people, Omulo and his colleagues organised several small meetings to prepare for the mammoth gathering where they would speak with one voice. Amala[252] noted the lead-up meetings for YKA, which they called "Lundha Conference," often held in Marenyo *bar* Local Council Hall. Marenyo was ten miles from Maseno. It became significant to conceal the identity of the genuine leaders, hence the adoption of the term *piny owacho* (The world has spoken). The origin of the term is attributed to Owen by Amala:

---

250. Owen, Letter to Heywood, 27 June 1927.
251. Okero, Personal interviews, 2020.
252. Amala, *Paroni Gik Mosekadho*, 51.

> Owen revealed to them the mysterious terminology the white men used saying the "government said" . . . He instructed them to say in their response to the government's enquiries, *piny owacho*, the "world" (people) has spoken (My translation from Dholuo).²⁵³

In an incident when the District Commissioner (DC) received an unsigned letter on African grievances from their meeting in Marenyo, Amala observes, they claimed to have recorded what "the world had spoken" in Marenyo.²⁵⁴ Curious to find the ground from where the world spoke, DC sent investigators to Marenyo. But they did not find the mouth from where "the world" had spoken. They hoped to confuse the white people on who their spokesperson was and on the source of their words, just like the term "the government said." That is why they always said *"piny owacho"* (The world has said).

On 23 December 1921, leaders gathered for a general meeting at Lundha in Gem. Chiefs Ng'ong'a Odima of Alego, Daniel Odindo of Asembo and Odera Ogada of Gem preferred Lundha. Apart from being Omulo's Chief, Ogada was a former Maseno student who became chief in 1916.²⁵⁵ That the meeting drew a large number from the entire Nyanza was significant. While Omulo calculated that 8,000 people attended,²⁵⁶ Ogot maintains that 9,000 people took part, which was "an impressive figure at the time given transport problems and given the fact that no general mobilisation of all the Luo had ever been attempted for any cause before."²⁵⁷

Meanwhile, a few Africans, not willing to support the protest, misinformed the state about the meeting. Odinga singles out Jairo Owino, the interpreter, also known as the eyes and ears of the government.²⁵⁸ Jairo informed the commissioners that the people were assembling for war. Hence, the state mobilized to crush the meeting. Fearing this imminent confrontation, Okwiri

---

253. Amala, 15.
254. Amala, 51.
255. Anderson, *Church in East Africa*, 69.
256. Omulo in Okaro-Kojwang, "Origins and Establishment," 115.
257. Ogot, *History of the Luo-speaking*, 13.
258. Odinga, *Not yet Uhuru*, 75.

and other elders hid Chief Ogada from the government to avoid his arrest, since the government accused him of fomenting the unrest.[259]

In the ensuing encounter, the Luo leaders appealed to the Christian conscience and reason of the administrators. Odinga[260] narrates how Okwiri engaged DC Montgomery, a brother to Field Marshal Montgomery, on why they gathered. Okwiri spoke for the elders, insisting that the gathering was neither Odindo's nor Ogada's, but the people's, *Piny Owacho*, and the people were there to make their future policy. He challenged Montgomery's assertion that they were preparing for war, proving they had no weapons, nor had they taken war postures, for they met in an open space with no club or spear. The DC inspected the crowd for weapons, invited by Okwiri, but failed to find any. Yet the crowds frightened the authorities.

Having confirmed this was not an insurrection, the DC demanded to know the people's complaints. But they declined to address him, insisting on having their own meeting first. According to Odinga, Chief Ogada said: "We want to hold our own *barazas*. After we have conferred together, we will bring our views to the District Commissioner and if necessary, they can be referred to the Senior Commissioner."[261] To break the stalemate, Jacob Ochola proposed to deliver the proceedings of their meeting in a letter. Surprised they could write, the DC left to wait for their letter, which Okwiri delivered to him two days later.

During the night meeting, the chiefs raised their concerns, though with slight differences of emphasis. For instance, Chief Ogada equated the word "colony" to "occupy," lamenting that the government had decided to deem them as *wasumbni* (slaves). He complained that placing women on government labour affected their health because some had miscarried. The chiefs banned the free things given to colonial officials for the entertainment of chiefs, DOs and DCs. The officials demanded people's food such as chickens, rams, sheep and oxen. He did not wish his people to work on public roads by the order of free labour. Ogada was emphatic:

> As regards our taxes, they used to be sh. 3. Mr. Ainsworth told us that the amount would be increased to sh. 5; we agreed. Then

---

259. Odinga, 25.
260. Odinga, 26–27.
261. Odinga, 26.

the government increased it to sh. 8. It is very heavy. Besides, we do not want our women taxed. Then we want title deeds to our land. The government has begun to eat in our country. You ask where? Mr. Smith has settled in Yala, and he is the first of the Europeans to come and live there.[262]

The Luo people associated the sudden cruelty of the administration with the declaration of Kenya as a colony. The meeting refused this form of direct rule. They wanted to be autonomous, as they had been when they were a protectorate, or like the Baganda.

Through this united action at Lundha the Luo leaders, writes Ogot, formed the Young Kavirondo Association as the mouthpiece for the Africans, with Jonathan Okwiri as chairman, Benjamin Owuor Gumba as Secretary and Simeon Nyende elected the Treasurer.[263] These officials met the Nyanza Provincial Commissioner, Mr. Tate at Nyahera Kisumu, in February 1922 and presented a Memorandum outlining the grievances and demands of the Luo people:

> Establishment of a separate legislature for Nyanza as an autonomous administrative unit, with an elected African president at its head, to avoid the reasons and abuses of direct administration.
>
> Abolition of the Kipande (identity card) which was regarded as a denial of freedom of movement, tying people to undesirable jobs on European farms.
>
> Reduction of the hut and poll taxes to exclude women from taxation.
>
> Building of a government school in Central Nyanza, and the general improvement of educational facilities in the whole province.
>
> Revocation of the crown colony status, with Kenya to remain a protectorate.
>
> Increase of wages for Africans in general, and chiefs in particular.

---

262. Ogada, YKA Memorandum, 1922.
263. Ogot, *History of the Luo-speaking*, 717.

Abolition of indiscriminate forced labour, especially among women, children, and old people.

Dissolution of the labour camps which had been set up at Nyahera, Rabour, Yala and Pap Onditi; these camps were the source of much hardship and the reason for frequent raids into villages by government officials in search of workers and free food, with resulting corporal punishment.

Granting of individual title deeds to land to allay the fear of possible European settlement in Nyanza, some Nyanza land having been alienated for settlement at Muhoroni.

Creation of a paramount chief for the Central Nyanza and South Nyanza Districts, similar to Mumia in North Nyanza.

The association galvanised the people into unity around the Memorandum, through the subsequent meetings in Yala, Maseno and Nyahera and drafted the constitution of the Luo state, a constitution they presented to the governor, Sir Edward Northey, at Nyahera on 8 July 1922. The governor explained to the association that the change from protectorate to colony had nothing to do with introducing a registration system or the rise of taxes. He was being clever. The officials raised the matter of people's unpaid supplies of thatching grass. The DC stated that the money was ready, and a decision was to be made whether cash should be given, or seeds purchased for them. Besides, they did not want women taxed.[264]

Omulo's discernment for action is clear in his involvement in the planning, forming, and activities of the YKA between 1921-1923. These actions, which constituted the first serious attempt to unite all the Luo people in Nyanza into a mass movement, were radical and political but rooted in the Christian faith. In this movement they achieved unity in a hitherto fragmented Luo society.

4.7.1.3 Indirect Campaign Against Injustice

In May 1927 Omulo received a tax demand addressed to Owala, son of Oburu, the registered head of the Owiti Kraal. At that time, he had thirteen siblings, nine sisters and four brothers, but one of them, Denge, had died. His brothers

---

264. Young Kavirondo Association Memorandum 1922.

were: Jason Wahore, son of Aduol was living in Mombasa, James Aweyo son of Orem was living in Kisumu, and Ateng' son of Wanga was living in Kitale. Omulo's rural home tax obligations fell on him, as his father's heir. The tax note he received read:

> Colony and Protectorate of Kenya
> --------------- N. Gem (un-P)
> Hut Tax Census 1927,
> No. 45.
> Name / Owala/o Oburu
> Women 4
> Huts 5
> Anke 2
> Total demanded was 48[265]

The government published tax laws, decrees, and demands in English. Tax collectors capitalised on people's ignorance of English and the fear instilled by the officials on the people through cruelty. They charged the hut taxes according to the number of houses belonging to adults in the kraals. Many young Luos left the reserves for waged employment because of taxes. Those workers paid their poll taxes at the source, which were recorded in their *kipande*. The family solidarity among the Luo made a brother stand by his brother in debt.

Although Omulo found this tax demand note exaggerated, requiring taxes for five huts and two adults (poll), he paid to avoid the taxman's brutality. The government officials had earlier burnt down defaulters' huts who vanished as the taxmen approached. Other times they confiscated livestock. But whenever taxmen found nothing of value, they would jail defaulters and force them to serve their terms with hard labour. The tax officials' enthusiasm forced citizens to pay taxes for their absent relatives. Individuals had to pay either the hut tax or poll tax.

Owala paid up taxes for two of the huts of Aduol and Wanga, paying twenty-four shillings off the dowry received from Jo-Umani for Asenath Ngalo, Aduol's daughter. But in 1927, Owala held Omulo responsible for the balance as the head of the family. So, Omulo had to pay for his hut, Ateng's and Omole's huts, as well as Jason and Aweyo's poll taxes, a total of forty-eight

---

265. The official cancelled the above details written in pencil or with initials.

shillings. Even though they were all working and should have paid their taxes, he sent forty shillings (of his monthly pay of fifty shillings)[266] by the end of May, promising to settle the balance later.

During the KTWA meeting at Maseno on 22 June 1927, Omulo made an official complaint of this tax injustice in the presence of the Nyanza Senior Commissioner, Archdeacon Owen, and Rev. Pleydell of CMS. The meeting, besides addressing the first business of the day, "Crimes of violence manifesto," spent more time discussing grievances in connection with tax collection. Bringing to the fore these complaints triggered more complaints, for there had been widespread abuse by the tax officers. Omulo stated:

> I have many times seen complainants going to the DO's office with complaints that the tax has been collected twice, once in the reserves from the relatives of men at work outside the reserves and again from the man where he is working for in their case a tax is refunded. Methods of tax collection are causing the people great annoyance.[267]

Shadrack Osewe from Sakwa Location raised a similar case. Osewe complained of being forced to pay taxes for his half-brother, Ezekiel Joram Atego, who was working in Nairobi beginning in 1919 and had been home only once in 1922. He paid taxes for the years 1922, 1923, and 1924 since they registered him under their father Myuwero. For 1925 he requested his brother to send him the money. To his surprise, Osewe learned that Ezekiel had paid his 1924 tax himself in Nairobi. Unfortunately, there was no mechanism for Osewe to demand a refund.

In Omulo's complaint, Owen found a person who was credible and respected among the Luo, one who gave him the best illustration of the complaints. He took down Omulo's statement and wrote to the Senior Commissioner (SC), Mr. Dobbs, demanding an investigation and action. To pressure the government, by exposing its injustice, he published the statement in the *East African Standard* and *Mombasa News*, of 29 June 1927. Both newspapers were widely read in Kenya and abroad.[268]

---

266. The district supported their own deacons for one year at fifty shillings per month. Kavirondo Ruri-decanal Council Minutes, 12 December 1924.
267. Omulo, Statement taken by Archdeacon.
268. Dobbs, Letter to Owen, 12 July 1927.

Meanwhile, Dobbs noted that Owen had made an error in dating the tax demand for 1926, when Omulo pointed to the demand of 1927. Since Omulo lived next to the provincial headquarters in Kisumu, Mr. Dobbs summoned him to clarify his statement about paying taxes for others. Omulo states: "I told him the demand was for 1927 and that I had sent the forty shillings," not the complaint of 1926 which he harped on.[269] This was Mr. Dobbs's way of dismissing the case and discrediting Omulo. Mr. Dobbs called Omulo a second time, having interviewed Owala Oburu. This time the SC enquired about a cow Owala had sold to pay taxes, but that was for something different and not for the 1926 tax, as the officer insisted. Yet his complaint forced an inquiry, during which the local officials cancelled the item of two adults on the demand note using a pencil, clearing him of the year's tax to clear the case.

Having investigated the matter, Bishop Heywood affirmed the administration's error in asking Omulo to pay for his brother's taxes. In his letter to the Archbishop of Canterbury, Heywood stated that the information he had received: "to my mind entirely clears Rev. R. Omulo from the charge of falsehood, and at the same time shows how the misunderstanding occurred."[270] The bishop emphasized: "All parties seem to be completely cleared of bad faith, and I am particularly thankful of this in relation to the native deacon concern."

4.7.1.4 Developing Luo Hymnody in Kisumu

As the head of the Anglican Church in Kisumu, Omulo was confronted with the need to develop the Luo liturgy and hymnody, which would anchor the growing number of Christians in faith. Besides, if the Anglican Church was to become indigenous, then developing a sound liturgy and music was imperative.

The Luo Anglican Prayer Book, *Kitap Lamo*, was a translation from the Anglican's Book of Common Prayer. It formed the backbone of the Luo liturgy Omulo used at K'Omulo, despite its being a partial translation. They made a complete translation possible in late 1930, after they translated the entire Psalter. Giving credit to Pleydell for translating *Kitap Lamo* of 1921[271] obscures Omulo's role in developing the Luo liturgy. Pleydell wrote a letter to Omulo:

---

269. Omulo, Statement taken by Archdeacon.
270. Omulo, Statement taken by Archdeacon.
271. Mojola, *God Speaks in Our Languages*, 216.

> Ndalogi aloso Muma machon to adwaro mondo ikonya. Kiyie ichak ilok Zaburi duto. Ndikgi e ex; book gi nukta matindo, eka korumo iboye matek ikowna e Posta. Mano tich madikonya ahinya, kendo dikony Luo bende.[272]
>
> Translation: I am translating the Old Testament these days. Kindly translate the entire Psalms. Write them in an exercise book written in small letters, wrap them well and send them by post. This will aid me greatly and help the Luo as well.

The Psalm's translation attributed to Pleydell was most likely an improvement of Omulo's draft. Jephtha Odonde, in a letter to Omulo from Kikuyu, mentions Omulo's translating the Psalms, knowledge of which was in the public domain.[273] The Psalter were a significant part of the prayer book, so Omulo made his contribution in developing the complete *Kitap Lamo*.

Developing Luo church music was an ongoing project which started with Pleydell at Maseno as early as 1908. It involved translating English hymns and songs into Dholuo. His time at K'Omulo allowed Omulo to test the hymns and create new church songs. What Lebaka's enquiry showed about the Lutheran hymnals can be said about the translated Anglican hymns, which even though they are worthy poetic hymns, had suppressed and restrained the people's emotions.[274] While Omulo and CMS intuitively translated the Luo hymns, without expert knowledge of translation theories, we can categorise their work with the help of the following modern translation theories: formal equivalence, functional equivalence, and Skopos theory.

In some translations, Omulo and his co-workers used a formal equivalence approach, where the translator focuses on the message in both form and content. The translator ensures that the message, in the receptor language, comes as close as possible to the unique elements in the source language.[275] The hymn "Abide with Me" by William Henry Monk (1823–1889), for example, followed this rule:

---

272. Pleydell, Letter to Omulo, 11 June 1934.
273. Odonde, Letter to Omulo, September 1934.
274. Lebaka, "Value of Traditional African."
275. Eugene Nida, *Toward a Science*, 159.

Original English wording	The translation in Wende Luo 9	A literal back-translation into English
Abide with me, Fast falls the eventide; The darkness deepens, Lord, with me abide. When other helpers fail and comforts flee; Help of the helpless, oh, abide with me.	*To bed kod an, piny koro yusona; Polo to chido, Yesu bed kod an; Ka onge moro madhi konyoa; Ja kony jochan iwoun to bed kod an.*	Abide with me, the night is approaching for me; As the sky gets dark, Jesus abides with me; I have no other to help me; Helper of the needy: Abide with me.

Figure 8: Translation of "Abide with Me" into Dholuo

Although there is a slight variation in the words or phrases used, the translators stayed close to the form and meaning to the English hymn, the source text. Thus, they made this translation in close approximation to the source text structure, similar to the approach by Nida and Taber,[276] known as formal correspondence, which calls for accuracy to the original text.

CMS missionaries and Omulo used rules akin to the dynamic equivalence theory in translating several hymns in *Wende Luo*[277] (Dholuo hymnbook) as well. The complex English hymns forced the translators to apply a rule that has become known as the functional equivalence or dynamic equivalence approach for other hymns. This translation approach is based on the principle of equivalent effect, in which according to Nida, "the relationship between receptor and message should be the same as that which existed between the original receptors and the message."[278] The translation of Frances Crosby's "Safe in the Arms of Jesus," (1868) makes an excellent example (see figure 9, below).

While translating Fanny's hymn, the translators changed the imagery from being safe in "the arms of Jesus" or "gentle breast," to Jesus guiding me, a change which addresses the existential fear of the spirit world. They tailored the message to the receptor's linguistic and cultural expectations and conveyed it with "naturalness of expression" so that Luo believers could relate

---

276. Nida and Taber, *Theory and Practice*, 22–28.
277. *Wende Luo* (Hymnal).
278. Nida, *Toward a Science*, 159.

to it. "Naturalness" for Nida is a key requirement, for it seeks to achieve "the closest natural equivalent to the source-language message."[279]

Original English wording	The translation in Wende Luo 105	A literal back-translation into English
Safe in the arms of Jesus,	Yesu kotaya pile,	When Jesus guides me daily,
Safe on His gentle breast;	Oritoa mang won;	He graciously cares for me.
There by His love o'ershaded,	An to kabedo bute,	If I stay near him,
Sweetly my soul shall rest.	Onge gi manyalo luor.	I shall fear nothing.
Hark! 'tis the voice of angels	Winji, Machalo dwonde,	Hark, like his voice,
Borne in a song to me,	Malaika mavero;	the Angels sing,
Over the fields of glory,	Weche mabiro ira,	words coming to me,
Over the jasper sea.	Weche mamiya mor.	words giving me joy.
Refrain:	Refrain:	Refrain:
Safe in the arms of Jesus,	Yesu kotaya pile,	When Jesus leads me daily,
Safe on His gentle breast;	Oritoa mang won.	He graciously cares for me,
There by His love o'ershaded,	An to kabedo bute,	If I stay close to him,
Sweetly my soul shall rest.	Onge gi manyalo luor.	I shall fear nothing.

Figure 9: Translation of "Safe in the Arms" into Dholuo

During translation, Omulo encountered the challenges of words that never existed in Luo, which they created and availed for common usage. For instance, the Luo did not need to count numbers exceeding one thousand, so Omulo and the team had to come up with a word *gana* for a thousand. So, translating 1867 Henry Alford's "Ten thousand times ten thousand" became, "*Ji gana gi gana*" in *Wende Luo No. 30*. These difficulties extended to translating songs with English idioms, phrases and words that had no equivalence in Luo. Yet the song in the original text had deep spiritual import. In this case Omulo and CMS approached translation in a theory equivalent to the Skopos theory. In the 1970s Hans J. Vermeer adopted the term *Skopos*, a Greek word for aim or purpose, as a technical term for translation and action of translating. Details of this theory is a book Vermeer co-authored with Katharina Reiss.[280] This was explicit in translating William O. Cushing's 1856 song "When He Cometh":

---

279. Nida, 166; Nida and Taber, *Theory and Practice*, 12.
280. Reiss and Vermeer. *Grundlegung einer allgemeinen Translationstheorie.*

English original	Literal translation into Dholuo
When He cometh, when He cometh	Kano duogi, kano duogi,
To take up His jewels,	Kuom kawo jewels'
All His jewels, precious jewels,	Mohero kendo mage.
His loved and His own.	Kaka otide mo kinyi.
Refrain	Refrain
Like the stars of the morning,	Ler ne no wak,
His brightness adorning,	gini Rieny gi e bergi,
They shall shine in their beauty,	'gems mag osimbone.
Bright gems for His crown.	

Figure 10: Literal Translation of "When He Cometh" into Dholuo

The hymn used the idiom of precious stones, gems, jewels, and crowns, all which were foreign to the Luo. A literal translation of the hymn into Dholuo (as in the right-hand column above) would not have made any sense. The translators produced the following translation:

Translation in Wende Luo 42(18)	Literal back-translation into English
Ka noduogi, Yesu Kristo,	When he comes, Jesus Christ
Kuom luongo nyithinde,	to call his children,
Jo mohere,	those who love him
jo mayiee,	those who believe in him,
Jo Kristo madier.	the true Christians.
Refrain:	Refrain
Gini pake gilala,	They will praise him forever;
Gini dende Jakonywa.	They will worship our saviour;
Ginimor ka gineno,	They will rejoice when they see;
Ruoth Yesu owuon.	Lord Jesus himself.

Figure 11: Actual Translation of "When He Cometh" into Dholuo

The translators substituted "taking home his jewels" with "children," "the jewels, gems and crowns" with "those who believe in him; the true Christians." This allowed the listeners to receive a direct message without the foreign English metaphors. The message of the song, according to the translators, was more about the Lord's return, expressed in a joyful homecoming than bringing treasure home. Here the translators applied Skopos theory, whose purpose, according to Munday makes the translation methods deliver an adequate result,²⁸¹ the result being the target text which Vermeer calls the *translatum*.²⁸²

The composition and use of spiritual songs that had no equivalents in English, was another significant development during this period. Of the 239 hymns in *Wende Luo*, thirty-nine had no English equivalent and the majority of those (eight out of ten) are in the section on the second coming (*Wende Luo* 42–52).²⁸³ This is because the second coming aligned to Luo belief in the world beyond the one we occupy. Ocholla-Ayayo observed the Luo idea of the upper world where they live and the underworld where they are destined.²⁸⁴ Earlier Baumann dealt with this belief among the Northern Luo, the existence of the underworld where life is like the one on earth.²⁸⁵

The music and liturgy were creative works of the Luo Christians whose effect, in the words of Chupungco,²⁸⁶ was to establish the link between culture and religion, resulting in as many liturgical forms as there are cultural concepts. The effect of developing Luo liturgy and music was similar to Triebel's observation, after collecting new Christian songs in Kiswahili for Tanzania, that indigenous music gives wings to the word of God to make it incarnate in Kiswahili.²⁸⁷ At K'Omulo, the Luo Anglican liturgy increased participation and attendance in Anglican liturgical church services and home prayers.

Omulo contributed to the development of Luo hymnody in the *Wende Luo*, songs in Luo. This comprised translated English hymns into Dholuo, sung using either English or local tunes. Spiritual songs composed by gifted Christians and local Anglican congregations were sung in the Luo genre. A major contribution was in developing a Luo hymn book. Before this, songs were hand-written or typed out on papers, and often sung from memory. Odonde pleaded with Omulo to urge CMS to publish a Luo hymn book, like the English or Kiswahili for the churches, for there were more hymns developed and not preserved.²⁸⁸ As a result, they published hymns, choruses

---

281. Munday, *Introducing Translation Studies*, 79.
282. Reiss and Vermeer, *Grundlegung einer allgemeinen*, 119.
283. *Wende Luo*, 42–52.
284. Ocholla-Ayayo, *Traditional Ideology and Ethics*, 172–173.
285. Hermann Baumann, *Die Dei Afrikanischen Kultur-Kreise*, 186, 193, 219.
286. Chupungco, "Die liturgie und bestandteile," 153.
287. Triebel, "Mission and culture," 238.
288. Odonde, Letter to Omulo, September 1934.

and spiritual songs collected in *Wende Luo*, together with the prayerbook in Dholuo, thereby preserving them for posterity.

4.7.2 CMS's Discernment for Action

This section discusses projects or organisations CMS was involved in from 1921 to 1945 in the Central Nyanza community. It also discusses how they resolved staff needs, sustained the developments they started and responded to injustices facing the people in Nyanza. Finally, it explains CMS's plans that embodied their theological insights.

4.7.2.1 African Agency

The increased deployment of African agency during this period had an ambivalent impact on the church. Everything depended on the leadership quality (as I explain below), because where the CMS posted competent personnel, it spurred the growth of the church.

Despite the evangelistic success registered from using African converts in the first period (1906–1920), the CMS had not screened or trained any workers for ministry, an approach that weakened the church and set the stage for unforeseen movements from within. The church lacked adequate leadership and a common identity to unite it. There are two reasons for this. First, the CMS relinquished the grassroots evangelism work to young converts without giving them adequate training, which created a weaker church, dependent more on the whims of the evangelists than solid teaching. It consigned the spiritual progress of the new church to inept preachers who lacked the requisite depth, which meant little spiritual growth. Second, Christianity in Nyanza during the 1920s and into the 1930s had no standardized institutional identity. Instead, the only models of evangelization that existed for Anglican Christians were multiple European mission stations and indigenous Christian *dalas*,[289] which African Christians set up as small Christian congregations under their "self-imposed charge."[290] As a result, the Anglican Church among the Luo exhibited not one identity but multiple identities, from which deviant movements emerged.

---

289. Hoehler-Fatton, *Women of Fire*, 71.
290. Ogot, and Welbourn, *A Place to Feel*, 24.

During the 1920s, the CMS strengthened the church by making deliberate efforts to recruit, prepare and deploy African leaders. They selected the best available Christians who lived up to the challenge of service. Omulokoli notes that the CMS devolved more responsibilities to African clergy, so that by 9 January 1929, the Registrar General registered Reuben Omulo for responsibilities in Kisumu and Yeremiah Awori in Butere.[291] In giving a title for those African priests, the council opted for the term "padre" (§4.3.1.2). In 1928, the CMS appointed six more teachers to be trained at Frere-town Divinity School.[292] The six were Owino and Esau Oywaya from Maseno, Simeon Nyende and Shadrack Osewe from Ng'iya, and Makonjio and Alfayo Odongo Mango from Butere.[293] However, Osewe dropped out while the rest finished and were posted to their home pastorates. The CMS trained two more Luo priests in 1934, Isaiah Ndisi and Ezekiel Apindi, who were both deployed in 1938.

This period set the framework for the indigenous African Ministry in Nyanza, which blossomed in the post-World War II period. But it left the proper care and support for African clergymen unresolved. Omulokoli[294] observes that CMS had not considered making policy on salaries, housing, and priests' support: "It was under this twin pressure of increasing govt taxes on one hand, and of family responsibilities, that some of the more prominent catechists went away for longer or shorter periods in search of wage-earning employment."[295]

4.7.2.2 Translation

CMS missionaries had translated and published the Gospel of Mark in 1911, and Luke and John in 1912. While A. A. Carscallen of the Seventh Day Adventist Mission (SDAM) translated the Gospel of Matthew in 1914, J. F. Clarke of Africa Inland Mission (AIM) translated the Book of Acts in 1915. Pleydell translated the remaining books and revised some of the earlier ones: Mark, Luke, John, James in 1917, Romans to Philippians and Titus in

---

291. Omulokoli, "Historical Development," 292.
292. Ogot, "Reverend Alfayo Odongo Mango," 99.
293. CMS Report 1929–1930, xxvii.
294. Omulokoli, "Historical Development," 293.
295. Omulokoli, 294.

1921; and John in 1924. He coordinated the publication of the whole Luo New Testament in 1926 by BFBS.

The first book of the Old Testament appeared in 1933. It was the work of Grace A. Clarke of SDAM, assisted by William Ogembo and Paul Mboya, and two other mother-tongue speakers named Sila and Apola. BFBS published the full translation of the Old Testament in 1953, which was translated by Clark of SDAM, Archdeacon Owen (CMS), and H. Capen (AIM). Canon Pleydell worked on the Book of Isaiah and the minor prophets. Justifying his reluctance to translate the Old Testament, Owen contended that converts needed more enlightenment to be ready for it:

> One of my rules is to translate a Hebrew figure of speech or idiom by an elegant figure of speech or idiom of the Luo. Failure to translate in the idiom of the people has already resulted in the emergence of a debased pidgin Luo which the people refer to as Dholuo mar Kitabu (Dholuo of the book).[296]

4.7.2.3 Education

Meanwhile, CMS's Maseno School needed stability at the head to prepare for the new era. Rev. Harold Stone Hitchen was the principal from February to December 1926, with one hundred sixty students in boarding. The number increased to two hundred at the end of 1927, which precipitated a crisis of principalship at Maseno.[297] CMS deployed the seventy-year-old medic, Dr. John Steadwell Stansfeld, from the hospital[298] to serve as principal until the arrival of Mr. Edward Carey Francis in 1928.[299] It was Francis who propelled Maseno School into what Richards described as "one of the most outstanding schools of East Africa from all points of view."[300]

Francis raised the standards by inspiring excellence in the school. In purging the school, he fell out with several teachers who didn't match his pace. The Luyia had weaker preparation for academic achievement, as Francis noted, when he addressed the Ruri-decanal Council in 1933, for only three

---

296. Owen, Letter to the Secretary, 9 August 1943.
297. CMS Executive Committee Minutes, 17–18 June 1928.
298. Richards, *Fifty Years in Nyanza*, 21.
299. Greaves, *Carey Francis of Kenya*, 17–19.
300. Richards, *Fifty Years in Nyanza*, 21.

Abaluyia had passed the entrance examination into Maseno School in 1935. This Francis attributed to, among other factors, poor staffing. To mitigate the problem, Francis recommended providing a separate Standard III at Maseno Junior School for the Abaluyia boys. Luyia entrants bridged the numerical gap, while maintaining the school's excellent standard.

Carey Francis, as Principal of Maseno School, brought the skills and leadership that CMS needed. As Principal from 1928, Francis became the Educational Secretary of Anglican Church educational work in Nyanza, hence he was the "intermediary between the schools and the department."[301] Government involvement in funding schools was one pillar in the Phelps-Stokes plan. In Nyanza, the support focused on the Elementary School. Mr. Webb, the government inspector of Schools for Nyanza, in his plan to standardize and exert control over rural education, selected one hundred schools in his charge for government help.[302] But for fear of ceding control of the schools to the government, CMS developed its own network connected to Maseno School under Francis. In 1929 Francis wrote:

> The archdeacon and Mr. G. S. Webb, Government Inspector of Schools for Kavirondo, tried an alternative plan. They selected 30 sector schools and financed only these, paying salaries, and putting in each year a certain amount of equipment. The Church managed the schools not aided by government. Such schools were gradually passed on to a committee and supervisor. They were soon guided from Maseno, which trained their headteachers.[303]

Despite the government's good intentions, it fell short of delivering the promised help to the selected schools, for in 1928 the government reduced the grants, prompting the Ruri-decanal Council to make a futile appeal to persuade the government to reverse its decision because of increased needs.[304]

Francis came to Maseno when CMS needed an educationalist with his skills. He upgraded Maseno School to such an extent that in 1930 and 1931 for the first time, their best students were admitted into Alliance High

---

301. Heywood, Letter to Director of Education, Nairobi, 22 April 1929.
302. Kavirondo District Church Council Minutes, 9 January and 6 February 1929.
303. Richards, *Fifty Years in Nyanza*, 22–23.
304. Kavirondo Ruri-decanal Council Minutes, 1933.

School, Kikuyu. Maseno School went to a secondary school status because an increasing number of students were forced to end their educational pursuit at Maseno. But a Maseno secondary school could, according to Francis, benefit them. Archdeacon Owen assured the Ruri-decanal Council of support from the government in approving a secondary school for all allied missions in Nyanza. Maseno gained secondary status in 1938.[305] Granting Maseno secondary school status, as observed by Richards, was highly significant: "Perhaps the most outstanding event in its history happened in 1937 when Maseno Central School was raised to secondary status so that there was no longer any need to send its best boys to the Alliance High School for further education."[306]

4.7.2.4 Ng'iya School for Girls

Having established a boys' school in Maseno, CMS considered an exclusive girls' school to match the boys' education in Nyanza. So, in 1920 Miss Edith Hill began the girls' school with ten girls, taught English language and sewing and, much later, Bible class.[307] Unfortunately, it did not last. Shortage of staff forced the school's closure in 1921. However, when the Ng'iya mission station was established among the Luo, the girls' school moved to Ng'iya.

CMS assigned Miss Fanny Moller to develop the school. With a grant from Australia to run it she opened it with fifty girls in January 1923 and doubled the pupil population a month later.[308] In the early days they conducted classes for girls in the church, which was divided into a class for older women in the morning and one for younger women in the afternoon.[309] Meanwhile, boys took their lessons under a tree. The elder women formed the first teacher training classes at Ng'iya. The girls went through the same Christian teaching as their male counterparts at Maseno. Miss Fanny Moller served as Principal throughout this period, from 1923 to 1952.

---

305. Greaves, *Carey Francis of Kenya*, 58.
306. Richards, *Fifty Years in Nyanza*, 23.
307. Omachar, "Contribution of the Church," 58.
308. Omachar, 59.
309. Omachar, 60.

4.7.2.5 Justice for the People

The people of Nyanza experienced widespread abuse by colonial officials during tax collection, which called for urgent resolution (the atrocities were discussed in §4.7.1.1). Although Owen knew of those injustices, he waited until he found a complaint in which he had confidence, which came when Omulo's complaint was presented to the KTWA meeting of June 1927. Omulo's case had the double strength which Owen sought to use: The problem was concrete and the complainant credible. Writing to the Archbishop of Canterbury, Owen stated:

> Here is one of our first deacons to be ordained, a man who held the very responsible position of Head Native Teacher in our Maseno School, and who now holds an even more responsible position as leader of the Native Church in Kisumu, victimised by his ignorance of the law a prey to unscrupulous tax collectors whose only desire is to get the tax in, even though their methods are not according to law, and it must be in the case of those who are incapable even of stating a grievance, so deficient are they in knowledge of procedure.[310]

Owen's aim in his letter was to point out the flaws of publishing the laws for Africans in English, which he argued caused victimisation, because even responsible men, such as Rev. Omulo, were not precluded from the problem. Owen blamed the corrupt officials for exploiting the ignorance of the locals because of a lack of communication. He also argued that the abuse and injustices were occasioned by the policy of publishing the Colony laws in English only, leaving it to district officers to explain the law to the local people. For Owen, that illustrated the evil resulting from denying the Africans the Colony laws in a tongue they could understand.

Omulo's report gave Owen a case to make against the colonial administration's injustice on the local people. Owen's primary approach was to demand investigation and corrective action by Mr. Dobbs, who served on the committee of the KTWA. Meanwhile, he reported this situation in a letter to the Chief Native Commissioner, the press, the Bishop of Mombasa, Canon Leakey, the African representative at the LEGICO, and Mr. Hooper,

---

310. Owen, Letter to Heywood, 27 August 1927.

the CMS Africa Secretary. In response, Owen laid out the detailed complaint from Omulo's statement made in Mr. Dobb's presence "that in 1926 the tax Collector had demanded of him the poll tax of THREE of his male relations who had left the reserves for work, and that he had been compelled to pay."[311] But the SC did not act as Owen expected. The SC did not acknowledge the receipt of Owen's letter, perhaps because Owen had made the matter public through the press.

To pressure the administration, Owen published the complaint in the *East African Standard*. He wrote:

> Under Hut tax, the Rev. R. Omulo gave instructions where in 1926 he was forced by tax collector to pay poll taxes (3) for members of the family who were earning outside of the reserves.[312]

They reprinted the same statement in the *Mombasa Times*. In the covering letter to the two newspapers, Owen stated: "I suggest that it is high time that the ever-recurring complaints of responsible Natives received investigation at the hands of the Press of the Colony."[313]

The stonewalling and refusal of the SC to respond to the memorandum forced Owen to mobilise the society to protest through KTWA. He reasoned that showing slackness in responding to complaints brought before the colonial administration, by such men as the Rev. Omulo, would erode "the confidence of our African Clergy and of our African Christians" in the government.[314]

Writing to the Chief Native Commissioner in Nairobi, Owen said: "I would be very grateful to you if you could tell me what section of the Hut and Poll tax ordinance, or what rule issued under the Ordinance empowers the collectors to demand that the tax shall be paid by relations of the person from whom the tax is due."[315] Owen was challenging the legality of the officials' activities against the Luo. He demanded "a serious effort to show the people that in the matter of tax collection we are as just and law-abiding at heart as we expect

---

311. Owen, Letter to Senior Commissioner, 24 June 1927.
312. Owen.
313. Owen.
314. Owen.
315. Owen.

them to be." He argued that in their unjust behaviour, the tax officials were as much lawbreakers as the subjects they accused of defaulting on taxes.[316]

Instead of an investigation and government action against the officers, they received denial and attacks. The government responded:

> Following the Senior Commissioner's investigation on R. Omulo's statement requested by Owen and the KTWA, his office found out that, "Omulo's statement was entirely untrue, the Rev. R. Omulo was not forced by the collector to pay poll taxes in 1926 on any of the male relations who were out at work, nor did he pay these taxes."[317]

The Chief Native Commissioner echoed the report of the SC that Omulo paid excess taxes by force, hinting at a possible confusion, and offered a solution, saying that when "a native pays his taxes twice, a refund is always made when the fact come to light."[318] The office called on Owen to take advantage of the LEGICO, where Rev. Canon Leakey represented African interests. Dobbs was aware of the potential men like Omulo had to dent the colonial authority's image of being humane. They broadcast these grievances throughout the world and in the reserves to raise discontentment.

Mr. Dobbs exploited the dating error made by Owen when he made Omulo's statement. For in reporting the case, Owen, including Pleydell, got the impression that Omulo was referring to 1926 taxes while he meant 1927. According to Owen, Omulo "did not actually name the year but used the past tense of the verb as the demand had been surrendered to him and he had sent the money."[319]

It was disingenuous of Dobbs to capitalise on the date mistake in the complaint as the sole basis for the charge against Omulo, for Dobbs was present when Omulo made the complaint at KTWA and had interviewed him to get the exact dates, yet refused to correct Owen's error. Even when Owen corrected the error, Mr. Dobbs did not budge. Instead, he attacked the reputation of both Owen and Omulo. He wrote to the Bishop of Mombasa, CMS Africa Secretary, and copied the Archbishop of Canterbury, saying:

---

316. Owen.
317. Dobbs, Letter to Owen, 12 July 1927.
318. Chief Native Commissioner, Letter in response to Owen's letter of 29 July 1927.
319. Owen, Letter to Archbishop, 17 August 1927.

> An episode like this where an ordained native priest of the Church Missionary Society (CMS) makes an untrue allegation does more than anything else to make the average white man despair of the efficacy of Christian teaching.[320]

Dobbs, whose family had a connection with CMS for three generations, and who was an active supporter of the society, castigated the society on account of this event, questioning the moral standards of the CMS: "how shocked I have been that an untrue statement like this could have been made by a leading Kavirondo Christian of this Society."[321]

With the case facts, Owen made a robust response to the denials of injustice and the later mischaracterization that cast aspersions on the reputation of Owen, Omulo and CMS's work in Nyanza. Having verified the facts of the case, Owen wrote to the Archbishop of Canterbury, through the Bishop of Mombasa, on 27 August 1927, restating the case as Omulo first reported it at KTWA in June. Owen argued that the SC's letter of 12 July worked to undermine the serious aspects and facts which Rev. Omulo's statement represented. They admitted injustice when the official cancelled the poll taxes on the demand note during the investigation.[322] The injustice in Omulo's complaint was the grievance, a symptom of his people's problems. The Bishop of Mombasa confirmed the excesses of the administration when he admitted:

> As regards the injustice occurring in connection with tax collection, I am afraid there is no doubt they occurred. Provision is made for rectifying them and I am sure the British officers concerned are most anxious to rectify them.[323]

Omulo's tax case of 1927 became the criterion for Owen's approach to injustice. Although the case did not gain fame in changing colonial policies, as it remained obscure, it became significant in laying a pattern for Owen's work for justice. Omulo's case permits consideration of the problems of initiative; of the focus of attack upon systems versus individual behaviour; of the necessity for an outcome; of political versus moral action. It permits

---

320. Owen, §3.
321. Owen, §4.
322. Owen, §7.
323. Heywood, Letter to Archbishop, 19 August 1927, §5.

continued examining of tactics to develop principles in engaging the administration, besides appreciating why denigrators of Owen called him "archdemon" instead of archdeacon.[324]

4.7.3 Interactions Between Omulo and the CMS on Discernment for Action

The interaction between Omulo and the CMS on the discernment for action is best described by using a musical metaphor. This implies performance, which refers to concrete human actors, doing a shared and embodied communicative act before and among a specific audience.

Omulo and the CMS collaborated in performing the gospel in Central Nyanza. They saw change in people's lives and the growth of an African Anglican church, attributing it to the manifest act of God in history that draws people into a living relationship with God and forms them into a community of faith. This community embodies God's will through their actions and a life of praise in society. It is alive in society through its praise of God and carrying out God's will. They not only confess but practise their faith, which is in harmony with an African philosophy: "Truth is simultaneously participatory and interactive. It is active, continual and discerning perception leading to action."[325]

The CMS's participation in mission was a transformative experience, seen in the conversion, commitment, and action of the Luo people. Using schools at Maseno, Butere and Ng'iya as means of evangelization, the CMS registered outstanding success in bringing the Luo in Central Nyanza to Christianity. They involved Africans such as Omulo in their outstanding performance, first as co-performers, as teachers who served at the mission schools. Then came the many others who echoed the performance of the CMS by opening schools and churches in their villages. They are the ones who held up the light among the Luo people and took the melody of the gospel to the multitudes. Up to 1920, they provided education in Nyanza, developed their own schools and churches outside the control of the CMS and the government. These schools

---

324. Lonsdale, "Political Associations," 608; Spencer, "Christianity and Colonial Protest," 48.

325. Ramose, *African Philosophy Through Ubuntu*, 50.

were clan-based provisions with amorphous structures, run according to the whims of the founders.

But after the Phelps-Stokes Commission, the CMS strategy had to be aligned with the government-imposed regulations to formalize and categorize schools in the rural areas.[326] The regulations also touched mission schools, pushing for reduced religious content and increased technical training, with the promise of government aid. So, the late 1920s and early 1930s focused on re-organizing education in Nyanza. For instance, they devoted most of the deliberations of the Ruri-decanal Council in Nyanza to education matters. Education improvement included girls' education, which got support from the African clergymen. Their appeal was persuasive, as they pointed to the grave consequences for the girls being left behind.[327] A good example of a harmonious joint performance was the building of Ng'iya girls' school: Under Canon Pleydell's direction, African church members physically put up the building, Chief Ng'ong'a of Alego gave contributions in terms of trees for roofing, the church women brought grass for thatching, and money for the building materials came from Australia.

Carey Francis headed the CMS's education department and the church councils that dealt with rural education matters. Developing education in rural Nyanza required a more centralized approach, although the Ruri-decanal Council played the intermediary role. They inspected all the rural schools and upgraded them to join the family of CMS schools. This was another case of performing together to affect society. The Africans learned from the CMS to play a tune that resonated with them. In education they reproduced that sound to their people, with significant results. Omulo straddled between the two approaches. Up to 1924 he performed in the same education team as CMS in Maseno. His move to K'Omulo in Kisumu in 1925 afforded him freedom to tinker with the school, engaging all African staff, using vernacular Dholuo and adopting the local name K'Omulo. This was a rendition that resonated with the Luo people, as they identified with their own school (§4.5.1.3).

---

326. Anderson, *Church in East Africa*, 83.

327. Kavirondo Ruri-decanal Council Minutes, 17 April 1928; Kavirondo Ruri-decanal Council Minutes, 1933.

Ramose's approach resonates with that of Hauerwas, which noted that Christian existence was neither a subjective experience nor a mechanical transmission of a "deposit of faith."[328] Instead, he saw it as "from start to finish a performance," since Christian worship requires "a performing God who has invited us to join in the performance that is God's life."[329]

The church needed to build an arch across the chasm between Anglican tradition (with its emphasis on theological teaching) and African culture (with its deep affinity for music and rhythm). However, the early missionaries, as observed by Dierks,[330] lacked the ability to compile indigenous hymnbooks, catechisms, or liturgical formulas. It was necessary to translate the Victorian and English worship hymns for morning and evening worship; hymns adhering to the liturgical cycle of Advent, Lent, and Holy Week; songs of adoration, salvation, and the second coming of Christ; assurance of salvation and Christian doctrine.

Canon Pleydell saw how necessary liturgy and music were for worship in the emerging church. As early as 1921, the SPCK had published Pleydell's version of the Luo Anglican prayer book, which was not complete but included many Psalms.[331] This version used by Omulo and the Christians at Maseno up to the 1930s was incomplete, because of the pending translation of the Psalms. Translating poetry, Psalms, and hymns, was a complex matter, requiring not only a good grasp of both Luo and English grammar (lexicon, phrases and idioms), but also of theology. Working with Omulo, Pleydell embarked on translating the Book of Common Prayer, the Anglican hymns and the Psalms into Dholuo. This challenge weighed on Pleydell, although he was forced to leave for England because of an illness that made him deaf. From England, Pleydell requested Omulo's help in translating the Psalms (§4.7.1.4).

Using music metaphors is akin to how "performance" as a concept has been used by theologians including Young, Hauerwas and Wells to describe the interpretation of Scripture and the nature of Christian existence.[332] To know God is to represent God on earth, to embody God's compassion and

---

328. Hauerwas, *Performing the Faith*, 75–77.
329. Kritzinger, "Mission Theology," 80–93.
330. Dierks, *Evangelium im afrikanischen kontext*, 37.
331. Mojola, *God Speaks in Our Languages*, 216.
332. Young, *Art of Performance*; Hauerwas, *Performing the Faith*; Wells, *Improvisation: The Drama*.

justice, and to defend and protect the weak and vulnerable. The Christian life should be a faithful and impactful performance of this melody in a particular context.

The Europeans expected mission-trained Africans to be purveyors of Christianity and Western civilisation among their own people. But Omulo and his fellow African teachers defied that expectation and appealed to the values of justice and fairness enshrined in Christianity, which the CMS did not teach. They expressed their understanding of faith in organising one of the earliest political oppositions to colonial rule. Surprised at the level of their articulation, the colonial administration could not ignore their demands. Therefore, they held a series of meetings to dissuade the associations from public engagement. Later meetings between YKA and the government officers became an intermediate structure to tackle the grievances of the people. The interaction between Omulo and the CMS has shown, as Ramose has said, that "truth is simultaneously participatory and interactive. It is active, continual and discerning perception leading to action."[333] We could describe this as "jamming" (as in a jazz performance), where recipients use their own instruments to play the same melody, but differently. They do so with variations, while performing the same melody.

In KTWA, the CMS (through Owen) and Omulo together erected a platform on which to challenge injustice in Nyanza. To guide African Christians in constitutional matters, Owen needed to keep their confidence, which would assure them their grievances would receive a fair hearing.[334] Hence, he wagered on the people's confidence in his capacity to verify facts and interpret the principles of equity and justice.[335] Owen noted:

> The Kenya Mission has done the Native great disservice by its steady and consistent inability to credit the Natives, or rather certain of them, power to say what they want, and to let them say it for themselves . . . Their voice would have more power and effect than a hundred Missionaries speaking on their behalf. I hold that the lack of confidence that characterizes the attitude

---

333. Ramose, *African Philosophy Through Ubuntu*, 50.
334. Owen, Letter to Senior Commissioner, 24 June 1927.
335. Spencer, "Christianity and Colonial Protest," 53; Owen, Letter to McKeag, 20 November 1931.

of many Missionaries in Kenya toward Natives is a positive barrier to Native welfare and the prosperity of the Native church and plays directly into the hands of those who do not wish the Native voice to be heard.[336]

Owen seized the role of midwifing the justice movement and sought to assist in areas where Africans were less effective in formulating issues, or in communicating grievances to the British public. The Luo deemed Owen's actions as responsibility, not paternalism.[337] However, his actions stirred the ire of his missionary colleagues when his actions did not comport with their wishes for the Africans.

Christian mission and existence, according to Kritzinger, is a "remixing" as they cross boundaries of religion, culture, gender, race, and class, by constantly imagining "alternative ways to sing, dance and perform the founding narrative (and basic melody) of Christian faith in new contexts."[338] Omulo's tax case presented Owen with an entry point to champion the African cause. The case gave him the mold that he would use in future cases against injustice in the government system. Owen's basic tactic was to raise a ruckus by launching a complaint against the local officials, then scale up the complaints to the officials above the ranks, calling for a check on the whole system. He did this in Omulo's case and in the Asembo Affair.[339] Then he mobilized the local community through KTWA to highlight the injustice and raise the local feelings. He would then share the issue with mission colleagues, not to call for coordinated action, but to remind his colleagues of Christ's mandate to individuals. Then he would appeal to English and world public opinion through the press. In Omulo's case, he used the local newspapers, but in the Asembo affair, it was the *Manchester Guardian* newspaper in Britain. Hence

---

336. Owen, "Memorandum on Native Education."
337. Spencer, "Christianity and Colonial Protest," 56.
338. Kritzinger, "Mission Theology," 83.
339. Spencer analyses Owen's approach in the 1931 case in Asembo. It was not enough to advise the district commissioner about the methods by which they chose Ismail Owuor as chief and by which Jason Gor was convicted. His approach also included securing legal advice, an appeal to the supreme court, communications with the chief native commissioner and the governor of Kenya, a draft for publication in the British press, discussions with his bishop, and joint strategy with African associates approximated to sufficiency. Spencer, "Christianity and Colonial Protest," 48–58.

Owen drew support for the plight of Africans through appeals to his public, both African and British.[340]

As pointed out before, Owen argued that "the publication of all the laws in English only leaving it to the District Officers to explain them to the Natives had resulted in very many abuses in the administration of the law."[341] By November 1920, the representative Council of the Alliance favoured the policy of publishing the laws in Kiswahili. Besides, the Anglican Church's policy was to publish all church laws and notices in Swahili. It also held the discussions in the synod in Swahili and English. Laws in a language other than English were significant in Owen's estimation, since that was the basis of good governance. So, Owen advocated direct access to "facilities for knowing what the law is, apart from the verbal statements of the Administration Officers." Otherwise, the people had to depend on those officials for getting information on the law.

We cannot judge the impact or relevance of Christian faith according to universal or independent criteria; it needs to be viewed as "compelling renditions, faithful performances"[342] in specific contexts. Hence, improvisation is essential, which is "the process of creating music in the course of the performance."[343] We can do mission as improvisation of the Christian performance of witness and service, within a context, and sustained by spirituality. The interaction between Omulo and CMS, explored through musical metaphors, shows that mission is improvisation, introduced by traditional Christian witness and service. The recipients contextualized it as they owned and shared the message. Such actions sustain mission, for in remixing and performing the melody in a local context, they draw the audience into resonating with the melody of the gospel themselves.

4.8 Reflexivity

In this section on reflexivity, we seek to answer whether Omulo and the CMS reflected on the impact of their decisions on the community. It explores how

---

340. Owen, Letter to chaplains' conference, 11 July 1933.
341. Owen, Letter to Heywood, 24 June 1927.
342. Hauerwas, *Performing the Faith*, 78.
343. Hauerwas, 79.

they reflected on the impact and result of their work and explains what they learned from their experiences. The section also explores the way those experiences shaped their ongoing ministry approach. In conclusion, the section explores the interaction between Omulo's and CMS's reflexivity.

4.8.1 Reuben Omulo's Reflexivity

Omulo reflected on his impact on the Luo. This section explains his reflection and what he learned from his activities in leadership during this period. How this experience shaped Omulo's approach within the mission is of immense importance.

4.8.1.1 Responding to Injustice

How did Omulo and his people respond to injustices by the colonial administration? They decided to form the YKA to confront the authorities and articulate their issues. At Nyahera, YKA officials met the Chief Native Commissioner who didn't allay their fears, so it became imperative to meet Governor Sir Edward Northey. In this meeting, the association demanded the government's response to their memo. Northey was brief, as he agreed to reconsider the government's *Native Policy*. But this approach was confrontational and drew a harsh reaction from the colonial administration. They saw it as part of the Africans' countrywide revolt. This wind of discontent among Africans worried the colonial government, which did everything to stop the uprising. Aware of the regime's capacity for violence and its readiness to crush any opposition, YKA chartered a distinct path. Nyanza had Archdeacon Owen to guide them in dealing with the regime.

On reflection, Omulo had to change his approach. They sought the support of the CMS by inviting Owen in July 1923 to become their patron. Owen's consent was on the condition that YKA changed its name and tactics, since Owen was cognizant of the peril in confronting the state, and the continued need for a united voice to speak on social justice issues.[344] As a result, in 1923 Owen helped transform the YKA into the KTWA, with a new constitution outlining its objectives (§4.7.1.3). The new association built a system of cooperation with the government.[345] The chiefs and the DCs became ex

---

344. Ogot, "British Administration," 246.
345. Ogot, 246.

officio members, with the senior commissioner as vice-president. Omulo and his people changed their earlier position of hostility towards the CMS on realizing they shared the goal of justice. And with the CMS in the KTWA, they developed an alternative approach in their agitation against atrocious government policies.

4.8.1.2 Songs and Hymns

Omulo's reflexivity is also shown when he guided the adaptation of Luo spiritual songs in the Anglican songbook. The well-arranged songs (hymns) that Omulo and the team worked on at K'Omulo initially lacked a cultural blend.[346] Culture is central in shaping both music and liturgy, hence developers need to consider it in church worship and music. Continuity of culture, as Friesen explains, is vital for the indigenous development of Christianity.[347] So, if the church were to develop an intelligible, theological, and cultural hymnody, translators had to pay due attention to the structure of indigenous music. In a letter to Omulo, Odonde complained of the difficulty people found in learning solfas.[348] What Omulo taught in Kisumu for church music, he learned from Pleydell in 1908. In teaching hymns, Pleydell would first translate two or three hymns, then teach the tone using solfas. Once they mastered the song, he would give out the lyrics on sheets of paper. Learners would then read after him, making several attempts at singing out the tune.[349] The singing of hymns was difficult for many Christians, and few mastered them without being prompted. Some English choruses had already been translated into Kiswahili and were being used in the school. Odonde recommended translating those songs into Dholuo since they used a cultural music style that did not need music notes. This saw the inclusion of eighteen choruses, besides short hymns composed by Luo Christians.[350]

---

346. Congregations and church choirs build a repertoire that is characterised by a cultural blend, polyrhythm, improvisation and four-part harmonic setting, which compels the entire congregation to dance to the music, and hence increases attendance and participation.
347. Friesen, "Methodology in the development," 92–94.
348. Odonde, Letter to Omulo, September 1934.
349. Ochieng' in Omachar, "Contribution of Church Missionary Society," 63.
350. *Wende Luo*, 177–180.

4.8.2 CMS's Reflexivity

This segment explores how CMS reflected on the impact and results of their work among the Luo. It further discusses whether CMS learned from their experiences, and how that self-reflection shaped their mission approach.

4.8.2.1 The Luo Mission Focus

The CMS's bias for the Luo people in the Nyanza mission caused consternation, planting seeds of animosity within the Anglican Church. While the population around Maseno, the CMS's central mission station, was mainly Luyia, the mission target groups were the Luo. The decision presented a problem of access, about which Pleydell wrote, "This part of the work has been our difficulty all along as we are not in an ideal situation to reach them, only quite a few Nilotic Kavirondo villages being reasonably near us."[351] The CMS developed the Maseno boarding school to accommodate Luo students whose homes were further afield. The Luo students became the majority at Maseno School. But as Omulokoli observed, although the medium of teaching in the day school was Dholuo, it had a majority of Luyia students, favoured by the proximity of their homes.[352]

They instructed in the Dholuo language, which both the missionaries and the Luyia learned. The language barrier did not hinder mission. For instance, more Luyias experienced education, with one hundred Luyia students attending the day school between 1910 and 1911. Those students, upon their return, taught their friends. Of the three hundred to four hundred members of the congregation on Sunday, very few Luo attended, and the majority were Luyia.[353] The Luyia at Maseno formed their casual workforce, most of their day school pupils and members of the local congregation.

Even though CMS developed a successful ministry to reach the Abaluyia people in North Nyanza,[354] that did not conceal the fissure created at Maseno. CMS ought to have been intentionally presenting the gospel in an even and inclusive manner. Using Dholuo for instruction and worship among the Luyia, even with Luyia catechists, soon became problematic. The Luyia, being the

---

351. Pleydell, Annual Letter, 25 November 1910.
352. Omulokoli, "Historical Development," 142.
353. Omulokoli, 142.
354. Omulokoli, 162–229.

majority in Musanda, abhorred the practice of being instructed in Dholuo, as was the practice in Maseno. So, when Jeremiah Otang'a, a teacher-catechist, gave instruction in Dholuo to Luyia families at Musanda in 1924, Luyia leaders warned him not to repeat it, although Jeremiah had practised and instructed in Dholuo all along. But they did not discipline him, for fear of conflicts flaring up with the Luo.

4.8.2.2 Ethnic Tragedy

CMS's inability to detect the underlying tribal tensions turned tragic. Those tribal and language conflicts persisted, dividing the church on tribal lines into the 1930s but they veiled the major problem, which was land. It was the core of the problem since it touched on ancestry, identity and belonging.

The CMS missionaries dealt with the conflict differently. For instance, when in 1933 the Anglican Luyias complained, as Omulokoli observed, that Carey Francis was employing Luo teachers in positions that should have been occupied by Luyias, he faced it head-on.[355] Francis insisted that he engaged teachers on merit and not on tribal quotas. He would not overlook capable Luos available in search of a non-existent Abaluyia.[356] Instead, Francis created a vehicle to solve the problem (§4.7.2.3) that quelled the storm.

Owen, however, left the cases to fester, so it was too late when he acted. In Musanda, where the majority Luyia shared the church with the Luo, the relations became tragic for the Luo minority, as conflict over Luo dominance in the church and threats of further encroachment on Luyia land came to the fore. Tribal altercation in the Musanda Anglican Church reached its crescendo on 21 January 1934, when the majority Luyia invaded the home of Rev. Alfayo Odongo Mango and set fire to houses, killing ten people, including Odongo himself.[357] According to Ogot, the years of unrelieved tension pitching the Luo against the Luyia in Musanda, exploded because the underlying issues of tribe, land and language remained unresolved, and got dragged into church relations.[358]

---

355. Omulokoli, "Historical Development," 280.
356. Kavirondo Ruri-decanal Council Minutes, 1933.
357. Kavirondo Ruri-decanal Council Minutes, 19 December 1934; Greaves, *Carey Francis of Kenya*, 47–49; Odinga, *Not yet Uhuru*, 69–70; Ogot, "Reverend Alfayo Odongo Mango," 108.
358. Ogot, "Reverend Alfayo Odongo Mango," 90–111.

Because of these animosities, the CMS first separated the worship services in the same church building, with the congregations worshipping along tribal lines. The Luyias worshipped first, followed by the Luos. But they soon abandoned that for a complete separation of church buildings, due to the ongoing flare-ups of the conflict. This was what led *Omwami* Arnold Talala to build a separate school and church for the Luyia adherents, leaving the Luo in the original building.[359]

The CMS attempted to resolve the issues. Rev. George Samuel Okoth, Rev. Jeremiah Awori, Rev. Isaya Musiga, and Rev. Mariko Oduor agreed that the land question was the divisive factor in the church, but they regretted that it was difficult to sort out.

The situation which had begun to deteriorate on 13 December 1931, when the Luyias tried to evict the Luos from Musanda, became dire in 1933. The Luo people thwarted the previous attack, and forced the Luyia to wait for an opportune moment to strike again. These animosities continued into 1932,[360] but a lull followed in 1933, characterized by reduced bickering, which deluded the administrators that the skirmishes had died out. In the Musanda Massacre of 21 January 1934 mentioned above Odongo Mango and his followers were burned alive during prayer.[361]

The massacre divided not only the Luyia and Luo peoples of Musanda, but it also pushed the charismatic Anglican adherents of the Roho fellowship out of the Anglican Church. Henceforth, Isaya Goro and Elijah Oloo, the surviving leaders, continued the Roho fellowship outside the Anglican Church and in 1941 they formed Dini Ya-Roho.[362] The claim of historians like Odinga, Ogot and Nundu that it was this incident that drove the Roho group out of the Anglican Church is plausible.[363] Had Owen intervened after the 1931 attacks and persuaded the colonial administration to pay more attention to the complaints of the Kager people among the Luyia, the outcome may have been different.

---

359. Butere Church Council Minutes, 26 July 1919.
360. Omulokoli, "Historical Development," 256.
361. Ogot, *History of the Luo-speaking*, 731; Hoehler-Fatton, *Women of Fire*, 63–66.
362. Hoehler-Fatton, *Women of Fire*, 82–85, 96.
363. Odinga, *Not yet Uhuru*, 69; Ogot, "Reverend Alfayo Odongo Mango," 103; Nundu, *Nyuolruok dhoudi Mag Ugenya*, 25–26.

4.8.2.3 Malanga Crisis

Malanga, in Central Nyanza, presented a unique set of crises for Owen. The Ojuodhi Luo, being in the majority, persecuted Jo-Umani (an assimilated Luyia clan) who were part of the Ojwando people. Owen sided with the majority Ojuodhi clan, and that also turned tragic.

At the beginning, the Anglican Padre Simeon Nyende and Chief Odera Ogada of North Gem attempted to block Silfano Ayayo from enrolling at Butere Teachers Center because he was Ja-Umani from the Ojwando clan. Owen intervened and got him admitted to be trained as a teacher and evangelist. But since Ojuodhi clans dominated Anglican schools and churches, Padre Nyende rejected Ayayo from serving in Malanga church because of his clan, despite his training and calling. After interrogating Rev. Nyende, Owen was convinced of unjust treatment of Jo-Umani and summoned a Rural Deanery meeting.[364] According to Wanyanga, Owen preferred to discuss those problems through the church structures.[365] The meeting resolved to have two separate services for Ojwando and Kagola people, with the former holding morning services while the latter holding services in the afternoon. But that only created a lull before a major storm, for Ojuodhi people refused to accommodate Ojwando and often caused them problems. Despite complaints they made, Owen took no further action.

But that changed after Sunday 28 March 1937, when Ojuodhi people desecrated the church. The Ojwando group gathered on that Sunday as assigned to them. Having their space increased their enthusiasm and commitment to Church. They brought tithes and thanks-giving offerings to the Lord. Their numbers increased as they admitted more children as catechumens. Then, as Wanyanga narrates:

> Strong Kagola men emerged from behind the thickets around the church armed with walking sticks (bakora) and leather whips made from the hide of hippopotamus, which were the weapons of choice. They descended on the people inside the church and beat them up. The gigantic men, ensuring nobody escaped, blocked the two exits. They beat up men, women and

---

364. An area formed by many parishes, usually under the jurisdiction of a priest, who is commonly referred to as a rural dean.

365. Wanyanga, *Triumph Through Faith*, 92.

children who were armed only with Bibles. At first there was yelling and crying from women and children, but this suddenly stopped when the men defended themselves and their women and children. They confronted their assailants on one-on-one combat. Strong women like Rosa Okuot Nyar Midenge joined the fight to help their men. The scene was chaotic. After a couple of minutes, the men and women in the congregation repulsed the ugly aggressors. Several people were injured, men, women, and children. There were injuries too, on the bouncers and musclemen of the Kagola clan. Chairs, pews, and tables were broken. Torn pages of Bibles littered the floor. Some people used Bibles as a weapon or armour. The tithes and offerings went missing. And although the aggressors were pushed out of the church building, skirmishes continued in the church compound.[366]

This was the end of Jo-Umani with the Malanga Anglican Church. They held their subsequent Sunday services under a gigantic tree in front of Petro Ongwen's home. Attacking the Ojwando in a church, beyond being a spiritual sacrilege, broke the law. That forced Owen's radical intervention.[367] The Rural Deanery meeting in Lundha Church reprimanded Padre Nyende and warned him of dire consequences for the hate and attack on the Ojwando people. They suspended him from serving them and gave Silfano charge over his people until they identified a padre prepared to serve *mwache*. Meanwhile, Owen assigned Padre Barnabas Weche, of Namasoli Anglican Church. Despite that, Ojwando people were no longer comfortable in the Anglican Church, so in 1940 Silfano and his people, Jo-Umani, seceded to the Seventh Day Adventist Church with all their churches and schools, which had been Anglican congregations.

Because Owen was reluctant to take sides on local politics and avoided engaging in tribal conflicts, he didn't act on Ojwando peoples' several complaints to him about injustice both in the church and society.[368] Had Owen addressed this issue earlier and acted to support the weaker Jo-Umani people, they may still have been Anglicans.

---

366. Wanyanga, 49.
367. Wanyanga, 102.
368. Wanyanga, 91.

The inability to unite the church and the decision to develop ministry strategy along tribal lines undermined the unity of Christian congregations, as evident in both the Musanda and Malanga cases. In such conflicts, Owen always appeared to support "the 99," the majority ethnic group, at the expense of the minority.

4.8.3 Interaction Between Omulo and CMS on Reflexivity

To explain the interaction between Omulo and CMS on reflexivity, this section uses some of the five relational "ideologies" constructed by Lochhead:[369] hostility, isolation, competition, partnership, and dialogue. They will help to clarify how their interaction developed from isolation to dialogue.

Lochhead's ideology of isolation occurs where a group sees itself as superior to others, with themselves in the light, while the rest are in darkness.[370] CMS missionaries became the voice of Africans against the injustices visited on them, even though missionaries were part of the dominant culture. About the tax injustices against Omulo's people, Owen sought to expose the ills through publicity and through mobilizing the public for action as the means toward a resolution. He accepted the sometimes conflicting, sometimes complementary, view of confidence in African abilities to represent themselves and to resist the existing colonial barriers that rendered them "inarticulate." During the transition, "those who are articulate must supply what is lacking."[371] But had he allowed Omulo to scrutinise the recorded statement, Omulo would have noted the date error that cost them the campaign against taxation. It was an isolationist relationship because Owen reflected a paternalistic view of his role and of the obligation to act on principle, which rarely aligned with the wishes of his mission colleagues or of the Africans.

The partnership ideology also helps to explain the CMS's and Omulo's relationship. According to Lochhead, partnership is when groups embrace one another, affirm a common interest, note their differences and similarities, and then forge meaningful cooperation.[372] Here, Africans provided the case of injustice, and the missionaries made the case. In this partnership they argued

---

369. Lochhead, *Dialogical Imperative*.
370. Lochhead, 8.
371. Owen, Letter to J. H. Oldham, 8 August 1926.
372. Lochhead, *Dialogical Imperative*, 24.

the case and challenged the state's injustice. Omulo's tax problem presented Owen with a concrete case, and he used it to justify issuing laws for Africans in a language they understand, for the CMS leader needed the confidence of Omulo and his people.[373] They showed their partnership relationship in Owen's mobilization of African participation on local justice issues. Oywaya affirms that Owen "encouraged African clergy to act to show Christian concern to the leadership of the government," which they took advantage of, addressing issues beyond what missionaries perceived.[374]

The dialogue ideology highlights another aspect of the relationship that sprouted between the CMS and Omulo. The atrocious colonial policies after 1920 had a negative impact on Omulo and his people. The Luo suspected the CMS missionaries were part of the plot. Owen's reaction of sympathy to the Africans was the CMS's show of concern, as it acted in love and benevolence towards Omulo and the Luo people.

Omulo's and the CMS's interactions, modelled Lochhead's dialogical imperative when they entered into a commitment to agitate against injustice.[375] Omulo and his people committed to channelling their grievances through KTWA, together with CMS, and sidestepping the Local Native Council, the channel through which the administration expected them to lodge their grievances. Owen, as a representative of the CMS, limited his campaign to Nyanza issues throughout his career,[376] venturing only on issues within his direct experience in Western Kenya. In acting together, the CMS and Omulo reciprocated commitment to each other, to demand action on events rooted in their own experience and which violated their principles.

Omulo's case gave Owen a model of campaign against injustice. Henceforth, any injustice cases brought to KTWA had to be scrutinized jointly for the facts, with a willingness to discuss solutions and a commitment to the value of an informed public. Owen's approach differed from that of J. H. Oldham of the International Missionary Council, who Spencer[377] notes, assumed the government's intent to act and so advocated allowing the state the opportunity

---

373. Owen, Letter to Senior Commissioner, 24 June 1927; Owen, Letter to Heywood, 24 June 1927.
374. Spencer, "Christianity and Colonial Protest," 56.
375. Lochhead, *Dialogical Imperative*, 93.
376. Spencer, "Christianity and Colonial Protest," 52.
377. Spencer, 58.

to do right. Omulo and Owen had a growing relationship, expressed in a willingness to accommodate mistakes and learn from them. So, when Owen erred in executing Omulo's tax case, a mistake that would have jeopardized the case, Omulo absolved him, willing to keep the close bond. Hooper noted, "occasionally he [Owen] has made mistakes, but as a general rule I believe that there is no missionary in Kenya who takes more pains to get to the truth."[378] Henceforth, collecting correct information before launching a justice campaign became imperative in KTWA. As a result, the Asembo affair in 1931 that involved Ismail Owuor succeeded because of the lesson learned.[379]

Their mutual self-giving transformed CMS and Omulo into part of God's community, as they entered a dialogical relationship. Connected as humans, they now sought God's justice together. Although they fought external injustice by the colonial regime together, the injustices within the Anglican Church, pitching the Luo against the Luyia, eluded CMS (§4.7.2.3). Had CMS remained true to non-racial policies, perhaps the ethnic altercations would have been minimal. The contextual reality in Kisumu was a paradox. CMS needed to express a non-racial, non-tribal faith but could not accommodate Africans in the European's church. Besides, CMS had to grapple with compliance to colonial colour-bar laws implemented in Kisumu, which contradicted CMS's indigenous church and non-racial church policies. But adhering to government's segregation policies was tragic. Separating the Kisumu Church on racial grounds tore the church's fabric in the eyes of the Africans. From then on, it became acceptable to discriminate based on the idiosyncrasies of a superior race, tribe or culture. And that became the default mode for both the Luyia and Luo churches. CMS failed to foresee tribal skirmishes stemming from her mission strategy in Nyanza, hence ethnic animosities metamorphosed into outright violent conflicts.[380] Aware of the danger of ethnic sentiments, Omulo at K'Omulo demonstrated Christianity could ameliorate ethnic or racial sensitivities. He favoured uniting the church under his charge through teaching the unity of faith in baptism, sharing of the table, and

---

378. Since land was a dominant theme in Kenya colonial protest, we should note that central, not western, Kenya was faced with land insecurity because of European settlement. The land issue, therefore, was distant from Owen's experience. He was, however, active in the land issues that the discovery of gold around Kakamega raised in the 1930s.

379. Spencer, "Christianity and Colonial Protest," 48–58.

380. Omulokoli, "Historical Development," 255–275.

worship. Being an urban multi-ethnic congregation aided in eliminating tribal barriers, for they were no strangers to each other. Omulo refused to exclude any gifted student at the school because of their ethnicity, as in Olang's case (§4.5.1.3). At K'Omulo he attempted to develop an inclusive Christian community despite the continued use of Dholuo as a medium of communication. Where CMS didn't discuss the Jo-Umani conflict over school access, Omulo came to the rescue, opening his school for the Ojwando children (§4.9.1.4).

4.9 Spirituality

At the heart of the praxis matrix is the spirituality dimension. This section uses the typology of Cannon and Foster, as indicated in §3.9.[381] It explains the dominant spirituality displayed by Omulo in this period. It also describes the dominant spirituality practised by the CMS missionaries at the same time. The last part of the section explains the nature of the interaction between their spiritualities.

4.9.1 Reuben Omulo's Spirituality

As Omulo embarked on his studies, the rational tradition of theologizing that characterizes the Anglican tradition influenced him. It was in studying Scripture that Omulo most experienced God's presence and guidance, thus discerning God's word for his life. In discussing the basic spiritual experience that motivated Omulo to take part in God's mission, this section describes three ways in which Omulo experienced the Holy Spirit working in his life.

4.9.1.1 The Sacramental Life

The period from 1921 to 1945 allowed Omulo to practice and share the spirituality he learned in Maseno. He attempted to replicate the "Christian environment" in the Anglican liturgical order in Kisumu, just as he practised and taught in Maseno.[382] In Maseno they prayed, studied the Scriptures, and sang spiritual songs, following the Anglican liturgical order. In Kisumu Omulo carried forward formal and organised worship, done both in the church and private homes. They permeated the practice of faith in every aspect of life in

---

381. Cannon, "Different ways"; Foster, *Streams of Living Water*.
382. Willis, "Reflection in 1949," 51.

Christian homes, where they entertained many Christian visitors. They took no meals without a thanks-giving prayer and developed a prayer formula for journeying mercies and meals. Heads of families led regular evening prayers at home, which began with an evening hymn, a Bible reading and often a repeating of the passage from the Sunday service readings. This was followed by supplication, in unison recitation of the Lord's prayer, intercession led by the head of the home, or anyone assigned, and united sharing the grace of our Lord.

The other feature of Christian practice was life in the liturgical cycle. They observed the Advent season culminating in Christmas marked with the joy of giving, with carol singing at church and from door to door. During Lent, Christians would forgo certain foods for forty days. The climax of the season was the sombre church services on Good Friday, followed by a joyous Easter celebration. Congregation members replicated this in their homes.

4.9.1.2 *The Spirit-empowered Life*

Omulo expressed his Holy Spirit empowered life in his missionary work. But this aspect was noticeable in his sensitivity to the spiritual realities affecting Christians in their daily lives. He gave such Christians help where CMS missionaries were ambivalent. Since Luo religion and Christianity acknowledged the spirit world in their worldviews, both had solutions. As Steyne notes, Christians acknowledge that God speaks in his Word with power, while the Africans experience this power in human spirit encounters.[383] But being a Christian, Omulo could not revert to traditional religious remedies, so he sought answers in Christianity. For example, he supported Mr. Onyango who had suffered from *sepe* (spirits possession) by conducting his wedding and praying for his release (§4.6.1.2). This expressed Omulo's charismatic faith.

4.9.1.3 *The Virtuous Life*

The devotional surrender in Cannon's typology can describe Omulo's spirituality. His personal difficulties in this period tested his resolve for mission service and priesthood. He lived a virtuous life despite family tragedies that could have forced him out. His son Owiti died in 1937 at K'Omulo School at the hands of his teacher Mr. Clement Odeny. His response in forgiveness and

---

383. Steyne, *Gods of Power*, 208.

embracing Mr. Odeny showed his commitment to Christ's teachings that had become his own. Omulo's teaching on forgiveness derived from the gospels:

> Omulo wacho niya: Wach mar Weyo nowetewa Motimonwa marach (Luke 17:3). Yesu nochikowa ni mondo wa we jomotimo nwa marach ka gilokre. To owacho ni ka ok gilokre wa pogre kodgi. Joma luwo Nyasaye ok ginyal chulo kuor kwom jomotimo nigi marach chik ariyo owacho kaka Nyasaye em janyiego machulo kuor. To Johana owacho kaka kane pod waricho Yesu nothonwa wan bende onego waluw Yesu kwom nguono ne. Eka onego walam nigi joma timonwa marach bende e wa ng'wonigi.[384]

> Translation: Forgiving those who wronged us Luke 17:3. Jesus said that we forgive those who wronged us if they repent. He also affirmed parting company with those who don't repent. Those who follow God's way do not take revenge on those who offend them. The second law shows how God is a jealous God and the avenger. But John said that Christ died for us while still sinners. So, we must follow the example of Jesus' grace. We must pray for those who wrong us and forgive them.

The essence of Omulo's teaching was that God commands us to forgive those who wrong us when they repent, that revenge offends God, who alone is the avenger. His basis for forgiveness, to which he invited his audience, was that Christ forgave us while sinners. This is the premise upon which we must act to forgive. His unwillingness to pursue justice through courts, seek vengeance, retribution, or even to judge Odeny was revealing of Omulo's faith.

The other level in Omulo and Odeny's relationships, other than faith, and comradeship at K'Omulo, was that they were kin (§3.3.1). It is plausible to infer Omulo's reaction to his Luo values, which he often weaved with Christianity. The Luo place great value on family moral laws, which, as Ochola Ayayo asserts, demands individual members to observe personal honour or good name (*Nying maber*) by doing justice.[385] Among the Luo, like other Africans, justice was about relationship and wholeness of relationship. This, Tutu observes, should restore good relationships, and not just punish the

---

384. Omulo, Reuben Omulo Notes, 72–73.
385. Ocholla-Ayayo, *Traditional Ideology and Ethics*, 184.

miscreant.[386] That Omulo was unwilling to pursue justice through courts or retribution, processes that were established according to Western (Christian) edicts then applicable in Kenya supports this notion. Odeny later became a headteacher of Uranga School, another CMS school.

Second, we see Omulo's virtuous life while developing the Luo hymnody. He encouraged the composition of spiritual songs, which he included in the Luo hymn book, together with the translated hymns. For Omulo, music was a significant element of spirituality since it bridged the chasm between African spirituality and Christianity. Even though religious hymns, as we know them, did not exist in the Luo traditional religion, music spoke deep into Africans' hearts. It was an intrinsic part of African daily life in the traditional dirges, praise, historical and merry songs. While in Christianity, Omulo understood that worshippers met God through liturgy in worship. He also understood that worshippers become witnesses of Christ as they gather, which agrees with Lieberknecht's conclusion that what distinguishes a congregation as the church of God is its music.[387]

4.9.1.4 The Compassionate Life

Of the manifestations of spirituality, it was the compassionate dimension of Omulo's spirituality that blossomed during this period. Omulo confronted colonial injustice against himself and his people on one hand and provided help for victims of injustice perpetuated by ethnic rivalries on the other hand.

The spike in injustice perpetrated by the colonial regime summoned a response based on Omulo's new faith. Since the issues affected him, Omulo demanded justice for his people by direct resistance in YKA. Later through KTWA, using indirect agitation, he pushed the colonial government to minimise abuses in their tax collection exercise (§4.7.1). It was a spiritual response to challenge abuses against people, for he stood for the oppressed at the cost of his reputation, following in the social justice tradition.

For the victims of persecution in Malanga 1938, the Ojwando people whose children could not access schooling, Omulo used his influence, opening a door for them at K'Omulo where they found refuge. Padre Nyende of CMS Malanga and Chief Ogada of Gem barred Ojwando children from

---

386. Tutu, *No Future Without Forgiveness*, 32.
387. Lieberknecht, *Gemeindelieder: Probleme und chancen*, 281, 283.

attending Malanga and Lwanda schools, which were the only schools in the area. In a cruel jest Nyende barred Ayayo, saying, "If you want to teach you must find a school for your own people where you can go and teach them foolishness . . . we can't mix with *mwache*."[388] But Chief Ogada would not allow any school to be built for the Ojwando people. For instance, when Joseph Okola, a Catholic catechist attempted to teach Ojwando people and children the Catholic doctrines, Wanyanga narrates: "Chief Ogada accosted him with his *askaris* (police) whips, tied him on a tree trunk and left Okola for dead. He whipped the children, scattering them across the villages."[389] Ogada was determined to bar Ojwando's children from education. Okola survived but defied the chief by continuing to teach underground. To those persecuted by the Anglican padre and Gem chief, Omulo opened an alternative school fifty miles away, which they seized with zeal. This was how Ayayo's people gained valuable education.[390] The irony was that Omulo from Ojuodhi clan differed with his kin Padre Nyende on persecuting the Ojwando (Jo-Umani). The Umani people had become Anglican Christians and so were brothers and sisters in Christ. Besides, his two sisters married Jo-Umani, hence Ayayo was his brother-in-law (§4.3.1).

This incident, among others, explains Omulo's spirituality in the social justice tradition. He developed these aspects while at Kisumu and continued during his pastorate service, as will become clear in the next chapter.

4.9.2 CMS's Spirituality

As explained in the spirituality segment of chapter 3, CMS represented multiple spiritualities because of the diversity of missionaries it deployed. The missionaries discussed in the last chapter continued to serve during this phase, so it will be important to explore whether their spirituality developed. Changes in the missionary policies during this period affected the spiritualities that missionaries espoused. It was during this period that CMS recruited Africans into pastoral service, replacing missionaries. CMS instead increased missionaries coming as experts in education, medicine and community work. This affected their way of being Christian missionaries, as it

---

388. Wanyanga, *Triumph Through Faith*, 42.
389. Wanyanga, 93.
390. Wanyanga, 40.

expressed different spiritualities and the role they played in shaping mission. This section describes four conspicuous types of spirituality in the life of the CMS missionaries.

4.9.2.1 The Compassionate Life

The most conspicuous spirituality among the CMS missionaries was the compassionate life. Its expression permeated through the projects they involved the missionaries in, including agriculture to educate the Africans to raise crops during the multiple famines ravaging Nyanza. It also included medical work done to help heal the sick with a hospital in Maseno, and clinics in Butere and Ng'iya. Education remained the chief act of compassion through which the missionaries expressed their spirituality among the Luo because of the transformation achieved. The support of the government was valuable. It aided in setting up and sustaining programs such as health and education. But soon it became a snare, following changes in the colonial arrangements from 1920.

Starting with Owen, the spiritual dimension as deeds of justice, showing kindness to victims of a small-pox epidemic, became CMS missionaries' trademark response in addressing difficulties Africans faced. CMS missionaries had no question about Christ's call to pursue political actions for justice, but there was a divide on the best approach to follow. First, they perceived the role of the church to be advocacy, such as calling out the state on injustices, which reflects the church's concern. Second, they perceived that the mandate of Christ was to seek the removal of the injustice. Owen belongs to this latter group, as shown in his tenacious and almost harassing involvement.[391] Writing to Mr. Parkinson at the Colonial Office, Owen said:

> I have been given the impression, mainly in Africa, that Africans must suffer administrative injustices in silence, that they must not cry aloud when they are hurt. If they say what is hurting them, they are called seditious. Anyone who attempts to voice the cry of a people who are almost inarticulate, is apt to be regarded, not as a peacemaker, but as a public nuisance. The Colonial Office has been a consenting party to every one of

---

391. Spencer, "Christianity and Colonial Protest," 52.

the legislative measures which are regarded by the Africans as unjust. I hold that the only thing which will enable the Colonial Office to embark on reforms is public opinion.[392]

Owen appealed to the English and world public opinion through the press, which provided Owen with his tactical answer. He reflected the spirituality of social justice by the organised resistance to colonial excess through the work of KTWA.

4.9.2.2 The Sacramental Life

Rev. Pleydell expressed CMS's spirituality in the Anglican liturgical tradition during this period as well. With a great number of CMS-approved congregations in Central Nyanza, Pleydell continued to avail vernacular material for liturgical worship, incorporating portions of the Book of Common Prayer in Dholuo and publishing hymns, which enabled worship among the congregations. At each gathering and worship, the congregations expressed a spirituality of sacramental liturgy developed by the CMS missionaries and passed on by the African Christians.

4.9.3 Interaction Between Omulo and CMS on Spirituality

The interaction between Omulo and CMS on spirituality is explained in this section through musical metaphors. It discusses spirituality as a melody performed first by CMS, then joined by Omulo and other participants. Explaining performance from an African standpoint, CMS were performers whose service embodied communicative acts with an audience among the Luo people and before God. Their acts of compassion, which were fundamental to their ministry, characterized their spirituality.

In response to the rising inhumane treatment, Omulo and his people appealed to their oppressors' faith, for they viewed the colonialists and missionaries as the same people. These abuses forced the CMS to make a decisive stand, to support Omulo and his people. They took a "prophetic" approach akin to one in the Belhar Confession, Article 4: "standing where God stands, against injustice and with those who are wronged."[393] Hence, Omulo and the CMS realized that Christian involvement in opposing injustice is an integral

---

392. Owen, Letter to Parkinson, 23 May 1931.
393. Dutch Reformed Mission Church, *Belhar Confession*.

dimension of discipleship. So, the CMS and Omulo, through KTWA, created an instrument to shield the Luo against colonial regime abuses during this period, thus developing a prophetic spirituality.

4.9.3.1 Deeds of Justice

If Christian existence, as Hauerwas states, is "from start to finish a performance,"[394] and if God is "a performing God who has invited us to join in the performance that is God's life"[395] then we should view action against injustice by the CMS and Omulo as their joint faith performance. Through the work of KTWA, which combined acts of compassion and open agitation during the crisis, they challenged the unjust action of the colonial government. Those acts demonstrated the spirituality in the tradition of social justice, acting with God for a just society.

Once receptors resonate with the melody of the performers, they improvise on the melody by "jamming" or remixing it. This describes the interaction between Omulo and the CMS in liturgical spirituality. At Kisumu, Omulo improved on the Luo Anglican liturgy of the prayer book and hymns, accommodating Luo spiritual songs that resonated with the people. Building on what Omulo inherited from the mission, they developed a spiritual approach that fit both the context and liturgical matters.

The notion of mission as improvisation points to the role of contextualisation, and the spirituality which sustains mission. Remixing and performing the melody resonates with the local context, which draws the audience to perform. Omulo and the Luo Christians were alert to the spirit world. Because of their traditional worldview, Omulo was cognizant of the Christian interaction with the spirit world (§4.6.1.2), for interpreting dreams and visions is a charismatic expression of spirituality. While Christianity and traditional religions share a "spiritual view of life" regarding beliefs in the spirit beings and the supernatural powers, they differ in the meanings they attach to beliefs and practices. What Christians and traditional religions believe, according to Steyne, must be "evaluated and submitted to the judgment of the Bible."[396]

---

394. Hauerwas, *Performing the Faith*, 75.
395. Hauerwas, 77.
396. Steyne, *Gods of Power*, 208.

But the CMS missionaries were tone-deaf to the spirit worldview; hence they did not appreciate the charismatic spirituality developing among their African adherents. Wanyanga narrates a crisis involving spiritual intervention that Owen avoided.[397] Following the attack on Ojwando people in Malanga Church by the Ojuodhi people (§4.9.1.4), Silfano Ayayo led the elders in fasting and praying for God's guidance. According to Wanyanga,[398] "Three elders, Musa Adongo, Mathayo Oduma and Ayayo, had a simultaneous vision in their dream. In the dream, something independently directed each to read Isaiah 66:22–23." Since they had not translated the Old Testament into Luo, they had to read in the English Bible in the catechist's custody:

> "As the new heavens and the new earth that I make will endure before me," declares the LORD, "so will your name and descendants endure. From one New Moon to another and from one Sabbath to another, all mankind will come and bow down before me, says the LORD" (Isa 66:22–23, NIV).

This vision perplexed the elders who sought an urgent interpretation of the message. Language limited their comprehension of the scriptural message, for they knew every word in the text except Sabbath.[399] For this reason, they sent three elders to Owen to unlock the dream and the Bible text. But, according to Wanyanga, Owen did not help them interpret the text, nor explain the vision.[400] The elders concluded either Owen did not know its interpretation, which was not plausible, or he just declined to help.

To Owen the Luos were a simple and uncritical folk, whose worldview allowed them to interpret natural phenomena, besides belief in the supernatural. Hence, he was reluctant to encourage dreams and Old Testament text application in this manner. With a letter, Owen directed them for answers to A. A. Carscallen, the head of the Seventh Day Adventist Mission in Gendia, South Nyanza, where the Umani delegation arrived in August 1939.[401] Hence, this Sabbath vision and Owen's letter guided the Ojwando people into the SDA out of the Anglican Church.

---

397. Wanyanga, *Triumph Through Faith*, 107–109.
398. Wanyanga, 107.
399. Wanyanga, 107.
400. Wanyanga, 108.
401. Wanyanga, 108.

4.10 Overview on the Encounters in this Period

This chapter has examined the raft of changes in Central Nyanza society between 1921 and 1945 because of colonial policies. It featured the negative impact these policies exerted on society. As a result, Nyanza people protested, appealing for a reconsideration. But they had to adjust to survive. These changes affected the CMS too. The government became more intrusive as they regulated education, which was their main missionary approach. It forced CMS to adjust its mission policies and lend support to the Africans, instead of backing the colonial regime. One cannot underrate the gravity of the 1923 Devonshire White paper's impact on the colony and CMS mission. While it made the African interests the priority of the Colony, the slow pace of obtaining African independence agitated African leaders. Against this backdrop, CMS and Omulo carried on mission work to set up the African Anglican Church in Central Nyanza.

The mission praxis of Omulo and the CMS mission explained in this chapter showed fresh insights during this period, which built on the activities discussed in chapter 3. During this period Omulo transitioned from teaching at Maseno to heading a mission station at Kisumu, which in his honour became K'Omulo. The chapter discussed his mission innovation by using the seven elements of the praxis matrix.

Faced with post-war challenges, CMS speeded up her indigenized church policies. With diminished resources and fewer missionaries, CMS recruited specially skilled missionaries to upgrade their flagship programs, such as major schools and hospitals. At the same time, they increased the number of African agents, both in pastoral and mission staff. CMS trained and deployed them, allowing the church to be more and more African.

The chapter explained the impact of CMS's mission approach on the African Anglican Church. CMS espoused a faith that emphasized believing and confession, which produced many nominal Christians. The chapter discusses the innovative movements that emerged within the Anglican Church, representing unique expressions of Christianity that rejuvenated a waning church in Central Nyanza. The main ones are the Roho and the East African Revival movements. While the Roho adherents formed their own denomination, the CMS integrated the Revival movement within the Anglican Church (§§5.4.2 & 5.9.2). This chapter explained Omulo's efforts to contextualize and indigenize his faith, building on what he learned from

CMS missionaries. Omulo's development of the liturgy and the setting up of K'Omulo represented a fresh mission approach. A storm of ethnic skirmishes, which occasioned splinter groups leaving, hit the African Anglican Church.

Had not Omulo and his people protested the colonial policies, presented their memorandum for change to the colonial government, and formed YKA, the CMS approach to social justice would have been different. African action put a wedge between the CMS and the government. The CMS had to choose sides on the scale of justice. Besides, they had to weigh their Victorian worldview against the Scriptures and the actions of the regime.

The increased pressure on the Africans thrust both the CMS and Omulo into responding to injustice in the Luo society. Omulo developed a justice spirituality, which became a key aspect of mission in this period. Through Owen, the CMS refined its praxis of justice. They flourished together in justice spirituality, which became a hallmark of the Anglican Church in Central Nyanza for many years to come.

This chapter provided ingredients with which the CMS set up the African Anglican Church in Central Nyanza. During this period, CMS recruited African agents, proved their leadership capacities, and trusted them with the church. Challenges facing the church during this period persisted into the following years when the church was completely under African authority.

CHAPTER 5

Independence Stage: Tracing Interactions Between the Forms of Mission Praxis in Central Nyanza from 1946 to 1970

5.1 Introduction

This chapter explores the mission praxes in Central Nyanza from 1946 to 1970 (§1.6). These mission praxes are constructed against the background of a raft of policy changes by the colonial regime enacted after 1945. The changes were aimed at lifting the status of Africans, who for their part piled pressure on the state, demanding better education, prosperity, and independence from colonial rule. It explains the mission praxis during the independence stage of the Anglican Church in Central Nyanza, by first constructing the praxis of Reuben Omulo as a mission innovator, then the praxis of the CMS as the change agent, by using the praxis matrix in its seven dimensions (§§1.6, 3.1 & 4.1). Each section concludes by tracing the interaction between those two praxes and examining how each of the seven dimensions of the matrix, representing their intentional transformative ideas and actions, responded to, or corresponded with, each other (§§3.3 & 4.3).

5.2 Key Events: Political, Economic, and Cultural Features of the Period

Just as declaring Kenya a colony triggered events that shaped the period between 1921 and 1945, post-WWII events sparked significant movements that heightened societal aspirations in Central Nyanza. With an increased and insatiable appetite for education, the population became impatient for self-rule; hence the nationalism euphoria as people were prepared to engage the government to achieve their demands. The changing attitudes toward colonialism in England leading to India's independence in 1947 imprinted a sense of urgency for independence in African minds as well.

5.2.1 Societal Changes in Politics

The more than 10,000 demobilised WWII soldiers in Central Nyanza were plunged into dismay. The cost of living soared, consumer goods were scarce, and both local and central taxation increased. Meanwhile, the minimum wage in Kisumu remained fixed at twenty-eight shillings per month, so Africans agitated for better terms. New movements of African nationalism emerged to air African grievances. Ogot names the Ramogi African Welfare Association and the Nyanza Ex-soldiers Association, with the Kenya African Union (KAU) and the Luo Union as the most significant.[1] These groups supplemented many clans and sub-clans, but the group of Luo people in the Anglican Church found it necessary to revive the defunct *Piny Owacho* (§§4.7.1.2, 4.4.2.1 & 5.4.1.1).

During this period, the guarantees of the 1923 Devonshire White Paper needed to be better articulated, especially the composition of the LEGICO (§§3.4.1 & 4.4.2). The settlers, through the European Convention of Associations, and the Asians with the Indian Congress, dominated the LEGICO. Africans had governor-appointed missionaries, such as Beecher, to represent them. There was a new dawn when, in 1944, Sir Phillip Mitchell appointed Eliud Mathu. Following agitation for increased representation, Sir Everly Baring appointed Mr. F. W. Odede in 1954, joining Apollo Ohanga in the LEGICO. Other Nyanza political leaders in the LEGICO were W. W. Awori, J. D. Otiende, and Achieng' Oneko. Africans gathered under the

---

1. Ogot, "British Administration," 269.

Kenya African Union (KAU) in 1946, and in 1947 Jomo Kenyatta became its president.

The segmentary feature of Luo society coupled with the prowess of *Piny Owacho* (§4.7.1.2) became foundational in the political organization in Nyanza going into the post-colonial era. Ogot observed:

> What organised the Luo to be the political force they were was a non-political association – the Luo Union. Branches of the Luo Union had for many years existed in the towns of East Africa. But between 1950 and 1954, great efforts were made . . . to build an interterritorial organisation linking up all branches and at the same time creating organisations for Central and Southern Nyanza Districts.[2]

By 1954, the Luo Union in East Africa was formed, with Oginga Odinga elected its first president. Oginga used this position to launch his political career. Nyanza politics changed when the government enacted the African Representation Ordinance of 1956. During the 1957 general elections, Africans could, for the first time, choose their representatives in a direct election. Thus, political progress in Central Nyanza developed with complex webs of interrelations rooted in the Luo's history.

5.2.2 Demand for Education

The African war veterans, having encountered soldiers from other countries, demanded more access to education and better education. Not waiting for either the government or missionaries to act, they developed schools, resulting in the proliferation of independent schools by 1946.[3] The growing number of primary schools became a burden, since there were not sufficient secondary schools to absorb graduating pupils. Further, the government could not cope with the demand for teachers. Africans found support for better education in post-World War II opposition groups within British society advocating for better schools in the colonies. In 1948, the colonial government attempted to improve access to African education when it developed the *Ten-Year Plan*

---

2. Ogot, 270.
3. Otiende, Wamahiu and Karagu, *Education and Development*.

under the Colonial Development and Welfare Act.[4] The plan aimed at providing 50 percent of school-age children with six years of primary education,[5] and expanding secondary schools in a limited manner, raising the number from two to sixteen in ten years.[6] Waste in primary schools was limited by giving grants-in-aid in proportion to qualified teachers, not to the number of schools in the district or province.[7] This was an attempt at improving the quality of a previously compromised education due to unplanned expansion and lack of supervision. The plan further included an adequate supply of teachers to establish twenty-four elementary Teacher Training Centres.[8]

Africans rejected this plan for failing to open higher education to Africans; neither did it make primary education compulsory, which Africans wanted. The government had no funds, and the local authorities could not raise enough funds to offer compulsory education. Instead, it increased the number of bursaries from sixty-three to two hundred for Makerere College.[9]

In March 1949, the government appointed the Beecher Committee, headed by Leonard Beecher, the African representative in the LEGICO. The Committee was to resolve the failure of the Ten-Year Plan and recommend that the government address the rapid expansion of African schools. It was to "inquire into the scope, content and method of African education, financing and African teachers' salaries."[10]

The committee established that the education system was very uncoordinated because it lacked proper supervision, inspection and control.[11] They also established that there was uncontrolled primary school expansion

---

4. Beecher, *African Education in Kenya*, 22–25.

5. Beecher, 23; §96.

6. Beecher, 23–24; §§102–103.

7. Beecher, 23; §101.

8. Beecher, 23; §101.

9. Makerere University in Kampala, Uganda was established in 1922 as a technical school. In January of that year, the school was renamed Uganda Technical College for Carpentry, Building and Mechanics. It became one of the oldest and most prestigious English Universities in Africa. It expanded over the years to become a Center for Higher Education in East Africa in 1935. In 1937, the College started developing into an institution of higher education offering various other courses in medical care, agriculture, veterinary sciences and teacher training. In 1949 Makerere became a constituent college of the University College of London, through which it offered courses leading to degrees courses in London. https://www.mak.ac.ug/about-makerere/historical-background; Beecher, *African Education in Kenya*, 25; §112.

10. Beecher, 2.

11. Beecher, 50–54; §219–36.

compromising quality, which made secondary school provision inadequate, leading to a lot of wastage. Besides, Beecher also noted that the number of trained teachers was inadequate; in 1948, there were 2,748 trained teachers compared to 2,852 untrained teachers.[12]

The Beecher Committee made one hundred forty-eight recommendations,[13] which included placing primary and intermediate schools under District Education Boards to ease the financial burden on local authorities and maintaining cooperation between the government and voluntary agencies (churches) as a basis for teaching "Christian Principles."[14] They asserted the necessity of religion-based education. Beecher also recommended that they should consider independent churches as Recommendation 1 "Voluntary Agencies."[15] In its Recommendations 2, 3, 4, and 6, the report called for providing strict supervision to control primary school expansion and stop the opening of independent schools.[16] The Beecher report in Recommendation 7 urged expanding and improving teacher training facilities to improve the quality of teachers and weed out untrained teachers.[17]

Recommendations 31–37 emphasised giving Africans practical education: technical, agricultural and commercial.[18] Beecher knew the Africans preferred literary to practical education, so he went to great lengths to justify this recommendation. The report recommended establishing only sixteen secondary schools, based on the estimation that by 1957 only 29 percent of African children were to go beyond Standard IV and less than 5 percent to secondary schools.[19]

In recommendations 39, 40 and 41 the report called for restructuring the system of education to the 4:4:4 system, i.e., four years primary school, four years intermediate school and four years secondary school.[20] Even though the

---

12. Beecher, 43.
13. Beecher, 55–77.
14. Beecher, 49; §214–218.
15. Beecher, 55; §246–255.
16. Beecher, 58–59.
17. Beecher, 58.
18. Beecher, 66–69.
19. Beecher, 64; §284.
20. Beecher, 69–70.

Beecher Committee had a broad mandate to develop education for Africans, it perpetuated racial segregation in Kenya's education.[21]

Njoroge and Gathigia observed that Africans vehemently rejected the reforms recommended by the Beecher Committee,[22] save for the setting up of the Royal Technical College in 1956 to offer advanced courses in engineering, scientific and related subjects.[23]

The rejection of the Beecher Report prompted the United Kingdom to set up the Binns Commission of Education in 1952, through the Secretary of State for the colonies and the Nuffield Foundation. It was to evaluate the educational policy and practice in British Tropical Africa territories. It examined wastage in the upper echelons of the Education Department. For Kenya, the Commission questioned the internal efficiency of African education and its ability to discuss their needs.[24] Its recommendations influenced teacher education development both in the colonial and post-colonial periods.

In withholding English learning from Africans and recommending vernacular instruction, in the view of Africans the Beecher Report, observed Gikandi,[25] reinforced racially-based education and confined the Africans to their ethnic reserves.[26] Besides, the state of emergency from 1952 rendered implementing both the Beecher and Binns reports difficult.

Sessional Paper Number 10 of 1965 saw education more from an economic perspective than as a social service aimed at alleviating a shortage of skilled domestic workers. The government wanted to create economic opportunities for its citizens.[27] From this political framework, the government derived the influential Kenya Education Commission of 1964, called the Ominde Commission. Through this commission, the independent government aimed at solving the perpetual twin problems of the quality and accessibility of education. The commission surveyed the existing educational resources and advised the government in the planning and implementation of new national education policies. The Ominde Commission Report recommended a unified

---

21. Beecher, 2.
22. Njoroge and Gathigia, "Treatment of Indigenous Languages," 77.
23. Bogonko, *History of Education*.
24. Sifuna, *Development of Education*.
25. Simon Gikandi, "Editor's Column: Provincializing English," 8.
26. Gikandi, 8.
27. Sessional Paper No. 10 of 1965.

education system,[28] which espoused the notion of community-initiated *harambee* (self-help) schools to speed up access. It endorsed free primary education for all, and expansion of secondary education by building more secondary schools through pooling together resources.

By 1968, the *harambee* secondary schools outnumbered government-aided secondary schools in seven out of eight provinces. Of the 361 unaided schools, 247 were *harambee* schools. The secondary schools expanded because of community and private sector initiatives, with no grants from the government.

This political, economic, and social survey of Central Nyanza context between 1946 and 1970 lays the ground against which this study explores Reuben Omulo's and CMS's mission praxes and the interaction between them. As in earlier chapters, the analysis of their praxes covers the seven dimensions of the praxis matrix.

5.3 Agency

The period between 1946 and 1970 marked the final stage of establishing the Anglican Church in Central Nyanza. This section explores the agency of Reuben Omulo and the CMS missionaries, building on the last two chapters. It illustrates the assertion by Archbishop Festo Olang' that Omulo became one of the most influential Africans in the development of the Anglican Church and education in Nyanza.[29] This segment discusses Omulo, his crucial breakthroughs, and the role power relations played in his journey. The section further discusses the agents of transformation among the CMS missionaries deployed to Nyanza, besides explaining their relationship to the people they served. And it explains the measure to which their social, economic, and class position, in relationship to the "others," influenced their approach. This section also explores the interaction between Reuben Omulo and CMS to explain how their encounters affected Christian witness in Central Nyanza.

5.3.1 Reuben Omulo's Agency

The last phase of Reuben Omulo's service in the church includes his most transformative years. It was a transition moment for him, after thirty years

---

28. Ominde, *Kenya Education Commission Report*, part 1.
29. Provincial Unit of Research, *Rabai to Mumias*, 80.

in CMS service. At fifty years of age, Omulo had a grown family and an established home at Marenyo in Siaya. His sons had left Nyanza. Malaki Otieno worked in Nairobi beginning in 1944. Gilbert Oduor left for India in 1948. Christina married Musa Amoke, the leader of the revival movement in Nyanza, in 1949. Janet was married in 1953, Edwina in 1956 and Malaki in 1959. By 1970, Omulo and Leah had twenty-eight grandchildren; he served the Anglican Church until his death in 1974.

The CMS deployed Omulo to work in rural pastorates after WWII. During this period, he served for three rounds in Ndiru Pastorate Kisumu (1945–1948 and 1962–1964), and Ngere created out of Ndiru (1965–1966). He served another three rounds in Ramula, Siaya (1948–1952, 1957, and 1964–1965); and Regea created from Ramula (1952–1956). Omulo also served two rounds in Yenga Siaya from 1958 to 1962 and from 1967 to 1970, from where he retired. While in Ramula and Regea, he worked from his home, but had to live away in the parish house during his service in Ndiru and Yenga.

Omulo used the transition from Kisumu to set up his home in Marenyo. He moved from his first kraal next to his father's, to build a new kraal, along Rabuor to Yala road.[30] Taking advantage of land reforms following the Swynnerton Plan of 1954[31] (§5.4.1.2), Omulo guided his people during the land demarcation exercise.[32] He gained larger land portions, as Owiti's heir (§3.3.1), enough land for him to practice modern agriculture. Omulo seized the opportunity, venturing into planting cash crops such as bananas and coffee, along with subsistence crops such as maize, groundnuts, and beans (§5.4.1.2).

Apart from agricultural policy changes, the colonial regime allowed Africans to trade alongside Asians and Europeans. In the late 1950s and 1960s, Omulo became part of the leadership of the Gem Traders Society (§§5.4.1.2 & 5.4.2.2). It was through this group that he and Leah got involved in regional trade. Leah Omulo conducted their business as a fishmonger, buying dried fish from Mwanza in Tanzania for sale in Kenya.[33] The trading

---

30. Joseph Otieno, Personal interview, 21 and 23 September 2020.

31. The Swynnerton plan was an colonial agricultural policy published as a government report in 1954 in Kenya, with a goal of intensifying the development of Kenya Colony's agricultural practice.

32. Swynnerton, *Plan to Intensify*, 10.

33. Ochieng', Autobiography written in exile, 28.

group introduced her to the fish trade during their stay in Kisumu, where she had a stall at the Jubilee Market. According to Opondo,[34] Tanzania had not imposed price controls on their large stock of dried fish, which ensured a reasonable profit margin. Traders needed lorry transport from Mwanza to Kisumu, which was monopolized by the Indian wholesalers, relegating Africans to mere agents whom they supplied.[35] Leah bought fish and distributed it to markets outside Kisumu in Ng'iya, Alego, Majanji Ugunja and Gem for better prices.[36]

Upon his transfer to the Ndiru pastorate in 1945, Omulo encountered the members of the East Africa Revival Movement (EARM) fellowship. Although well acquainted with the movement, which began in Maseno in 1938, and its leaders, it was not until his Ndiru pastorate that he worked with them. He soon encountered a revivalist in his home, for his wife became a member of the EARM at a Maseno revival meeting in the mid-1940s. Leah was not alone; Felesia Adwar, the wife of Jason Wahore, Omulo's stepbrother, also joined the movement and became her confidant and partner in faith. Later, Christina Omulo's daughter also was converted at one of the Revival Movement's mini-conferences in 1948 at Ulumbi, Gem. Christina was young and her transformed life spoke to many younger people to follow Christ. Christina's marriage to Amoke was significant, in increasing EARM adherents in Omulo's family. In due time, Omulo was converted into the revival movement in December 1950 when he attended a revival meeting at Chulaimbo in Maseno (§5.9.1.2).

5.3.2 CMS's Agency

During this period, the number of missionaries in church service continued to decline as they increased services at the schools and hospitals. The two significant players during this time were Bishop Leonard James Beecher and his predecessor, Bishop Richard Crabbe. The Anglican Church made significant strides during the 1950s, for Beecher did more towards indigenization of the church, and thus he has been described as "the architect of Kenya's

---

34. Opondo, "Fishers and Fish Traders," 183.
35. Opondo, 181.
36. Opondo, 179.

ecclesiastical integration and independence."[37] Under him, CMS appointed two African Assistant Bishops, Obadiah Kariuki and Festo Olang'.[38]

In 1953, Bishop Reginald Crabbe retired as the bishop of the Diocese of Mombasa and Leonard James Beecher CMG (1906–1987) succeeded him.[39] Bishop Beecher was the first Archbishop of the Province of East Africa, comprising Kenya and Tanzania, from 1960 to 1970. Beecher was schooled at St. Olave's Grammar School and Imperial College London. Leonard Beecher, born near the London docks, had come to Kenya in 1927 as a science teacher at Alliance High School. He married Gladys Leakey, a daughter of Canon Harry Leakey, in a Kikuyu language service in 1930.[40] This created a link between the pioneer missionary tradition and local Kikuyu. Beecher was CMS's missionary in Mombasa Diocese from 1930, working in the Highlands. He became the Archdeacon of Mombasa and a Canon in 1945 and an Assistant Bishop of Mombasa. Geoffrey Fisher, the Archbishop of Canterbury, consecrated him as bishop on 25 July 1950 (St. James's Day) at St. Paul's Cathedral.

He was criticized for the 1949 Beecher Report, which recommended an eight-year base for African education, ending with the intermediate exams and an elitist secondary education for a few. It is doubtful that the government would have accepted any recommendations made within the limited resources available. Beecher became Archdeacon in 1945, Assistant Bishop of Mombasa in 1950 and Bishop of Mombasa in 1953, upon the retirement of Bishop Crabbe.

In 1960, at the inauguration of the church of the Province of East Africa, comprising Kenya and Tanganyika, Beecher became its archbishop.[41] The Archbishop of Canterbury installed Beecher at the new province's inauguration service on 3 August 1960 at Dar-es-Salaam.

A prominent member of the Royal African Society, he retired in 1970 and died on 16 December 1987. The archbishop was perceived as pro-Kikuyu as he settled in their ancestral land, Limuru, upon his retirement. His bones, and

---

37. Cole, *History of the Church*, 14.
38. Cole, 84.
39. Provincial Unit of Research, *Rabai to Mumias*, 114.
40. Provincial Unit of Research, 90.
41. Provincial Unit of Research, 89.

those of his wife, lie at the cemetery of All Saints Limuru church compound, with an inscription on his gravestone reading:

> Leonard James Beecher 1906–1987, Archbishop of East Africa (1960- 1970), together they worked for the Lord in this their beloved land.

In Nyanza, Rev. Alfred Stanway succeeded Archdeacon Owen in 1945, but they changed the designation to Rural Dean of Nyanza. Stanway had been converted to faith through a discussion given at St. Paul's Fairfield by the late Rev. C. H. Nash. From that time onwards, he dedicated his outstanding gifts to the service of Christ. Following studies at Ridley College, the Archbishop of Melbourne made him deacon in 1934 and ordained priest in 1936. They accepted him as a missionary in the Diocese of Mombasa in 1937. CMS transferred him to Nyanza in 1945 as the Rural Dean after serving on the coast for some years.[42]

Stanway moved to the African Council Secretariat in 1948 after serving in Nyanza for three years. Omulokoli notes that Stanway's key focus was restructuring the church administration of the region.[43] Unlike Owen, who moved the Archdeaconry office and residence to Ng'iya, Stanway returned the office to Maseno, and Stovold maintained it there. This was now an office with staff to manage personnel, the administrative staff. In the 1950s, most of the mission's administrative work was still being done by the missionaries. But the Ruri-decanal Council office decided "to set up in Nyanza an RDC office with an African clerk because it is quite obvious that Europeans are still doing clerical work that could be done by Africans."[44]

He separated the tasks with a clerk for ecclesiastical and educational matters. By 1945, he had employed two more African staff and raised their support from multiple sources. Even though collating Canon Awori was in recognition of his past contribution, it signalled the breaking of a new dawn of indigenous leadership in the church. Stovold succeeded him as the Rural Dean of Nyanza from 1948 to 1950, serving as the Missionary Adviser to Nyanza Rural Deans in 1953 and as Archdeacon of Western Kenya from 1954 to1955.

---

42. Cole, *History of the Church*, 71–72.
43. Omulokoli, "Historical Development," 306.
44. Omulokoli, 306.

Archbishop Festo Habakkuk Olang' (d. 1995) was born at Ebusakami, Maseno, and since there were no birth registers in those days, he claimed 11 November 1914 as his date of birth.[45] His father was Eterwa, and his mother was Emisiko Sambaya; she was the senior wife of the four wives his father had. His brother was Okwiri Eterwa, and he had two elder sisters. As a child, the family moved from Maseno to the Kano plains on the eastern side of Kisumu Town, Nyamasaria. They moved here to find ample grazing land since he had many cattle. They never went back to Bunyore.

Olang' was educated at Kisumu at the St. Stephen's Pro-Cathedral Kisumu, where the primary school called K'Omulo existed.[46] His first teacher was Reuben Omulo, who enrolled him in K'Omulo.[47] After K'Omulo, where he received faith in Christ, Olang' went to the Maseno School and Alliance Secondary School to complete his schooling.

In December 1937, he married Eseri Twera, the daughter of Joshua Olume, who was a member of the Church of God in Kima.[48] At Maseno, Olang' joined the EARM after his conversion in 1939.[49] CMS sent him to work in Butere to help lift the standards of the Luyia students teaching girls.[50] In January 1944 he joined St. Paul's Limuru.[51] In 1955, the Archbishop of Canterbury consecrated Festo Olang', Obadiah Kariuki, Deng Atong of Sudan and Yohan M. Omari of Tanzania as the first African Bishops in the East African region.[52] CMS formed the diocese of Maseno in 1961. The Rt. Rev. Festo Olang', who had been the suffragan bishop, then became its first bishop. Since Kisumu was the name of the Roman Catholic diocese, it was proper for CMS to use Maseno, the first home of the African Anglican Church in Nyanza. At the end of 1965, CMS consecrated Bishop Evan Agola as assistant bishop of Maseno.

In 1970, after a long consultation, CMS divided the diocese of Maseno into Maseno North and Maseno South, covering Central and South Nyanza. That same year, Kenya became a province of the Anglican communion. Beecher

---

45. Olang', *Festo Olang' An Autobiography*, 1.
46. Provincial Unit of Research, *Rabai to Mumias*, 22.
47. Olang', *Festo Olang' An Autobiography*, 5.
48. Olang', 11.
49. Olang', 14.
50. Olang', 16.
51. Olang', 18.
52. Olang', 30.

retired early to usher in a Kenyan Archbishop; thus Bishop Olang' of Maseno was elected the first African Anglican Archbishop.

5.3.3 Interaction between Omulo and CMS/Anglican Church

The interaction between CMS (Anglican Church) and Omulo involved serving the church alongside the missionaries and church leaders in the diocese serving his people. Omulo's relationships with the missionaries and church leaders can be described using these relationship metaphors: face-to-face, shoulder-to-shoulder, back-to-back, and in front and behind, already described in §§3.3.3 and 4.3.3.

As partners relate *face-to-face* where they enjoy each other's company and experience conflicts, they move towards embracing and celebrating each other. Did Omulo enjoy the missionaries' intimacy and support in the face of challenges? Festo Olang' became the church leader in Nyanza from 1957 as a bishop. He had a special relationship with Omulo, who had introduced him to the Christian faith as a student at K'Omulo in 1928.[53] While the Revival Movement gained legitimacy with experienced and revered clergy like Omulo joining the fellowship, some clergy castigated them.

When relating *shoulder to shoulder*, colleagues look in the same direction and share the same goals, values, hope and vision. Such shoulder-to-shoulder partnership showed itself at various levels of the church's life: the pastorate and the congregation or the church, and underneath, in the sub-pastorate and various groups. Meanwhile, the sub-pastorates were under lay readers. The lay readers were teachers or evangelists. Since Nyanza had a spontaneous planting of Christianity, the churches needed better guidance in doctrine and organization of congregations, which made the pastorate approach vital. In Kenya the notion of pastorates began in the 1930s, with Maseno, Kisumu and Ng'iya, but they embraced these as a way of organizing the church. They became vital in the church's life for the increase in numbers and health of the Christians.

Commitment to a partnership requires *back-to-back* loyalty. Loyalty is a bond that binds the partners to faithfulness when together and when apart. The measure of a relationship is what partners do behind the other's back.

---

53. Olang', 2.

Here we ask if Omulo trusted the CMS enough to turn away from his people. And could the CMS rely on Omulo? CMS missionaries in Kenya were firmly against diocesanization (§4.5.2.1) and spoke of "the very great danger of such policy in Kenya. Diocesanization would not be received well in parts of Africa."[54] Wilson Cash seemed unaware that originally Uganda had been in a unique position to the other African missions, apparently not realizing the control that the missionaries had.[55] For example, in 1940, Cash held up Uganda as a fine example of diocesanization functioning well.[56]

In a relationship, partners walk *in front or behind* as partners in leadership. During times of hard decisions, they oppose each other until one of them leads in decision-making. The impression in the relationship between Omulo and the CMS is that missionaries gave leadership, while Omulo and his colleagues followed. While CMS and the African Anglican Church involvement in higher education diminished, Omulo saw education as the best way to position his children for independence. He saw it as a duty and the best investment a society can make for its future, which resonates with the manifesto of his confidant Ohanga who said a society's responsibility "is to prepare and equip its progeny reasonably for the duties and obligations which in due course it will be their responsibility to bear and for those opportunities that lie ahead."[57] Omulo sponsored his son Gilbert Oduor to study medicine at Medical University in Madras, India. Omulo made it a priority that Oduor reminded him of: "*Parie kaka kanene an thurwa kuro ne iwacho ni ibiro uso oponge mondo itera loka.*"[58] (While I was still at home, you promised to sell off your mills to take me abroad.) In other words, he made sacrifices to position his son for an independent Kenya which would need educated people.

5.4 Contextual Understanding

This section explains how the change agents understood the context of Central Nyanza. The understanding of the social, political, economic and

---

54. Farrimond, "Concerning the Development," 231.
55. Cash, Letter to Stephenson, 17 June 1930.
56. Cash, Letter to Bishop, 13 December 1940.
57. Ohanga, "Election Campaign Manifesto," 3.
58. Oduor, Letter to Omulo, 6 October 1951.

cultural factors shaping society shows the peculiar analysis the recipient made of their context. It discusses how they "read the signs of the times" and factors influencing their decision to adopt the innovation. The second part discusses how the CMS analysed the social, political, economic, cultural context of Nyanza, and how those factors shaped their perception and approach. The last part of this section explores the nature of the interaction between Reuben Omulo and the CMS regarding their understanding of the context.

5.4.1 Reuben Omulo's Contextual Understanding

This section discusses the context of Central Nyanza under political, economic and educational themes. It focuses on how the Luo people, and Omulo himself, analysed their context. Of significance is how Omulo read the signs of the times and responded to the factors that shaped their society, hence influencing his position.

5.4.1.1 Politics

The end of World War II affected the social and political atmosphere for Omulo and the people of Central Nyanza. Over 10,000 demobilised soldiers returned to a district experiencing harsh economic conditions. The smallest wages in Kisumu, which remained fixed at twenty-eight shillings per month, did not correspond with the soaring cost of living and scarcity of essential goods. And by raising both local and central taxes, the government exacerbated living conditions.

Although the impetus for nationalism among Africans began before the war, many Africans awakened to it during their deployment. Veterans formed new organizations to engage the government over a range of social issues. But a group of Luo people associated with the Anglican Church, to which Omulo belonged, opted to revive the defunct *Piny Owacho* (KTWA). Yet, unlike the 1920s, when Omulo got involved in politics along with his colleagues, old Maseno students and teachers, engagement in this era called for direct national political engagement.

Missionaries ceased to represent Africans when, in 1947, Sir Phillip Mitchell nominated Apollo Ohanga as the second African Member to the LEGICO, joining Eliud Mathu, who was nominated in 1944. Omulo associated with Ohanga at several levels. Ohanga was Omulo's kin and, like him, was born in 1913 at *got* Regea. Their association with CMS was even a stronger bond. Like Omulo, Ohanga studied at Maseno School and later taught at Maseno for a long time. Both shared the revival faith (§4.5.2.2). Formation of the first African political party in Kenya was, according to Ogot,[59] linked to Eliud Mathu's nomination to the LEGICO. The lack of a political party impaired his effectiveness; hence, the educated Africans sought to create one similar to the Indian Congress and the European Convention of Associations. Thus, in 1945, they formed the Kenya Study Union, but changed its name to the Kenya African Union (KAU) in 1945. KAU was not set up in Nyanza. It was aloof because its leadership organized activities around Nairobi. It was Kikuyu dominated, hence treated with suspicion in Nyanza. Nyanza's political leaders in the LEGICO were W. W. Awori, J. D. Otiende, Achieng' Oneko and Walter Odede who did not share the practical ideals, nor were they keen on the problem of politics that occupied *Piny Owacho*.[60] Instead, their interests were national issues.

Political events affecting other parts of Kenya reverberated in Central Nyanza, even though it was not at the epicentre. For instance, the detention of Mau-Mau leaders fighting for land rights in Central Kenya included Mr. Odede and Achieng' Oneko from Central Nyanza. Since over 50,000 of Central Nyanza's adult population worked elsewhere, the district experienced an ever-rising political tempo, reflecting the political events in the major cities of the colony.[61]

Ohanga's political influence in Central Nyanza was discernible. He championed the government's multi-racial policy created under the 1954 Littleton Constitution and promoted a Central Nyanza political party. But both ideas were used to lock Ohanga out of representative politics.

First, in 1954, Ohanga sought to promote multi-racial government policy in Central Nyanza, which called for the integration of all races into the government. But the multi-racial policy divided Central Nyanza leaders. While some agreed with Ohanga, Luo Union leaders led by Oginga Odinga opposed the policy.[62] They termed those who embraced the policy conservatives, while progressives opposed it, hence starting what appeared to be an unending

---

59. Ogot, "British Administration," 26.
60. Ogot, 264–265.
61. Corfield, "Origins and Growth," 216.
62. Ogot, "British Administration," 272.

political duel between the conservatives and progressives in Central Nyanza. In 1957, the state made Ohanga a minister in the multi-racial government.

Second, in 1955, Ohanga mobilised prominent Luo leaders in the district, urging them to form a Central Nyanza political party. This party was to support a multi-racial government. Again, Mr. Oginga led a group that opposed the idea, but failed when the policy got majority support. So, the Luo leaders formed a Central Nyanza political association, the African District Association (ADA), which was registered in 1956.[63]

Although ADA was not active after its formation, as Ogot observes, the government's publication of the African Representation Ordinance of 1956, which allowed a direct General Election in early 1957, gave it the impetus to change Central Nyanza's politics.[64] It is ironic that in the 1957 General elections, Oginga seized ADA and deposed Ohanga as the Central Nyanza representative with the support of the intelligentsia and the urban dwellers.[65] So, in 1960, when the Kenya African National Union (KANU) was formed, ADA became its Central Nyanza branch. KANU was the party that won Kenya's independence in 1963.

By providing leadership in the political sphere, The church played a significant role in stabilising the society following the change in social order in Kenya before and after independence,. The measures CMS took in indigenizing and establishing an independent Anglican province minimised the potential fallout after national independence. This chapter highlights CMS's response to the agitation for independence and the role African Christians played.

5.4.1.2 *Agriculture and Trade*

The effect of WWII on African peasant producers in Kenya should be understood in the context of the colony's economic difficulties triggered by the 1930s Depression. But this Depression did not affect farmers in the African reserves of Central Nyanza as it did the settlers and Asian traders. African farmers were insulated from the economic disruptions the country

---

63. Ogot, *History of the Luo-speaking*, 762.
64. Ogot, 767.
65. Ogot, 769.

experienced because of the capitalist economy. This was the backdrop in which Omulo engaged in the rural pastorate.

Anderson and Throup propound that WWII exacerbated the 1930's economic meltdown, leading the state to introduce a raft of agrarian policies to salvage the situation.[66] The measures comprised encouraging African production as a way of maintaining revenue, although the state never relinquished commitment to settler production.

Since the Swynnerton plan classified the African reserves as "suitable" for balanced mixed farming, Smith noted that it became necessary to merge land fragments into larger single holdings.[67] On these lands, the government issued individuals with registered freehold titles. Implementing the plan motivated individuals to gain more land, which created a landed and landless class in the society.[68] They considered such a differential a normal step in the evolution of a country for, by supplying labour for wages, the landless would gain from improved wages. Thus, Alila acknowledged a degree of economic specialisation creating "economic" size holdings for high-value cash crops and with a reasonable livelihood for the landless.[69] But first, land registration was a necessary administrative measure to define who were the owners and who were the land tenants.[70] This proved impractical on account of the area's ecological and socio-economic heterogeneity.

In this post-WWII period, agitation for individual land titles waned. Advocates against individual land titles, among them Jairo Owino, rejected titles on the grounds of it being contrary to Luo customs. They further claimed that it limited the farmer's control over his own land,[71] but land tenancy seems to have been the underlying reason. During their settlement into Central Nyanza, the Luo allowed subdued people the usage of land as tenants. If they issued individual titles, then the tenants were now entitled to land titles among people who make a total claim to the land. This issue further complicated the plan's implementation. Hence, the available economic security for

---

66. Anderson and Throup, "Africans and Agricultural Production," 329.
67. Smith, Overview of Agricultural Development," 126–135.
68. Swynnerton, *Plan to Intensify*, 10.
69. Alila, "Kenyan agricultural policy," 40.
70. Moris, "Agrarian Revolution," 89.
71. Alila, "Kenyan agricultural policy," 49.

Nyanza, writes Alila, was in long-term wage employment outside Nyanza.[72] One consequence of the Depression was the laying off of farmworkers, hence limiting avenues for making money through wages. This gave a premium to primary education.

5.4.1.3 Education

The Luo had been captured by the desire of gaining education since 1906 when CMS arrived in Nyanza. Omulo and fellow clergy acknowledged:

> As the key to everything in this world is education, so we natives of this country our failure which generally spoken about is due to lack of education . . . We are noticing how the number of boys who are in need to enter the school is increasing year by year.[73]

This impetus became urgent with the end of WWII, when veterans could no longer wait for the mission and government but developed their own schools. Having encountered soldiers from other countries, the war veterans demanded more access to, and better education for, Africans. Hence, the Beecher report was of immense importance. To Africans, the Beecher Report entrenched racial segregation in Kenya's education system.[74] It disappointed them because the government failed to expand African education opportunities and because, at the same time, it offered an inferior education that would cause Africans to remain at the bottom of the educational pyramid.[75] The Report emphasized quality rather than quantity, meaning that enrolment would grow slowly.

To restructure education as suggested by the Report to the 4:4:4 system (i.e. four years primary school, four years intermediate school and four years secondary school), meant that the majority of the Africans would end schooling after four years of primary, or at the intermediate level.[76] Beecher designed each stage as a complete course to make sure that students sat for exams after each level and that each stage prepared them for the labour market.

---

72. Alila, 28.
73. Byrne, "Memorandum of KTWA," 2.
74. Beecher, "African Education in Kenya," 2.
75. Beecher, 64.
76. Beecher, 69–70.

The clergy of Central Nyanza wanted the best education available in the world for their children. Why should their children not get the same quality education that Europeans and Asians received? Omulo shared the patriotic vision of competent educated Africans in a memo to Sir Cunliffe:

> We are certain that much money which we pay in form of taxes is going out of our country through foreign communities who are on Government service. If our own people were to maintain these positions, the money would not have gone out of the country, but our people cannot hold the positions due to a lack of good education. We realize how important technical education is, but there should be no confinement of general education as it is at present.[77]

The people of Nyanza had experienced Maseno School and Alliance High School, model schools with high standards, set up by Carey Francis. Murray states that Francis wanted to raise a crop of elite Africans that the administration should co-opt.[78] Omulo had for many years developed a feeder school for Francis at Maseno, K'Omulo in Kisumu, hence the worry that Beecher's recommendations would derail the foundation set for African education.

Even though the government did not envisage higher education for Africans, the people's wish for higher education was insatiable. They were ready to fund their children's university education abroad with their own resources. The Report limited the number of students proceeding beyond Standard IV to just 29 percent of African children and the number of children proceeding to secondary school to less than 5 percent. The people did not find this acceptable. They were further disappointed when only sixteen secondary schools were to be established by 1957.[79] Africans no longer waited for the government and built their own secondary schools.

Africans opposed Beecher's recommendations when tabled in the LEGICO. All African representatives voted against the report, including Mr. Mathu who was a member of the committee and signed it, but who renounced

---

77. Byrne, "Memorandum of KTWA."
78. Murray, "Archdeacon W. E. Owen," 669.
79. Beecher, "African Education in Kenya."

its recommendations on the floor. Commenting on the report's rejection during the parliamentary proceeding, Mr. Dugdale said:

> First, let me say that Mr. Mathu, the leader of the Africans on the Legislative Council, was himself a member of the Beecher Committee and did, in fact, sign the Report. Second, that the Africans voted against it in the Legislative Council is, I think, only an occurrence which happens often in this House when people vote against something because of certain facts in it rather than because they object to the whole thing itself. They voted against it because of certain aspects with which they disagreed, particularly the payment of teachers.[80]

Dugdale hoped for further discussion of the matter to agree. Despite the protests by Africans, the majority in the LEGICO passed the Report.

5.4.2 CMS's Contextual Understanding

This section discusses How CMS analysed the Central Nyanza context under the themes of politics, economy and education. It further explores how the perceptions of these factors by CMS missionaries and church leaders influenced their approach to ministry among the Luo.

5.4.2.1 Politics

Although Beecher followed in the tradition of missionaries who represented Africans in the LEGICO, he pressed the government to appoint Africans and not missionaries to the LEGICO.[81] As a result, it appointed Eliud Mathu in 1944, followed in 1947 by Apollo Ohanga, a Maseno teacher. CMS missionaries' support of African elevation earned them the settlers' taunt of seeking "to raise the native into the position of a spoiled child," a process which would "undermine the foundations of empire."[82]

By involving itself in the colonial affairs in the 1950s by working with and for the colonial state, CMS posed the problem of the mission being identified with the state's policies. Stanley mentions that a nationalist KAU

---

80. Dugdale, "Kenya (African Education)," 1303–1312.
81. Richards, *Fifty Years in Nyanza*, 63.
82. Ogot, *History of the Luo-speaking*, 762.

representative, visiting Britain in 1952, had warned CMS of this danger.[83] Sensing this danger, the society dispatched its Africa secretary, Canon Cecil Bewes, to Nairobi.[84] Bewes's visit to Kenya reflected the view of CMS General Secretary Max Warren that the best hope for CMS's future in its African fields lay in its strategic engagement on these political issues and with the government, settlers, and Africans. According to Stanley, Warren projected that if a church would one day rely upon African leadership, then it could not afford to alienate its African supporters.[85]

5.4.2.2 Agriculture and Trade

The CMS missionaries had invested hope in the Devonshire Declaration. They expected the government to adhere to its tenets of "African paramountcy" and eventual independence of the country under Africans. Implementing this edict, they had hoped, would restrain the state's wholesale restructuring of Kenya in favour of the European community.

Even though WWII had a profound effect on Kenya's social, economic, and political order, Anderson and Throup observed that the overt consequences often ascribed to the war actually emerged from the balance of power struggles of the 1930s, pitching African elites against settlers and the state.[86] The impact of the war, they contend, must therefore be evaluated considering the Depression of the 1930s and its political and economic effect on Africans and settlers.[87]

During the Depression, the settler-economy project, as the backbone of the colonial economy, faced imminent collapse.[88] Many of the farmer settlers experienced financial hardships, unable to service their mortgages or capitalize on their farms. This shook their political unity as the more efficient producers refused the prospect of subsidizing their challenged counterparts.[89] Aggravating the situation were lower commodity prices for agricultural produce that rendered the settlers' production uneconomical, thus forcing more

---

83. Stanley, *Missions, Nationalism*, 187.
84. Nicholls, Letter to Cecil T. F. Bewes, 18 December 1952.
85. Stanley, *Missions, Nationalism*, 187.
86. Anderson and Throup, "Africans and Agricultural Production," 327.
87. Anderson and Throup, 327.
88. Lonsdale, "Growth and transformation"; Lonsdale, "Second World War."
89. Anderson and Throup, "Africans and Agricultural Production," 328.

of them out of business. The Depression placed the entire future of the colonial state in jeopardy, because inefficient settlers failed to deliver the goods.[90] The regime had to develop rather than depress African production if it were to avoid collapse. For this reason, Governor Byrne considered abandoning the settlers saddled with financial burdens in favour of the more prosperous African commercial farmers and traders. But Byrne dodged the fundamental problem in the mid-1930s by suppressing the rise of African capitalists. He used the revenue accruing from peasant producers to subsidize the recovery of inefficient settlers with loans from the Land Bank.

During WWII, Anderson and Throup observed, the settlers experienced an immeasurable economic recovery.[91] With their debts to the commercial banks repaid, the settlers purposed to stay afloat by diversifying from monoculture into well-capitalized mixed farming. But their revival renewed rivalry with African farmers over control of the economy, which reached a crescendo in 1952 with the declaration of "the Emergency."[92] To tone down this rivalry, the colony under Philip Mitchell attempted to create a multi-racial society departing from the pre-war policy of propping up the settlers.

In 1954, the regime authorized R. J. M. Swynnerton to devise a plan for developing agricultural policies and services for African areas with high potential, known as the 1954 Swynnerton Plan.[93] The plan, Alila argues, considered re-settlement as a solution to agricultural problems since people had settled on most of the land.[94] But it focused on intensifying agriculture in existing areas, and providing the requisite resources to the African farmers. But for Nyanza, the plan recommended land consolidation, an increase in agricultural advisory staff, and set targets for cash crops. In Central Nyanza, CMS worked with the government to help the African Anglican Church benefit from the policy change. To carry out this plan, the colonial government received a £5 million grant from the British government.[95]

---

90. District Commissioner Nyeri 1/4, South Nyeri District Annual Report, 1930.
91. Anderson and Throup, "Africans and Agricultural Production," 344.
92. Mitchell, *African Afterthoughts*, 211.
93. Swynnerton, *Plan to Intensify*, i.
94. Alila, "Kenyan agricultural policy," 39.
95. Moris, "Agrarian Revolution," 82.

5.4.2.3 Education

As the chairman of the committee, Beecher had an immense influence on the resulting report. He revealed his imperial leanings by upholding a racial education structure that confined Africans at the bottom of the education pyramid. Africans were to focus on manual and technical education in the Owen model of Booker T. Washington's Tuskegee College. It only allowed a select few for higher education, unlike what their white counterparts received in the Carey Francis model.

Since Beecher recommended that each stage be a complete course, it ensured that those leaving school were competent to take active roles in society. So, each stage ended with a major examination, which implied that Africans would sit for exams after fewer years of instructions than their white counterparts. Beecher's report recommended the creation of an elite African group of 26 percent, not useful for enhancing the Africans' quest for learning and personal development, but useful for the imperial agenda. The Beecher Report concurred with the Phelps-Stokes and the Ten-Year Developmental Plan for educating Africans. It laid the foundation for the regime's education policy, biased towards meeting rural society's needs.[96] Of significance, CMS cooperated with the government to expand and improve teacher training facilities to increase the number of trained teachers.[97] For Nyanza, CMS agreed to train teachers at their schools in Butere, Ng'iya and Maseno.

Other than technical instruction, the government had no vision for higher education for Africa. Even though Beecher knew the Africans preferred literary to practical education, his report proposed Africans be given practical education.[98] However, the Royal Technical College was established in 1956 courtesy of the Beecher Commission.[99]

The Beecher Report's recommendations laid the foundation for the government's policy on African education until the last year of colonial rule. And it did not follow further developmental plans because the pace towards independence sped up, but significant changes took place in piecemeal fashion before independence arrived.

---

96. Beecher, "African Education in Kenya," 66–69.
97. Beecher, 58.
98. Beecher, 66–69.
99. Beecher, 25.

5.4.3 Interaction Between Reuben Omulo and CMS on Contextual Understanding

Omulo and CMS based their interaction during this period on the continued evangelism among the Luo. The CMS approach spurred a dynamic and complex set of interactions drawing in the government. These included different levels of colonial administration and the white settlers, whom they had to face together. This section uses a selection of relational ideologies constructed by Lochhead, classified as "hostility, isolation, competition, partnership and dialogue" to assess the nature of the interaction between CMS and Omulo, on areas they agreed, differed, and cooperated.[100]

5.4.3.1 Education

Omulo and the CMS acted in partnership according to Lochhead,[101] for they united in the interest of African education, noting their differences and similarities, and then forged meaningful cooperation. In preparing for the independence of the Anglican Church, the CMS feared saddling the church with the management of schools, and so involved government in two crucial areas.

First, the cost of developing and operating schools was going to overwhelm the African church. From his experience at K'Omulo, Omulo and his fellow clergy had acknowledged in their memo to Cunliffe:

> We are not ignorant, we know that education facilities require much money, but the chance of making money is forbidden to us, and if we have not got much money, our education will not increase.[102]

It was therefore prudent for the government to fund African education, for which demand increased after the war. Beecher's recommendations placed responsibility for primary and intermediate schools on the government through District Education Boards (DEB).[103] This included provision for equipment and facilities, where it could levy taxes to support education.

---

100. Lochhead, *Dialogical Imperative.*
101. Lochhead, 24.
102. Byrne, "Memorandum of KTWA," 2.
103. Beecher, "African Education in Kenya," 49.

Through the DEBs, the government would control primary school expansion, thus reducing any further opening of independent schools.[104]

Second, both Omulo and the CMS feared that the emerging church would drain its resources on school support instead of using resources for the church workers. The shortfall of teachers due to lack of training and capacity to pay them limited the CMS's ability to sustain required standards at some schools. Inviting the government to run schools allowed the missions to focus on religious education, for involving the state affected the syllabus. While Omulo and the CMS agreed on the reduced religious content, their reasons for it differed. For the CMS, schools were no longer needed as religious centres with the development of the churches. For Omulo and his colleagues, the increased academic content would better prepare their children for higher education.

The mission agencies remained in African education as sponsors, which involved independent churches, school outfits and missions supporting joint school projects. Beecher[105] acknowledged the role of independent churches in meeting educational demand based on Christian principles. The polity agreement by mission agencies of 1907 no longer mattered to CMS. Hence, CMS urged the government to include them in its support for schools as "Voluntary Agencies." The Alliance of Protestant Churches, a conglomeration of various Protestant churches, was keen on advancing education acquisition in Kenya. It sponsored the founding of various primary and high schools in Kenya. In the post-war period, the Alliance chose the name UNION to symbolize joint ownership of the schools among its members. Hence, such primary schools were created in Kisumu, Kitale, Eldoret and Nakuru. In 1956, churches started the Kisumu Union school by merging K'Omulo, the Salvation Army school and others. They then transferred it from the St. Stephen's Cathedral church premises to its present location between Kisumu Day High and Kibuye Mixed primary school. Kisumu Union perpetuated the tradition of elite African Protestant schools.

5.4.3.2 Re-ordering Society as a Dialogue

Omulo and CMS had to answer the question: How could the "Native Anglican Church," as they called it in Nyanza, learn self-reliance? This period was

---

104. Beecher, 58–59.
105. Beecher, 55.

characterised by the suppression of African enterprise in the country and within the church. CMS adopted Owen's concern for "tribal cohesion" through developing the "entire race." It was an attempt to suppress class formation and thwart the emergence of African capitalists.[106] This logic exposed Owen's paternalist inclination, which guided the interaction between CMS and Omulo, described in Lochhead's ideology of isolation.[107] Isolation occurs where a group sees itself as superior to others and directs its action without their concurrence. But as Murray observed, other CMS missionaries such as Carey Francis rooted for, and encouraged, the rise of African entrepreneurs.[108]

CMS had to align with the colony's post-war changes. They included the state's changed attitude towards African production, resulting in the success of African traders and farmers.[109] But the African producers disrupted society in two ways, affecting the interactions between Omulo and CMS.

The first was on land tenure. Anderson and Throup suggested the African proto-capitalists would provoke social order instability in the reserves, following the increase of "selfish individualism" at the expense of the long-standing communal solidarities that undermined Africans' land tenure.[110]

The second was a shift from the KTWA welfare approach to development. Owen worked through KTWA to lift the entire society and, at the same time, create a unified voice to negotiate for justice. But during this time, individual entrepreneurship advanced by Carey Francis attracted Christians. It focused on creating wealth through growing high yielding cash crops, better education, better pay and jobs, and trade. For this purpose, in 1942, Omulo joined progressive leaders in Nyanza to form the Kavirondo Traders and Lands Union (KTLU). KTLU held its first meeting on 10 October 1942, where under the chairmanship of Mr. Z. I. A. Nyandoja, they discussed the new government requirements on the selling of grain, problems about fishermen, avoiding using donkeys for transporting grain, and livestock development. Eliud Mathu and Apollo Ohanga, African Representatives in LEGICO, addressed the Nyanza Traders and Lands Union (KTLU)'s next meeting in

---

106. Murray, "Archdeacon W. E. Owen," 669.
107. Lochhead, *Dialogical Imperative*, 8.
108. Murray, "Archdeacon W. E. Owen," 669.
109. Anderson and Throup, "Africans and Agricultural Production," 344.
110. Anderson and Throup, 342.

May 1947. Among the agenda items were: "*Kufikiri jambo la kufanya makusudi ya kukusanya mimea yote ya Nyanza kwa namna moja*" (To consider how to achieve the grain allocation for Nyanza in a united way, as Agenda 3) and "*Kufikiri umoja wa KFA*" (Consider a united African Kenya Farmers Association KFA, as Agenda 6). By the late 1950s and early 1960s, Omulo also became a member of a smaller group they formed, the Gem Traders Society, whose officials were Samson Kidha (Chairman), Sila Omolo (Treasurer) and Apollo Ohanga (Secretary).

The people further split the trading groups along tribal lines, with Mr. Oginga Odinga leading the Luo to form the Luo Union. According to Ogot, Odinga Founded Luo Thrift and Trading Corporation (LUTATCO) in 1946 to offer a solution to African (Luo) social and economic disabilities.[111] They organized business along ethnic lines to promote Luo entrepreneurs.[112] It targeted the educated Luos, teachers, peasants, urban proletarians, and traders from all of East Africa. They sought a commercial revolution for the economic emancipation of the Luo people. To Odinga, LUTATCO had a uniting effect, relying on Luo identity.[113]

The third was the political order. By 1945, the economic success of African proto-capitalists propelled them into the political scene, previously the domain of teachers and scholars. The 1940s appointment of Mathu and Ohanga as African representatives to LEGICO gave legitimacy to the colonial regime as partners but was soon to change in favour of the proto-capitalists.

5.5 Ecclesial and Religious Scrutiny

This section describes how the adopters perceived their "former" religion and culture to explain what drew them to Christianity. It also explains how the change agents (CMS) envisioned the churches in Central Nyanza. It begins by discussing issues Omulo encountered while establishing an independent African Anglican Church among the Luo. Then it explains the CMS's preparation for the indigenous Anglican Church's operations without direct European leadership. It discusses the CMS's influential public contacts and the factors

---

111. Ogot, *History of the Luo-speaking*, 755.
112. Ogot, 756.
113. Odinga, *Not yet Uhuru*, 76–77; Ogot, *History of the Luo-speaking*, 757.

that shaped the CMS's approach. The section concludes with the interaction between Omulo's and the CMS's ecclesial scrutiny to show the nature of their encounter.

5.5.1 Reuben Omulo Ecclesial Scrutiny

Establishing the African Anglican Church was Omulo's lived experience. It began through indigenizing ministry staff, demonstrated in leadership when he developed K'Omulo in Kisumu. He sustained it with sacrificial service in the pastorate. The pastorate offered a different dynamic, for it was rural with villages scattered across the fields. They had interspersed schools; thus, they needed a fresh approach.

Spontaneous evangelism, carried out with unaided African agency, characterized the "gestation" period (1906–1920), while developing emerging church institutions such as churches and schools marked the "juvenile" period (1921–1945). These approaches could no longer advance the Anglican Church in central Nyanza, for the CMS had given up school control to the government.

5.5.1.1 *United Church*

The EARM members were the most committed members of the congregations. They made up most of the local church teachers and the bulk of the congregation. Omulo seized the potential in lifting the commitment of nominal church members and spurring growth as well. Church growth in the Anglican Church during this "mature" period (1945–1970) was the dynamic expression of EARM. The movement leapt into prominence as the element shaping the African Anglican Church under African leadership.

In joining the EARM, Omulo affirmed the power it wielded in Central Nyanza Deanery. On the EARM's impact on the Anglican Church, Reed reached this profound conclusion:

> No missionary who served in East Africa between the 1930s and the 1970s could be indifferent to or ignore the Revival; it was simply an integral part of church life. Some missionaries felt uncomfortable with it, as they were not at home in an African form of Christianity. Some felt threatened by it, as Africans questioned their attitudes toward racial superiority and leadership.

Others entered it wholeheartedly and found in it, deep Christian sharing and friendship, and spiritual renewal and liberation.[114]

Personal evangelism became the hallmark of EARM. Reed observed that they scattered from the fellowship, preaching Jesus and testifying to what Christ had done for them.[115] They were bold and laboured in teams, preaching on all pathways, roads, homes, and villages and hired trucks to deliver them to their preaching centres.

As a padre in the Pastorate, the EARM forced Omulo and the Anglican Church into an ecclesiastical debate. The debate was about the place of the EARM in the church, and the authority of clergy over the EARM. First, should the revival movement stay within the Anglican Church or form its own organization? Nzioki identified this to be a nagging question the EARM faced between 1945 and 1957.[116] Two groups within the EARM opted to leave the Anglican Church because of controversies within the EARM. In 1946, Welbourn and Ogot observed, the Bildad Kaggia group deserted the Anglican Church to form a non-denominational church.[117] By 1948, Kaggia had a significant following in Central Nyanza, *Jokaggia* (Followers of Kaggia). Their emphasis was on confession of sins, speaking in tongues and spiritual healing. They refused the Anglican Prayer Book and parts of the Bible that deal with Jewish customs and practices. In 1955, Kaggia registered his church, The Voice of the Worldwide Salvation and Healing Revival.

Then the followers of Ishmael Noo left as well. Disillusioned, they severed their relationship with the Anglican Church after they left the mainstream EARM. Noo followers believed that only the first wives kept their marriage vows and should remain in marriage.[118] Also, the saved women left their unsaved monogamous husbands. From 1945, claims Nzioki,[119] the church raised questions about the fidelity of Noo's congregations. Eventually, Noo formed The Christian Universal Evangelical Union In 1948, a church he led

---

114. Reed, *Walking in the Light*, 36.
115. Reed, 12.
116. Nzioki, "Development of the Anglican Church," 165.
117. Ogot and Welbourn, *Place to Feel*, 31.
118. Mwangi, *Missio Dei*, 78.
119. Nzioki, "Development of the Anglican Church," 164.

until he died in 1960. His group drew followers from the EARM and the Anglican Church in Sakwa, Asembo, Uyoma, and Yimbo.

The greater challenge Omulo had to face regarding his position in the church came from the remaining EARM members who were further split into *Johera*, based at Maseno, and *Joremo*, based in Ramba. *Johera* comprised the younger intelligent Luo padres, recently graduated from Limuru, which included Matthew Ajuoga who emerged as the groups' leader. For *Johera*, the EARM was an integral part of the church support since Christians ought to separate themselves from sin and not from the body of Christ. *Johera* propounded, as Ogot and Welbourn observed, since the visible church was Christ's body, *Johera* must espouse her authority and tradition.[120] *Joremo* had considered separation from the mainstream church necessary for spiritual survival.[121] They, therefore, gained the name *Kuhama (Wahamiaji*, pilgrims) for the movement's main tenets was separation from the world. But *Joremo* made significant changes from 1948 after their Uganda mission, during which, according to Amoke, the members resolved to keep the Fellowship within the Anglican Church like their Ugandan counterparts.[122] They thus had the obligation to support the church to which they belong. Although they had an uneasy relationship with the leadership, this improved once they settled to stay in the Anglican Church.[123] The EARM remained a community within the church, even though they did not integrate with the rest of the Christians.

Under these conditions of division by faith within the pastorates, Omulo taught a broader understanding of the church as the body of Christ and the ecumenical trait of the body. He taught catechism for *"Hearers" Classes*:

> Kanisa en riwrwok mar jolup Yesu madier, tiende ni riwrwok mar jopinje duto mag ogendini duto kata dhok duto moyie kwom Rwodhwa Yesu Kristo koda ma noyie chon. Ka ma Yesu Kristo nitie, kanyo nitie Kanisa Makatholika.[124]

> Translation: The church is the body of Jesus' true followers, that is the worldwide body of all ethnicities and languages who

---

120. Ogot and Welbourn, *Place to Feel*, 38.
121. Mambo, "Revival Fellowship (Brethren)," 112.
122. Amoke, "Musa Amoke Life Story," 7.
123. Ogot and Welbourn, *Place to Feel*, 32.
124. *Catechism for Hearers' Classes*, 15.

believe in our Lord Jesus Christ and others who have believed. Where Jesus is there, the Church exists.

For Omulo, the church comprised believers in Christ, i.e., those baptised, without regard to their salvation status. Jesus was central to his understanding of the church, hence followers of Jesus, among whom His presence dwells regardless of their origin or language they spoke. These form the body of Christ, as Omulo argues; "Paulo olunge ni ringer Yesu" (Jokorintho 1, 12:20) (Paul calls it the body of Jesus, 1 Cor 12:20).

Omulo further taught:

> Onge kanise mang'eny mopopogre opogre . . . Jolup Yesu madier duto luwo Yesu, kendo yie mondo Roho Maler mar Nyasaye otelnigi. Timbegi kaachiel gi yoregi kwom loc mar Kanisa opogre to giduto gin Oganda mar Kanisa Achiel Makatholika. Onego geherre kendo gikonyre ng'ato gi ng'ato.[125]

> Translation: There are different churches . . . loyal followers of Jesus would follow him and allow the Holy Spirit to guide them. Traditions and emphasis of different church traditions may differ, but they are one community of the Catholic Church. They should love and aid each other.

The church in Omulo's teaching was ecumenical, for though they followed different traditions, the unity of the body was important to him.

5.5.1.2 Authority of Clergy

Omulo faced the EARM challenge of priests as spiritual leaders. It presented the question of clergy authority over the fellowship. For *Johera*, the church was supreme, making the priests as its leaders special. Hence, they urged the fellowships' leaders (laity) to submit to the priests, ordained ministers out of love, as espoused in John 3:34–36, John 4:16 and Revelation 2:2–4.[126]

But *Joremo* held that the EARM leadership should not yield to the clergy and that its lay leadership was supreme over the clergy. They met at Ramba, under the Nyanza team which comprised Musa Amoke, Jeconia Okelo, John Mariko Ade, Gideon Opala, Hezekiah Oduwo, Samson Chilo, Peter Alaka,

---

125. *Catechism for Hearers' Classes*, 15, §3.
126. Ogot and Welbourn, *Place to Feel*, 37.

Solomon Okawo, John Onguko, Sila Oyola and Sila Nyawanda.[127] However, Musa Amoke emerged as their leader.[128] With the blessings of Bishop Crabbe and the Rural Dean, Rev. Festo Olang', *Joremo* held an official corporation meeting with the Anglican Church at Maranda in 1953.[129] This implied that the highest-ranking African clergy in Nyanza submitted to the lay leadership of *Joremo*. Ajuoga,[130] leading *Johera*, rejected this decision, arguing against lay people having authority over clergy.[131]

Olang's injunction to the priests among the EARM was "*kuvua upadre*"[132] which could be translated: "Set aside clerical authority." He and several senior clergymen, Canon Esao Oywaya, Canon Reuben Omulo, Rev. Evan Agola, among others, yielded their ministry to the group opinion. The laity's questioning clergy was not sacrosanct; Olang' had an occasional difference of opinion running deep. Notes Olang', what the members objected to were clergymen who elevated their theological training above questioning by the laity.[133] But Olang' advised the clergy in the EARM, including Omulo, as follows:

> Never to be angry with the questioner, even the assailant. To lose your temper is evidence to her you have indeed fallen from grace. Instead, be very polite, and give the person a chance to explain his or her point of view. Once this is done, they will have to think hard about what they really mean and perhaps also give you a chance to answer for yourself.[134]

It disappointed Ajuoga and *Johera* that the Anglican leadership didn't discuss doctrinal controversies which attained crisis proportions during the height of the EARM era.[135] Although Ajuoga cites clergy authority as a reason for conflict with Anglican leadership, he articulates in his fifteen-page document[136] that Olang' denied that "any specific point of doctrine, led to the

---

127. Amoke, "Musa Amoke Life Story," 8.
128. Mwangi, "*Missio Dei*," 77.
129. Nzioki, "Development of the Anglican Church," 166.
130. Ajuoga, Interview with Nzioki, 26 July 1984.
131. Ogot and Welbourn, *Place to Feel*, 42.
132. Olang', *Festo Olang' An Autobiography*, 35.
133. Olang', 35.
134. Olang', 35.
135. Pickens, *African Christian God Talk*, 93.
136. Pickens, 97.

separation of the church of Christ in Africa, *Johera*, in early 1958."[137] Omulo affirmed that, having attended their convention in Maseno, and concluded that the plausible reason for the cleavage was *Johera's* contention that laity cannot have authority over the clergy in religious matters, a position espoused by *Joremo*. Such divisions were inconsistent with Omulo's position regarding the church as a united body.

5.5.2 CMS Ecclesial Scrutiny

After WWII, the African Anglican Church made significant strides towards both indigenization and independence. CMS built the African Anglican Church on the foundation laid in the earlier pioneer period. They premised it on independence, indigenization, and ecumenicalism. For in 1945, with the approval of the Standing Committee of the Synod, Bishop Crabbe implemented the 1944 constitution with its accompanying regulations from the level of Rural Dean downwards.[138]

5.5.2.1 Indigenizing the Anglican Church

The Venn principle of an indigenous Anglican Church remained the CMS's undergirding philosophy in Central Nyanza. CMS missionaries, therefore, endeavoured to replicate the Venn principle of the 1860s in Jamaica and Sierra Leone, a policy aimed at withdrawing missionaries and filling the positions with converts. Venn's policy justified that the outcome of CMS's twenty-five-year work in Sierra Leone was not by accident. It resulted from deliberate effort.[139] It was, though, the Sierra Leone and West Africa experi-

---

137. Pickens, 34.

138. Omulokoli, "Historical Development," 305.

139. Wilbert R. Shenk in his article, "Henry Venn and Mission Thought," observed the differing ways Venn's success has been judged. For example, Stephen Neill noted, "the first attempts to carry out the principles of Venn's dictum proved almost wholly disastrous. The establishment of the 'Native Pastorate' in Sierra Leone in 1860, with the complete withdrawal of the missionaries from participation in the affairs of the pastorate, inflicted on the church a paralysis from which a whole century has not availed to deliver it." See *A History of Christian Missions*, Pelican: Harmondsworth 1964, 260. T.S. Johnson, the first Sierra Leonean bishop, in 1937, maintained that missionaries, contra Neill, did maintain control far too long and that at the expense of the maturing of the church. Eugene Stock reaches a more measured judgement, calling Venn's Sierra Leone experiment a qualified success Stoke, *History of the Church Missionary Society*, 445–449. In 1867 Venn was drawing a comparison between two concrete cases, Sierra Leone and Jamaica. The contrast was obvious. Should Venn be held accountable for how his insights and policies were applied or misapplied?

ence that matched East Africa, for there, local agents replaced missionaries. CMS staffed and managed the entire Niger mission with over one hundred teachers and catechists in 1867, plus twenty-five ministers, and a black bishop. Further, Venn observed that the local agents, with local support, cared for the nine parishes, and a grammar school headed by a local principal, serving a hundred pupils. Bishop Crabbe nurtured the seed Bishop Heywood planted in ordaining the first group of indigenous Christians, thereby transforming the church into an independent African Anglican Church within the Anglican Communion. But Beecher focused on indigenizing the church; thus, he has been described as "the architect of Kenya's ecclesiastical integration and independence."[140]

5.5.2.2 *Independent Churches*

As political independence swept across Africa, CMS also prepared to hand over power to the churches they started. The church had become self-governing, thus ready to inherit both missionary and African initiated institutions. These independent churches have continued to grow and at present remain part of the Anglican Communion in which they now dominate in numbers.[141]

The Anglican Communion is not a centralized institution. Its provinces decide most issues for themselves. The acceptance of the principle of "subsidiarity" was emphasized at the 1998 Lambeth Conference, as expounded in the *Virginia Report*.[142] This notion has two sides: a province cannot force another province to follow a particular course, neither can a province prevent another from charting its chosen course. But they can use discussions, advice, and arguments, since each church, being indigenous, seeks to understand God's call in its own culture.[143] The church, though, belongs to a wider fellowship, expressed in its being linked to the Church catholic (universal). However, these churches, contends David Cash, are not independent but interdependent. An interdependence is demanding, "in some matters to give

---

140. Cole, *Cross Over Mt. Kenya*, 14.
141. Farrimond, "Concerning the Development," 264.
142. Summarized as "a central authority should have a subsidiary function, performing only those tasks which cannot be performed at a more immediate or local level." Lambeth 1998 Resolution: Section III.3.
143. Farrimond, "Concerning the Development," 266.

each other a little more time and space for thought."[144] Breaking communion is the only sanction available to the Anglican Communion churches in a disagreement with each other. The Nigerian church feared that disputes with Western churches would cost it financially. Historically, the West has done little to allay such fears. By 1946, under Crabbe (§5.3.2), CMS had developed the African Anglican Church as a province independent from Canterbury, with its own instruments for governance, such as a constitution that proposed how to govern the emergent church. The 1944 Diocesan Constitution did not become official until 13 July 1949, when the Seventh Synod received and adopted it.

The increase in African personnel exceeded the Europeans, pointing to an imminent shift to Africans' greater participation. Although Africans trained their own ministers, paid for their own buildings, housed their pastors and evangelists, and contributed to the central expenses, the missionaries still dominated the church, stifling the growth of indigenous forms of Anglicanism. Farrimond observed in Africa a self-extending church, which in places was self-supporting, but was nowhere self-governing.[145] This was a flop in Venn's assessment:

> CMS neglected Venn's vision of the euthanasia of mission, of bringing mission-agency control of the African church to an end. The CMS itself became a vehicle of white domination over the churches it had helped found. But then again, under the more recent leadership of Max Warren and John Taylor, the society had begun once more to work out a definite mission of reparation, this time perhaps for some sins and failures of Western missions in the first half of the twentieth century.[146]

For this reason, Barrington-Ward criticised Cash, presenting him as part of the problem, and also criticized Warren and Taylor as pursuing an unenlightened policy.[147] In Kenya, Hooper should share the blame, although as

---

144. *Archbishop of Canterbury's Letter to the Bishops of the Church of England*, June 2003, http://www.lambethconference.orglacns/articles/34175/acns3485.htmi.
145. Farrimond, "Concerning the Development," 263.
146. Barrington-Ward, "My Pilgrimage in Mission," 62.
147. Barrington-Ward, 62.

the General Secretary of CMS Cash had to carry the ultimate responsibility. Hetherington points out that:

> The period between the wars was characterized by almost universal support for the idea that it was necessary for Britain to stay in Africa, either indefinitely or until particular reforms had been achieved.[148]

Cash was a child of his time, but the CMS needed leadership that could see beyond prevailing prejudices.

In dioceses which contained Anglicans who were the fruits of other missionary work, or large expatriate congregations, Farrimond argues, diocesanization (§4.5.2.1) involved coming to terms with Anglicans who held different beliefs and worshipped in different ways.[149] Kenya as an Anglican province was formed out of dioceses with a complete CMS background, of the evangelical tradition.

5.5.3 Interaction Between Reuben Omulo and CMS on Ecclesial Scrutiny

This section describes the dynamics emerging from the interaction between Omulo and the CMS by using Schreiter's syncretism model as a framework.[150] The model enables a discussion on the response to the incoming religion and identifies the dynamics emerging from their interaction, showing points at which they agree, cooperate, or differ.

Schreiter identifies one distinctive feature of exploring syncretism as "solutions at which a culture arrives because of trying to incorporate new messages, codes and sometimes signs into the culture."[151] So, the Luo people, in incorporating Christianity as taught by the CMS, adopted the *kusoma* Christianity, characterized by people attending church in order to read.[152] These are the Christians Omulo came to serve. All they had was what the evangelist, teachers and catechists had given them. Even so, they exhibited a spiritual gap between their belief and practice. The EARM tenets defined what Christianity

---

148. Hetherington, *British Paternalism and Africa*, 154.
149. Farrimond, "Concerning the Development," 265.
150. Schreiter, *Constructing Local Theologies*, 165–180.
151. Schreiter, 174.
152. Anderson, *Church in East Africa*, 111–112.

became in Central Nyanza, which Reed explains, changed "irrevocably the Christian Church in East Africa; it made the Faith of Jesus its own, at home in an African homestead and city.[153] Its beliefs and customs became part of the expression of faith that has lasted until today, even after the original fire has died down." The revival movement helped clarify existing opacity in their faith, which occurred because Christianity was dominant.[154] Since signs and codes convey specific meanings, they can fill existing meaning gaps besides organizing the meaning when introduced in a culture.

CMS and Omulo interacted on the policy of creating an indigenous Anglican Church. Omulo supported the notion of indigenizing the church, hence choosing service in the church over other offers. For Omulo it began with his ordination and service but reached a climax when in 1955 the Archbishop of Canterbury consecrated Festo Olang' along with three others to become the first African bishops in the East African region.[155] Schreiter cautions against a syncretism where the weakened local cultures replace its sign systems with the dominant invading culture's sign system when changes are incomplete, at the risk of sudden indigenization.[156] On this point, Omulo and CMS agreed. They continued a gradual increase of African influences on rituals and practices in the Anglican Church. This represented an incremental transformation of the African Anglican Church into an African entity, under local leadership, but connected to the global Anglican Communion. Omulo, like other padres, had an affinity to the exotic and European symbols of religion. They were not keen on improvising Anglican emblems of service, and thus appealed to Bewes for:

> Help in matter of purchasing articles such as the Chalise, plates and cups for the Holy communion. Price out here is very high and new pastorates find it impossible to get them.[157]

In their view, the due regard for the church would diminish if they used local, commonplace utensils while celebrating Communion. Omulo and his

---

153. Reed, *Walking in the Light*, 13.
154. Schreiter, *Constructing Local Theologies*, 175.
155. Olang', *Festo Olang' An Autobiography*, 30.
156. Schreiter, *Constructing Local Theologies*, 175.
157. Bewes, Letter to Stanway, 28 June 1945.

colleagues understood that certain aspects of the faith should not be tinkered with but be retained as was received, this being one of them.

Whereas Warren contended that "the Church anticipated political independence, in itself a spiritually important demonstration of respect for the capacity of Africans to rule themselves,"[158] Omulo and Africans padres in Central Nyanza, fascinated with the Anglican communion, seem to disagree on the idea of an independent church. In their meeting with Bewes in 1946, they sought a closer understanding and relationship with CMS London.[159] They judged that in an independent African Anglican church, they were being neglected, and feared that CMS was forsaking them when they needed their encouragement most. The padres argued, "Our church is still young and backward in many ways. We are grossly handicapped and sometimes growth is near impossible without closer understanding and support from a parent body."[160] In their submission, Omulo and his colleagues were not ready for the independent diocesan proposal by the CMS. They cited as handicaps: training for padres and inadequacy of staff. Hence, they called for ongoing cooperation with the CMS and the Anglican Communion.

Cross-cultural interaction is important in leadership training for mission and so allowing Olang' and Madoka to go for further studies overseas was a good step towards the African leadership development by CMS which would lead to a self-governing Kenyan church.[161] In June 1946, Rev. Festo Olang' left Kenya for a year's course at Wycliffe Hall, Oxford. That same year, in July, Rev. Allen Madoka left for the London College of Divinity and Rev. Josiah Magu took over the leadership of Kabete school.[162] The value of such a program to the young church was obvious. Omulo and his colleagues urged Bewes, representing CMS, to continue the program in which:

> A few selected clergymen would be given a further overseas training for pastoral work, and we must thank you and the CMS

---

158. Warren, *Crowded Canvas*, 69.
159. Bewes, Letter to Stanway, 28 June 1945.
160. Bewes.
161. Kagema, "Leadership Training for Mission," 114.
162. Owen, Letter to the Secretary, 9 August 1943.

London for having given a chance to three of our Padres, who had already been to Europe.[163]

Omulo revealed how, as clergy in Nyanza, they had saved 20,000 shillings in a fund started for this purpose, which they requested CMS to renew and continue. Warren concludes that the deliberate diminution of the metropolitical authority of Geoffrey Fisher, the Archbishop of Canterbury was the most fluent act of statesmanship during his tenure.[164]

5.6 Interpreting the Tradition

Considering the questions raised in the earlier three dimensions of agency, contextual understanding and ecclesial scrutiny, this section discusses how both Omulo and CMS interpreted tradition and the Scriptures in the period 1946–1970. It begins with how Omulo understands Christianity in relation to the Luo cultural tradition and examines the Christian message he developed. Then it examines how these same dimensions influenced CMS's way of (re)interpreting the Bible and their theological tradition. It explains a special formulation of the Christian message and how these theological insights shaped CMS's approach. It winds up correlating how CMS and Omulo interpreted tradition, in areas they agreed, disagreed, or collaborated.

5.6.1 Reuben Omulo's Interpreting Bible and Tradition

This segment discusses how Omulo interpreted the Bible in relation to the Luo religious tradition, and considers the questions raised by the earlier three dimensions. It discusses marriage issues facing Christians in the pastorate. The segment also explores how Omulo planned Christian messages.

5.6.1.1 Christian Marriage in the Pastorates

Marriage among Christians in the pastorates was a defining challenge for padre Omulo, both on a personal and ministry level. Luo Christians struggled to reconcile marriage, as Christianity taught it, with the marriage understanding of their Luo customs. What would be the place of polygamy and

---

163. Anglican Padres Central Nyanza Deanery, (APCND) "Petition presented to Canon Bewes," 2.

164. Warren, *Crowded Canvas*, 69.

divorce? Omulo's interpretation of the Bible and tradition was intended to mitigate the negative impact of Christian marriage teaching and practice on the church's witness.

The African Anglican Church held that holy marriage was for baptized couples only and that this was: "a lifelong and indissoluble union irrespective of the conditions unto death"[165] (Canon I of Marriage). It excludes all others, is between one man and one woman, and is for procreation and mutual help and comfort. So, divorce was out of the question, for "If such a marriage be declared valid, it is consequently indissoluble."[166] The church did not recognize unions of the unbaptized. These teachings were to prepare a Christian for holy Christian marriage (*harusi*) done in a church, following the procedures set by the dioceses: a padre counsel, marriage banns announcement and a church wedding.[167]

Omulo had worked with Archdeacon Willis to develop the book explaining and introducing God to the Luo, which was used by the catechumens (§3.6.1). He was among the African clergy who developed the revised *Catechism for Hearers* of 1948, which contained the African Anglican Church's teachings on marriage. Hence, Omulo espoused the teaching which instructed Christians on marriage.[168] But the contextual challenge Church members experienced in divorce and polygamy came from the African perspective of marriage. The post-WWII Owen, according to Murray observed that only 30 to 40 percent of Anglican marriages in Central Nyanza remained monogamous.[169] A case in point:

> While expanding Christian work to the frontiers of Yenga Pastorate, Omulo worked with Mzee Daniel Oginde, Ja-Usonga, now a jadak[170] at Kagonya. He married Nereah Ogega nyar ka-Puny' in a harusi at Yenga pastorate.

---

165. "Canon Law of Marriage," Canon I of Marriage.
166. Canon Law of Marriage," Canon II of Marriage.
167. *Sheria za Kanisa juu*, Anglican Bishops of East Africa, Reuben Omulo private archive.
168. *Catechism for Hearers' Classes*, 24; see also §5.6.2.1.
169. Murray, "Archdeacon W. E. Owen," 644.
170. The term *jodak* has been earlier identified as people who come to settle, or land clients. Without these people, perhaps the Luo system of exogamy would have run into difficulties much earlier since they would not have achieved the need for social reproduction. Ocholla-Ayayo, *Traditional Ideology and Ethics*, 135. Oginde's father had migrated from Usonga

An industrious Oginde gained great wealth from his cattle trading business, besides farming. Soon his in-laws, Jo-Kapuny, offered a second wife to help care for and grow his wealth, but it was social support to his host society as well. A man of his means customarily married many wives. But it conflicted him. The demands of his Christian faith and service clashed with this legitimate customary demand. He adhered to his catechism vows and refused to fulfil his societal responsibility. But Jo-Kapuny would not yield and incessantly sent women one after another, without success. In their new strategy, the elders accused Nereah, his wife, of jealousy and refusing to allow her husband to marry. Besides, they blamed her for kicking out the other women. Afterwards, the Puny elders made another try. They brought him a three-month pregnant woman for a wife, Nereah's kin, as her *nyar-ot*. Again, Oginde was obstinate, standing in his Christian persuasion. But Nereah confronted him, threatening to commit suicide. This threat broke Oginde, for suicide was anathema among the Luo.

Left with no room to wiggle, Oginde sought padre Omulo's spiritual guidance. How would he protect his excellent relationship with the Puny' clan among whom he sojourned and stay true to his Christian faith? To preserve Mzee Oginde's faith and keep his societal status, Omulo allowed him to marry the second wife. Although this offended the church, it enhanced his status in this society and therefore Christian witness. Oginde paid for the marriage with a diminished role in his budding teaching and preaching ministry in the church. Besides, he had to forthwith forego receiving Holy Communion, being a godparent at baptism or a witness at a wedding. But Omulo kept him in other church services. He served as the chair of the building committee and in management and mobilizing resources for the church.[171]

An analysis of Omulo's interaction with Oginde shows how his teaching to catechumens clashed with the society's position.[172] Sometimes his actions were not congruent with his teachings, implying the esteem he gave to the witness of the gospel. Omulo taught that marriage is God's ideal for man and woman. It defined its boundaries thus:

---

to Ugenya where his sister was married. His in-laws permitted him land to cultivate, and he soon married one of the Ugenya Ka-Puny girls who bore him Oginde and other children.

171. Fredrick Oginde, Personal interview, 23 February 2021; Mbala, Personal interview, 11 August 2021; Joyce Oginde, Personal interview, 11 August 2021.

172. *Catechism for Hearers' Classes.*

Ka dicwo ok okendo kata dhako ok okend, ooyo ok giketho cik Nyasaye. Jo moko ok kendgi kata kendi ni mondo giti tij Nyasaye maber moloyo, jo moko nikec ok gihero kata ok giyudo.[173]

Translation: If a man does not marry, or a woman is not married, no, they have not offended God's law. Some people do not marry or are not married so that they work for God better, others because they did not like or did not find a partner.

Teaching that marriage was optional and not for everyone collided with the Luo position that all Luo should be married, for boys' and girls' goal in life is marriage.[174] Since marriage is a social construct, fear of the consequences and not God's will guide the Luo. Fearing the ghost of the unmarried would demand of their folks a reason why they allowed her to go to the grave before marriage. Ocholla-Ayayo submits:

> This also emphasizes how necessary it becomes for a girl to be married before death . . . The same is also true with a man over the age of eighteen who dies before marriage. He cannot be buried inside the homestead. The burial will take place outside the homestead fence.[175]

While Omulo taught marriage as an optional and individual decision, he would not allow his son Malaki Otieno to stay unmarried.[176] At thirty-seven, Otieno was still unmarried. Omulo not only found a bride for his son in Alice Ohowa but negotiated for their marriage according to the Luo customs, even though he didn't join them at a crucial visit to the brides' home. Omulo writes:

> Wadhi malanga Reuben, Jason Wahore, Owala Opata, Obare, . . . waduogo ka nyako owachona ni ok abi tedo ni wuodi kochiko wang'e kuoma.

> Translation: We went to Malanga, Reuben, Jason Wahore, Owala Opata, Japuonj Obare, . . . we returned with the message from the girl that she will not marry his son who cannot face her.[177]

---

173. *Catechism for Hearers' Classes*, 23, §1–2.
174. Wasawo, "We Understand but Darkly," 67.
175. Ocholla-Ayayo, *Traditional Ideology and Ethics*, 143.
176. Alice Otieno, Personal interview.
177. Omulo, "Omulo 1959 Diary."

Alice stalled Omulo's efforts, insisting on the son's proposal in a face-to-face meeting. They solved this and Malaki wedded Alice in November 1959.

5.6.1.2 Polygamy

Although Canon Horstead did not advocate for polygamy but claimed to show Africans' sentiments, he propounded: "monogamy is not a fundamental tenet of Christianity and that just as the Western church disputes the ethic of war so we would dispute the ethic of monogamy."[178] So, the Anglican Church's teaching against polygamy raised misgivings and debates, sometimes expressed in revolt, as Christians adhered to both church and Luo customs. For instance, the *Catechism for Hearers' Classes* book listed the ills of marrying many wives, which appealed to the intellect more than the spiritual.[179] It elevated love as the goal of marriage over children:

> Nikec kendruok ok en mar nywolo nyithindo kende, to bende ni dicwo gi ciege onego giherre adier. Ng'ato ok nyal hero ciege madwong' adier koda mon mamoko bende.[180]

> Translation: Marriage is not only for procreation, but also for love between husband and wife. A man cannot love his first wife and love other women in the same way.

Hence, love became the basis of marriage, which means that consent of those involved and not force by the family should determine marriage. Besides, married life continued in love, as was written in the *Catechism for Hearers' Classes*:

> Nyako ok onego cun gi dicwo e kendrwok. Nyasaye dwaro dhano, dicwo gi nyako mondo oyiere giwegi kendo giherre.[181]

> Translated: We should not force a woman to marry. God wants man and woman to agree and love each other.

---

178. Horstead read this paper to the Advisory Committee on African Education at Edinburgh house on 19 May 1933. The paper was an outcome of months of study and collaboration with students of Fourah Bay College. African clergymen of Sierra Leone and Bishop Gelsthrope of Niger were consulted. Horstead, "Marriage and the Christian Church," 2.

179. *Catechism for Hearers' Classes*, 24, §7.

180. *Catechism for Hearers' Classes*, 24, §7.

181. *Catechism for Hearers' Classes*, §§8–10.

This *Catechism for Hearers' Classes* booklet further argues that spouses would not harm each other out of love, and one would do nothing that shames a spouse they love. But the love for God supersedes other loves, including love for a spouse. Thus, Omulo taught love as an overarching purpose of marriage.

But in the Luo mind, as in most African minds, the paramount purpose of marriage would be the continuity of the family, hence, without children no marriage is complete.[182] This notion centres children in marriage, so not having or wanting more children justifies seeking children by another woman. Many wives would acquiesce in their husband's extra marriage. Mzee Oginde's case above is illustrative.

Omulo taught also that every woman needs her own husband, which is not possible where one has married many women.[183] This clashed with Luo customs of socialisation, which attached great responsibilities to polygamy. Each wife had her own house in the homestead, and each was allocated her milk cows, land for farming and a granary. Mama Nereah valued the social equilibrium, which called for sharing, and believed that polygamy for a person of means was a social duty.

Omulo argued, in teaching the church's catechism, that in countries where men marry many wives, they force girls to marry older men, which is an offence against the girls.[184] This position claims the Luo impute a low value to their women and girls. And it implies women are forced to marry in polygamous homes. The case of Oginde undermines this notion, for many of the women given him for marriage were willing to marry him, but he turned them away. When they got the opportunity, they could not stay.[185] Wasawo postulates that the standing of the man among the Luo is derived from how he ran his homes, how peaceful and prosperous his family was.[186] Such reasoning could not supplant polygamy, rooted in the Luo customs. If able, Luo men would marry a second, a third, and even more wives.

Omulo, in teaching about polygamy, invoked God's displeasure with it, on the grounds that it was not God's plan for humankind. This was the

---

182. Horstead, "Marriage and the Christian Church," 3; Ocholla-Ayayo, *Traditional Ideology and Ethics*, 141.
183. *Catechism for Hearers' Classes*, 24, §7.
184. *Catechism for Hearers' Classes*, 24, §7.
185. Joyce Oginde, Personal interview.
186. Wasawo, "We Understand but Darkly," 67.

theological reason given to the Christians. But, by now, Christians had read the Old Testament Scriptures, and in those texts didn't discern God's displeasure in polygamy. They thus challenged the teaching of monogamy as the basic rule of marriage.

The church acknowledged the practice of polygamy in the biblical narrative but argued:

> In the beginning, God did not rule that man should marry only one wife. There is no such law. But God gave Adam one wife. Moses allowed Israelites to marry over one wife because of their stubbornness of heart. Abraham or Moses, along with other prophets, were not given law to only marry one wife . . . no, God waited for Jesus to give this law.[187]

Hence, the Bible allowed the teaching of polygamy to be made in context. The church's justification for monogamy was that it constituted Christ's main teaching to his followers "*Yesu to no waco niya: Ni ji ariyo kende e ma nyalo bet ringrwok achiel* (Mat.19:5)" (Jesus said, only two people can become one flesh (Matt 19:5).[188]

For the church's teaching was: *Ng'ato ok nyal bedo ja lup Yesu mar adier ko kendo mon ariyo . . . mani en ketho cik mar Yesu*[189] (one could not follow Christ and be polygamous . . . he would break Christ's commandments). Here is the case: Oginde became *jaketho* (offender) of Christ's laws according to Omulo and had to go through discipline (§5.6.2). *Joketho* (offenders) in the eyes of the church was wider than perpetrators of polygamy. Omulo had to reschedule restoration prayers in Ngere, Ndiru Pastorate for sanctioning Stela Auma and Tereza Achola. Both had wedded in church *harusi* as first wives, but their husbands married other women later.[190] These women became transgressors due to their husbands' offence of marrying second wives after doing *harusi*.

Church leaders used the Old and New Testament Scriptures to persuade catechumens and Luo Christians to change their view of polygamy and adopt

---

187. *Catechism for Hearers' Classes*, 24, §§3–4.
188. *Catechism for Hearers' Classes*, 24, §5.
189. *Catechism for Hearers' Classes*, 24, §6.
190. Ngere Group, Letter to Omulo, 28 May 1951.

monogamy as compatible with following Christ, thus, making those who become polygamous offenders of Christ's law.

5.6.1.3 *Divorce*

The state, through the church, tasked padres to officiate marriage and endowed them with powers to recommend divorce. The padres recommended divorce, acting on the decisions of their Pastorate Councils. While at Regea pastorate Omulo wrote to the DC in Central Nyanza Kisumu, approving the dissolution of Mr. Ajuang's marriage:

> RE: Claudio Ajuang' s/o Demba.
>
> Dear Sir,
>
> The above named was married in July 1944. Then his wife offended him, forcing them to separate. For this reason, I am asking you to let him divorce his wife on stipulated divorce terms. We investigated this matter as the Pastorate Committee, and to grant divorce if satisfied.
>
> Reuben Omulo Chairman (pastor in charge).[191]

Since it only took the padre's letter for the DC to enact a divorce, Christians discovered easier ways of dissolving their marriages, which was not as stringent as the stated Christian codes or in the Luo customs. For example, John Adera turned to the church to divorce his wife, Julia Athieno. The Pastorate Standing Committee in August 1954 discussed John's request for divorce from marriage to Julia, from whom he had separated. John's grounds were:[192]

1. Ne oketho giga mang'eny ahinya e yo mar wang'o gi mach . . .
2. En dhako ma wiye tek ok owinja . . .
3. Jo odwa ok dware.

Translation:

1. She burnt and destroyed my personal properties.
2. She is a stubborn wife who does not obey me.
3. Our family no longer wants her.

---

191. Omulo, Letter to the DC Central Nyanza, 5 November 1952.
192. Omulo, Letter to the DC RE: Divorce, August 1954.

But Julia, in response, debunked and challenged John's reasoning by stating:

1. Ne gin gik maricho richo mane odong' ka koro wapogre gikmoko, kendo en ema ne omiya thuolo mar wang'ogi.
2. Wich teko- onge gimoro ma asetimo manyisa wich teko, nikech tije duto mag mon onge mane otama. Bende ne wachiemo mana kode emesa kochakore e kedwa nyaka chieng' moriemba. To dhako ma wiye tek bende dichiem go chuore e mesa ka ok giwinjore?
3. Joodgi kane oyudo barua moa ir joodgi eka koro dhaw nitie. Ng'eny weche ne hinyo a edho jonyuolne. To mano ne Julia ok odewo nikech jakend en Mr Adera ok jonyuolne.[193]

Translation:

1. These were things of little value, left over after our separation. Indeed, he permitted me to burn them.
2. On stubbornness, there is no evidence to show my stubbornness because the customary demands of a woman I have fulfilled. We always ate at the same table from the day of our marriage until the day he sent me away. But can a stubborn woman eat with her husband at the same table if they have not agreed?
3. Our quarrels started after he got a letter from his family. Most of the issues came from his parents. But these did not bother me because I married Adera and not his parents.

The committee found no reason in church, Luo customs or civil law that would grant the divorce on these grounds, hence the committee passed that Julia "return to her home and marriage." But John's family would not swallow the verdict. Hence, Omulo referred the case to the Maseno dean.

Divorce was rare among the Luo except at the early stages of marriage before *riso*. *Riso* is a ceremony done by the Luo to consummate marriage after a couple of years of coming together.[194] It followed a period where the man's family scrutinized the woman's suitability for marriage in that home. They raised questions that could inhibit marriage, for the Luo are "a patrilineal exogamous society as commanded by their normative beliefs. All marriages

---

193. Omulo, Letter to the DC RE: Divorce, August 1954.
194. Ocholla-Ayayo, *Traditional Ideology and Ethics*, 141.

MUST take place outside the sub-tribe groups."[195] A marriage within the sub-tribe would evoke immediate group sanction, the couple banished, and their house burned.[196] Wilson stressed: "No other crime in Luo was treated as seriously or as immediately or as effectively as the law of incest."[197] Once the family of the man were satisfied that no inhibition existed, the couples' marriage would be consummated.

Ocholla-Ayayo further contends that, even though the Luo considered marriage after *riso* permanent, they provided grounds for divorce.[198] Wilson correctly distinguishes between "divorce" and separation in the Luo marriage.[199] Hence, separation was a common occurrence, observed Wilson, and "it made little difference to a man if his wife went away with someone else, because he knew she must someday come back to him because her father would not dare accept second bride-wealth cattle."[200] But other divorce conditions besides the pre-*riso* ones are antisocial and often hard to prove.

5.6.1.4 Approach to Ministry

Christian witness guided Omulo in handling the people of Kagonya in his Yenga pastorate. This differed from his colleagues. For instance, since Rev. Ezekiel Apindi was averse to women married without *harusi*, he would not greet or allow a woman who had not done *harusi* or in a polygamous family to cook or serve him meals.[201]

But Omulo allowed latitude regarding church rules on polygamous practitioners, focusing instead on inviting them into God's Kingdom. Joice Oginde has testified, "Omulo baptized me as a newly married woman, although a third wife to Daniel Oginde. He insisted I could not stay married to him if I only had one name."[202] Omulo took Joice through catechism and baptized her at Miyare church of Yenga pastorate in 1958. This was a huge accommodation, since Omulo was required to seek the bishop's permit to baptise her, according

---

195. Ocholla-Ayayo, 135.
196. Ocholla-Ayayo, 136.
197. Wilson, *Marriage Laws Customs*, 137.
198. Ocholla-Ayayo, *Traditional Ideology and Ethics*, 141.
199. Wilson, *Marriage Laws Customs*, 130.
200. Wilson, 130.
201. Aloo, Personal interview, 22 September 2021.
202. Joyce Oginde, Personal interview.

to Canon X:2, the same "provided always that the native customary union involving polygamy was entered into, in a state of ignorance."[203]

Omulo did not use baptism as a device to block those the church considered as "offenders" (polygamists). Instead, he applied it to include those excluded as "errant" members by giving them the means to enter God's Kingdom of those born again. For, he maintained the catechism teachings of the Anglican Church, that through baptism one became a Christian, hence born again. He contended that God gives that second birth in answer to the prayers at baptism, regardless of one's earlier status:

> Giwacho ka Adam noketho chenye notho, eka nythind gi ok nonyuolgi gichunye negingi ringruok, gi rieko, kendo ekagiwacho nonyuole diriyo onwang'o chuny, to e weche nogogo ok wanyal puonjogi ka adier, ok wanyal neno gima nie igi. Yesu no wacho weche mang'eny kwom ngero, eka nyuol manyien en wach ma Roho Maler donjoni ng'ato miye hero dwaro gima Nyasaye dwaro.[204]

> Translation: Some say that when Adam sinned, his spirit died, so his offspring were born with spirit, body, and soul. We cannot separate them or see what is in them. Jesus spoke often in parables; hence, new birth occurs when the Holy Spirit enters someone who seeks God's will.

Here, Omulo mentions that Jesus's usage of the term could have been as a parable. Salvation comes by faith in Christ, Omulo maintained. Hence, Christians should focus on Christ's new kingdom. He wrote:

> Yesu otemo nyiso wa ngima manyaka chieng' kaka obet, eka nikech wachni dwong' ahinya, wakiya. Bende kanono kaka (nwogn) kidwaro nyise piki piki kaka obet kinyisogi weche manyienigi to bang'e okia pikipiki. To wangeyo kaji opogore moko ok dwar gik mag ringrewa, moko dwaro gik mag Nyasaye. Yesu owacho joge gidwaro gi mag Nyasaye nikech Roho, ok nikeck kido minyuologo ji.[205]

---

203. Anglican Church of Kenya Constitution 2002, Canon X:2, 75–88.
204. Omulo, Omulo Notes, 83.
205. Omulo, 84.

Translation: Jesus tried to teach us what eternal life means, but we can't comprehend such a grand theme. For instance, when you describe to someone what a motorbike is, at the end he would not comprehend a motorbike out of these unfamiliar words. We are though aware of human differences. Some want earthly things, while others want godly things. But Jesus said that the Holy Spirit, and not because of human nature, will make his followers want God's will.

Omulo taught his people through the Scriptures and logical persuasion to change their view of polygamy. And even though he encouraged them in catechism teachings to adopt monogamy, Omulo understood that change would come with new birth by faith. Thus, he stressed that new birth occurs in a person's spirit and is a mystery to us. It is a work of faith that humans cannot fathom.[206] It is observable here that Omulo walks the slippery path between strict Anglican rules and Luo customs, where he makes a genuine missional posture of negotiating non-negotiable positions with love for his people – in David Bosch's words, "creative tension" and not compromise.[207]

5.6.2 The CMS's Interpreting Bible and Tradition

How the CMS, represented by the African Anglican Church leadership, (re)interpreted the Bible and their theological tradition is the focus of discussion in this segment. The discussion occurs in light of the questions raised by the earlier three dimensions. It examines whether there were unique formulations of the Christian message arising in that context and how those theological insights shaped the church's approach.

5.6.2.1 Christian Marriage

The Anglican Church articulated her position on monogamous and lifelong marriage (*harusi*) that its members must espouse, in Canon I: Of Marriage and provided further detail in the catechism books.[208] The church maintained that African marriage could not raise to the level of Christian marriage

---

206. Omulo, 82.
207. Kritzinger and Saayman, *Mission in Creative Tension*.
208. "Canon Law of Marriage."

(*harusi*) because it had the potential to be polygamous or dissoluble. Neither could baptism of one party elevate African marriage.[209]

Rambui's case affirmed the church's misgivings that African marriages, as "potentially polygamous or dissoluble."[210] Stovold had to deal with a complex marriage case from Omulo while serving at Ramula Pastorate in 1949. In 1935, Safania Rambui married in a church *harusi*.[211] But he married another woman by the Luo customs in 1937, a wife he now wanted the church's help to divorce in 1949. There was no justifiable reason in the Luo custom to dissolve their marriage. But in a terse response, Stovold wrote: "*Haiwezekani kwa mtu aliye kwisha oa mke wa pili. Sorry*" (It cannot happen, this man had married a second wife).[212] It is puzzling that Stovold did not grant this request, even though the church did not regard Luo's customary marriage as permanent. Since the church regarded a second marriage as null, a situation in which a man is requesting a divorce from a second wife should have provided a pastoral moment to restore a fallen brother and re-affirm his family.

5.6.2.2 Divorce

Even in a case of *harusi* for baptized members, the church allowed divorce, for it recognized civil courts' conditions for granting a decree of nullity as valid grounds. In the *Resolution 118 on Divorce: The Family in Contemporary Society* of the 1958 Lambeth Conference, the Anglican Church pronounced its stand on the divorce issue, affirming the role of secular authorities in annulling marriages. The state's grounds for divorce may not have been compatible with the church's teaching or Luo customs. Often, they may have granted divorce decree sought where, in the church's view, the marriage was invalid. For instance, the church allowed nullification for an *unbaptized* person(s) since they regarded such marriages as invalid.[213] In addition, the church, guided by 1 Corinthians 7:2–15, held that one may not have *harusi*, solemnizing one's marriage in church, if they have repudiated their baptism by renouncing their membership in the church.[214]

---

209. "Canon Law of Marriage," Canon II: Native Customary Union, 2.
210. "Canon Law of Marriage," Canon II: Native Customary Union, 2.
211. Oyolo, Ramula to Rural Dean, 8 October 1949.
212. Stovold, Letter to the Pastorate, 11 October 1949.
213. "Canon Law of Marriage," Canon II: 1.
214. "Canon Law of Marriage," Canon II: 5.

The Anglican Church taught monogamy and expected Christians to comply, for the church took disciplinary action if there was any lapse from the marriage standard. Horstead lamented that the teaching was given through negative order and discipline, which require divorced people to be dissociated from membership for at least three months, after which they would be restored, as the pastor deemed fit.[215] But they would bar the member from communion and burial inside the church.

But in Central Nyanza, as elsewhere in Africa, this teaching raised questions of inconsistency. For while they did not view marriage as a sacrament, as the Roman Catholic Church does, *harusi* was unbreakable while the partners were alive. Hence divorce was not possible; although sometimes they annulled a marriage, they did not allow or recognise divorce.

With the enactment and continuous amendments of the *African Christian Marriage and Divorce Ordinance*,[216] church marriage shifted from being a religious to a legal act, whose procedures, limits, and realms were state determined. For instance, in ACMDO:

> Celebration of Marriage: Marriage may be celebrated in any licensed places of worship by any recognized minister of the church, denomination, or body to which such place of worship belongs and according to the rites and usage of marriage observed in such a church . . . to which such last-mentioned recognized minister belongs, provided that the marriage be celebrated with open doors between the hours of 8 am and 6 o'clock in the afternoon. In the presence of 2 witnesses besides the minister.[217]

Since love was essential for a monogamous marriage, then legislating love would be a problem. It would link the church with state policies. Hence, it was possible to view this standard of monogamy as part of the dominant British civilization that was inherent in Anglican theology and practice, a Christian standard going back to the early church. There were doubts among

---

215. Horstead, "Marriage and the Christian Church," 2.
216. Governor of the Colony, *African Christian Marriage*.
217. Governor of the Colony, §23.

the converts whether "the monogamous life is the only possible one for a true Christian community."[218]

5.6.2.3 Polygamy

Earlier on, the church did not understand the importance of polygamy to the people's way of life, argued Olang', hence it ignored polygamists without helping them to understand the message.[219] Further, Olang' advanced monogamy as ancient and essential for full church membership, for which the church could not compromise. In the same position, the 1958 Lambeth Conference emphasised Christ's teaching, which bore witness to monogamy as the "divine will for every race of men." It invited the church members to seek God's guidance and, through study, to develop its witness and discipline.[220] But the Conference acknowledged the church's challenge of introducing monogamy in societies where polygamy was part of a vital social and economic fabric.[221] Of relevance, the Conference associated the problem of polygamy with the limited opportunities for women in society. So, the 1958 Lambeth Conference urged the church to advance women's status with all within its means, and education in particular.[222] Thus, in the Lambeth 1958 Resolution 120, The Family in Contemporary Society–Polygamy, the Anglican Church pronounced its position on polygamy. But since the polygamy issue remained unresolved, the conference referred it to the Advisory Council on Missionary Strategy.[223]

5.6.3 Interaction Between Reuben Omulo and CMS on Interpreting Tradition

To show the nature of the interaction between Omulo and CMS about interpreting tradition, this section uses Schreiter's "dual religious systems" model to describe the responses to the incoming cultural and religious impulses and discuss the different dynamics of the encounter. To Schreiter, dual systems develop as parallel models emerging from the contact of cultures and

---

218. Horstead, "Marriage and the Christian Church," 1.
219. Olang', *Festo Olang' An Autobiography*, 22.
220. Lambeth Conference 1958, 120a, c.
221. Lambeth Conference 1958, 120b.
222. Lambeth Conference 1958, 120d.
223. Lambeth Conference 1958, 120e.

emphasize the conflictual aspect of cultures.[224] A dual system emerges when an invading culture is considered incomplete by the receiving culture, because the sign system it deploys cannot address the same things as the receiving culture's sign system.

The padres, Omulo and CMS shared the notion about the status and involvement of women in the church. CMS and the church viewed opening opportunities for women as a solution to polygamy.[225] Owen and the CMS dedicated their time to lifting African women's status, upon whom they laid the foundation of the new style of Christian family.[226] Omulo, and the Luo Nyanza padres, called for more opportunities because:

> Women are hopelessly backward and the little that is being done is inadequate. We understand that men without women are mere carts without wheels. We plead for more women missionaries to come and teach our women.[227]

The CMS and Omulo agreed to cooperate in promoting women in Central Nyanza. By 1956, the CMS had established a girls' boarding school with 130 girls representing the very low number of girls getting an education.[228] During that meeting Omulo requested of Bewes that London make women's education a priority, since CMS had done extraordinary work in boys' education. In their recommendation to the Nyanza Deanery on women's work, Omulo and Mwanda trained them, so that in their monthly meetings, elder women guided and counselled younger mothers, encouraging them to send their children to school. They also appointed women to find out issues about widows and orphans, and girls' fellowship.[229]

In Schreiter's second type of dual religious system, the CMS's response to women's empowerment represented the invading culture as challenging the value of the sign system of the local culture.[230] Omulo's and the CMS's promotion of women created a new societal challenge. For instance, the

---

224. Schreiter, *Constructing Local Theologies*, 178.
225. Lambeth Conference 1958, 120c.
226. Murray, "Archdeacon W. E. Owen," 644.
227. Anglican Padres Central Nyanza Deanery, "Petition presented to Canon Bewes."
228. Omachar, "Contribution of the Church," 64.
229. Omulo and Mwanda, Ramula Pastorate Report, 3 §a.
230. Schreiter, *Constructing Local Theologies*, 178.

educated girls soon became social misfits. Mrs. Apindi testified that as an educated woman she missed out on the cherished and sanctioned tradition of escorting brides from their parents' house to their marital home.[231] That illustrated the problem educated girls in the Luo society faced. Men and their families avoided educated girls, whom they assumed only knew how to read but couldn't cook or dig. The preference for uneducated girls discouraged girls from going to school.

In his third type, Schreiter discusses a situation where the invading culture (in this case, CMS Christianity) offers new sign systems that are accepted by the local culture, although they find them inadequate.[232] The church recognized annulling of marriage by a civil court, and in a marriage: "where either party was permanently impotent, or incapable of consummating the marriage, at the time of the marriage."[233] The Luo Christians found this grounds for annulling marriage to comport with Luo customs. Annulling marriage became inevitable when couples had no children, since marriage was for procreation. While couples could not find out impotence before a *harusi*, such a marriage may end up annulled, if they noticed such anomalies in the period preceding the *riso* ceremony. Even then, dissolution would only occur after mitigating measures failed. Ocholla-Ayayo describes such measures as follows:

> A wife may report to her parents that the man is impotent (*buoch*), that was traditionally sufficient reason for divorce since there is no guarantee for social reproduction of the lineage. But there is room for reconciliation on this point. If it happened in the village where the impotent man had a brother, the wife was persuaded not to disclose it, but to look for one of her brothers-in-law or clansmen in the relation of brother-in-law to cohabit secretly with her.[234]

---

231. Omachar, "Contribution of the Church," 64.
232. Schreiter, *Constructing Local Theologies*, 178.
233. "Canon Law of Marriage," Canon IV: Nullity, §a.
234. Ocholla-Ayayo, *Traditional Ideology and Ethics* 141–142. The children produced would be legally and socially children of the husband. This man's activities would remain top secret. Such cohabitation must occur with the clan and among the husband's kindred.

If a woman is *lur* (barren), a man may demand *nyar-ot* (relative of the elder wife, see §3.3.1), instead of asking for a divorce. The only difference here is, they must send the normal bride's wealth as at any other marriage, although there will be no hurry. But dissolution must be granted if the woman rejects the thought of a secret lover. So, Luo Christians realized the *harusi* did not give sufficient time for couples to examine and prevent marital issues that might lead to annulling marriages once consummated. Besides, for *harusi* marriages, the church prohibited certain customary solution, such as polygamy, or having secret lovers, which was seen as adultery. In addition, after *riso*, a Luo marriage may last longer than *harusi*, which is supposed to be indissoluble lifelong.

Although the Luo Christians valued *harusi* in church, they followed the Luo customs as long as it did not conflict with church norms, while addressing their fears of dissolution. These customs included background checking to avoid marrying relatives and dowry as the seal of marriage. Omulo's daughter Janet Awuor's case is illustrative. She eloped with Apollo Ogolla, which offended Omulo's honour as a priest. He cited it as two offences in his letter to them. To get over the issue, Omulo met Apollo's relatives, as the Luo tradition demanded, negotiated dowry and called on them to expedite the process to get over with it. But since they violated the church code, a church would not permit a wedding. Omulo directed:

> Ni jokristo gi jokristo kokaore ok gitim kendgi e Kanisa to githi ndiko e Registrar's office. Bang'e kagi hero japadre dhilemonegi chieng' moro.[235]
>
> Translation: If Christians take each other, the padre will not wed them in the Church but would go to the Registrar's office. Later, if they would, the priest can bless their marriage.

This advice shows Omulo's efforts to be a Luo Christian while dealing with both Christian and Luo customs on marriage. It also demonstrates Schreiter's fourth type of dual religious system, where the invading and local sign systems are dealing with two different things. The Luo, as a receiving culture, kept aspects of their marriage customs to deal with emergent issues.[236]

---

235. Omulo, Omulo 1954 Diary.
236. Schreiter, *Constructing Local Theologies*, 178.

5.7 Discernment for Action

This section focuses on the concrete steps of faith taken by both CMS and Omulo in the community in the period under discussion. It explains the cultural decisions involved in Omulo's world and the decision-making structures and patterns that existed for him. Then the section discusses the concrete faith projects the CMS missionaries undertook – the plans they made to embody their theological insights into the community. Both Omulo and the CMS mission developed a holistic view of mission. The last segment in this section discusses Omulo's and CMS's discernment for action on what they agreed on or disagreed on and their points of collaboration.

5.7.1 Reuben Omulo's Discernment for Action

In assuming duties at the pastorate from Kisumu, Omulo faced the challenges of untrained church teachers, EARM and establishing an African Anglican Church. Those challenges defined his service. He began service in the pastorate at a time of transition. After 1944, the CMS realigned and unified churches in the new diocese. Omulo arrived at the pastorate during this restructuring under Deans Stanway and Stovold, during which the diocese set up pastorates out of the old mission station (§5.6.2).

5.7.1.1 Training at the Pastorate

For mission work to thrive in the Nyanza Archdeaconry, the twin challenges of the inadequacy of ministers and untrained church leaders needed urgent attention. The clergy to Christian ratio, as Stanway noted in 1946, was unacceptably low.[237] In all of Nyanza, Omulokoli estimated, each padre oversaw an average of 1,000 congregants.[238] But despite this overwhelming burden on the padres, there were "12,000 children baptized in infancy who are not yet confirmed and at least 1/3 of them are in some church class."[239]

Following their evaluation, padres Nehemiah Mwanda and Omulo[240] noted the Ramula pastorate had challenges. The church leaders did not prescribe a time for worship and had no timetables. So, the congregation did not gather

---

237. Stanway, Letter to Cecil Bewes, 29 April 1946.
238. Omulokoli, "Historical Development," 333.
239. Stanway, Letter to Cecil Bewes.
240. Omulo and Mwanda, Ramula Pastorate Report, 3, §2.

at specific times for service. Worse still, the churches did not adhere to the CMS standard procedures espoused in *Amri na Sheria*.[241] Since most of the churches had no registers, record keepers made no weekly entries, service details, or other required entries. Serving as lay readers was, sometimes, unrewarding, for the church groups failed to make out monthly payments for their teachers. However, Rawa and Ngere in Ramula Pastorate were exceptional. In most churches, women rarely attended their monthly meetings. Mwanda was concerned that few churches had seats for their congregants and had not registered their plots.[242] Worse still, only Ngere, Kambare, Kahera and Lung'a had built staff housing. He also regretted losing his Bible, eaten by a goat when he slept at a lay reader's home.

Since CMS focused on training padres, the challenge of training lay leaders fell on the padres. So, in 1950, Omulo had to train the church leaders he worked with in the Ramula pastorate. They tailored their training around the gaps identified in the pastorate, which represented problems across the deanery.

Working with Rev. Nehemiah Mwanda from the Ambira pastorate, Omulo developed the following subjects suited to church leaders for his Ramula pastorate:

1. Establishing time for service.
2. Maintaining clear attendance registers.
3. Verifying cards early before hearers appear before examiners.
4. Visiting Christians in the villages.
5. Conducting Sunday prayers on time, at 9:30 or 11:30 a.m., and the leaders preparing beforehand.
6. Registering church land and building the premises, such as the minister's house, toilets, etc.
7. Burying Christians: a. the baptized, confirmed using Psalms b. catechumens without Psalms.
8. Baptizing the ill about to die, but if they get well, they should be subject to regulation.
9. Electing and inducting church elders and wardens, making good offering bags.

---

241. *Amri na Sheria* -- Laws and Regulations, 1 August 1941.
242. Omulo and Mwanda, Ramula Pastorate Report, 3 §2, f.

10. Ensuring all lay readers have "amri na sheria."
11. Examining issues of people in the margin: a. second wives who become Christians, b. second wives' enquirers, c. widows, d. needy women.
12. Ordering churches in this diocese and church committees – how they are led.
13. Determining things village churches should do as they compete – like choirs and other competition they would agree on.
14. Organizing parental meeting with two parents (man and woman) except where the man is absent.
15. Examining the usage of church money and church groups' funds.
16. Listing names of ministers in a book not on papers that disappear.[243]

They trained the following numbers of lay readers (*jopuonj*), church elders or wardens and women leaders in the following churches: Ngere (111), Kambare (40), Ramula (86), Ulumbi and Rawa (89), Ndiru Kahera kit mikaye (44), Magwar Lung'a (77), Bimos Lela (35), Chulaimbo (121), Ndiru (57). The report showed that a total of 671 leaders were trained.

Omulo and Mwanda identified an urgent need to encourage the church workers, including church group leaders, village church teachers and women in all their meetings.[244] Thus, they recommended that the deanery take appropriate action. Although they noted progress in Ramula compared to other pastorates, Mwanda urged Omulo to help the Ngere congregations improve.

5.7.1.2 Pioneering New Churches in the Pastorates

While the Anglican Church had taken root in the Ndiru, Ramula and Regea pastorates where Omulo served, the Yenga pastorate presented a classic case of the unchurched areas in Central Nyanza. He served Yenga first between 1958–1962 and 1967–1970. During his first tour, he reached the furthest edges of the pastorate, bordering Busia district, pioneering the church. It is Okere's testimony that Omulo baptized two hundred people, following a period of instruction.[245] Since the church was large enough to accommodate

---

243. Omulo and Mwanda.
244. Omulo and Mwanda, 3, §3.
245. Okere, Personal interview, 11 August 2021.

catechumens, Omulo ordered the clearing of the bush next to the church for the event. On this ground, the Kagonya parish's primary and secondary schools stand today. Omulo trekked to most of these centres, preaching and instructing enquirers. Nicholas Mbala, whose father, Daniel Oginde, worked with Omulo, adduced that while at Aboke, Omulo worshipped and baptized people under an *ober* tree at Ageng' centre.[246] This became a place for worship, where St. Stephen's ACK church is built today. Omulo repeated this pattern of bringing people to worship, regardless of whether there was a building, for what he did at Ageng' he repeated in Got Rembo. There, Margaret Omolo testified, Omulo baptized her under a tree, which was the ground upon which Got Rembo ACK church of Kagonya Parish was established.[247]

5.7.1.3 *Developing Secondary Schools*

Africans in Central Nyanza could not wait for the government to establish secondary schools. So, they pressed the government to allow them to expand their sector schools into Secondary Schools. Omulo was a member of the first Ambira School committee meeting that proposed the development of Ambira Secondary School in 1958.[248] This followed the recommendation of the DEB that also recommended the creation of Maranda and Onjiko Secondary Schools.

5.7.1.4 *Resourcing the People and Church*

The concern for sustainability made Omulo and pioneer Church leaders change from Owen's welfare approach to open enterprise in trade and farming.[249] African farmers looked up to Omulo and other priests, by virtue of their position in the society and the church, for direction. For in a KTWA meeting with Sir Cunliffe, Omulo and the clergy of Nyanza lauded the government efforts in improving African agriculture; however, they lamented:

---

246. Mbala, Personal interview, 11 August 2021.
247. Mbala.
248. Minutes IV, Proposal of a Secondary School, 25 July 1958.
249. Murray, "Archdeacon W. E. Owen," 656.

The maize and other crops which they advise us to grow are sold at low prices … Maize has no profit.[250] Therefore, we beg that the Government may see its way of allowing us to grow coffee, for it is a valuable crop.[251]

The regime granted their desire in the Swynnerton Plan, which Omulo took full advantage of, and grew coffee for cash. He encouraged Gem people to join in coffee farming and managed it through the farmers' cooperative in Yala. The Gem people, led by padre Nyende, had earlier rejected the regime's attempt on cotton, given that cotton's profitability was dismal.[252]

5.7.1.5 Managing Schism

The Anglican Church, the deanery leadership, turned to Omulo to help. He was in charge of the Ramula pastorate, when in 1958 the Johera group of clergymen, led a walk out of the Anglican Church to form the Church of Christ in Africa (CCA) (see §§5.8.2.1 and 5.8.3). Ramula was the epicentre of the crisis, and his Gem people were the ringleaders. He would minimise the impact of CCA, which was exploiting clan loyalty to win followers. Canon Osodo, then a teacher at Anyiko School, attests to how Omulo helped him stay in the Anglican Church after his entire clan and family at Uriri defected to CCA at the end of 1957.[253] He testifies that under threat of attacks and ostracization, Rev. Omulo's admonition made him remain faithful to the Anglican Church. Since Osodo was not ready to leave teaching for church ministry, he recruited Amos Otiang', then a cobbler at Yala, to serve their three families. Canon Otiang' as a lay reader rebuilt the Uriri Anglican Church from the ruins of CCA. Otiang' later trained and was ordained as a priest. He died in 2009 as a canon of the Anglican Church. The Anglican parish and school at Uriri in Gem now stand because of Canon Osodo and Otiang' under the

---

250. Anderson and Throup, "Africans and Agricultural Production." Observe the cost of maize supplied to the Maize Control at 4/90 per bag. But from January 1941 to June 1942 the average monthly price of maize sold by Africans at Kisii only once reached 4/90 per bag, while in Yala it exceeded this figure in only four of the eighteen months. The price of 8/96, which was introduced in January 1943, was far above the prevailing free market prices during 1941 and the first half of 1942.

251. Byrne, Memorandum of KTWA, 3.

252. Nyende, Interviews with Harry Reed, 25 September and 29 October 1973.

253. Osodo, Personal interview, 24 September 2020.

guidance of Omulo. For this resilience, in 2017 Osodo was made Canon of Maseno West Diocese.

5.7.2 CMS's Discernment for Action

Nyanza Archdeaconry served the four ecclesiastical districts of Maseno, Kisumu, Butere and Ng'iya, which CMS changed into the three districts of Maseno, Butere and Ng'iya in 1940.[254] African clergy were chairmen of each of the three districts: Ezekiel Apindi for Maseno, George Okoth for Ng'iya and Jeremiah Awori for Butere.[255] Once CMS enacted the 1944 constitution, it reorganised its operation units as pastorates.

5.7.2.1 Church Restructure

CMS increased the number of pastorates in Nyanza by subdividing these units into smaller pastorates. The padres headed the pastorate, with a Pastorate Council, to assist in their daily work and governance. For efficient action, CMS instituted the Pastorate Standing Committee to execute the Pastorate Council's decisions. To devolve power further down, CMS divided the pastorates into sub-pastorates, which stimulated activities at the grassroots level. Lay readers who were teachers or evangelists led the sub-pastorates. Each sub-pastorate had its council and a standing committee. Below the sub-pastorates were the group congregations responsible for several churches and congregations. The Group Congregational Council (GCC) governed them.[256]

The African Anglican Church established in 1944 (see §4.5.2.1) developed a hierarchy and order of governance.[257] The primary bodies were the pastorate, known as the congregation or the church. Underneath were the sub-pastorates and the group churches. They granted each level a measured authority in descending order to the lower levels, hence realigning the congregations of the Anglicans church. Each church in a group had three delegates in the GCC. But where small groups had three or fewer churches, four delegates from each church represented them.[258] Each council of a group had a chair

---

254. Nyanza Rural Deanery Council Minutes, 12 November 1940.
255. Nyanza Rural Deanery Council Minutes, 22–23 August 1945.
256. Group Congregational Council, 1943, DMN Files.
257. Omulokoli, "Historical Development," 327.
258. Nyanza Rural Deanery Council, Standing Committee Minutes, 17–18 November 1943.

and members from feeder churches, where issues were first dealt with before ascending the ladder.

5.7.2.2 Code: *Amri na Sheria*

To offer a foundation upon which the church was to run, Omulokoli posits, CMS instituted "Laws and Regulations of the African Anglican Church in the Diocese of Mombasa" (*Amri na Sheria* in Kiswahili) authorized on 1 August 1 1941.[259] These laws addressed pastoral issues focusing on baptism, confirmation, holy communion, and marriage. They dwelt on marriage procedures under the sub-themes of registrations, banns, and polygamy. Thus, they blended biblical injunctions with Anglican Church traditions, while accommodating the indigenous customs. Hence, in the *Amri na Sheria*, CMS attempted to empower her African staff to work in a unified way.

5.7.2.3 Clergy Terms of Service

The Anglican Church in Nyanza engaged a large army of paid and non-paid workers working with the few clergy in the pastorates. Omulokoli contends that the church had difficulties in paying padres and staff, for neither the bishop nor CMS accepted responsibility for the African priests.[260] The bishop insisted that unless the Africans had tried on their own to solve the problem, he would not aid them, even if he had the means. Omulokoli observed:

> Guarded approval was given to the suggestion to try it out to see regardless of whether it yielded the promised results. In recommending it to the church, both Owen and Stanway were not in favour of appeals for such funds or any other church funds being made to those considered "notorious backsliders." Nevertheless, this approach resulted in a balanced budget for the year 1945.[261]

During this period, the African Anglican Church attempted to define a formula for employing and training clergy. As the church established a pattern of giving and receiving resources, she set guidance on salaries for clergy and their terms of service and guidelines for retirement, known as

---

259. Omulokoli, "Historical Development," 329.
260. Omulokoli, 313.
261. Omulokoli, 317–318.

Kujiuzulu kwa ma padre, as well.[262] The guidelines demanded retirement, either at age fifty or after thirty years of church service, whichever came first. And subject to medical fitness, they would give the clergy an extra fifteen years, at the discretion of the committee.[263] However, a padre would have to take compulsory retirement at age sixty-five or after forty-five years of service, whichever came first.[264]

5.7.2.4 Literature

The church had important literature published and made available to congregations during this period. BFBS published, as Mojola notes, the complete Luo Old Testament translation in 1953, crowning the translation work by Clark of SDAM, Owen and Pleydell of CMS, and H. Capen of AIM (§§3.7.2 and 4.7.2).[265]

CMS and the church developed a course to instruct Christians seeking baptism in the book *Njia ya Uzima* (The Way of Life). They divided the book into three levels: *Catechism for Hearers* for six months, *Enquirers* for a year, and Catechumens also for a year. Stanway suggested binding the *Hearers* and the *Enquirers* manuscripts into the Catechumen's book because of the numbers requested.[266] In 1945, the dean reported Nyanza to have had 6,632 Enquirers, 4,522 Catechumens, 2,391 Baptisms, and 1,876 Confirmations, hence 15,421 were under the church's instruction.[267] In 1948 there were 6,000 Hearers, 5,858 Enquirers, 3,672 Catechumens. There were also 2,069 infants baptized, 3,221 adults baptized, 3700 confirmations, 21,137 communicants and 15,576 children in Sunday school classes. They confirmed 3,400 candidates in the first half of 1949.

5.7.2.5 Clergy Training

Bishop Beecher focused on training African leaders for the church. During his tenure, the Divinity School experienced rapid growth.[268] To continue

---

262. Omulokoli, 318.
263. Bewes, Letter to Stanway, 28 June 1945.
264. Omulokoli, "Historical Development," 319.
265. Mojola, *God Speaks in Our Languages*, 216.
266. Bewes, Letter to Stanway, 28 June 1945.
267. Stanway, Letter to Cecil Bewes, 29 April 1946.
268. Kagema, "Leadership Training for Mission," 117.

training the clergy, he worked with other Protestant churches such as the Presbyterian and Methodist churches. Beecher saw the

> Need to make provision for two types of instruction, there was first the teaching of theology which could be given inter-denominationally, and secondly there was the preparation for ordination. Here the responsibility for the form that such instruction should take lie with each of the co-operating Churches, whereas in the case of the former, the school would have authority to issue a certificate of Theology to all its successful students irrespective of their denominational affiliations. The school would have its own Board of Management.[269]

Bishop Beecher hoped that what was a temporary experiment between the three churches could move forward to a more permanent condition.[270] Hence, he asked the Board of the Divinity School that met at Limuru to agree to the following formal statement, which came to St. Paul's: "This Board rejoices at the possibility of working with the Presbyterian and Methodist Churches in East Africa to train African clergy."[271]

5.7.3 Interaction Between Reuben Omulo and the CMS on Discernment for Action

To explain the interaction between Omulo and the CMS on the discernment for action, this section uses musical metaphors as it refers to concrete human actors doing shared and embodied communicative acts before and among a specific audience. This implies performance, the term contemporary scholars such as Young, Hauerwas, and Wells, use to describe Christian existence.[272]

In assuming duty at the pastorate from Kisumu, Omulo was confronted with CMS churches and schools that were spontaneously created. They were unplanned and did not operate according to the norms of the CMS mission strategy that established churches from mission stations of Maseno Kisumu and Ng'iya in Central Nyanza.

---

269. Beecher, "African Education in Kenya," 11.
270. Beecher, 12.
271. Board Of Governors Meeting Minutes, 11 September 1953.
272. Young, *Art of Performance*; Hauerwas, *Performing the Faith*; Wells, *Improvisation: The Drama*.

The converts in Nyanza were not passive recipients of Christianity. They took part in shaping the message, as well as propagating Christianity, for Maseno students and their teachers introduced the church in the remote centres of the district. Explaining performance from an African standpoint, Ramose remarks: "Truth is simultaneously participatory and interactive. It is active, continual and discerning perception leading to action."[273] This resulted in churches led by people not versed in doctrine or CMS ecclesiastical tradition.

But the most incisive spread was the spontaneous response of the EARM members within the church. This transition triggered growth away from the mainline Anglican Church. There were factions within EARM, who, out of disaffection, left to form their own groups, saying, "I migrate with Jesus; I migrate from the church; I migrate from all secular councils."[274] Where possible, Omulo, in collaboration with CMS, encouraged them to stay in the Anglican Church, but where the cleavage was inevitable, they worked together to build fresh congregations.

Certain pastorate Christians, as Rev. Mwanda observed, preferred EARM's meetings to the Anglican Church's services and training.[275] Here was a classic example of a "jamming it up" performance. By using their own "instruments," the EARM members played that same melody, with variations, but kept the same frequency. Since they did not align the fellowship to any formal organization, they needed to maintain independence from any mission board or church denomination.[276] The EARM developed crucial lay leadership, with experience in planning revival conventions and supporting their members. They managed their finances as a fellowship, parallel to CMS or the pastorates, by instituting tithing for their membership. They called this collection, *Mfuko ya Bwana* (the Lord's bag) and used it to support members in need, hospitality, and funding mission conventions.[277]

There was a dissonance between Omulo, his people, and the CMS missionaries on the point of African education. The Beecher Report showed

---

273. Ramose, *African Philosophy Through Ubuntu*, 50.
274. Gehman, "East African Revival," 47.
275. Omulo and Mwanda, Ramula Pastorate Report, 3.
276. Amoke, "Musa Amoke Life Story," 7–8.
277. Mambo, "Revival Fellowship (Brethren)," 115.

most CMS missionaries aligned to the government's vision, as in the Beecher Report. Omulo and his people craved higher education for their children; thus they built secondary schools, not waiting for the government's promise or looking to CMS.

Omulo and CMS agreed on the spiritual state of Christians needing instruction and guidance, including lay-leaders and church leaders, the army of volunteers who supported the church. This wish for African church leadership enabled decentralization of the church through the creation of smaller ecclesiastical units and their assumption of more power than they had previously wielded. Insufficient indigenous staff managed pastorates or even trained the church leaders to run the churches.

The interaction between CMS and Omulo during this period was clear in the double interchanges of roles. Omulo served as the CMS missionary in charge of Kisumu but changed roles when he came into the pastorate under African leadership. Hence, he underwent a transition from leading to being led by the new African leadership. There is another interchange of roles. Omulo had brought Olang' to faith at Kisumu in 1929, opening him to Christianity.[278] Now he was submitting to Olang's leadership first as his Rural Dean, then as his Bishop from 1964 to 1970, swapping authority.

5.8 Reflexivity

This section on reflexivity explains how the adopters and the change agents reflected on the impact of their decision on the community in the period 1946 to 1970. It describes how each, Omulo and CMS, reflected on the result of their work and what they learned from their experiences. The section ends by discussing the interaction between Omulo's and CMS's reflexivity in areas where they agreed, disagreed, or collaborated.

5.8.1 Reuben Omulo's Reflexivity

This section discusses Omulo's progressing reflection during his work in the pastorate. Of importance is his conversion to EARM and seizing the opportunities availed by the change of government policy on trade and cash

---

278. Olang', *Festo Olang' An Autobiography*, 2.

crop farming for sustainability. It touches on how these changes influenced his ministry.

From 1918 onward Archdeacon Owen was Omulo's mentor, and in 1924 Owen trained him for ordination. Owen, writes Murray,[279] was ambivalent on spiritual matters but was keen to show faith in wider social problems, and was not inclined to pastoral ministry or evangelism. Omulo shared Owen's orientation as a student learns from his teacher. But Omulo came to value spiritual ministry during his pastoral service as a padre in Kisumu. The dire need in the pastorate made this experience invaluable for him. Like Owen, in the beginning, Omulo was cautious of the EARM's spiritual hubris, although they surrounded him both at work and home, and their lives affected him. However, his position changed during his pastorate service. It is possible to attribute this change to the freedom for personal reflection after Owen's death in 1945. It is plausible, however, that the EARM leaders' imposing presence in the pastorate, and in his life, made him more open to engaging with them. Considering that the EARM members formed the core of church membership and volunteer teachers, they could tilt his position on revival. Omulo appreciated the EARM's zeal for personal evangelism and commitment to the pastorate.[280]

Making the "Native Anglican Church" in Nyanza self-reliant was another major concern for Omulo and his colleagues. Depending on the missionaries, CMS espoused different approaches (§§5.3.2.1 & 5.3.3), to which Africans had mixed views. Owen, among others, opined that African clergy and evangelists, such as Omulo, must learn to be content with what their congregations afforded them from what they collected. Omulo adhered to this Owen-imposed anti-capitalist position for most of his service years, despite developing financial support links within CMS,[281] which Owen discouraged. He argued that the church should not be rich, implying that padres would get lazy with riches.[282] Remaining poor, in Owen's view, earned the church

---

279. Murray, "Archdeacon W. E. Owen," 656.
280. Reed, *Walking in the Light*, 12.
281. Nyanza Rural Deanery Council Minutes, 6 December 1944.
282. He praised Esau Oywaya for his sacrifice, upon returning from war-time services as a chaplain, of accepting only £30 a year as a pastor, after getting £96 per year with the armed forces. Oywaya, ordained in 1929, claims that his salary went down from eighty-five shillings a month to fifteen shillings when he left teaching at Maseno School to become a clergyman.

independence, besides shielding her from becoming a "capitalist" enterprise.[283] Hence, Owen propounded a self-reliant and buoyant church as the partner of self-reliance in secular affairs through KTWA. But Carey Francis, among others, held a unique position, which called on Africans and priests to be involved in enterprises of trade and farming of cash crops. From 1946, Omulo cashed in on the changed government policies towards African involvement in the economy (§§5.4.1.2, 5.4.2.2 & 5.4.3). Supported by the younger clergy and Christians who were not apologetic for capitalist enterprises, Omulo's change was complete, and he became an advocate of free African enterprise (§5.4.1.2).

5.8.2 CMS's Reflexivity

This segment evaluates the impact of the work of CMS mission, by discussing their experience establishing the African Anglican Church in Central Nyanza. It discusses how the choice of the Venn policies and the CMS missionaries' attitudes affected the African Anglican Church. It questions the effectiveness of the CMS approach to the church transition.

While the CMS missionaries in Nyanza were quick to create a self-propagating church, which to that extent was self-supporting, they were reluctant to allow it to be self-governing. CMS, adopting Venn's dictum, had critics who considered it disastrous for the local church. For instance, Neill postulates:

> The establishment of the "Native Pastorate" in Sierra Leone in 1860, with the complete withdrawal of the missionaries from participation in the affairs of the pastorate, inflicted on the Church a paralysis from which a whole century has not availed to deliver it.[284]

Whereas Neill blamed the delay for the independence of the Sierra Leone church on the sudden handing over to African agents, Bishop T. S. Johnson differed, contending that it retarded the church because of protracted missionary control.[285] In Venn's defence, Eugene Stock posits that Venn's Sierra Leone

---

283. Murray, "Archdeacon W. E. Owen," 667.
284. Neill, *Christian Missions*, 260.
285. He became the first Sierra Leonean bishop in 1937.

experiment was a qualified success.²⁸⁶ Hence, Venn could not answer for the way subsequent generations applied, or misapplied, his insights and policies.

Most CMS missionaries in Kenya were against diocesanization and spoke of "the very great danger of such policy in Kenya."²⁸⁷ By 1942, the Missionary Conference was still dominant, even starting an enquiry into the doctrine of the church, showing the power the missionary Standing Committee wielded until 1953. Farrimond asserts CMS missionaries neglected Venn's vision of ending the mission's control of the African church, for they had become agents of white domination.²⁸⁸ But diocesanization gained increased acceptance, as Hetherington points out:

> The period between the wars was characterized by almost universal support because it was necessary for Britain to stay in Africa, either indefinitely or until particular reforms had been achieved.²⁸⁹

The delay in preparing Africans for church leadership resulted in the worst schism in the Anglican Church in Kenya. Ong'ombe affirms that *Johera* refused to be silenced by the African church leadership but apportions blame for the schism to both the CMS European leadership and the new African church leadership, who refused to accommodate divergent African views.²⁹⁰ They probably did not adequately prepare the congregations doctrinally to withstand the schism of 1958.

5.8.2.1 *The CMS Reaction to Cleavage*

In hindsight, the 1957–1958 Anglican Church's cleavage should have been handled with much more grace. This schism, remarks Hastings, remains the "most considerable in scale and unlike any other separation this century."²⁹¹ For it wrenched from the African Anglican Church eight priests and one hundred and thirty congregations with 16,000 communicants.²⁹² And at the

---

286. Stoke, *History of the CMS*, 445–449.
287. Handley D. Hooper, Letter to Cash.
288. Farrimond, "Concerning the Development," 263.
289. Hetherington, *British Paternalism and Africa*, 154.
290. Ochola Ong'ombe, Interview with Nzioki, 30 July 1984, 181.
291. Hastings, *History of African Christianity*, 127.
292. Barrett, *Schism and Renewal in Africa*, 12.

time of its registration, the Church of Christ in Africa (CCA) had nine padres and was estimated to have 20,000 members.[293]

The tragic consequence of the schism, Baur proffers, was the rivalry between two factions of the EARM manifested in the confrontation between Bishop Olang' and Deacon Matthew Ajuoga.[294] This occurred at two levels: the subordination to ecclesiastical authority and the rekindling of ethnic animosity within the church.

The new African Anglican Church leadership resolved to bring all functions of the EARM under *Joremo*, being the larger and that to which the reputed clergy belonged. But *Johera*, under their leaders Mathew Ajuoga, Philip Okungu, Meshack Owira, Nathan Sila Awuor and Oganda, rejected the proposal.[295] For their disobedience, Rev. Peter Hawes, the new Rural Dean for Central Nyanza in 1956, judged them heretics. As a result, Olang' suspended Rev. Awuor. That was the first instance of insubordination.

In the second incident, Ajuoga undermined Bishop Olang's authority. Ajuoga's successful appeal to Beecher against the suspension of Rev. Awuor, who had been victimized for associating with *Johera*, divided the church's leadership. Beecher reinstated him, but it ruined the chances for reconciliation among the factions.[296] Besides, it fractured the relationship between church leaders in Nyanza and the diocese on one hand and Ajuoga and his groups on the other.[297] According to Nzioki, *Johera* continued to defy the church's draconian new rules, imposed to stop them from holding meetings or conventions. They were not to write to the Bishop in Mombasa either.[298]

Johera's third insubordination was in their encounter with Bishop Beecher in May 1957. Beecher cautioned the *Johera* leaders to stop "preaching their nonsense" and upheld the sanctions Olang' imposed.[299] A defiant and irate Ajuoga warned that the bishop would have been back in the UK with no church to dedicate if *Johera* and *Joremo* left the church.[300] In June 1957 Bishop

---

293. Ogot and Welbourn, *Place to Feel*, 56.
294. Baur, *Years of Christianity*, 482.
295. Nzioki, "Development of the Anglican Church," 168.
296. Pickens, *African Christian God-Talk*, 97.
297. Ogot and Welbourn, *Place to Feel*, 44.
298. Nzioki, "Development of the Anglican Church," 171.
299. Ogot and Welbourn, *Place to Feel*, 53.
300. Joseph Omollo, Interview, 26 July 1984, 171.

Beecher withdrew the licenses of Rev. Ajuoga and Rev. Owira and reported them to the police as insurrectionists,[301] claiming that, if they couldn't obey the Anglican Church, they should register their own society.[302] Ajuoga's disappointment in the Anglican leadership, as Pickens noted,[303] led to the catastrophic schism they had laboured to avoid.[304]

The rift widened with the 1955 appointment of Olang', a Luyia, as the bishop of Nyanza. The appointment raised concerns among the Luo priests because of the animosities between the Luo and Luyia Anglicans in Nyanza.[305] This went against what the Luo priests of the Central Nyanza deanery expected, who thought Olang', a Luyia, took an opportunity that should have been given to a Luo; for although he was a Luyia, Olang'clarified, "I had successfully hidden from the Europeans that I was in fact a Muluyia. I had passed myself as a Luo."[306]

In another account, Nzioki suggests, Luo priests feared being victimized by Olang'.[307] They had accused him of favouring the Luyia priests when he was the Rural Dean. The young *Johera* clergy did not accept it as mere coincidence, alleges Ogot,[308] that several Luo priests retired during Olang's incumbency. Olang' got Simeon Nyende (ordained 1930), Isaya Ndisi (ordained 1938) and Samuel Okoth (ordained 1924) to retire, while promoting Luyia clergy of the same age, for example, making Canon Esau Oywaya (ordained 1930) archdeacon in Eldoret and promoting Jeremiah Awori (ordained 1924) to canon and rural dean.

Even though the comparison seemed legitimate, older Luo clergy such as Omulo (ordained 1924) were still serving in the pastorate. Besides, Oywaya deserved his promotion, having served as rural dean in Nairobi from 1947 on and having requisite experience for the task. But because of the fewer

---

301. Joseph Omollo, 50.
302. Nzioki, "Development of the Anglican Church," 172.
303. Pickens, *African Christian God Talk*, 93.
304. Ajuoga, Interview with Nzioki, 169.
305. Ajuoga, 40, 41.
306. Olang', *Festo Olang' An Autobiography*, 14.
307. Nzioki, "Development of the Anglican Church," 167.
308. Ogot and Welbourn, *Place to Feel*, 38.

number of clergymen serving the North Nyanza Deanery,[309] it is plausible that Olang' kept the older Luyia priests in service to maintain mission momentum. Central Nyanza had a larger pool of priests to draw from for its many pastorates. Although these factors undermine the ethnic bias motive claimed by *Johera*, Olang's ethnicity remained a nagging issue that could have contributed to the schism that created the CCA.

5.8.3 Interaction Between Reuben Omulo and CMS on Reflexivity

While Omulo's and CMS's actions in the society led to transformation, reflection reveals that the impact of their actions was both positive and disruptive. This section uses a set of relational ideologies constructed by Lochhead, classified as hostility, isolation, competition, partnership and dialogue, to explore how the reflexive journeys of CMS and Omulo related to each other.[310] Were they changing in the same direction? In different directions? Or at cross purposes?

Omulo and the CMS went in different directions on resolving the complaints of *Johera*. This division within the Anglican Church disappointed Padre Omulo.[311] Omulo attended one of the banned *Johera* meetings at Maseno, seeking to understand their position, after which he advised the deanery leadership to dialogue with them. But the CMS-backed church leaders ran out of patience and brought down their entire ecclesiastical weight on them. Relating to *Johera*, the church acted in hostility, according to Lochhead's ideology, even though Omulo urged a dialogue relationship.[312] The leaders, Padres Ajuoga, Meshack Owira and Simeon Nyende (Omulo's cousin), and a majority of the congregations and communicants joining the CCA were from Omulo's Gem location. Among those who joined CCA were Omulo's three brothers, James Aweyo, Jason Wahore and Ateng' K'Owiti.

By trying to bring back *Johera*, Omulo and CMS acted in line with the partnership ideology as defined by Lochhead, where groups embrace one another, find a common interest, note their differences and similarities, and

---

309. In 1956 there were fifteen Luyia clergy in one rural deanery with eight pastorates. Omulokoli, "Historical Development, 407.
310. Lochhead, *Dialogical Imperative*.
311. Osodo, Personal interview, 24 September 2020.
312. Lochhead, *Dialogical Imperative*.

then forge meaningful cooperation.³¹³ During this schism, CMS and Omulo worked together to prevent the collapse of the church. While CMS backed the church leaders despite their error in judgement (§5.8.2.1), Omulo supported the leadership of Olang' for different reasons. He had brought Olang' to faith; besides, he did not support the Luo clergymen out of justice and fairness and refused to join his Luo and Gem clergymen in revolt. With the support of CMS, Omulo worked to rebuild the Anglican Church after the cleavage (§5.7.1.5).

Omulo and CMS were at cross purposes regarding the goal of the church's mission in Central Nyanza. Omulo worked to honour Luo and African customs within Christianity, thus undermining imperialism exhibited by missionaries. Their imperial inclination led to the CCA breakaway. In Lochhead's set of "ideologies," protagonists are in competition when they perceive each other as a threat.³¹⁴ *Johera* considered CMS and the Luo clergymen like Omulo, who disapproved of their actions, as a threat. Enmity characterizes such a relationship, manifested in negative rhetoric, observable in the cultural, as already shown, or ideological differences of clericalism.

Scholars discussing indigenous religious movements in the colonial era have imputed political motives of opposition to imperial oppression on the rise of CCA, in what has become the pattern.³¹⁵ According to Ogot, this schism emanated from the religious controversy emanating from Ajuoga's opposition to CMS's imperialistic leanings.³¹⁶ Although the CCA emerged against the backdrop of rising multiple non-missionary religious movements in Nyanza, these movements, according to Lonsdale, perceived the European missionaries as the auxiliary arm of the colonial government.³¹⁷ In that sense, Africans reacted against imperialism in the missionaries' actions.

Pickens dismissed Ogot and other scholars who attribute political motifs to the schism, arguing that it is an all-too-common reductionism of a more complex problem.³¹⁸ Pickens articulates Ajuoga's position that schism fol-

---

313. Lochhead, 24.
314. Lochhead, 24.
315. Balandier, *Sociologie actuelle de 'Afrique noire*, 417–487; Lanternari, *Religions of the Oppressed*, 19–62.
316. Ogot and Welbourn, *Place to Feel*, 40.
317. Lonsdale, "Political History of Nyanza," 350.
318. Pickens, *African Christian God Talk*, 30.

lowed the failure of African leadership to discuss doctrinal controversies, which festered and broke out at the height of the EARM.[319] The *Johera* narrative, maintains Pickens, emerged out of theological activity within Ajuoga's Christian experience.

The interactions between Omulo and CMS were characterized by their wish to see the church established in Central Nyanza. If the church had paid more attention to imperial, ethnic tendencies and embraced dialogue, a better outcome would have been ensured in the experience in the Central Nyanza Anglican Church.

5.9 Spirituality

As shown in previous chapters, a model differentiating between six types or streams of spirituality, as advanced by Cannon and Foster, is useful to explore the role of the spiritual dimension in the matrix.[320] For Cannon and Foster, these streams are not exclusive, for most believers experience their faith in terms of more than one of them. This section explains the spirituality that Omulo displayed in the period after WWII. It also describes the spirituality of CMS, explaining the spirituality that CMS missionaries practised and the dominant spirituality among them. The last part of the section explains the nature of interactions between Omulo and CMS on spirituality in this period, to describe where they agreed, collaborated, and differed.

5.9.1 Reuben Omulo's Spirituality

This period best showed Omulo's ongoing conversion experience into Christianity. Since he encountered Christianity at Maseno, Omulo had been moving towards a profound ideal through spiritual disciplines, whose purpose, according to Foster "is the total transformation of the person."[321] Through such disciplines (§§4.4.2.3 & 5.4.2), Omulo experienced a deeper understanding of the divine through meditation, prayer, solitude, and such other disciplines that he shared with other believers as confession, worship guidance and celebration.

---

319. Pickens, 61, 88–99.
320. Cannon, "Different ways of Christian prayer," Foster, *Streams of Living Water*.
321. Foster, 62.

5.9.1.1 Deeds of Justice

True service, according to Foster,

> indiscriminately welcomes all opportunities to serve" because all service is important. And this "rests contented in hiddenness... is free from the need to calculate results... can serve enemies as freely as friends... knows that the 'feeling to serve' can often be a hindrance... is a lifestyle... acts from ingrained patterns of living.[322]

The case of the milk boy O'kubasu *nyakwar (grandson)* Wadore is instructive of the value Omulo placed on education as a help out of poverty. Omulo intervened upon learning of O'kubasu's expulsion from school. The expulsion was because of an altercation between the headmaster and Wadore, protesting his grandson's heavy punishment. Omulo's plea to the teacher allowed O'Kubasu to be readmitted. He again pleaded with Wadore not to bar O'Kubasu from going to secondary school in Maseno.

Omulo explained, "Very well, he has known how to read and write in *Lunyore*. Now he should learn other languages, including English, with other boys from distant places at Maseno."[323] Wadore refused to allow him to go ahead, but his wife, in disagreement, sought the help of Rev. Omulo, who coming to Ebukolo, rebuked Wadore: "*Wadore ang'o marach kodi we nyathini osom?*" (What's the matter with you Wadore? Let the boy [go to] school?) This time, Omulo assigned a social worker, Margaret Ogolla *nyar* Maseno, to be the boy's guardian through the secondary school stage. Had Omulo not intervened on behalf of O'kubasu, he would not have completed school.[324] O'kubasu's grandfather was a Luyia neighbour of the Gem, who supplied milk to Omulo. O'kubasu lived with his grandfather in Ebukambuli, having lost his mother at age seven. He testifies that Omulo intervened three times to change the trajectory of his life for the better. Education is what Omulo wanted for his Gem children, and he wanted it for all, including his Luyia neighbours. He was patient with them and acted in humility to guide this one, O'kubasu, to an education.

---

322. Foster, 112.
323. O'kubasu, Personal interview, 16 August 2017.
324. O'kubasu.

In another instance, Omulo's spirituality was shown to have a justice dimension, in the land case of Odonde's family. At age thirteen, Mr. J. Odonde was orphaned, and Omulo asked to educate him. Odonde's grandmother was reluctant to let him go, fearing ill might befall him, but Omulo insisted that the lad would be more helpful to her with education than anything else. The grandmother yielded, allowing Omulo to hand Odonde over to missionaries at Maseno. He trained in music and could play any tune on the piano.[325] At Alliance High School in 1934, Odonde helped compose and develop hymnody for the African Anglican Church (§4.7.1.4). Upon returning to Ulumbi in the 1950s, Odonde found their family land occupied. During his absence, his mother had moved to stay with other relatives to avoid being alone. Omulo took his case to the Land Adjudication Court and litigated until they returned it to Odonde and his family.

Foster's description that true service builds community certainly applies to Omulo: "It quietly and unpretentiously goes about caring for the needs of others.[326] It puts no one under the obligation to return the service. It draws, binds, heals, builds. The result is the unity of the community."

5.9.1.2 Other Spiritualties

Omulo often rose early to pray, study the Scriptures and read books as a discipline. In prayers and meditation, done in openness and solitude, Omulo made space for something larger, for God transforming his life.[327] One time upon returning from farming, Leah Omulo found him still reading. She rebuked him in jest, saying "get off your books, go get your car, on which Ugenya women are drying their millet."[328] While at Yenga, Omulo's car had broken down and was abandoned at the vicarage, so the village women found it a convenient spot to dry millet before grinding.

Omulo invited his flock in the pastorate into this space of prayers. K'Ochieng' narrates how Omulo visited his grandfather, Ishmael Odhiambo, where he led them in singing "*Yesu kotaya pile orito a ma ng'uon*" (Safe in the arms of Jesus) then spontaneously prayed for them before inviting them

---

325. Ombaka, Personal interview, 10 August 2021.
326. Foster, *Streams of Living Water*, 113.
327. Foster, 30.
328. Alice Otieno, Personal interview.

to join in the Lord's Prayer.[329] He would encourage Christians in meditation through the hymn lyrics, his priestly prayers and encouragement from the Scriptures. Omulo used the Scriptures in his life and to correct his grown children. In a letter, he corrected them over their offending him:

> Ketho ariyo tek nono. Kendo kelo mana mirima to mirima ok en mar Nyasaye to oa ka saitani. To gima ok nikare en ketho, to Nyasate noketo yo achiel en yor lokruok kwom richo kaka Daudi e Zaburi 51:10. Yie ulok paro no obed paro maber manyanlo konyou Tito 2:11 mwe paro mae Tito 1:15.[330]

> Translation: It is hard to resolve two mistakes. And it only brings anger, which is not of God but from Satan. What is not right is sin, but God gave us one way, which is repentance, like David in Psalm 51:10. Please change your minds to good thoughts that can help you Titus 2:11 to leave the thought in Titus 1:15.

It was Flora Okonji's testimony that, while preparing them for confirmation at Ndiru pastorate in 1945, Omulo cautioned pregnant women not to steal their neighbours' vegetables or crops in farms.[331] The child will be born a thief, Omulo proffered, since one can pass traits to their unborn babies, hence he urged them to pass on only excellent traits.

Genuine pioneer work exposed Omulo's spirituality as devotional surrender when, at the advanced age of sixty, he sacrificed more in the field than expected. He continued to endure sacrifices in the mission field, where he could have lived comfortably in retirement in the home he built. His previous physical experience was horrifying: ill-health (§4.3.3.4), loss of his parents at same time (§3.3.1), loss of his firstborn (§4.3.1), and lack of means during his pastorate service. He could not have borne such challenges without divine help. When the church transferred Omulo to Yenga from Regea, Janet, his daughter, expressed her dissatisfaction at his accepting ministry assignments to remote places far from home. Awuor was impressed at Omulo's zeal for church service. At age sixty-five, he should have retired according to AAC's new terms. But he was still doing pioneer mission work, expanding

---

329. K'Ochieng', Personal interview, 23 September 2020.
330. Omulo, Omulo 1954 Diary.
331. Okonji, Personal interview, 28 December 2019.

the church mission where none existed. Awuor preferred he worked nearer home. Protesting, she wrote:

> Ok onego bed kamano eka in bende ionge kod paro ngima mari kaka onego iyud chiemo mari . . . Ibiro dok kendo echandruok kaka isechandori Ramula kod Lundha.
>
> Translation: Don't you worry about your life, how to get food . . . Are you going back to suffer like you endured in Ramula and Lundha?[332]

When he did not heed her protest, Janet Ogola[333] advised that he get a caretaker to make his meals. Once more, she persuaded Omulo to work near home and supervise his budding business. For her, the church pay was not worth risking an old man's life for. It was dismal and never paid on time, leaving one hungry.

Foster's depiction of an attitude of true service makes it appear difficult to achieve, but discipline allows it to work its way into our lives.[334] Humility will build and grow as one's practice becomes habit.[335]

In this regard, Joice Oginde described Omulo as follows:

> Omulo ne en ng'a ma muol kendo no winjo ji kata matindo . . . and na dhi ire ka adwaro batiso to ne an dhako maduong' to ne otisa . . .[336]
>
> Translation: Omulo was humble and accessible to all, even young people. I went to him seeking baptism; he baptized me even though I was an adult.

Through his experience of the EARM, Omulo displayed the spirituality of evangelical tradition. At Chulaimbo, Maseno in 1950, where an estimated 6,000 people attended the convention, Omulo was convicted by the Scripture theme of the conference, "God wants all men saved" which was drawn from 1

---

332. Ogolla, Letter to Reuben Omulo.
333. Ogolla.
334. Foster, *Streams of Living Water*, 111–112.
335. Carr-Chellman and Kroth, "Spiritual Disciplines as Practices," 33.
336. Joyce Oginde, Personal interview, 11 August 2021.

Timothy 2:3–4, and he got saved.[337] He joined in the fellowship of people he knew well, who had preceded him in the revival, who included Festo Olang', Apollo Ohanga, Samuel Ayany, among others.

5.9.2 CMS's Spirituality

Bishops Beecher and Olang', as leaders of the mission, expressed the dominant spirituality practised by the CMS in this period. The spirituality among them was mainly deeds of justice and compassion, but a liturgical spirituality also continued to be seen in the life of missionaries.

5.9.2.1 Deeds of Justice

The mainstay of CMS missionaries' spirituality was service as a spiritual discipline. Foster distinguishes between self-righteous service and true service, both of which were discernible among them.[338] The imperial leanings of the CMS missionaries cast aspersions on the motive of their service, thus making their impact ambivalent.

For instance, Bishop Beecher was a paradox regarding the race issue. While advancing the imperial agenda, he openly challenged imperial racism as well. In the Beecher Report, he reinforced the racial divide by keeping the Africans at the bottom of the pyramid to technical education. His report further limited African access to higher education to 26 percent, being useful for the imperial agenda. This expressed self-righteous service, which Foster notes, derives from human efforts, which are selective and without sensitivity.[339] The Report insisted on meeting the state's need, even when to do so destroyed the Africans' aspirations.

On the other hand, Beecher also undermined the imperial goal, both in the political sphere and in the church. In the LEGICO, Beecher declared: "If Europeans claimed to have an interest in the demarcation of African land, Africans should also sit on the White Highlands Board as interested parties."[340] While in the church he defended Olang' against white missionaries rejecting

---

337. Omulo by joining the EARM, was considered "saved," a term describing his conversion experience, as mentioned by Amoke, "Omulo's testimony," 4 August 1991; see §4.5.2.2.
338. Foster, *Streams of Living Water*, 112.
339. Foster, 112.
340. Richards, *Fifty Years in Nyanza*, 33.

his leadership who said: "I cannot have a black man laying his hands on my children's heads in confirmation."[341] Bishop Beecher rebuked them:

> My brothers, we have come to Africa to live alongside the African, to share our faith with him and to worship with him. If we cannot bring ourselves to meet with him here, we shall certainly have to meet with him in heaven. So, if you cannot accept him here in Kericho, it is time for you to pack and go home.[342]

In both cases, Beecher exhibited the spiritual discipline of true service, which Foster contends welcomes the opportunity to serve all without discrimination. For in these incidents, he served enemies as freely as he did friends. Following the Kericho incident, Olang' admitted, "I had no more difficulty in Kericho. People received me respectfully as their bishop and I often stayed most comfortably in the homes of the white Christians."[343] What was true of Beecher here was true of other CMS missionaries, who acted in care for the Africans' needs, even when that impinged on lifestyle, by not saddling them with the obligation to return service. In this spiritual discipline of true service, CMS missionaries bound, healed, and built a unified community.

During this period, Africans agitated to be free from British rule. To survive, the church appointed African bishops. The nationalism issue conflicted Olang', who was the representative of both the African Anglican Church and CMS,[344] for during the Emergency between 1952 and 1960, he faced African activists who rejected Jesus as a "white man's God". Olang' writes, "I was even accused of receiving pay for what I preached. The white man is paying you, they said."[345] He also experienced prejudice from certain missionaries who would not accept his authority as their bishop because he was black.[346]

But Olang' was emphatic: "We wanted to be free of the British too, but Christian could not turn against Christian."[347] Olang' expressed a spirituality of brotherhood that barred him from turning against Christian brothers,

---

341. Olang', *Festo Olang' An Autobiography*, 32.
342. Olang', 32.
343. Olang', 32.
344. Olang', 29.
345. Olang', 31.
346. Olang', 32.
347. Olang', 31

either of different races or ethnicity. His chaplain was the CMS missionary Rev. Richard Spurina and in Beecher, Olang' found a wise and faithful friendship he could always rely on.

5.9.2.2 Evangelical Tradition

Rev. Festo Olang' encountered revival preachers while teaching at Maseno School, during the missions which began in 1938. The revival teams preached about new life in Christ, leading his distinguished colleagues, such as Apollo Ohanga, John Onguko, Jacob Bwire, Samuel Ayany and Gawo, to join the EARM. He states, "one of my own pupils who did so was Hezekiah Oduwo."[348] Oduwo, in the 1940s, became an eminent team leader. Olang' was converted into the revival movement at Maseno in 1939. He asserts, "I came to see that the Lord was entering into my life in a new way."[349] It convicted Olang' of his sins of dishonesty. In repentance he paid back eleven shillings for the value of the stationery he took, for which Carey Francis the principal gave him a receipt.[350] Such action startled many, yet it was not unique to Olang', as other EARM members also confessed to crimes, paid restitution for stolen goods, and reconciled relationships. According to Reeds such actions of Olang' had a moral impact on society. He continued in the fellowship into his ordained years and remained in the main fellowship, *Joremo*.[351]

5.9.3 Interaction Between Reuben Omulo and the CMS on Spirituality

To explain the interaction between Omulo and the CMS on spirituality, exploring where they agreed, disagreed, or cooperated, this section uses musical metaphors. Explaining performance from an African standpoint, the CMS were performers whose service embodied communicative acts with an audience among the Luo people and before God.

Both CMS and Omulo espoused an "evangelical tradition" spirituality, in Foster's typology, which was clear in the revival movement. We can view this spirituality of revival as a melody performed first by the CMS, then joined

---

348. Olang', 13.
349. Olang', 14.
350. Olang', 14.
351. Reed, *Walking in the Light*, 12.

by Omulo and other participants. The interaction between Omulo and the CMS under revival occurred in church leadership. As CMS Bishop Olang's trip to Ceylon in 1957 endeared the fellowship to him, while he discovered its moral impact in the church leadership.[352] Hence, mission as improvision is sustained by spirituality. The notion of "performance" is an appropriate metaphor for mission since it is carried out in front of and among a particular audience. Besides, it involves concrete human actors, whose actions are shared and embodied communicative acts. It is thus possible to do mission as improvisation of the Christian performance of witness and service, on the nature and limits of contextualization and sustained by spirituality.[353]

Improvisation is remixing and performing the melody to resonate with the local context, which draws the audience into the performance. First, it was Omulo's spiritual leadership leading Olang' to faith in 1929,[354] and once revival came in the 1930s, Olang' preceded Omulo and later in 1950 welcomed him into the fellowship. Olang' in 1953 became Omulo's episcopal senior upon becoming a bishop. Bishop Olang' guided Omulo in the crisis of leadership struggle that pitched the priests against the laity in the revival's leadership fellowship. Although the priests were leaders in the church, the CMS adopted Olang's position of humility in service. We can understand this form of interaction as in a performance where, once receptors resonate with the melody of the performers, they improvise on the melody by "jamming" or remixing it.

If Christian existence is, as Hauerwas states, "from start to finish a performance,"[355] and if God is "a performing God who has invited us to join in the performance that is God's life,"[356] then we should view action against injustice by Omulo and CMS as their joint faith performance. And disagreements that resulted in schisms, as dissonant, for Omulo and the Christians disagreeing with their treatment (§§4.9.3 & 5.6.3) performed their own tune, different from CMS's.

---

352. Reed, 34.
353. Hauerwas, *Performing the Faith*, 79.
354. Olang', *Festo Olang' An Autobiography*, 2.
355. Hauerwas, *Performing the Faith*, 75.
356. Hauerwas, 77.

5.10 Overview of the Encounters

Upheavals in Kenya in the post-WWII era resonated with the changes in Central Nyanza society. This chapter considered the African agitations for a better future, which compelled the government's hand to institute reforms that benefited the population. These were a wide range of changes touching on economic, social, and political issues that affected the church as well. The shift in economic policies in the post-war setting opened opportunities for Africans to take part in trade and cash crop agriculture. But Africans rejected the education reforms of the Beecher Report. They continued demanding greater access to education and called for quality higher education for Africans. In the political sphere, Africans replaced not only the missionaries as their legislators in the LEGICO, but the government also stepped up their numbers. Those reforms, which started with providing for direct election of their representatives, culminated in independence in 1963.

For fear of being saddled with the outrageous government policies, CMS strained to delink itself from the colonial state and to work for African independence. The CMS continued to win the diocesanization process, as seen in chapter 4, which began with indigenization and which brought into the mission service many Africans as priests and as teachers. It was in this period that CMS made the church independent, by creating structures of the pastorates and allowing it to be governed by Africans. But the church remained part of the Anglican communion.

This chapter discussed both Omulo's and CMS's mission praxis, utilizing the seven elements in the praxis matrix, in the transition period that led to the establishment of a robust Anglican province by 1970. It explored the establishing of the African Anglican Church into an independent and self-governing church of the Anglican communion. It examined the challenges the new church encountered in staffing and the breakup that divided it, discussed Omulo's transition into the pastorate and focused on his agency as a padre and community leader of significance, and explained his developing mission praxis in a changing Central Nyanza context. The dominant types of spirituality were evangelical revival spirituality and deeds of justice, manifested in Anglican Church leaders such as Omulo being members of the EARM.

Exposed in this chapter are the ironies of the EARM. While the EARM, through its zealous evangelism, increased the membership of the church, injected spiritual life in the pastorates, and became a reliable source of both human and financial resources, it became the springboard of controversies attending the tragic 1958 schism in the Anglican Church in Central Nyanza. EARM was the ground on which church teaching (catechism) was entrenched in the pastorates, whereas the movement forced theological debates that dominated the church around that time.

The chapter also considered the intersection between Christian faith and tradition on marriage issues such as polygamy and divorce on which the church had to pronounce itself in Lambeth resolutions.

CHAPTER 6

Theological Reflection

6.1 Introduction

This chapter discusses select issues emerging from the encounters analysed in chapters 2 to 5. The list of the lingering issues facing the Anglican Church in Kenya is not exhaustive. I chose the following themes for final reflection: African agency in mission, mission praxis, translation of the vernacular text, the gospel message, and being an indigenous church. In this chapter, I reflect theologically on each of these issues, thus addressing questions about forms of mission praxis that continue to affect the church that emerged in Central Nyanza in the period from 1905 to 1970.

6.2 African Agency

We credit CMS missionaries with starting the Anglican Church in Central Nyanza, while the evidence adduced in this study reveals the critical contribution of African agency. This study has shown (§§3.3.3 and 4.7.2.1) that when CMS began its Nyanza mission in 1905, it depended on European missionaries, but that they were too few to meet the demand for workers. First, CMS turned to Ugandan converts but later deployed Maseno students to bridge the personnel gap. Faced with a further decline in personnel and resources during the post WWI period, CMS made drastic policy changes from their Eurocentric missionary approach, to draw invaluable mission personnel and resources from the Africans. It was a drastic change for the CMS missionaries because, due to their paternalism, they had delayed implementing Venn's indigenous Church ideal, which they held to theoretically from the start. But after WWI they had no option. As the numbers of European missionaries dwindled, CMS increased the number of Africans deployed, both in pastoral and mission service. In that period, Omulo transitioned from teaching at Maseno School to heading a CMS mission station at Kisumu (§4.5.1.3). To merge gains from indigenization, where they engaged Africans as priests and missionaries, CMS progressed to creating independent dioceses, organised into pastorates under African leadership. Such initiatives required fresh impetus and new personnel to succeed, which the East African Revival Movement (EARM) provided (§5.5.1.1). The EARM, through its zealous evangelism, increased the number of members of the church and injected spiritual life into the pastorates, thus becoming a reliable source of both human and financial resources.

While Willis credits the entire work of evangelization and education in Nyanza to the Luo convert teachers,[1] this study showed that ordinary people in a mass movement, which was spontaneous and non-clerical, did the bulk of the work (§3.8.2). It was spontaneous because no mission officials planned it. The young Africans, Maseno students, became evangelists who built schools and churches in their own homes, resulting in a mass movement to Christianity.[2] Wright discovered that his new converts in Kisumu gathered men, women, and children together to teach them the gospel in the vernacular. Involving African agency spurred a spontaneous growth of schools and multiplied the number of Christian catechumens (§3.8.2).[3] According to Pleydell, over two hundred catechumens a day would join at Maseno, such that by 1918 Nyanza had 5,706 of the 11,534 catechumens in the entire Diocese of Uganda.[4]

The ACK should latch on to the point Willis argued: "Not only must Africa be evangelized by the African but . . . every native Church must be built up by its own sons."[5] McGavran's position rejects the characterization of mission as

---

1. Ogot and Welbourn, *Place to Feel*, 24.
2. Anderson, *Church in East Africa*, 34–45; Pirouet, *Black Evangelists*.
3. Fredrick H. Wright, General Letter, 4 February 1914, 2.
4. Pleydell, "Mass Movement in Kavirondo," 133.
5. John J. Willis, "African Church in Building," 37.

comprising education, evangelism, medicine, famine relief, world friendship, etc., without a focus on the disciples' witness.[6]

Besides being spontaneous, the movement was also non-clerical. As this study has shown, lay Christians evangelised Nyanza during the inaugural (1905–1920), indigenization (1921–1945) and independent (1946–1970) periods. Clericalism, compatible with Church of England tradition, which placed little weight on the priesthood of believers, would have locked the laity out of missions. In Uganda, observes Gehman, the church leadership came under the Christian chiefs.[7] Although the church being under chiefs led to exponential growth, as the entire tribe became Christian through the chief's conversion, it established in the minds of Africans the association of church service with authority, which made the laity subservient. The CMS considered creating an elite group of Christian leaders out of chiefs' sons in Kenya. They envisaged training Luo chiefs' sons at Maseno School and using them to lead their society to Christianity,[8] but the fact that the colonial government recruited Maseno students as civil servants thwarted that endeavour. Besides, the pace of the spread of education and the egalitarian doctrine preached by the CMS missionaries rendered the approach futile.[9]

I attribute the collapse of clericalism in Nyanza at that early stage to ethnic competition and the spread of the EARM. First, strong chieftainship did not exist among the Luo. They were organised in clan segmentary units, which were forever multiplying out of jealousy and competition with each other. The inter-clan competition made each clan develop its own institutions to prepare their members for opportunities within the colonial government and not the mission.[10] Thus, by taking the elite out of church service, evangelism was left to the laity. As a result, converts who were not clergy carried out evangelism along ethnic lines, an approach that not only delivered Christianity into the hinterland but justified establishing the Anglican Church along ethnic lines. However, exploiting segmentary unit competition was a tragic irony. It exposed the weakness of a Church Growth missiology (theory and practice),

---

6. Fanning, "Church Planting Movements," 3.
7. Gehman, "East African Revival," 49.
8. Willis, "Reflection in 1949," 51.
9. Ogot, "British Administration," 255.
10. Onyango, *Gender and Development*, 97–98.

in that it encourages fast church growth on an ethnic basis, without realizing how that often lays the foundation for later ethnic-based clashes and schisms (in churches as well as in politics). Besides, it raises the theological question of the relationship between unity and mission.

Secondly, the EARM "reaffirmed the responsibility of the laity in the church."[11] According to Taylor, the movement emphasised individual witness as the most important aspect for its members.[12] So, the EARM created an indigenous church structure in which Christian communities were organised in clusters around a household head, who may be a senior teacher, civil servant, or a Christian of means.

Given a choice between empowering laity or clergy for evangelism, the ACK should bank on the laity, for the reasons adduced in this study. While Kagema argued that "Evangelization cannot be fully achieved if there are no trained people to carry on the task"[13] and suggested that the success of the ACK Evangelism Decade would depend on the ability to train her leaders, the clergy or pastors.[14] McGavran differed, propagating a "spontaneous expansion of churches" because it links expansion with growth points among the people.[15] Such growth points remain unbroken when people become Christians. Expansion does not depend on outside help, only on training. Such people's movements characterized by group decisions, argues McGavran,[16] is the natural way of growth throughout most of history around the world.

6.3 Mission Praxis

Multiple mission praxes became evident during the inaugural, indigenization, and independence stages of creating an African Anglican Church, reflected in the symbiotic encounters discussed in chapters 3 to 5 of this study.

---

11. Gehman, "East African Revival," 49.
12. Taylor, *Growth of the Church*, 102.
13. Kagema, "Leadership Training for Mission," 69.
14. Kagema, 70.
15. McGavran, "Church in Every People," 184.
16. McGavran, 178.

6.3.1 Evangelism

During the inaugural stage, the CMS missionaries' mission praxis was dominant as they set up Maseno School (§3.7.2). But this study has shown that Africans built most of the schools and churches. Converts mimicked the missionaries by building, deep in their villages, their own schools that also acted as churches. Nyanza depended on its own resources.[17] After WWI, CMS reduced her direct involvement in evangelism by focusing on stabilising the mission institutions such as schools and hospitals through their specialised staff. Besides, CMS sought the colonial government's financial aid to run them. During the period of indigenization, Omulo showed fresh insights into his mission praxis. He transitioned from teaching at Maseno to heading a mission station at Kisumu, where he developed his mission praxis in the *Dala* approach of K'Omulo, with an African orientation (§4.7.2.1). Omulo improved on the Anglican liturgy at K'Omulo centre, where he balanced Christianity's demands with traditional responsibilities. He contextualized and indigenized his faith by building on what he learned from CMS missionaries (§§4.5.1 & 4.8.1).

In the independence stage, CMS avoided saddling the new church with the expenses of running schools and seized the government's offer to fund schools (§5.2.2). With the implementation of the 1949 Beecher Report, CMS handed schools over to the government under the District Education Board (DEB), allowing them to focus on the church. Again, the East African Revival Movement (EARM) played a key role in this period to ground the African church. Whereas EARM members entrenched the church's teaching (catechism) in the pastorates, the movement forced theological debates that dominated the church around that time. Olang' acknowledged that EARM wielded power in the Anglican Church during that period.[18] In the earlier periods, schools attracted people to Christianity. According to Anderson, *kusoma* Christianity, where people went to church *kusoma* (to read), was initially the main mission praxis.[19] The Christians adhered to teaching by evangelists, teachers and catechists, resulting in a formal faith that had a spiritual gap. However, according to Reed, the revival "changed irrevocably

---

17. Ogot and Welbourn, *Place to Feel*, 24.
18. Olang', *Festo Olang' An Autobiography*, 34.
19. Anderson, *Church in East Africa*, 111–112.

the Christian Church in East Africa; it made the Faith of Jesus its own, at home in an African homestead and city. Its beliefs and customs became part of the expression of faith that has lasted until today, even after the original fire has died down."[20] In their new approach the EARM, through team planned strategy, held conventions that were spontaneous and informal.[21] These comprised their public witnessing. Africans bore the task, while missionaries supported them from behind the scenes. The conventions, when localized, were attended by about two hundred people, but when national they were attended by thousands. The CMS made the church independent and re-structured how the dioceses were organised into pastorates, installing Africans in governance, although this church remained part of the Anglican Communion.

We have lauded CMS mission methods for the success of the mission among Luos. However, the evidence adduced in this study revealed more factors that led the people in Central Nyanza to accept Christianity. There was creative tension between the Luo tradition and Christianity, which was evident in the interaction between the mission praxes of Omulo and the CMS. The previous three chapters have shown how religious and non-religious outliers in Central Nyanza shaped the mission interaction and the understanding of the Christian message in significant ways.

For instance, Omulo's Gem people decided on embracing the Europeans before they arrived in Nyanza. Given the grounding in Luo religious customs and resolute unity among the Luo, Mr. P. H. Clarke was pessimistic that the Luo would become Christians, saying, "I know these people (the Luo), and I tell you frankly you must not expect to see any sort of result of your work for at least 10 years."[22] Willis' dialogue with the Kisumu Roman Catholic priest in 1904, with a Sunday congregation of some forty people, is revealing. Enquiring if those were Luos, the priest promptly replied: "Luo? not one. They are quite hopeless. You might as well attempt to convert sheep."[23] But what made Gem people of Central Nyanza, and Omulo's father, accept Christianity was the admonition of diviners inspired by *Juok* and *Nyasaye*. *Juok*, now regarded as

---

20. Reed, *Walking in the Light*, 13.
21. Reed, 32.
22. Willis, "Reflection in 1949," 39.
23. Willis, 39.

demonic, was their guiding light to Christianity (§3.4.1). According to Ogot,[24] some *jobilo* (Luo diviners) foretold the coming of the Europeans emerging from the sea, and advised the people against showing hostility to them lest they incur the wrath of the ancestors. The Luo interpreted Hobley's punitive expeditions as the wrath they were to avoid. Hence, the Luo people welcomed the Europeans, cooperated with the administration, and expected great things from "the white man." The prodding by the seers explains why Luo people converted in droves when CMS established a mission in Maseno. We can liken the diviners to the Magi, who used their knowledge of stars to find and worship Jesus (Matt 2:1–12).

The promise of prosperity in the colonial regime drew the Luo people to Christianity. To embrace mission, therefore, was indicating acceptance of the imperial regime. CMS was to the Luo a means to that goal, while that embrace motivated missionaries to engage the Luo as "civilising" agents. The offer of education was of mutual interest to Omulo's people and CMS. While CMS used education for evangelism, Omulo and his people saw it as new opportunities for advancement proffered by the colonial order. The demand for schooling led to a literary revolution and a quick spread of Christianity among the Luo.

6.3.2 Translation and Vernacular Liturgy

CMS focused on the translation of the Scriptures and the liturgy to reach the soul of the Luo. By translating the Bible and developing valuable liturgy and teaching material in Dholuo, CMS missionaries grounded the converts in their new faith, bridging the past with the present. With more vernacular Scriptures available, many Christians read them and came to know God for themselves. The translation and development of liturgy and teaching materials continued throughout all three periods (§§4.7.2 & 5.7.2.4).

Some important issues emerged concerning translation. For instance, most historians attribute the translation work to Pleydell and Owen, among other missionaries, yet this research has documented the vital involvement of Omulo and other converts in vernacular translation work (§4.7.1). Willis attempted to understand the Luo worldview and infuse it with scriptural meaning, in order to proclaim Christianity. He acknowledged belief in God

---

24. Ogot, "British Administration," 249.

as a common ground between Africans and Europeans, and found significant good in Luo religious life, but sadly exposed his imperial prejudice by choosing what to accept among the Luo beliefs.[25] Because they did not pay adequate attention to Luo beliefs, the CMS missionaries ended up imposing new terms on the Luo Christian lexicon, like the translation of the term Holy Spirit.

CMS missionaries translated "Holy Spirit" into Dholuo, within the framework of translating and understanding God. Mojola observed that, while translating God in the Luo Bible, the translators grappled with how to translate the term "Holy Spirit."[26] Some translators preferred *Roho Mtakatifu*, the Swahili translation for the Holy Spirit. The Swahili word for Spirit is Roho, which is derived from Arabic and related to the Hebrew *Ruach*, while *Mtakatifu* is the Swahili word for holy. Meanwhile, the Luo Catholic translation settled for *Muya Mahagios*, which is Holy Breath (*Muya* means breath or steam and Mahagios is transliterated from the Greek word *hagios*, meaning holy). However, CMS popularized *Chuny Maler*, which meant clean heart. They used variant translations among the central Luo people such as the Acholi (*Cwiny Maler*) and the Adhola (*Chuny Maler*). In Luo culture, *chuny*, the heart, is the site of a person's intellect, ethical emotions, and wisdom,[27] to be distinguished from the physical heart (*Adundo*).

Despite the incongruence of using *Chuny* (heart), where a word for spirit (*juok*) existed, the translators reached a compromise among themselves, to introduce a new term, *Roho Maler*.[28] Missionaries introduced this alien term into the Luo vocabulary, which was useful for Christian purposes only. So, translating the Holy Spirit in Dholuo as Roho Maler contradicted Owen's translation technique, which was to prevent a pidgin Luo from emerging.[29] This was a paradox, for while claiming to avoid creating a jargon unique to Luo Christians, the translators did exactly that. By coining the term Roho Maler they were developing a *"Dholuo mar Kitabu"* (Luo of the Book). The term has now been in the Luo Christian lexicon for over a century. Thus, having been "Christianized," it gained theological and doctrinal momentum,

---

25. Willis, Annual Letter, 24 November 1910.
26. Mojola, *God Speaks in Our Languages*, 218.
27. Ocholla-Ayayo, *Traditional Ideology and Ethics*, 52.
28. Mojola, *God Speaks in Our Languages*, 218.
29. Mojola, 217.

so that Mojola doubts whether coining a new term, however exact, would be acceptable.[30]

In the Luo context, while introducing "Roho" aided the spread of Christianity, it distorted the basic structure of the Luo understanding of deity. By expunging *Juok*, the Luo Christian lexicon was impoverished. Although a word for spirit, *juok*, existed in Dholuo, just as in English, it is puzzling that the translators introduced a new phrase the Luo had to learn. It is a further puzzle that Omulo did not correct the missionary translators on this issue. *Roho Maler* was not only an alien term; by using it for Holy Spirit, it obscured the converts' prior core understanding of deity. The ACK cannot and should not shy away from mending this tear. For a Luo setting, we need not fear calling the Holy Spirit, *Juog Nyasaye* (God's Spirit), therefore knowing God in terms of Spirit (*Juok*) (§6.5).

6.4 The Luo Gospel Message

The Christian message responded to both the spiritual and social needs of the Luo people. The previous chapters explained the impact of CMS's mission approach on the African Anglican Church. The theological question to ask is: What did the Christian gospel say to Omulo and the Luo people as they transitioned from African traditional religion to Christianity in the era of colonialism? I suggest the gospel spoke to them in an eschatological tongue, whose message addressed their immediate life issues and the hereafter. The gospel message of the Kingdom of God spoke in a language of justice on earth and life everlasting in heaven.

6.4.1 Gospel of the Hereafter

In the inaugural stage of the church, Willis centred his preaching on God: "Nyasaye in heaven where we are all headed" (§3.6.1).[31] To Willis, the African did not understand the Christian hope of "the life of the world to come,"[32] but he saw the possibility for introducing the gospel,[33] "for the Luo was acquainted

---

30. Mojola, 217.
31. Willis, "Reflection in 1949," 43.
32. Willis, 49.
33. Willis, 49–50.

with the notion of life after death long before hearing the message of the Christian Gospel."[34] Willis thus integrated their knowledge of life after death with the doctrine of the one God and the eternal Son of God (§3.6.2).[35]

Because the Luo were concerned with the ultimate destiny of the soul or of humankind, the eschatological hope had significant meaning to them. The gospel of Jesus answered this quest for a new home in heaven, an *Injili mar dala mawendo* (gospel of the new home). The Luo recipients of the message were animistic, whose cosmology comprised three worlds, the sky, the earth and the underworld.[36] But Ocholla-Ayayo explains the underworld within the concept of *Juok*, where humans exist in two worlds: the world of the living, the upper world, *piny man malo*, and the world of the dead or the world of the spirits, *joma Piny man mwalo*.[37] These two worlds are alike in many respects (see figure 12).

The Luo gospel listeners found clarity about the hereafter in the Gospels. Omulo and the Luo people were not passive about the gospel message preached among them. Apart from teaching and translating the Scriptures into the vernacular (Orawo, Omulo and the Maseno students), they read and heard the gospel in the vernacular and believed it. CMS espoused a faith that emphasized believing and confession, which produced many nominal Christians. Those Christians came to faith for reasons other than spiritual ones, mimicking prayer, and Scripture reading, but without experiencing a deeper transformation.

However, what the first converts heard during the inaugural and indigenization stages spoke to the immediate challenges of colonialism, thus resulting in the *Kusoma* gospel. Maseno students came out as Christian converts, but without believing.[38] Being a Christian for them meant knowing the Bible, preaching like the missionaries, behaving as prescribed, singing Christian hymns, having one wife, reading, and not drinking beer or working on Sundays.

---

34. CMS Report, 1911, 64.
35. Willis, "Appeal to the African," 33.
36. Ogot, *History of the Luo-speaking*.
37. Ocholla-Ayayo, *Traditional Ideology and Ethics*, 171.
38. Wright, General letter, 30 August 1910.

Theological Reflection

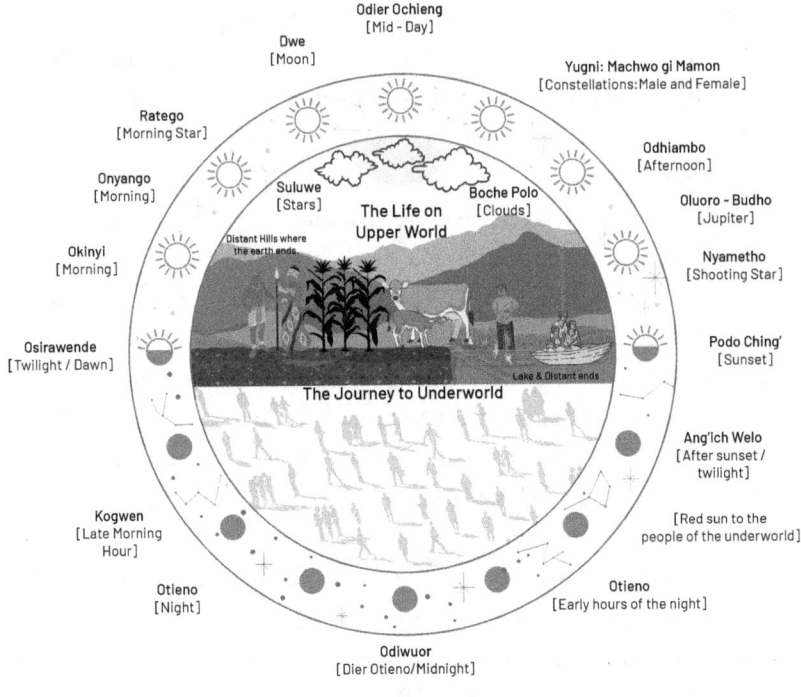

NOTE: We can note in the Luo Phylosophocal thinking, life is conceived as a continuity. Natural objects such as the sun, the stars and the moon can be utilized by man, i.e., the Luo system of naming, the wayconstellations are used to determine season, periods of rain, of cultivation, of harvesting.

Figure 12: Chart of the Traditional Luo Universe[39]

In response to this, innovative Christian movements emerged within the Anglican Church (chapters 4 and 5). The main ones were the Roho and the East African Revival movements. While the Roho adherents formed their own denomination, CMS integrated the Revival movement within the Anglican Church (§§5.5.3 and 5.9.2).

Apart from the East African Revival Movement, which was sanctioned by the CMS and spread across east Africa, there were other unique expressions of Christianity that rejuvenated the waning Anglican Church. According to Gehman, they affirmed their faith in the doctrinal teaching of the church learned at catechism but focused on particular biblical truths which eluded

---

39. Adapted from: Ocholla-Ayayo, *Traditional Ideology and Ethics*, 171.

many official priests.[40] The EARM stressed a puritan gospel whose message forbade alcohol drinking, smoking and adultery. EARM, in their preaching, cautioned against such statements as: *Jakong'o idong'* (drunkard you are stranded) and *jachode idong'* (adulterer, you'll be stranded) and instead preached hope in Christ.

The message of the gospel and the challenges it presented to aspects of Luo culture, especially about life after death, became a linchpin for the present societal order. They stressed that one entered bliss in the next world on account of one's life before death, and hence justice in the world mattered. Ocholla-Ayayo observed that, for the Luo, life now and life after death were alike.[41] That is why they used expressions like *Chieng' wanarom; Tel idhi maknwa piny* (We shall meet again; proceed and occupy the land for us).

This philosophy shaped the Luo's ideology and ethics. It inspired the Luo laws that valued honesty, dignity, generosity, and frankness in a case. Ocholla maintains that the Luo based their morality on metaphysical beliefs, but their ethics were rationalistic.[42] Ocholla notes that immorality implied disgrace, but also a sin, since it jeopardized the spiritual welfare (*chira*) of the family, village and clan of the community. But with certain misdeeds (*kwer*) the rationalistic and absolutistic value of the ethics had gravity.[43] So, drawing from this knowledge and their readings of the Gospels, the Luo Christians developed not only a message of the coming Kingdom but also new ethics to govern their lives as a people of God's Kingdom in this world (§§4.5.2.2 & 5.6.1.4). We should understand their reaction to colonialism and injustice from this premise.

6.4.2 Response to Colonialism

Christian converts in Nyanza interpreted the message of Christianity in justice terms, and as a spiritual response to their context. Omulo and the Luo people confronted European imperialism on two fronts: The colonial administration and colonialists within the mission.

---

40. Gehman, "East African Revival," 52.
41. Ocholla-Ayayo, *Traditional Ideology and Ethics*, 42.
42. Ocholla-Ayayo, "Vyouj Cloveka a Jero," 209.
43. Ocholla-Ayayo, 209.

Some CMS missionaries, in their fight against the colonial authorities, found allies among the Luo, as this study has shown. Owen mastered his approach to serving justice for Africans by working with converts from Maseno (§§4.7.1.2 & 4.7.2.2). He believed that the colonial system had potential benefits for both the colonizer and the colonized. Thus, Africans should be aided to see the better side of colonial rule and not view it as mere exploitation. Owen[44] acknowledged the exploitative character of colonialism in Kenya but saw the possibility of harnessing its positive features, so that the state does not betray its imperial trust by promoting the interests of international or national capital over local African interests. Had not Omulo and his people protested the colonial policies, presented their memorandum to the colonial government for change, and formed YKA, the CMS approach to social justice would have been quite different. African action put a wedge between CMS and the government. CMS had to choose sides on the scale of justice. They were forced to weigh their Victorian worldview and the actions of the regime against the clear message of the Scriptures.

The negative impact that colonial policies exerted on the society examined in chapter 4 showed a raft of changes in Central Nyanza society during that period (1921–1945). Those changes affected the CMS too, as the government became more intrusive by regulating education, which was CMS's main missionary approach. Hence, the people of Nyanza protested, appealing for a reconsideration. But the Luo to adjust to survive. For example, CMS opted to support the Africans, instead of backing the colonial regime. CMS's key achievement on the side of African interests was negotiating the 1923 Devonshire White Paper (see §4.2.2). The paper made African interest the priority of the Colony, even though it slowed the pace of obtaining African independence. Against that backdrop, CMS and Omulo carried on mission work to set up an African Anglican Church in Central Nyanza. The ACK must also respond to the societal challenges affecting Christians today by demanding justice and fostering social advancement for her members.

In the intersection between Christian faith and Luo traditional beliefs, the missionaries held on to their Victorian worldview to "civilise" the Luo. In the inaugural stage, Willis attempted to understand the Luo worldview and infuse it with scriptural translation to proclaim a relevant Christianity.

---

44. Owen, "Empire and Church," 245.

He acknowledged belief in God as a common ground between Africans and Europeans, and found significant good in Luo religious life, but exposed their imperial prejudice in choosing what to accept among the Luo belief.[45] The CMS missionaries' reticence to the spirit world caused them to reject the Holy Spirit movement within the Anglican Church. Once the CMS dismissed the concept of *juok* and African spirits, it had to isolate the charismatic movement within the Anglican Church. However, Hoehler-Fatton observes that an indigenous charismatic Christianity, akin to that promulgated in grassroots *Gandan synagogi* in the late nineteenth century, had already taken root before the start of European missions.[46] So, when the Holy Spirit was manifested in the Anglican Church from 1912, it was an indigenous and charismatic Christianity.

Missionaries identified those who demonstrated the Holy Spirit as *Jo-Roho* (people of the Holy Spirit). The Roho members' experiences were similar to *juogi* (spirits) possession, hence the missionaries linked them with the *Lang'o* spirits, perhaps because the missionaries could not distinguish the Holy Spirit (Roho) from the indigenous spirits. For this reason, the missionaries criticised and rejected the Roho movement, to deter Anglican Christians from espousing the Holy Spirit. The indigenous spirit possession movements proliferated in Uganda, Tanzania, and Kenya in the latter half of the nineteenth century, which, according to Hoehler-Fatton, made the CMS missionaries reject the charismatic expression of faith in Nyanza.[47] For instance, during the nineteenth century, the Nyabingi cult of south-western Uganda whose leaders were women, "manifested a stylized trembling movement, ventriloquism and the ability to hold a dialogue with spirits in an esoteric language and falsetto."[48] Then, in 1914, Mumboism emerged in Central Nyanza, with a call to return to Luo religion. Mumboism and other such cults, which Anyumba associated with *juogi nam* (Lake spirits), erupted around the time, as did *juog Lang'o*, the spirits that possessed Luos in their fight with Nandi warriors, whom they vanquished in a series of bloody raids.[49]

---

45. Willis, Annual Letter, 24 November 1910.
46. Hoehler-Fatton, *Women of Fire*, 206.
47. Hoehler-Fatton, 72.
48. Hopkins, "Nyabingi Cult," 259.
49. Anyumba, "Historical Dimensions," 8.

European missionaries assumed the right to set the standards, and they ejected out of the Anglican Church those who had received the Holy Spirit. Owen, Pleydell and Leach rejected Anna Inondi and her colleagues, even though they considered themselves Anglican Christians.[50] Missionaries labelled them Jo-Roho (or Anti-Kristo), while Rev. Odongo Mango, their leader, contended they were *jogo mose yudo Roho Maler* (those who have revived the Holy Spirit).[51] Rejecting those who received the Holy Spirit was an act of coloniality. CMS missionaries had the example set by George Pilkington of CMS Mengo Uganda. Pilkington, having been baptized in the Holy Ghost, embraced the charismatic movement among the Ganda Christians, and promoted the filling with the Holy Spirit, thereby sparking the Ganda revival of the 1890s. The Ganda Christians experienced the Holy Spirit's power, which drove them to become missionaries themselves.

Anglican theology among the Luo must also concern itself with the traditional "last things": death, judgment, the intermediate state, heaven and hell. These religious views on the afterlife, as expressed in the Scriptures and based on Judeo-Christian faith, may still speak to the inner being of the Luo. For when the gospel teaching on human destiny is allowed to dialogue with traditional and contemporary African cultural ways of representing life after death, theology would address pressing issues among Anglican Luos. The theological reflection on the afterlife would provide a picture of the last things through the Scripture, and the church's teachings.

6.5 Indigenous Church: Theological Link with the Past

The Anglicans in Nyanza have had an affinity for the exotic and for European style in worship and architecture. Hence, it has faced the challenge of grounding the faith in African customs. Inherited church structures and mission policies continue to hinder the development of a creative mission philosophy, liturgical formulations, and a structural organization of the church.

---

50. Hoehler-Fatton, *Women of Fire*, 68.

51. Hislop corroborates this claim against his report: "A name came into use for those people who followed Lawi; they did not adopt this name themselves, but most people used it. The name was JO-ROHO MALER (a mixture of Kiswahili and Luo) meaning the people of the Holy Spirit." District Commissioner /North Nyanza/O/1 Report on the Disturbances, 2.

Omulo and fellow converts understood the missionaries not to have proclaimed a strange God. This made their transition to Christianity easier. And the vernacular Scriptures as God's words removed the ambiguity in the Luo religion. The Christian faith they proclaimed was complex in doctrine, such as the Trinity, which led to higher demands of adherents on morality, monogamy, and Western practices (§§5.6.2.3 & 3.6.1). And yet the Luo of central Nyanza chose Christianity over Islam, which was closer to African culture. Omulo was open to the new understanding of God that Christianity proffered, while noting the incongruences that ran against the grain of his Luo understanding. This made the God of Christianity as proclaimed by the missionaries a new entity, which they could not relate well to their past understanding. Omulo lived in the two worlds of the empirical and *Juok*, which is the transcendent world of spirit. The Western theology of the missionaries made peace with the Enlightenment (with its firm divide between the empirical worlds and the transcendent world or spirit world) and assumed a firm division between them, but Omulo experienced the transcendent world of *Juok* as an everyday reality, as the worldview and backdrop within which he experienced and interpreted the New Testament's message of the Triune God: Father, Son and Holy Spirit.

Adopting Nyasaye as God's name in Christianity, emptied of the *Juok* notion, had the effect of separating Luo converts from their entire history and heritage. It is inexplicable that Omulo did not correct Willis, Pleydell and Owen about the Holy Spirit while translating the Bible and developing the liturgy. Dismissing *Juok*, the African past, as demonic and rejecting the African charismatics, was the crown of coloniality. Omulo and his colleagues sought connecting ideas and practices that would link their Christian faith to their ancestral past, centred in the concept of God (*Juok*). Their faith, like cut flowers in a vase, had no link to their past. In his subversive reaction to missionaries' impulses, Omulo latched on to certain aspects of his Luo experience and reconfigured them in Christian terms. CMS missionaries' theology, being based on post-Enlightenment philosophy, conceived only one spirit, the Holy Spirit, whereas Omulo and the Luo people accepted the reality of a plurality of spirits.

Omulo's question, which Luo Anglicans are still asking, remains: "Does another God exist?" Since the answer is "no," the inexorable inference is to recognize the ethnic perception of the divinity, in this case *Juok*, and accepting the universal notion revealed through the Scriptures. By doing this, we set up a link, like Paul did for the Athenians who worshipped God as the "Unknown God" (Acts 17:23 NKJV). Paul related the Athenians' religion to Christianity, first through the deity they venerated, then through their createdness. Where God has not shown himself, human beings – out of the sense of God within themselves – build altars to worship "the Unknown God" (Acts 17:23. NKJV). Hence, humans can only worship God to the extent of God's revelation. Ratzinger wrote, "If God does not reveal himself man is clutching empty space."[52] And yet, we may never describe God in the same way to everyone, without recognizing their particular situation and experience. This God whom Paul preached to the Athenians as their creator – whom they were groping towards and, if possible, to find – was a critical link between Christianity and the Athenians. I view the link established through God and creation as a solid contact, as opposed to the process of Hellenizing or Christianizing African deities.[53] It is more reliable compared to using metaphorical terms regarding ancestors. What Paul declared of the Athenians, who defined God through their experience in their unique poetry, applies also to the Luo, who perceived God as *Juok* and Nyasaye. God did not cease being their creator when they gained fresh knowledge of God and of the means of salvation. For, even in their pre-Christian state, "He is not far from each one of us" (Acts 17:27 NKJV).

Omulo honoured the custom of venerating ancestors by giving his elder son the name Owiti, which was *nying juok ma kakwaro* (ancestral name). In the naming of children,[54] the Luo refer to the spirits (*juogi*) existing beyond the immediate life on earth. They believed dead parents or guardians passed on ancestral *juogi* to their progeny. Naming his son Owiti implied that Owiti, Omulo's son, acquired his grandfather's spirit because of the ancestral name of the *nying-Juok* (the name of Juok or the name of his parental spirits.[55] This suggests that, through the *juogi-kakwaro* (ancestral spirit), the living dead were alive in the family. Apart from that, Omulo gave each of his five other

---

52. Ratzinger, *Spirit of Liturgy*, 21.
53. Mojola, *Bible Translation and Culture*, 82–91; Okot p'Bitek, *Religion of the Central Luo*, 50.
54. Ocholla-Ayayo, *Traditional Ideology and Ethics*, 182.
55. Ocholla-Ayayo, 182–184.

children *nying juok mar chieng* (spirit names from the sun), thus linking them with *Juok* (§4.6.1.2).

Following Omulo's precedent, I recommend we recover the term *Juok*, and use it for Spirit. That is, change the translation of *pneuma hagion* in the New Testament from Roho Maler to *Juog* Nyasaye (God's Spirit). The concept of *Juok* should be the shards we pick up and piece together into a patchwork, a mosaic speaking of the ancient Luo experience with a new understanding of God's work. The conception of *Juok* is the existing tie between the Luo past and the present in Christianity. Not translating the Holy Spirit in terms of *Juok* reflected a worldview reticent to acknowledge indigenous spirits. For a postmodern Luo people seeking purpose in their spiritual past, Africa needs to grow biblical scholars who can translate and revise the biblical text from their vernacular. As Elly Gudo states, "Christianising Biblical terms denied local African communities' opportunities to use terms that could make them do theologies in vernacular."[56]

Since there is no culturally universal Christianity, we need to forge a Christianity steeped in local history and accustomed to different cultures. It is in Juok that God could become authentically Luo, expressing the form of local Christianity encouraged by Andrew Walls. Walls acknowledged African theological potential, since African theologians oscillate between the world of experience and the transcendent world.[57] We need not fear a deeply local Christianity, for when God became human, in our case, God became Luo. We should therefore allow Luo history and culture to frame our idea of God for a specific moment and place.

Some Luo people have discarded Christianity as "the white man's deceit." However, they can, as Omulo did, discover how to link their faith to their African past. This means piecing together that past with the present and showing the linkage of this faith with their heritage.

6.6 Conclusion

In this chapter, I have synthesised some key issues arising from the encounters analysed in chapters 3 to 5 and reflected on them theologically. These

---

56. Gudo, Personal interview, 22 October 2021.
57. Walls, "Expansion of Christianity," 792–799.

are issues of concern for the ACK today, as identified in the earlier chapters. The thesis suggested that the church should focus on empowering the laity as her agency for missions. Advancing the priesthood of believers may replenish the dwindling numbers faster than the present focus on clericalism. Mission praxis must reaffirm culture and speak to the core needs of the people. The church must avoid mimicking foreign mission approaches without contextual consideration, while affirming that they are part of a worldwide Anglican communion.

I have invited the church to consider restoring into the Luo lexicon some valuable terms lost in earlier translation. In formulating her message, the church ought not to let go of its eschatological message, with its double accent on God's heavenly kingdom and justice on earth. This chapter summarised my research findings on intricate issues in mission praxis during the establishing of the Anglican Church in Central Nyanza.

CHAPTER 7

Conclusion

Since this is primarily a historical study of the encounters between mission praxes, it does not focus on suggesting the way forward. But in concluding this work, I answer three sets of questions:

1. What are the issues this research could not discuss and hence what topics do I recommend for further study?
2. How do I evaluate the use of the praxis matrix in the study of mission, to determine whether the approach works well or needs improvement?
3. What has this study meant to me?

Apart from these responses, I will give a general overview of the research, highlighting the findings and appraising the research objectives. I end the chapter with an overall concluding statement of the study.

7.1 General Overview of the Research, Highlighting the Findings

7.1.1 Overview of the Research

This research looked at the mission dynamics in Central Nyanza by examining the transformative encounters between mission praxes that gave rise to the Anglican Church in Central Nyanza between 1905 and 1970. Using the praxis matrix, this study made an incisive analysis of the rich history over that period, whose findings the contemporary church can find helpful for her mission praxis.

In chapter 2, the research discussed Luo migration from South Sudan into the East African region and to the present settlement around Lake Victoria. This movement of people triggered ethnic conflicts, population displacement and the establishment of new settlements in the Nyanza region. The research explicated the forming of the Luo nation, forged through assimilation of the Bantu settlers they found in the Victorian gulf. Out of the disintegrating societies, new integrated ones emerged, developing oral traditions meant to explain the origins of the Western Kenya peoples. The Luo society found its societal cohesion from this formation process, not from a pure ethnic origin but from the ability to assimilate. Hence it is ironic that the Luo created an elaborate genealogy to prove the common origin of the Luo, while proof exists that they assimilated Bantu and other Nilotic groups within their society. During this period, the Luo did their first inculturation of the notion of God, by adopting the name Nyasaye.

Chapter 3 explored the mission praxes of Omulo and CMS for the period between 1906 and 1920, by means of the dimensions of the praxis matrix. The chapter identified the inaugural mission praxes during the establishment of the Anglican Church in Central Nyanza. It brought the two sets of praxis into a dialogue to explain the nature of their interaction during the emergence of the church.

Chapter 4 covered the indigenization stage of the church between 1921 and 1945. This was a time of major social upheavals, characterised by political changes that ushered in a harsh colonial regime. The chapter examined the impact colonial policies had on people in Central Nyanza, and how they responded to accommodate these changes.

Chapter 4 also explored the mission praxes of Omulo and CMS between 1921 and 1945. This was the period when CMS began indigenizing the church in Nyanza by appointing African leaders. Here Omulo improved mission school under the government recommendation of the Phelps Stoke Commission, which welcomed children from denominations other than CMS and from mixed ethnicities. This research showed the Luo people's response, initially by revolt and organised cooperation, between people and government. It was a spiritual response, which weaved faith and social action, the forerunner of a justice spirituality.

Chapter 5 highlighted the upheavals in central Nyanza in the post-WWII period, from 1946 to 1970. The church in Nyanza transitioned from the indigenizing stage to the independence stage, during which the church became an independent diocese with African leadership and organised into pastorates. The chapter centred on the mission praxes of both CMS and Omulo, using the seven elements in the praxis matrix, to show how they contributed to establishing, by 1970, an independent Anglican province within the Anglican communion. CMS mission praxis shifted in this period from schools to pastorate churches. Without enough workers, CMS turned to the EARM for assistance. The CMS continued to win the diocesanization process that began with indigenization, which introduced African padres and teachers who moved into the pastorates under African governance.

In chapter 6 this book discussed, from a theological perspective, some issues of concern for the ACK today, identified in chapters 2 to 5. These included African agency in mission, the preached message of the gospel and to the converts' ears, the challenges of translation and the link that Omulo made between his Christian faith and his Luo identity.

7.1.2 Findings of the Research

The founding of the Anglican Church among the Luo was not incidental but resulted from the mission praxis of CMS missionaries, which not only won converts but also organized them into churches. At first, such churches were under the missionaries' direct control, but they were later placed under the control of nationals. This research has not only shown the hitherto concealed mission praxes of indigenous Christians, in our case Omulo, but showed how intricately interwoven the mission praxis of the CMS was with the mission praxis of the converts, from the very beginning – and how those praxes constantly influenced each other.

This research noted that earlier studies acknowledged their inability to bring to the fore the voices of indigenous Christians. Missing from the discourse was the contribution of African mission agents to establishing the church, the pioneer generation of indigenous Christians involved in the emergence of the church in Nyanza. Focusing on the mission praxis of Omulo, a convert trained and recruited to serve in the CMS mission, this research has documented his work, which remained obscure, despite being known and acknowledged in the Anglican Church of Kenya.[1]

---

1. Provincial Unit of Research, *Rabai to Mumias*, 80.

This study explored how transformative encounters shaped the mission praxes that led to the establishment of the Anglican Church in Central Nyanza. The interplay between Omulo's and CMS's approaches to the Luo people revealed a creative tension between Luo customs and Christianity. It revealed how religious and non-religious outliers in their societies shaped the interaction with the Christian message in significant ways. For Omulo, it was an attempt to balance Christianity's demands with traditional responsibilities, and so situate the Luo in Christianity, while for Willis of the CMS, it was an attempt to penetrate the Luo worldview and infuse it with Scripture and "civilisation" to allow them to proclaim the Christian faith. Although Omulo affirmed the missionary teaching on polygamists, he differed with the missionaries' treatment by demanding that victims be granted more latitude and hence strengthened Christianity.

At the centre of chapter 4's discussion is Omulo's innovative mission, traced with the seven elements in the praxis matrix, when he transitioned from teaching at Maseno to heading the K'Omulo mission station at Kisumu. This was Omulo's effort to contextualize and indigenize his faith, building on what he learned from CMS missionaries. The research exposed Omulo's unacknowledged or suppressed mission praxis, his role in Bible translation and the development of a contextual liturgy. One example was his role in translating the Psalms and the development of Luo hymns, which grounded the church during the period between the world wars. Omulo improved on the liturgy, which had been translated earlier, to align it to the Luo worldview, creating new hymns and spiritual songs.

The study identified in Christianity a message distinct from its educational and social aspects, which attracted the Luo people. Even though the CMS mission started by using Europeans to evangelise the Luo, circumstances forced the extensive use of African agents. The findings of this research were that CMS began evangelising and educating the Luo, but that young African teachers, among them Omulo, did the actual evangelising work. Education, as the CMS's dominant evangelism model, could not have succeeded without the Africans' participation. Offering education mutually interested Omulo and CMS. While CMS used education for evangelism, education was to the Luo people a ladder to the new opportunities that the colonial regime offered.

This research has shown the critical role played by diviners and seers in the Luo people's decision to accept Christianity. For despite the CMS approach of Bible translation and inculturating action, the setting up of schools and Westernisation, Omulo's people of Gem had decided to embrace the Europeans even before they arrived. CMS only confirmed what their seers had prepared them to believe.

The research showed how CMS reacted to colonial atrocities by changing her policies to stand with the Africans against the colonial regimes. This included international lobbying that resulted in the 1923 Devonshire White Paper, which made African interests paramount and organised the converts into a pressure group, the Kavirondo Taxpayers Welfare Association (KTWA). Both Omulo and CMS, in responding to injustice, developed a justice spirituality, which became a key aspect of their mission praxis in that period. And through Owen, CMS refined its praxis of justice, which has become a hallmark of the Anglican Church in Central Nyanza. Those experiences helped both Omulo and the CMS missionaries realize the need for Christian involvement in justice matters as an integral dimension of discipleship.

This research picked out what Omulo saw in the CMS praxis, which affirmed what he already believed. That gave him grounds to link pre-Christian Luo customs with Christianity. Chapter 5 of this study discussed Omulo's transition into the pastorate and focused on his agency as a padre and a leader in the society, explaining his developing mission praxis. It also discussed Omulo's role at the intersection between Christian faith and Luo marriage customs such as polygamy and divorce, on which the church had to pronounce its position in Lambeth resolutions.

The dominant spirituality of the emerging Anglican Church in Central Nyanza was an integration of evangelical revival spirituality and deeds of justice, manifested in Anglican leaders such as Omulo being members of the EARM. While the EARM increased the number of church members, renewed the dwindling faith of many, and became the bedrock of both human and financial resources for the pastorates, the movement also fostered bitter controversies that led to cleavages in the church such as the tragic 1958 schism. The praxis of EARM raised fierce theological debates that dominated the church during this period, despite formally championing the church's teaching (catechism).

The book acknowledged the role of the laity in establishing the church and recommends empowering the laity for missions in the ACK today. It further advanced that mission praxis must reaffirm culture and speak to the core needs of the people, to avoid converts being like cut flowers dislocated from their cultural roots. It identified what it considers an error in translating the term Holy Spirit in Dholuo. It is recommended that the church restore the term *juok* into the Luo Christian lexicon and change it as suggested. The book recommends that the church should reaffirm the Bible's eschatological message, with its double accent of God's heavenly kingdom and justice on earth. If the origin was vital for their identity on earth, one's sure destiny should give confidence to the faithful about the concerns of life.

The research also explained how Christianity met the spiritual needs that the Luo religion was less able to fulfil. Chapter 3 discussed the Luo people's second experience in the inculturation of their deity, this time by CMS missionaries, when they presented the God in Scriptures as a Luo God Nyasaye. This convinced Omulo and fellow converts that the missionaries did not proclaim a strange God. The success in vernacular translation inadvertently diminished the dominant missionary role, as it elevated the role of local agents. The Africans believers picked up the vernacular Scriptures and soon became missionaries to their own people. Translating Christianity and availing the vernacular Scriptures as God's words removed the ambiguity in the Luo religion, making it easier for African agents to spread the gospel within their society.

In discussing the impact of CMS mission approach, chapter 4 identified a faith that emphasized outward believing and confession, which produced many nominal Christians. It also explicated the innovative movements that emerged in reaction to that nominal faith within the Anglican Church. The new movements represented unique expressions of Christianity that rejuvenated the church in Central Nyanza. They included the Roho movement and the East African Revival Movement (EARM). While the Roho members later formed their own denomination, CMS integrated the Revival movement within the Anglican Church.

7.2 Appraising the research objectives

The academic aim of this study has contributed to new missiological insights into setting up the Anglican Church among the Luo in Central Nyanza through:

- Documenting the unfolding mission praxis of Rev. Reuben Omulo, a Kenyan pioneer Anglican, as exhibited in his life and ministry.
- Using a praxis matrix to explore the encounters between CMS mission praxis and Reuben Omulo, this research has shown the value of this method in doing mission research.

Thoughts advanced in this study should allow the Anglican Church of Kenya (ACK):

- To have a clearer understanding of her mission history,
- To appreciate and reclaim the formative role played by Luo mission innovators such as Omulo and
- To rethink its present mission praxis by employing a praxis matrix.

7.3 Evaluation of the Praxis Matrix in the Study of Mission

I must now evaluate the efficacy of the praxis method for studying mission. The areas for scrutiny will include the praxis matrix, encounters, the choice of Reuben Omulo and the historical periodization.

This study has shown the value of the praxis matrix for missiological research. I propose this method for future missiological research. I found the praxis matrix helpful in guiding my research to ask who Omulo was, how he analysed his context, what his worldview was, how he interpreted Scripture, what actions he took, his analysis of the church and tradition, his reflection, and his spirituality. I also found the praxis matrix helping in guiding my research to ask who the missionaries were, how they analysed the context, what was their worldview, how they interpreted Scripture, what actions they took, their analysis of the church and tradition, their reflection, and their spirituality.

The praxis matrix allowed me to look at the presuppositions and prejudices of both Africans and Europeans, and to sense how those were affected by the missionary approach and their representations of African people. Most documents in the archives tell the stories from missionary and European perspectives, and hence show the dominant voices of the time. But through these encounters, because one can discern alternative experience, we can read, according to Kritzinger, between the lines; or behind the text; or read the text "against its grain" to hear the silenced voices or "observed" others, whose direct voices we do not hear.[2]

I am indebted to the CMS archives document at the University of Birmingham, which I pieced together like shards to tell a fuller story and present a bigger picture of the mission encounters. Sources such as letters, reports, registers, artefacts, and diaries provided evidence for my investigation. I found in the CMS missionary archives invaluable data that helped me piece together elements of Omulo's life, work and thinking that no documents written by African agents, church or himself availed.

Using the three-step process was an effective way of gathering detailed information about the Omulo and CMS praxes. This is the "encounterology" approach Kritzinger coined, which analyses two related praxes and the nature of the encounters between them (dimension by dimension).[3] It has four key components: the a) systematic study of the b) encounters between c) different praxes in a d) specific context. I meticulously pursued all four components, which allowed me to view mission praxis from multiple dimensions and angles. Hence, I could appreciate how different aspects of Omulo's and CMS's experiences, thoughts or actions were shaped. This is important to understand why they acted in a certain way. The overlapping aspects of the praxis matrix proved a challenge. I found it difficult in each of the seven elements of the praxis matrix to identify aligning events or actions in Omulo's and CMS's praxis for analysis or comparison. But where they aligned, the interaction between the praxes was easy to observe.

7.4 Issues this Research Could Not Discuss

There were issues noted in this research that the study could not fully discuss. These issues may be important in understanding the church and are significant for mission studies. I outline them in this section and make recommendations for further research on them.

---

2. Kritzinger, "Faith to Faith."
3. Kritzinger, "Faith to faith."

In the unfolding encounters during the different stages of establishing the church, this research noted several ethnic conflicts. Those conflicts led in some instances to the expansion of the church, but in most cases to cleavages and division. In some instances, it led to people leaving the Anglican Church. Both the leadership and the congregations were affected by those conflicts, for such disagreements undermined the gospel message. I recommend further exploration of the impact of inter-ethnic encounters on the growth of the Anglican Church in Nyanza should be conducted. Such was beyond the purview of this study.

The impact of colonialism was ever-present, yet nuanced, throughout the period of establishing the Anglican Church in Nyanza. The encounters in this research showed various ways Africans coped with or resisted colonialism, until independence *(uhuru)* finally arrived. However, the current emphasis on coloniality argues that, even though colonialism as a political-economic system has disappeared, many key features of that system persist in postcolonial Africa: "The actors change, but the script seems to be unchanged."[4] I recommend a missiological study to interpret and evaluate the history of the ACK through a decoloniality prism.

This research focused on the mission praxes that established the Anglican Church in Nyanza between 1905 and 1970. It would be intriguing to explore the mission praxis that sustained and expanded the ACK (now different dioceses) since 1970, to see which new encounters shaped its ongoing development.

The Anglican Church in Nyanza inclines toward keeping its inherited church structures and mission policies, which continue to affect the church's mission philosophy, liturgical formulations, and outreach in context. I recommend a study to evaluate how the present structural formation, in conformity with the Anglican communion, inhibits mission in the Kenyan context.

This study referred to the influence of Islam among the Luo but could not give attention to it. There are at least three reasons why Christian-Muslim relations in Nyanza should be researched. First, Islam was the first foreign religion to arrive in the region and it seems that it influenced the formation of the Johana Owalo Nomia Luo Church, which is usually considered a breakaway denomination from the Anglican Church. Second, the factors

---

4. Katongole, *Sacrifice of Africa*, 15.

that caused Maseno students, led by Jairo Owino, not to embrace Islam but Christianity need to be further explored. Third, there have been Luo Muslims in Nyanza since the nineteenth century and Islamic centres with Luo converts have endured to this day, which means that there is regular contact between Muslims and Christians among the Luo. I recommend a study to explore the influence of Islam on Luo people in Nyanza and how the nature of the encounters between Christians and Muslims impacts their relationship.

7.5 What the Study Has Meant to Me

In 2013, Pastor Tobias Otieno Ayayo (Omulo's nephew), called me to his home at Oyani Migori County and gave me several photographs of Omulo's experiences as a priest and of his visits to London, which Omulo had given him. He then stated, "Omulo had done significant work in building the church and establishing education in Nyanza. I want you to write his story for people to know what he did." I was overwhelmed with this charge, not knowing where to start. I finally decided to subject the life and work of Omulo to academic study, hoping to find enough information from the annals of history to construct his story. Although Tobias is not alive to receive what has come out of my study, I am relieved and fulfilled that I have been able to present Reuben Omulo and his mission praxis to the world.

I found my grounding as a Luo while doing this study. The research allowed me to establish a stronger connection to my ancestors than I had before, being Omondi son of Otieno, Otieno son of Omulo, Omulo son of Owiti, Owiti son of Oburu, Oburu son of Mijeni, Mijeni son of Jeje, Jeje son of Adhaya, Adhaya son of Ojuodhi, Ojuodhi son of Ragem, Ragem son of Ochielo, Ochielo son of Omolo, and Omolo son of Ramogi Ajwang'.

My family were among the early Christians, brought to faith through the first CMS missionaries to Western Kenya. My grandfather, Rev. Canon Reuben Omulo, joined the CMS mission in 1908 and was one of the students of Rev. J. J. Willis, a CMS missionary, later Bishop of Uganda (1912–1934). Omulo was his student, who then taught at Maseno and became one of the six from Nyanza to be ordained as Deacons in 1924. In 1925, CMS sent him to open an African Anglican Church in Kisumu.

This research made me discover myself as a pioneer missionary among unreached people groups. For the length of my service, I bragged about "pioneer ministry" – until I carried out this study. I identified with the first struggles of John J. Willis in Vihiga and Maseno, and with the pioneering work of Reuben Omulo in Kisumu and in the pastorate. I also identify with the tension of leaving the privileges of home and enduring hardship until a church is formed. Hence, I discovered myself to be in the line of God's pioneer missionaries, and that my work is completing what they began, not laying a new foundation. In my more than thirty years of involvement in missions among unreached peoples, I have developed into a referenced indigenous mission leader, with influence in mission and the church. I learned that my calling to missions is not my own but an extension of God's mission in Africa, carried out first through J. J. Willis, A. E. Pleydell, Reuben Omulo and many others after them.

Thirty years on, The Sheepfold Ministry (TSM) has established mission work with one hundred mission workers in the northern Kenya region, southern Tanzania, and Northern Mozambique. We chose areas where the church had very little impact, or where it had never existed, to carry out pioneering cross-cultural missions. Thus, we have inserted a Christian presence where no such contact had been made.

The Somali and Swahili people have been Muslim for over one thousand years. To expect them to flip faiths in just ten years would be untenable. Their culture and life have been so intertwined with their religion. We have therefore adopted a long-term strategy. There are areas where, in thirty years, we have seen no converts; but we have built bridges and laid foundations for future witnesses.

In the late 1990s, TSM had a tremendous opening in work among the Sakuye of Northern Kenya. Mzee Abagana, their local seer, foretold the coming of African preachers to their secluded community. Our two missionaries arrived during his lifetime. This field has seen a significant number of people turn to Christianity.

7.6 Concluding personal remarks

In my MTh research thesis,[5] I wrote about the significant contribution of nationals to mission work. In it, I aimed to bring their voices to the table of

---

5. Omondi, "Contextual Missiological Study."

missions. Continuing in a similar line for my PhD thesis, I wished to explore the contribution pioneer nationals made to establishing the Anglican Church in Nyanza. Hence, I chose the mission praxis of Reuben Omulo, a pioneer clergy, one of the first Christian converts in Western Kenya through the CMS, and one of the first six African priests to serve through CMS from 1924.

I integrated this study into my life's journey and identity. It is in line with what adult education scholar Stephen Brookfield proposed, namely that reflective practitioners research their assumptions by seeing practice through four complementary lenses: the lens of their autobiography as learners of reflective practice, the lens of other learners' eyes, the lens of colleagues' experiences, and the lens of theoretical and research literature.[6] He further states how reviewing practice through these lenses makes us more aware of the power dynamics that infuse all practice settings.

I am interested in how our (that is, Kenyan nationals') collective experience in missions can improve mission praxis within our changing context. The church needs to rejuvenate its mission work in Africa. This can be done only if we take note of – and give serious attention to – current contextual and missiological changes. Such a process should draw largely from the nationals' perspectives, which is what I strived to achieve with this book. It is what I will continue to strive for.

---

6. Brookfield, "Book Reviews."

APPENDIX 1

The Luo Migration

The Southern Luo

Scholars striving to explain the Luo of Kenya have focused on three major premises. First, earlier scholars, adopting a linguistic approach, classified the Luo as Nilo-Hamites. Lindblom,[1] Seligman et al.,[2] Baumann,[3] Crazzolara,[4] and Kohler[5] concurred with Evans-Pritchard's Nilotic-Hamite's categorization of the Luo. But modern scholars reject this categorisation, on the account of the "Hamitic hypothesis," which assumed African inferiority, that Edith R. Sanders exposed as a fallacy.[6] Safholm[7] opines, "it is certain that this name has been imposed on them"; Ocholla-Ayayo[8] also states that it has no meaning in Luo. In its place, scholars have embraced the term Nilo-Saharan. We classify the Luo in Kenya and Northern Tanzania in the Nilo-Saharan group of languages, found in Eastern Africa, areas east and north of Lake Victoria, spreading westward as distant as the Niger basin in Mali, West Africa. Nilo-Saharan, according to Greenberg[9] is one of the four groups of languages on the

---

1. Lindblom, *Use of Stilts*.
2. Seligman and Seligman, *Pagan Tribes*.
3. Baumann, *Die Volker Kunde*.
4. Crazzolara, *Lwoo*.
5. Kohler, "Die Ausbreitung der Niloten."
6. Edith R. Sanders, "Hamitic Hypothesis," 527.
7. Safholm, "Nilotic Religion," 232.
8. Ocholla-Ayayo, *Traditional Ideology and Ethics*, 14.
9. Greenberg, "Nilo-Saharan Languages."

African continent, others being the Afro-Asiatic, Khoisan, and Niger-Congo. The assumption of a common ancestral language connects the Nilo-Saharan languages, further to which Greenberg found a genetic unity when he proposed their classificatory study in 1963. In this classification, Mojola recognizes the Luo as the Western Nilotic language group, also called the "River Lake Nilotes," thus differentiating them from the Eastern (or Plains) and Southern (or Highland) Nilotes.[10]

Second, scholars preferred to classify the Luo with a term from within, and then resorted to the style applied by the German intellectual and linguist Wilhelm Heinrich Immanuel Bleek.[11] Bleek noticed the common use of the root term or stem–*ntu* among South African languages. Adding the prefix *Ba* to become *Bantu* meaning people, he coined the term Bantu to refer to the entire group of languages that use this term, or as Mojola asserts, "share significant grammatical, morpho-phonological, lexical and semantic features."[12] These scholars made the case for referring to the Luo people as *Jii*, meaning "people"; among them are historians such as Ogot[13] and linguists including Mojola.[14] Ogot accepts that the *Jii* peoples belong to the Western Nilotic language family.[15] By using the *Jii* term, he identifies the Luo in central Nyanza with those in southern Sudan. *Jii*, according to Mojola, include:

> The Alur, who live in the Okoro and Padyere counties of West Nile in Uganda and in the Mahagi District in Eastern Congo, where most of them live, the Acholi who live in Northern Uganda and on the border of Southern Sudan, the Ocholo (Shilluk) who live along the West Bank of the White Nile from Lake No where they had settled at Wipaco between 1031 and 1058 CE. The Luo who live in the Bahr el Ghazal Province of the South West Sudan who usually refer to themselves as the descendants of Podho, the Shatt or Thuri together with many offshoots in Bahr -el Ghazal: the Pari or Lokor in Equitorial

---

10. Mojola, *God Speaks in Our Languages*, 207.
11. Bleek, *Comparative Grammar*.
12. Mojola, *Utu, Ubuntu & Community*, 3.
13. Ogot, *History of the Southern Luo*.
14. Mojola, *God Speaks in Our Languages*.
15. Ogot, *History of the Luo-speaking*, 24.

Province, the Anywaa (Anuak) who call their country which is situated along the banks of the rivers in the Southern-East Sudan and West Ethiopia, Pach Anywaa; the Naath (Nuer) and Jieng' (Dinka) both living in Southern Sudan; the Padhola who live in Tororo District of Eastern Uganda; the Paluo in Bunyoro, and who live in Tororo District of Eastern Uganda; the Labwor in eastern Uganda, the Paluo in Bunyoro and the Luo who live in western Kenya and northern Tanzania.[16]

Thus, linguists and historians have not solely used the term *Jii* to refer to the Southern Luo but also to their kin found as far north as Southern Sudan and as far south as the North Mara Lake district of Tanzania.

Third, as the Luo migrated southward and encountered groups of different languages, they insisted on being called *Joluo* (the Luo people), rejecting other names given them. The word Luo has multiple etymologies as Ocholla-Ayayo contends:

> If we say the Luo, we often refer to the southern Luo people (the Kenyan Luo), or refer to the Luo language, or to the people we generally call Nilotes. But the words luwo, lupo, or luw, means to speak, to follow, or to come after. We can say Iluwo lep mane? This may be translated as "what language or tongue do you follow (speak)?" The term lupo also means fishing, luwo rech, to follow fish, or luwo dhako (riso) a party at the Luo marriage ceremony, which takes place after a woman has returned to her kin's home, with the riso ceremony following.[17]

Based on this linguistic evidence, the term *Joluo* comes from either the word *jolupo*, which means fishermen, or *luwo dhok*, meaning "following cattle." We would refer to those whose routine tasks involved fishing as *Jolupo*, *Jalowo* or *Janewo*.

Of the Western Nilotes, it is the group that moved to Central Nyanza, and dispersed from there to northern Tanzania, identifying themselves as the Luo people. Besides, dialects, language of operation, and national name,

---

16. Mojola, *God Speaks in Our Languages*, 207.
17. Ocholla-Ayayo, *Traditional Ideology and Ethics*, 14.

bind not only the Western Nilotic groups in Uganda but link them to their ancient kin in the north as well.

Cradle of the Southern Luo

In determining the cradle of the Southern Luo, scholars had relied on oral traditions and "the Nilotic cultural uniformity" with their relations in the Sudan. According to the oral tradition, Dino or Odimo the Luo leader, Dengdit the Dinka leader, Gilo of the Anuak and Nyikang leader of the Shilluk-Luo, together, migrated from "Dhowath" to their first homeland. Westermann relies upon the Shilluk folklore when he accounts for the Shilluk migration from their cradleland on the Bhar-el-Jebel in CE 1500 to their present home.[18] But Seligman depended on the manifestations of material culture, language, and head shape to show the origin of the Nilotes as east of the Great Lakes.[19] Springing out of "Dhowath" were two northward migrations of the people. The first were the Nuer-Luo and the Dinka, and the second, the Shilluk, Anuak, and then the Luo. But Crazzolara,[20] after evaluating traditional evidence and myths, suggests the land to the south of Lake No to be the cradle of the Nuer and the Dinka and the Luo groups. Crazzolara's account is plausible since the Nuer and the Dinka did not move far from this homeland. Instead, it was a fraction of Luo that moved northwards to become the Shilluk. The later groups broke away from them in intervals. They dispersed into divergent directions: Bor Belanda to the west, the Anuak to the east, while the Acholi, the Alur, the Palwo, among others including the Luo, migrated to the south.

It was this southward journeying group that got into contact with the Bantu and Nilo-Hamites. This study notes but contrasts with Roberts[21] preposition of link through "blood groups" of the northern Luo and those in the diaspora. Roberts stressed the frequency for a large array of blood groups for the Nuer, Dinka and Shilluk. He also acknowledges the genetic arguments of

---

18. Westerman, *Shilluk People*.
19. Seligman and Seligman, *Pagan Tribes*.
20. Crazzolara, *Lwoo*.
21. Roberts, "Serology and History," 302.

the blood group data to uphold tradition and myths of the common ancestry of the northern Luo.[22]

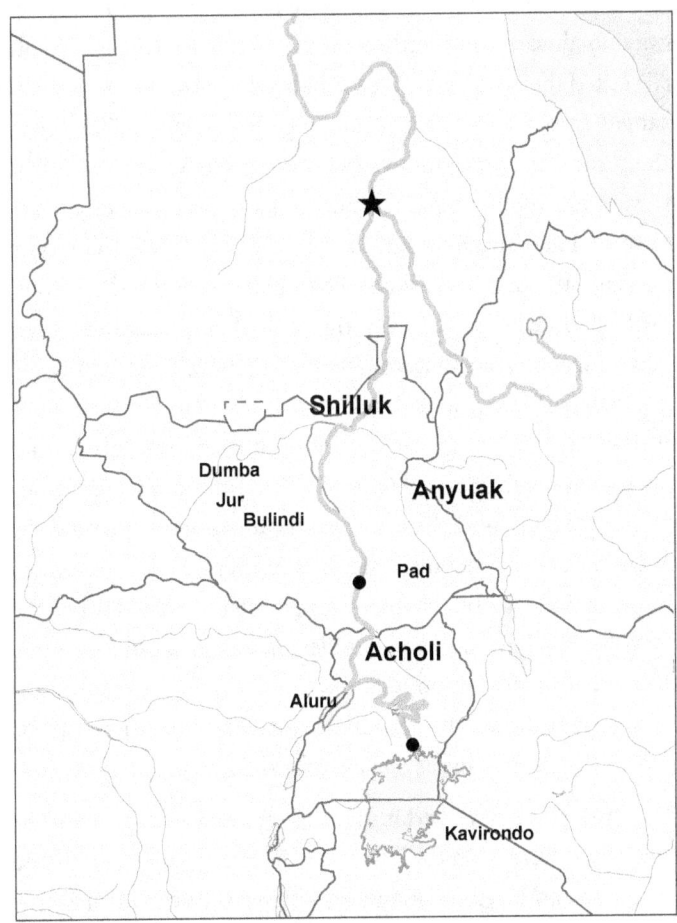

Figure 13: Luo Migration Path from South Sudan to the Lake Victoria Region[23]

Ogot situates the cradle of the *Jii* (western Nilotes) in the Upper Nile basin and to the west of the Bahr-el-Jebel in the Eastern Bahr-el-Ghazal region.[24]

---

22. Ocholla-Ayayo, *Traditional Ideology and Ethics*, 15.
23. By ShillukinUSA – Own work, CC BY-SA 3.0, https://commons.wikimedia.org/w/index.php?curid=22976055.
24. Ogot, *History of the Luo-speaking*, 23.

It is the territory of many lakes such as the Nyibor, Anyii, Yirol and Shabe, from where many groups of the *Jii*-speakers later dispersed. The majority migrated northwards and southwards, while the rest stopped in the original motherland. The Naath (Nuer)-Jieng' were first to leave, moving a scant distance away northwards and settling on the southeastern tip of Bentiu. This dispersal settled the proto-Jieng' at the Bahr-el-Ghazal Bahr-el-Jebel (White Nile) triangle, according to Ogot[25] occurring between about 500 and 100 BCE. While the proto-Luo communities (who landed by God Nam according to custom) went elsewhere to their south and east, perhaps along the Sobat or down towards Lake Turkana. But the proto-Luo left Jebel-Ghazal moving southwards about CE 85, to inhabit Shambland region. The second major cluster of *Jii*-people estranged from the proto-Jieng'-Naath between c. 500 and 100 BCE. Ogot[26] avers that we can break up the cluster into three groups along linguistic and geographic lines.

Ocholla-Ayayo attributes the Luo migration to the "great quarrel" as they turned towards the Bahr-el Ghazal.[27] The Nilotic researchers including Westermann,[28] Seligman,[29] Crazzolara,[30] and Ogot[31] confirmed this story through circumstantial details. Ndeda[32] enumerates the reasons for their migration to include the search for pasture for livestock and water, unending conflicts within the Luo clans and families, and external aggression. Internal factors were the increase in population, the stress on the environment, and natural disasters, such as famine and diseases. Eric Baker notes the external aggression of the Ethiopians as a trigger for the Luo dispersion:

> The Ethiopians have certainly conquered various parts of the Sudan at different times. In the fourth century, they conquered an ancient and civilised kingdom which has its capital at Meroe near Khartoum. In recent times, in 1888 King John of Ethiopia

---

25. Ogot, 23.
26. Ogot, 24.
27. Ocholla-Ayayo, *Traditional Ideology and Ethics*, 15.
28. Westerman, *Shilluk People*.
29. Seligman and Seligman, *Pagan Tribes*.
30. Crazzolara, *Lwoo*.
31. Ogot, *History of the Southern Luo*.
32. Ndeda, "Nomiya Luo church," 93.

and in 1901, a raiding party of Ethiopians was reported to have come as far south as Karamoja.[33]

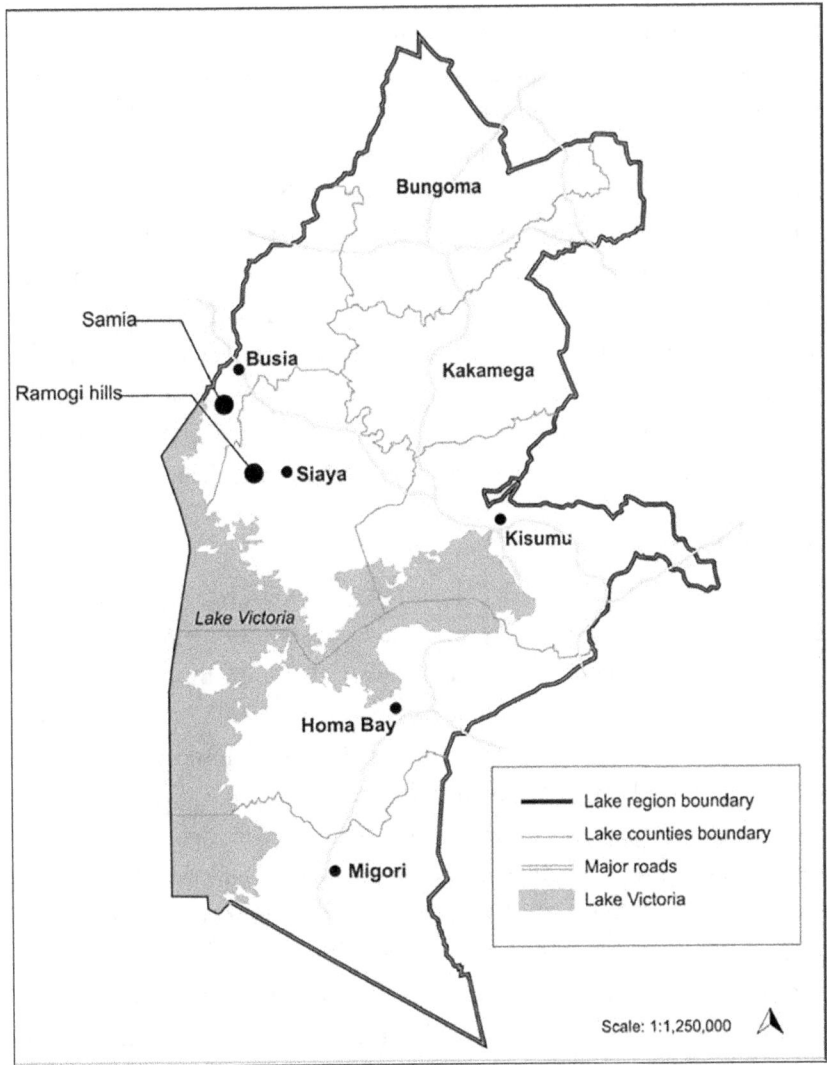

Figure 14: Luo Migration into Central Nyanza Adapted from Ndeda[34]

---

33. Baker, *Short History of Nyanza*, 7.
34. Ndeda, "Population movement."

With these compounds of factors, southward migration was unavoidable. Ocholla-Ayayo observes, out of the major Luo groups in southern Sudan (Shilluk, Nuer, Dinka and Anuak), the first fracture groups shifted eastwards to Ethiopia, while others went further west towards Chad, and the last groups migrated southward to northern Uganda.[35] Ogot notes that historical records show the southern migrations developed from four primary groups: the Acholi, Paluo, Alur and Padhola.[36] From here they panned out in two directions: the Acholi, and the Busoga but arrived in Nyanza in four waves.

The first Luo group to migrate into a Central Nyanza were the Joka-Jok. Then the Owiny group (Jok-Owiny), in a second wave, followed the Joka-Jok into Alego. The Ugenya-Omolo group was in the third wave and sojourned in Alego. But the Gem-Omolo proceeded south into Yimbo, where they tarried for three to four generations. Four other independent clusters: the Kano, Sakwa, Asembo and Uyoma, came in the fourth wave and settled in the Uyoma peninsula after a brief stopover in Alego. By the early eighteenth century, the Southern Luo clusters had arrived in Central Nyanza.[37]

Joka-Jok (Joka-Juok)

Ogot estimates the arrival of the Joka-Jok in Western Kenya to be between CE 1490 and 1517.[38] Following the Nile from southern Sudan, they went northward to the land of the Shilluk. Some settled along this route, which is clear from the linguistic communities living across these vast tracts of South Sudan. From the Shilluk land more groups journeyed towards the east and south, travelling through Anyak towards Acholiland and Padhola in Uganda. They found an open plain of savannahs like those of southern Sudan. Some took up residence there, while others continued their southward journey. The group that settled in the Pajok region triumphed and set up a minority Luo rule over the local Madi people. Meanwhile, the journey to Western Kenya began from Acholiland in northern Uganda, led by Ramogi Ajwang', the Luo warrior elder. Ndeda[39] notes that it was the largest migrant community on

---

35. Ocholla-Ayayo, *Traditional Ideology and Ethics*, 16.
36. Ogot, *History of the Southern Luo*, 38.
37. Ogot, *History of the Luo-speaking*, 34.
38. Ogot, 485.
39. Ndeda, "Population movement," 93–94.

record. Their course took them between modern-day Bugwere and Mbale, towards modern Tororo and the Teso region. Crossing the River Sio, they entered today's Samia at Bukangala. The Luo migrants made Ligala in Samia their first settlement in Western Kenya and lived there for three generations.

A part of Joka-Jok, the Jok Owidi sub-group, stayed in Samia and established a settlement they called Kisumo. But the majority continued their journey to the Ramogi Hill at Kadimo. The river Yala borders the area to the east, and the Yala swamp to the north, and Lake Victoria to the west. It has a fertile stretch of grassland for grazing Joka-Jok livestock. The elevation of Ramogi Hill, like a watchtower, provided secure spots to sight any invader. At the Ramogi Hill, the Luo established the Kadimo Empire and their first permanent settlement in Kenya Luo in the early 1500s.

Joka-Jok comprised the Alego, Seje and Nyinek clans. From Ligala they spread to Got Ramogi in Yimbo and later to Alego. Following protracted disagreements, Joka-Chwanya (a sub-group) moved across the Winam Gulf to South Nyanza, and as Ochieng[40] notes, one group occupied Asembo, Gem and Sakwa. The eighteenth century saw new Luo migrants in Uyoma, forcing a section of Joka-Jok to Seme, Nyakach (in Kisumu County) and further out to South Nyanza and Tanzania. There are two clan clusters of Joka-Jok who moved into Western Kenya:

1. The Pajok clan cluster: Alego, Nyakach, Komwa, Konyango, Kagwa, Kano, Ramogi and Kanyinek.
2. The clans that left from Alur land were: Kanyala/Nyangori, Kanyikela, Karabuor, Kayadoto, Kamot, Kagan/Kowino, Kamageta, Kajulu, and Komenya.

In three generations after the arrival of Joka-Jok, the Luo people had spread from Ramogi Hill into various corners of the Western Kenya region. They inhabited the territories to the north and south of the Lake Victoria gulf, hence neighbouring Abaluiya and the Nandi to the north and Maasai, Abakuria and Gusii to the south.

---

40. Ochieng', *Outline History of Nyanza*, 23–25.

Jok-Owiny (Joka-Owiny)

The second wave of Luo migration took place between 1590 and 1670, from Western Uganda. At the time Joka-Jok were moving from Acholiland towards Western Kenya, the clusters of Owiny-Padhola and Omolo groups moved further south to Busoga (in Bukoli) region. Jok-Owiny established strong links to the people of Northwestern Uganda, the northern margins of Bunyoro. According to Ndeda,[41] Jok-Owiny travelled along the western borders of Mount Elgon, through Mbale and Tororo, to arrive at Padhola from Pubungu. Having settled in Busoga for some generations, they spread wide and mingled with their hosts.

A few lineages from Bukoli moved westwards into Central Busoga where they organised several principalities, known as the Mukama movement. But the majority departed from the east or northeast in three clusters: the Owiny, Omolo and Padhola clans. At the time they were establishing themselves into sizeable communities in Bukoli, Jo-Kajok had settled in the Samia-Yimbo region.[42] Later, out of Busoga came two major cluster groups of Owiny and Omolo, with the Owiny group leaving first, followed by the Omolo groups. The Owiny-Padhola groups moved to Samia, where they settled for a generation. The Padhola, in a reverse migration, settled in the present-day Padhola, where both Luo and Ateker migrants from the north joined them.

But towards the end of the sixteenth century, Jok-Owiny began their movement into Western Kenya in two groups. Cohen and Atieno-Odhiambo[43] observe that these Bukoli groups came into Nyanza through the south and central Busoga in Uganda, the humid savannah, and the dry grasslands of eastern Uganda to the higher areas of Kakamega District. First, the Adhola group settled in Padhola (Uganda). This group moved across Samia-Bugwe, imposing their rule on the Bagwe, who referred to them being conquerors as Karuoth (royal clan). Second, the group led by Owiny moved southwards to Samia. Owiny died at Bakangala in Samia. It was his grandson, Owiny Sigoma, who led the group from their sojourn in Samia to their new settlement in Sigoma Alego in the Nyanza. Jok-Owiny clans were the Karuoth, Kogelo, Kanyigoro, Kanykwaya, Kanyakwar, Karapul, Kakeny, Kajwuodhi,

---

41. Ndeda, Population movement," 94.
42. Ogot, *History of the Luo-speaking*.
43. Cohen and Atieno-Odhiambo, *Siaya: The Historical Anthropology*, 18.

Kowili, Kadimo, Ndere, Kaluo, and Kadhola. Ochieng' names the progeny of Owiny to be the Kadimo, Kowil, Wanyenjra in Yimbo, Kogelo, Karuoth, Karapul, Kanyabol and Agoro found in Alego, the Kanyakwar in Kisumu and the Kamot and Konya in Kano, Kisumu County.

According to Ogot[44] Jok-Owiny followed in the footsteps of Jok-OJok, into the Samia, Yimbo and Alego regions. A generation elapsed during their journey between Budola and Alego. Alego had become the gateway of the immigrants into the region. The region experienced political turbulence, during which the earlier inhabitants got subjugated, assimilated, and driven out in the wake of the Luo incursion. But the Jok-Owiny exacerbated the political tensions at their arrival. A real conquest of the region had begun. The Owiny clans fought over the region to gain political dominance, but this proved difficult. As a result, three of their clans moved southwards to Yimbo, whereupon they set up their own state of Kadimo. It marked an era of Luo expansion history in Nyanza with aggression and conquest. The newcomers not only impinged on the territory of the Bantu people but also on areas occupied by the earlier Luo settlers. A power struggle soon festered within Jok Owiny group, forcing a split in the Samia-Bunyala area, and as Odinga[45] notes, Gwaga (Owiny Sigoma's cousin) led a group to Ugoma (Port Victoria), where they settled in Kadimo, subjugating the local Wahaga, Wagugwa and Walany. They were in turn defeated by another Owiny party led by Munyejra, Owil and Dimo, who invaded and conquered Kadimo. The Bantu inhabitants attempted to resist the newcomers' insatiable appetite for land. For instance, when Jok-Ojok established another settlement at Nungo, the Abaulwani, Abamatsi, Abanyekera, and Abaamba attacked them in organised resistance, but they repulsed, subjugated, and ruled the attackers. The Dimo, Wil and Munyejra journeyed south, settling among the Alego Mur clan between Nyandiwa and Mur Malanga. The Dimo group proceeded to Kadimo and found the *Joka-Jok*. Although the Luo had been in Kadimo for several generations, the local Bantu groups still owned the land. The Dimo provoked bitter conflicts over land, forcing the Bantu groups to yield to the Luo rule, while others fled to Samia and Bunyala.[46] Oral traditions among the Abasamia and

---

44. Ogot, *History of the Southern Luo*.
45. Odinga, *Flame of Freedom*, 74.
46. Odinga, 75.

Banyala affirm that followers of Dimo and Owiny Sigma travelled to Alego leaving the Ababongo people in Bunyala.

The Luo push into other parts of Alego was with both tact and force. Owiny Sigoma, with his brothers Ager and Ogelo, journeyed to *Ruoth* Seje's settlement, east across River Nzoia. *Ruoth* Seje welcomed and settled them at Sigoma (named after their leader). Seje acted on condition they become his subjects and assimilate to be Jo-Alego. Ager accepted these terms and married Seje's daughter. But Owiny Sigoma was at pains to relinquish the superior status, the *Karuoth* title, given to them by the Samia-Bagwe. This resulted in the prolonged *Seje-Karuoth* tussle. Owiny Sigoma toppled Seje and ruled over Alego. But his later harsh rule caused a revolt among Jo-Alego, who dethroned and drove him out. To restore his rulership, Owiny gathered his forces from Bunyala invading Alego, but met firm resistance. Seje had become more organised, wiser, and better mobilised to contain any such attacks. Seje and his people enlisted the aid of the recent arrivals, Jo-Ugenya group from Samia. They annihilated the Jok-Owiny group, killing Owiny Sigoma, thus ending his tyrannical rule.

Jok-Omolo

Jok-Omolo characterized the third migration movement, arriving in early CE 1600. They separated into two groups and shifted south towards Got Ramogi in Acholi. Coming through the Alur, the Pakwach-Pawir country, they went through eastern Busoga into Nyanza. According to Acholi tradition, Omol was the ancestor of the Jok-Omolo:

> Ochielo the father of Gem and Ugenya was the son of Omolo, who they identified with Rwot Omolo Ococ, the last of the Pawir Kingdom, before its disintegration . . . They appear to have developed this tradition in Budoola camps and which suggests the Jok-Omolo may be related to Crazzolara's and Reuben Anywar's the Jo-Pugwenyi (Ugwenyi) and Ragem.[47]

Jok-Omolo were part of the Luo-speakers who left Pakwac-Pawir, following the collapse of the Pawir kingdom. As the traditions showed, wars, prolonged drought and famine forced the dispersal to the east before branching

---

47. Ogot, *History of the Luo-speaking*, 494.

north and south into eastern Uganda and Western Kenya. The Leading clan the Jok-Omolo group was the Gem-Omolo. Gem claimed the royal lineage of the Luo. He was a prince whose mother was the famous Queen Daca, and entrusted with various royal regalias including rainstones (which Cwa-Nyabong'o had confiscated from the Madi King of Koc-Paga), the revered royal drum called *ladwol*, and a bowl with four legs called *wer* by Cwa-Nyabong'o. Ogot[48] observes that, between CE 1559 and 1586, Gem secured the throne of the Koc-Pagak kingdom through these royal regalia. He divided the kingdom into two, naming the western state Koc-Ragem after himself, and the eastern one, Koc- Labong'o after Cwa-Nyabong'o (Gem's half-brother Cwa). This explains the bent among the Omolo-Gem clans towards *ruoth*-ship among the Luos. Ogot notes: "As the first Lobong of Madi Opei *ruoth*-ship, the Gem people and their leader had a special place in the chiefdom which included being responsible for the chiefdom-wide Jok."[49]

Odinga adduces the origin of the Gem clan to be among the Alur group and suggests they could have been part of a larger Jok-Omolo group that included the Jo-Pugwenyi, part of them settling in Teso and among the Padhola of Uganda.[50] But Ogot claims they were a splinter group from Acholiland, which in search of pasture went west to Alurland.[51] They arrived in Banda, Busoga, where they practised fishing among the neighbouring lake islands. They also learned how to make shields. This moulding of their culture in Busoga prepared them for warfare in later years. Ndeda states that between 1540 and 1600, the Omolo group settled at Banda for three generations.[52] By CE 1600, the Jo-Gem group of Jok-Omolo opted to move from Busoga but left behind a smaller group led by Gor. Jo-Gem spent two generations around Akek, in Samia, before proceeding south across Bunyala into Kadimo in Nyanza. Traditions show that Jo-Gem stayed for several generations before migrating to Western Alego under the leadership of Rading' Omolo in CE 1760.

Jo-Ugenya's party, of the Jok-Omolo group, moved from Banda to Alego in two large waves, according to Ogot.[53] Okiyo, Nywa, Teg and Deje, founders

---

48. Ogot, 513–514.
49. Ogot, 516.
50. Odinga, *Flame of Freedom*, 76.
51. Odinga, 649.
52. Ndeda, "Population movement," 94.
53. Ogot, *History of the Luo-speaking*, 16.

of the Kateg and Kanyamwa clans, led the first group that crossed from Samia to Western Alego and settled at Uhui, Sigoma and Gangu. As a group they fought fierce battles, allied to the Seje, against Owiny Sigoma. The second movement of Jo-Ugenya arrived in Alego, led by Boro and Puny. They met the Abachonga during their sojourn at Sifuyo and Rwambwa, in Samia. Waljak (Ger, the brave one, the founder of Kager clan) followed their Jo-Ugenya kin, and together they forged a war alliance. The Abachonga and Ugenya-Waljak defended their kinsmen against the aggression of Owiny Sigoma and his armies in Alego. Odinga attributes their prowess to superior military tactics and strategic manoeuvres, by which they crossed the River Nzoia and decimated Sigoma's army.[54]

According to Ogot from CE 1700 to the second half of the nineteenth century, part of the Jok-Omolo group lived in mud-walled villages, looking after cattle and practising a limited form of agriculture.[55] They began a sedentary existence, changing from a pastoral life to mixed farming with an increased emphasis on agriculture. But as pressure mounted with the inflow of other Luo groups, a section of Jok-Omolo sought fresh territories further east and from the lake shores into upper areas then occupied by the Bantus. Ogot again notes that some drifted southward to Uyoma, and others crossed the lake and settled in South Nyanza.[56] The Omolo-Gem group is composed of Jok-Adet (Gem), Joka-Nyada, Jok-Ochia (South Nyanza) and Jo-Unami (Samia). Jok-Omolo clans include (a) the Ragenya clans clusters: Rager, Boro, Kakan, Kanyada, Ugenya, and Kanyimach; and (b) the Kakwenda clan clusters: Kochia, Gem Kowili, Agoro, Sare, Koguta, Gem-Rae, and Kadiro.

Joka-Wango

By 1700, the Luo groups that had arrived in the first three migration waves had settled. During this quiet period, the fourth and final wave of migrants arrived. This caused an imbalance in the settlements. The migrant group was called Jo-Kawango. The Jo-Kawango or Joka-Wanga sub-group are the product of interaction between the Luyia and Luo clans. They were part of the Joka-Jok, whose journey originated from Alur. While the Joka-Jok contingent

---

54. Odinga, *Flame of Freedom*, 77.
55. Ogot, *History of the Luo-speaking*, 518.
56. Ogot, 27–28.

proceeded to Nyanza, they sojourned in Western Kenya. Jo-Kawango are a heterogenous group made up of Asembo, Uyoma, Suba and Kajulu. Jo-Asembo are believed to be the progeny of the Padhola. Ancient histories of Jo-Sakwa and Jo-Uyoma link them to the Wanga dynasty.[57] During their sojourn, they interacted with the Tiriki ethnic group, who soon moved to Madungu in Wanga. According to Huntingford, "the origin of the Wanga confirmed by tradition is clearly the inter-lacustrine people of Western Uganda."[58] Huntingford affirms the anthropological work of K. R. Dundas in linking the Wanga to the Ugandan inter-lacustrine Hima-Bito group.[59] The Hima are the descendants of earlier migrating Nilotes and the Bato were a Luo speaking Nilotic group that arrived with migrants from the north.

Out of the Kawango Luo group it was Owila, brother of Wanga nicknamed Ja Oyuma (hence Uyoma), who first migrated into Nyanza. The Sakwa are descendants of Sakwa, the wife of Wanga, who followed them. Ogot argues, "Luo traditional accounts are unanimous that the rulers of Wanga kingdom were of Luo extraction, of the Owila and Matar groups who represent the dominant clans in the sub-nationalities of Uyoma and Sakwa . . . who journeyed from Budama via Busoga and Busia."[60] Joka-Wango, referred to as Jo-Suba because they migrated together with the Girango people, are included in the assimilated Luo groups such as the Rieny and Abakunta.[61] Of the Jo-Kawango clans, the Sakwa are the most prominent, comprising the Kagwa, Kamgwenya/Waganjo, Waumi, Kanyamwanda, Kaler/Kamageta, Kamiyawa, Kamnaria (Surwa), Kakmasia, and Nyasmwa. But that these people intermarry is a sign that the broader clan of Sakwa comprises descendants with no common ancestry.

---

57. Ogot, *History of the Luo-speaking*, 535.
58. Oliver and Mathew, *History of East Africa*, 89.
59. Dundas, "Wawanga and other tribes," 19–75.
60. Ogot, *History of the Luo-speaking*, 538.
61. Ogot, 575–576.

APPENDIX 2

Research Guiding Questions

Guideline of questions to ask respondents about Reuben Omulo.

The praxis matrix will be applied to study Rev. Reuben Omulo (1895–1970), a pioneer missionary who served during the pioneer time of mission enterprise in Central Nyanza.

Agency:

- Who is Reuben Omulo Owiti who got involved in CMS mission?
- What social or class position did he occupy in the Luo society of Central Nyanza?
- Who were the interlocutors who shaped his approach?
- What is his sense of identity?

Contextual understanding:

- How did Omulo understand his context: social, political, economic, and cultural factors that influence the situation in which he worked and lived?
- How did he "read the sign of times," discerning the positive and negative powers at work in his society?
- How did he assess or analyse society?
- What tool, if any, did he use?
- What were his biases and interests? Was he aware of how these influenced their context?

Ecclesial scrutiny:

- How did Omulo relate to the church in the region?

- Was he aware of other religious communities and how they influenced the present situation?
- How did he relate to the churches active in the community?

Interpreting the tradition:
- How did Omulo interpret Scripture and the Christian tradition in his context?
- How did his sense of his contextual understanding and his ecclesial scrutiny influence his contextual theology and the shape of his local theology of mission?

Discernment for action:
- What kind of methods activities did Omulo employ or design in his attempt to erect signs of God's reign in the context?
- How did he plan and strategize this purpose?
- How did this relate to other groups and the community?
- What aims do they pursue in transforming the community?

Reflexivity:
- Was there an interplay between the different dimensions of Omulo's mission praxis?
- How did he hold them together?
- How did he reflect on his prior experiences and modify his praxis by learning from mistakes and achievements?
- What was his role in transforming society?

Spirituality:
- In this area we ask whether the spirituality at the heart of a particular mission praxis can best be characterised as:[1]
    - contemplative
    - sacramental
    - devotional
    - "faith seeking understanding"
    - Pentecostal

---

1. See Cannon, "Different ways of Christian prayer"; Foster, *Streams of Living Water*.

- "deeds of justice"
  - a combination of (some of) these
- How does the inspiration (in-breathing, empowering) of the Spirit set in motion and guide this specific form of participation in God's loving outreach to the created cosmos?

APPENDIX 3

The Canon Law of Marriage

(As was operational in the Mombasa Diocese 1931)

Contents:
1. OF HOLY MATRIMONY
2. OF THE MARRIAGE OF UNBAPTISED PERSONS
3. OF NATIVE CUSTOMARY UNIONS
4. OF NULLITY
5. OF CERTAIN IMPEDIMENTS TO THE SOLEMNIZATION OF MATRIMONY
6. OF MIXED MARRIAGES
7. OF IMPEDIMENT TO HOLDING ECCLESIASTICAL OFFICE
8. OF DIVINE SERVICE AFTER CIVIL MARRIAGE
9. OF THE ORDERING OF THE MARRIAGE SERVICE

Canon IV: Of Nullity

The Church recognizes as valid grounds for the granting of a decree of nullity by a Civil court any one of the following conditions:

a) where either party was permanently impotent, or incapable of consummating the marriage, at the time of the marriage or

b) where the parties are within the prohibited degrees of consanguinity

c) where either party at the time of marriage was of unsound mind or subject to recurrent fits of insanity or

d) where the former husband or wife of either party was living at the time of marriage and the marriage (including a marriage by native law and customs) with such previous husband or wife was then in force or
e) where the consent of either party to the marriage was obtained by force or fraud in any case in which the marriage might be annulled on this ground by the law of England; or
f) where there was defective form in the marriage itself, that is to say if both parties had knowingly and wilfully acquiesced in its celebration.

APPENDIX 4

CMS Memorandum 1901

The Three Main Stages in the Writing of the 1901 "Memorandum on the Constitution of Churches in the Mission Field."

Underlined sections of version "A" indicate the concept is missing or put less strongly in the final version.

	Rough Memorandum "A"	Review Version "B"	Final Version "C"
Key Points	• CMS Cannot form churches but can advise (A1) • CMS can only cooperate with view to churches being in communion with Anglican Churches, holding creeds and sacraments and historic episcopate.	• (B4) • (B6)	• (C4) • (C7) adds full Lambeth Quadrilateral, recognises that independent churches may choose reunion that interrupts communion. (C7)
	• 34th article should apply - these Churches can adopt formularies and modes of worship. • Native assistant Bishops, wither with a race / language jurisdiction or a territorial one, are first step to Dioceses under Native bishops [(A6) • Native Diocesan Bishops should then be appointed over territorial Dioceses. (A7, A10) • There may be clergy and even assistant Bishops with "subordinate Church organization" for particular races. (A8) • Dioceses would be formed together into provinces, not for small areas, ideally forming national churches. (A9,A13). • Native Diocesan Bishop can be appointed over areas containing "white clergy and laity." (A11) • "It being one object of the Christian Religion not to separate races but to bring them together in Christ." (A11) • And over areas with "large Heathen population"	• Specifically for areas with non white majority (B5) • (B8, B9) Substantial extra jurisdiction. • Territorial division implied but not specifically stated (B9) • Implied but not specifically stated (B9) • (B10, B11) but reference to national Churches dropped. • (B14) • "One object of which is to unite different races in Christ and not separate them. (B12. • (AB15).	• Different present situation detailed more carefully but same thrust as B5 (C5,C6). • Added idea of some English assistant bishops to show that it is not just a post for natives" (C9,C11) • If it be assumbred ... "none but territorial" clearly expected but not the rule (C11) • Effectively back to A8 (C11) • As B10, B11 (C12, C13) • Extended into discussion of relation of races in new dioceses (C15, C16)) • (C16) • (C18) adds that evangelism to surrounding "heathen" is the work of the local Church which CMS should assist with "men and money." (C19)
	• Self support and independence should not be linked, either can come first. (A13)	• (B16) • CMS should "take it's part in all diocesan and other movements towards the development of the Church in it's missionfields." (B18)	• (C19) • Adds both "home and abroad." (C22)
Present Situation	• CMS Native Christians are 'de facto members of the church of England.' (A4)	• (B5)	• (C5) • Details of how present bishops are appointed. (C10)
Definitions and accepted goals		• CMS "native Church Organisation" was to administer and support local affairs and to "train the Native Christians for future ecclesiastical independence" (B2) • Missionary effort aimed at "independent Churches, or at least, of autonomous branches of existing churches." (B3)	• (C2) • Adds "in communion with the Mother Church." (C3) • Definitions of "Native", "Foreigner." (C0) • Church "external community of baptised Christians." (C0)
Provisos		• Native Episcopate "would be formed on the lines of the Primitive Church, and not necessarily on those of the Mediaeval or even English Episcopate." (B7) • Views of laity and existing groups of congregations should have a place in overall unity. (B17) • Assumes that "Church of England will remain loyal to the Holy Scripture, and to Apostolic Christianity." (B18)	• Changed to "characterised by the simplicity of "Primitive Church." (C8) • (C20) added care over patronage, also laity should have a voice in appointments of bishops. (C10) • Adds "Truth of the Gospel" of higher importance than all else. (C22)
Justification	• Native Bishops will help reunion. (A5)	• Not specific about Native Bishops but properly constituted Anglican Churches as a base for Native Christians to play a part in Reunion. (B6) • Particularly important that Indian Church be territorial. (B13)	• (C7) • (C17)
Details of application	• Where CMS works alone, NCC may be "embryo Church Councils", but where other Anglicans are present Church Councils will not be connected to a a society. (A13)	Dropped.	• A15 effectively reinstated. (C21)
		• Idea of very gradual transfer and long period of working together of white and native clergy and laity. (B12) • In India progress possible but notes complications of State / Church situation. (B13)	• Extended with specific hope of racial harmony (C14, C15, C16) • (C17)
Historical Background	• Native Bishops will help reunion. (A5)	• Introduction comments a quote from Venn (B1)	• (C1)

Figure 15: Abstract of Replies to Report and Constitution Memorandum

Bibliography

Adéẹ̀kó, Adélékè. "Theory and Practice in African Orature." *Research in African Literatures* 30, no. 2 (1999): 222–227. http://www.jstor.org/stable/3820568.
Ainsworth, John. "Memo Re: Native Labour. 13 Sept 1911." *Journal of African History* 14, no. 2 (1973): 237–255.
———. "On Native Treatment." *Leader of British East Africa*, 25 November 1911.
Ajuoga, Matthew A. Interview with Nzioki, 26 July 1984, Kisumu Town, Kisumu.
Alila, Patrick O. "Kenyan agricultural policy: the colonial roots of African smallholder agricultural policy and services." Working paper no. 327, Nairobi: Institute for Development Studies, University of Nairobi, 1977.
Aloo, Patroba. Personal interview by Paul Francis Omondi. 22 September 2021. Ng'iya, Siaya.
Amala, Robert N. *Paroni Gik Mosekadho mane Osetimore*. Kisumu: G.O Ombete, 2008.
Amoke, Christina J. "Omulo's testimony." Personal interview. 4 August 1991. Marenyo, Siaya.
Amoke, Musa A. "Musa Amoke Life Story." Unpublished. Reuben Omulo Private Archives. Marenyo, Siaya, 1999.
Amoth, Andrew. Personal interview by Paul Francis Omondi. 22 September 2020. Ulumbi, Siaya.
"*Amri na Sheria* – Laws and Regulations of the African Anglican Church in the Diocese of Mombasa," as approved by Bishop Crabbe, 1 August 1941.
Anderson, John E. "Education for Self-Reliance. The Impact of Self-help." Discussion Paper No.67, September 1968. Unpublished. Nairobi: University College.
Anderson, William B. *The Church in East Africa 1840–1974*. Dodoma: Central Tanzania Press, 1977.
Anderson, David, and David Throup. "Africans and Agricultural Production in Colonial Kenya: The Myth of the War as a Watershed." *The Journal of African History* 26, no. 4 (1985): 327–345. http://www.jstor.org/stable/181653.

Anglican Communion Office. "2022: Anglican Communion Mission Agencies." https://www.anglicancommunion.org/community/organisations.aspx.

Anglican Padres Central Nyanza Deanery (APCND). "A Petition presented to Canon Bewes, Secretary of CMS For Africa by The African Padres." Nyanza, Maseno. Reuben Omulo Archives, Marenyo, 1946.

Anglican Council in the Diocese of Mombasa. Reuben Omulo Archives, Marenyo, 1948.

Angogo, Rachel K. "Linguistic and Attitudinal Factors in the Maintenance of Luyia group Identities." PhD diss., University of Texas, 1980.

Anyumba, Owuor H. "The Historical Dimensions of Life-Crisis Rituals. Some Factors in the Dissemination of *juogi* Beliefs Among the Luo of Kenya up to 1962." Unpublished manuscript, 1974.

Auger, Peter. *The Anthem Dictionary of Literary Terms and Theory*. London: Anthem Press, 2010.

Ayany, Samuel G. *Kar Chakruok Mar Luo*. Kisumu: Lake Publishers & Enterprises, 1951.

Ayot, Henry O. *Historical Texts of Lake Region of East Africa*. Nairobi: Kenya Literature Bureau (KLB), [1977] 1990.

Baker, Erick E. *A Short History of Nyanza*. Nairobi: East African Literature Bureau (EALB), 1950.

Balandier, Georges. *Sociologie actuelle de 'Afrique noire, dynamique sociale en Afrique centrale*, Presses Universitaries de France, 1971.

Barrett, David. *Schism and Renewal in Africa: An Analysis of Six Thousand Contemporary Religious Movements*. Nairobi: Oxford University Press (OUP), 1968.

———. The development of Kenyan Christianity, in J. K. Mambo (Ed) *Kenya Churches Handbook*. Kisumu: Evangelical Publishing House, 1973.

Barrington-Ward, Simon, "My Pilgrimage in Mission." *International Bulletin Missionary Research* 23, no. 2 (1999): 62.

Baumann, Hermann. Die Dei Afrikanischen Kultur-Kreise, AC-7, 1934.

———. *Die Volker Kunde von Africa*. Essen: [1934] 1940.

Baur, John. *Years of Christianity in Africa: An African History 62–1992*. Nairobi: Paulines, [1994] 2000.

Bediako, Kwame. "The Roots of African Theology." *International Bulletin of Missionary Research* 13, no. 2 (1989): 58–65.

Beecher, Leonard J. *African Education in Kenya: Report of a Committee Appointed to Inquire into the Scope, Content, and Methods of African Education, its Administration and Finance, and to Make Recommendations*. Nairobi: Government Printer, 1949.

———. "The Future of Divinity School." in *The Bishop's Charge*, published by the Diocese of Mombasa, 1954.

Bernard, Russell H. *Research Methods in Anthropology; Qualitative and Quantitative Approaches*. 4th Ed. Lanham: Alta Mira Press, 2006.

Bevans, Stephen. *Models of Contextual Theology*. Maryknoll: Orbis, 1992.

Bewes, Cecil T. F. Letter to Stanway, 28 June 1945. Diocese of Maseno North (DMN) file, Nairobi.

Bleek, William. *A Comparative Grammar of South African Languages, Vols. 1 and 2*. London: Trubner & Co, 1862 (Vol.1) and 1869 (Vol. 2).

Blood, Arthur G. *The History of the Universities' Mission to Central Africa, Vol. III 1933-1957*. London: Universities' Mission to Central Africa, 1962.

Board Of Governors Meeting Minutes. 11 September 1953. Divinity School, Limuru.

Bogonko, Sorobea N. *A History of Modern Education in Kenya, 1895-1991*. Nairobi: Evans Brothers, 1992.

Borg, Walter R. and Meredith D. Gall. *Educational Research: An Introduction*. New York: Longman, 1983.

Bosch, David J. *Witness to the World. The Christian Mission in Theological Perspective*. Eugene: John Knox Press, 1980.

———. *Transforming Mission: Paradigm Shifts in Theology of Mission*. New York: Orbis Books, 1991.

Bradley, Candice. "Luyia." In *Encyclopaedia of World Cultures Volume 9: Africa and the Middle East*, edited by John Middleton and Amal Rassam, 202-206. New York: Macmillan Reference, 1995.

Brookfield, Stephen. "Book Reviews." *Adult Education Quarterly* 39, no. 1 (1988): 57-58. doi: 10.1177/0001848188039001010.

Buell, Raymond L. *The Native Problem in Africa, Vol. I*. New York: The Macmillan Company, 1928.

Bundy, C. *The Rise and Fall of the South African Peasantry*. Berkeley: University of California Press, 1979.

Butcher, H. J. E. "Kenya's Native Ministry." In *The Church Missionary Outlook*, October 1927.

Butere Church Council Minutes. 27 April 1918. DMN Files, Butere.
Butere Church Council Minutes. 26 July 1919. DMN Files, Butere.
Butere Church Council Minutes. 30 August 1919. DMN Files, Butere.
Butere Church Council Minutes. 28 May 1921. DMN Files, Butere.
Butere Church Council Minutes. 29 July 1922. DMN Files, Butere.

Byrne, Joseph. "Memorandum of KTWA to the Secretary of State for Colonies, Rt. Hon Sir Philip Cunliffe on his visit to East Africa, Through His Excellency the Governor." 23 January 1933. Reuben Omulo Archives, Marenyo Siaya.

Cannon, Dean H. "Different ways of Christian prayer, different ways of being Christian." *Mid-stream* 33, no. 3 (1994): 309–334.

Carr-Chellman, Davin J., and Michael Kroth. "The Spiritual Disciplines as Practices of Transformation. *International Journal of Adult Vocational Education and Technology* 8, no. 1 (2017): n.p. https://www.researchgate.net/publication/315475412_The_Spiritual_Disciplines_as_Practices_of_Transformation.

Cash, Wilson. Letter to Stephenson, 17 June 1930. *GN AS/2*.

———. Letter to Bishop of Iran, 13 December 1940. GNIPES.

Casson, John. "To Plant a Garden City in the Slums of Paganism: Handley Hooper, the Kikuyu and the Future of Africa." *Journal of Religion in Africa* 28, no. 4 (1998): 387–410.

Catechism for Hearers' Classes in Dholuo. Published for the Literature Committee of the Anglican Council in the Diocese of Mombasa, 1948.

Central Kavirondo District Annual Report for Kisumu, 1922. Kenya National Archives (KNA).

Chief Native Commissioner. Letter in response to Owen's letter of 29 July 1927. Church Missionary Society Archives (CMSA), Acc. 83 01.

Chief Native Commissioner. Letter to Owen, Office of the Chief Native Commissioner, 29 July 1927. Ref. No. 6/3/1/7 Nairobi. CMSA. Acc. 08/01.

Chupungco, Ansar J. "Die liturgie und bestandteile der kultur." In *Lutherischer Weltbund: Gottesdienst und Kultur im Dialog, Lutherisches Kirchenamt*, edited by A. Stauffer, 151–163. Berlin: Evangelische Haupt-Bibelgesellschaft, 1994.

Church Missionary Society Report. 1900, CMSA, G3.A7/05.

Church Missionary Society. *The Centenary Volume of the CMS for Africa and the East*. London: CMS, 1902.

CMS Executive Committee Minutes. 1 August 1904. CMSA G3.A7/04, Nairobi.

CMS Executive Committee Minutes. 17–18 June 1928. CMSA G3.A7/08, Nairobi.

CMS Missionary Committee Minutes. 30 November 1909. CMSA G3.A7/08, Nairobi.

CMS Gleaner. 1 October 1918. CMSA G3.A7/09.

CMS Report. 1911. CMSA G3.A7/05.

CMS Report. 1912. CMSA G3.A7/05.

CMS Report. 1917–1918: Elizabeth Chadwick, *Early Years in the Mission*, Chapter 10, CMSA. A7/08.

CMS Report. 1929–30. CMSA G3.A7/05.

CMS Report. 1940. CMSA G3.A7/05.

Cohen, David W. *The Combing of History*. Chicago: University of Chicago Press, 1994.

Cohen, David W., and Atieno-Odhiambo, Elisha S. "Ayany, Malo and Ogot: Historians in Search of a Luo Nation." *Cahiers d'Études africaines* 107/108

(1987): 269–286. https://www.persee.fr/doc/cea_0008-0055_1987_num_27_107_3406.

———. *Siaya: The Historical Anthropology of an African Landscape*. Nairobi: Heinemann, 1989.

Cole, Keith. "Theological Training in East Africa." Unpublished typescript, 1960.

———. 1970: *The Cross Over Mt. Kenya: A Short History of the Anglican Church in the Diocese of Mount Kenya, 1900–1970*. Nairobi: Diocese of Mount Kenya, n.d.

———. 1971: *A History of the Church Missionary Society of Australia*. Victoria: Church Missionary Historical Publications Trust, n.d.

Colenso, John W. *The Pentateuch and Book of Joshua Critically Examined*. London: Longman, Roberts, & Green, 1862.

Collard, Charles E. "Military Report of the Expedition" enclosed in letter from H. H. Johnston to Salisbury, 26 February 1900. FO 2/297, Public Records Office.

Colony and Protectorate of Kenya. *A Ten-Year Plan for the Development of African Education*. N.p.: Government printer, 1945.

Comaroff, John. and Jean Comaroff. *Of Revelation and Revolution: Christianity, Colonialism and Consciousness in South Africa, Vol. 2*. Chicago: University of Chicago Press, 1997.

Comaroff, Jean, and John Comaroff. "Africa Observed: Discourses of the Imperial Imagination." In *Perspectives on Africa: A Reader in Culture, History, and Representation*. 2nd ed., edited by Roy R. Grinker, Stephen C. Lubkemann, and Christopher B. Steiner, 31–43. Oxford: Blackwell Publishing, 2010.

Corfield, F. D. "The Origins and Growth of Mau Mau." Cmd 1030, 1960. UK Parliamentary Report. Public Records Office.

Coryndon Robert T. Letter to Secretary of State, 14 February 1924. Object of Kavirondo Taxpayers Welfare Association, enclosure in Public Records Office, CO 533/308.

Cox, Jeffrey. *Imperial Fault Lines. Christianity and Colonial Power in India, 1818–1940*. Stanford: Stanford University Press, 2002.

Crazzolara, Joseph P. *The Lwoo, Parts 1–3*. Verona: Museum Cambonianum, 1950.

Davidson, Randall T. "Archbishop of Canterbury Statement." *Church Missionary Review* (July 1915): 427.

Dealing, James R. "Politics in Wanga, Kenya c. 1650–1914." PhD thesis, Northwestern University, 1974.

Dierks, Friedrich. *Evangelium im afrikanischen kontext: Interkulturelle kommunikation bei den Tswana*. Gütersloh: Gütersloher Verlagshaus Gerd Mohn, 1986.

Diocese of Mombasa Native Christian Marriage and Divorce Ordinance Minutes. 22–23 February 1932. 16 CC, ACC, February 1932. Mombasa Diocese, Reuben Omulo Archives, Marenyo.

District Commissioner Central Nyanza Kisumu. *Annual Report 1899*. Kenya National Archives (KNA).
District Commissioner Central Nyanza Kisumu. *Annual Report 1900*. KNA.
District Commissioner Central Nyanza. 3/1, Kisumu District Archives. 1900–1916, KNA.
District Commissioner Central Nyanza. 3/2, Political Record Book. 1909, KNA.
District Commissioner Central Nyanza Kisumu. *Annual Report 1913*. KNA.
District Commissioner Central Nyanza Kisumu. *Annual Report 1917*. KNA.
District Commissioner Central Nyanza Kisumu. *Annual Report* 1918. KNA.
District Commissioner Central Kavirondo. *Annual Report for Kisumu 1922*. KNA.
District Commissioner Central Nyanza. *District Annual Report 1932*. KNA.
District Commissioner Kisumu. 1/ 3 /122 Agricultural Bank Loans 1930–40. KNA.
District Commissioner North Nyanza. 10/1/1, 1926–40. KNA.
District Commissioner North Nyanza. "Letter to Col. Anderson, DC," January 1934. 10/1/1: KNA.
District Commissioner /North Nyanza/O/1/1: "**Report** on the **Disturbances** at Musanda in Wanga North Kavirondo, in January 1934" by **Captain Hislop**, February 9, 1934. 74.
District Commissioner Nyeri, 1/4, *South Nyeri District Annual Report*, 1930, 2–9. KNA.
Dobbs. "Letter to Owen, Office of the Senior Commissioner Kisumu," 12 July 1927. Ref: no. 2179/62/3) CMSA. Acc. 08/01.
Dugdale, John. "Kenya (African Education)." *House of Commons Debate, 13 December 1950. Vol 482 cc1303–12*: https://api.parliament.uk/historic-hansard/commons/1950/dec/13/kenya-african-education.
Dundas, Kenneth R. "The Wawanga and other tribes of the Elgon District, British East Africa." *Journal of the Royal Anthropological Institutes* 43 (1913): 19–75.
Dutch Reformed Mission Church. *The Belhar Confession*. 1986. https://www.rca.org/about/theology/creeds-and-confessions/the-belhar-confession/.
Education Department, Kenya Colony and Protectorate. Annual Report of 1938, Tables V and XVIII.
Eliot, Charles N. *The East Africa Protectorate*. London: Barnes & Noble, 1966.
"Encyclical to the Anglican Membership in the Church of Nigeria, June 2003." http://www.lambethconference.orglacns/articles/34175/acns3486.html.
Evans-Pritchard, Edward E. "Luo Tribes and Clans." *Rhodes-Livingstone Journal* 7 (1949): 24–25.
———. *The Sanusi of Cyrenaica*. Oxford: Oxford University Press, 1949. doi: 10.2307/1156202.
Fanning, Don. "Church Planting Movements." *Trends and Issues in Missions* 6 (2009). https://digitalcommons.liberty.edu/cgm_missions/6.

Farrimond, Kenneth J. T. "Concerning the Development of Self-Governing Indigenous Churches 1900–1942." PhD thesis, The University of Leeds, August 2003.

Fetterman, David M. *Ethnography: Step by Step*. 3rd ed. Thousand Oaks: Sage Publications, 2010.

Fisher, Robert. B. *On the Borders of Pygmy-Land*. London: Marshall Brothers, 1935.

Foster, Richard J. *Streams of Living Water: Celebrating the Great Traditions of Christian Faith*. New York: Harper Collins, 1998.

Frazan. In District Commissioner Central Nyanza reports, 1913–1920, KNA.

Friesen, Albert W. D. "A methodology in the development of indigenous hymnody." *Missiology: An International Review* 10, no. 1 (1982): 83–96.

Furley, Oliver W., and Thomas Watson. *A History of Education in East Africa*. New York: NOK Publishers, 1978. http://www.jstor.org/stable/24769418.

Gehman, Richard. "The East African Revival." *East Africa Journal for Evangelical Theology* 5.1 (1986): 36–54. https://biblicalstudies.org.uk/pdf/Eajet/05-1_036.pdf.

Gikandi, Simon. "Editor's Column: Provincializing English." *Publications of the Modern Language Association of America/ PMLA* 129, no. 1 (2014): 7–17. http://www.jstor.org/stable/24769418.

Githige, Renison M. "The Mission State Relationship in Colonial Kenya: A Summary." *Journal of Religion in Africa* 13, no. 2 (1982): 110–125, doi:10.2307/1581206.

Goldsmith, Fredrick H., ed. *John Ainsworth, Pioneer Kenya Administrator, 1864–1946*. London: Macmillan, 1959.

Gollwitzer, Helmut. "Why Black Theology?" *Union Seminary Quarterly Review* 31, no.1 (1975): 38–58.

Gonzalez, Justo L. *Mañana: Christian Theology from a Hispanic Perspective*. Nashville: Abingdon, 1990.

Government Of Kenya Native Christian Marriage and Divorce Ordinance Minutes. 22–23 February 1931. 16 CC, ACC, KNA.

Governor of the Colony and Protectorate of Kenya. "African Christian Marriage & Divorce Ordinance." Cap. 144, Ordinance No. 44 of 1955.

Greaves, Lionel B. *Carey Francis of Kenya*. London: Rex Collings, 1969.

Groves, Charles P. *The Planting of Christianity in Africa, Vol. 4*. London: Lutterworth Press, 1958.

Greenberg, Joseph H. "Nilo-Saharan Languages." *Encyclopædia Britannica*, 2017. https://www.britannica.com/topic/Nilo-Saharan-languages.

Gudo, Elly I. Personal interview by Paul Francis Omondi. 22 October 2021. Nairobi, Kenya.

Guy, Jeff. *The Heretic. A Study of the Life of John William Colenso, 1814–1883*. Johannesburg: Ravan and University of Natal Press, 1983.

———. "Class, Imperialism and Literary Criticism: William Ngidi, John Colenso, and Matthew Arnold." *Journal of Southern African Studies* 23, no. 2 (1997): 219–241. http://www.jstor.org/stable/2637619.

Hailey, Lord. "Native Administration and Political Development in British Tropical Africa." 1940 Report 1940.

Hartwig, Gerald W. *The Art of Survival in East Africa*. New York: Africana, 1976.

Hastings, Adrian. *A History of African Christianity, 1950–1975*. London: Cambridge University Press (CUP), 1979.

———. *The Church in Africa, 1450–1950*. Oxford History of the Christian Church. Oxford: Oxford University Press, 1996.

Hauerwas, Stanley. *Performing the Faith: Bonhoeffer and the Practice of Non-violence*. London: Society for Promotion of Christian Knowledge (SPCK), 2004.

Hauge, Hans-Egil. *Luo Religion and Folklore*. Oslo: Universitetsforlaget, 1974.

Hay, Margaret J. "Economic Changes in Luoland: Kowe, 1890–1945." PhD thesis, University of Wisconsin, 1972.

Hetherington, Penelope. British *Paternalism and Africa 1920–1940*. London: Frank Cass, 1978.

Hewitt, Gordon. *The Problems of Success: A History of the Church Missionary Society, 1910–1942, Vol. 1*. London: SCM Press, 1971.

Heywood, Richard S. Letter to Archbishop of Canterbury, 19 August 1927. CMSA Acc. 83 07/08.

———. Letter to Director of Education, Nairobi, 22 April 1929. CMSA Acc. 83 07/08.

Hill, Mervyn F. *The Permanent Way: The Story of the Kenya and Uganda Railway*. Nairobi: East African Railway and Harbours, 1949.

Hobley, Charles W. "Report on Uyoma Expedition near Lake Victoria." Enclosure in H. H. Johnston letter to Salisbury, 5 February 1900. FO 2/297 PRO.

———. *Kenya: From Chartered Company to Crown Colony*. 2nd ed. London, Frank Cass, 1970.

Hoehler-Fatton, Cynthia. *Women of Fire and Spirit. History, Faith and Gender in Roho Religion in Western Kenya*. Oxford: Oxford University Press, 1996.

Home, Robert. "Colonial Township Laws and Urban Governance in Kenya." *Journal of African Law* 56, no. 2 (2012): 175–193. www.jstor.org/stable/41709959.

Hooper, Handley D. *Africa in the Making*. London: CMS, 1922.

———. In paper prepared by Cash for CMS Commission, 28 October 101932. G/APc2/6.

———. Letter to Archbishop of Canterbury, 21 February 1933. Archbishop Lang Papers, Lambeth Palace Library, London.

———. Letter to Cash, Extract of the response from Kenya Mission, 17/07/1934. GIAPc2/4.
———. Report to Group III Missions, 21 January 1934. G/APc 2/4.
———. Letter to Warren, 1944. 26171, GNIAg2.
———. Review in *Daily Leader* of British East Africa of Hooper's "Africa in the Making." n.d. In Hooper Papers, Acc. 85/F8.
Hopkins, Elizabeth. "The Nyabingi Cult of Southwestern Uganda." in *Protest and Power in Black Africa*, edited by Robert I. Rotberg and Ali A. Mazrui. New York: Oxford University Press, 1970.
Horstead, Canon. "Marriage and the Christian Church." Address to the Advisory Committee on African Education, Edinburgh House 19 May 1933. CMSA. G3/07/08.
Iliffe, John. *A Modern History of Tanganyika*. Cambridge: Cambridge University Press, 1979.
Itebete, P. A. N. "Language standardization in western Kenya." In *Language in Kenya*, edited by W. H. Whiteley. Oxford: Oxford University Press, 1974.
Jansen, Mechteld. "God on the Border – Missiology as Critical Theological Guidance for Crossing Borders." In *Mission Revisited: Between Mission History and Intercultural Theology*, edited by Volker Küster, 45–62. Berlin: LIT Verlag, 2010.
Jones, Thomas J. *Education in East Africa*, New York: Phelps-Stokes Fund, 1925.
Kagema, Dickson N. "Leadership Training for Mission in the Anglican Church of Kenya." ThD thesis, UNISA, 2008.
Katarikawe, James, and John Wilson. "The East African Revival Movement. MTh and MA thesis, Fuller Theological Seminary, 1975.
Katongole, Emmanuel, *The Sacrifice of Africa: A Political Theology for Africa*. Grand Rapids: Eerdmans, 2011.
Kavirondo District Church Council Minutes. 9 January and 6 February 1929. DMN Files, Maseno.
Kavirondo Ruri-decanal Council Minutes. 3 June 1922. DMN Files, Maseno.
Kavirondo Missionary Committee Minutes. 4 April 1923. DMN Files, Maseno.
Kavirondo Ruri-decanal Council Minutes. 8 February 1923. DMN Files, Maseno.
Kavirondo Ruri-decanal Council Minutes. 16 March 1923. DMN Files, Maseno.
Kavirondo Ruri-decanal Council Minutes. 3 January 1924. DMN Files, Maseno.
Kavirondo Ruri-decanal Council Minutes. 16 May 1924. DMN Files, Maseno.
Kavirondo Ruri-decanal Council Minutes. 17 April 1928. DMN Files, Maseno.
Kavirondo Ruri-decanal Council Minutes. 11 November 1928. DMN Files, Maseno.
Kavirondo Ruri-decanal Council Minutes. 9 December 1931. DMN Files, Yala.
Kavirondo Ruri-decanal Council Minutes. 8 February, 19 April, 7 June, 8 August, 20 September 1933. DMN Files, Maseno.

Kavirondo Ruri-decanal Council Minutes. 19 December 1934. DMN Files, Maseno.
Kavirondo Ruri-decanal Council, Minutes. 7 August 1935. DMN Files, Maseno.
Kavirondo Ruri-decanal Council, Minutes. 1937. DMN Files, Ng'iya.
Kavirondo Ruri-decanal Council, Minutes. 17 September 1937. DMN Files, Maseno.
Kenyon E. R. "Letter to Manley GT," on Lake Victoria, 9 July 1913. G3. A7/0 10, 1913.
Killick, Anthony B. ARC(MAWR) 3 Agri-3/62, "Notes for the enquiry into maize control, 1943." To the Secretary of Food Shortage Commission, 30 April 1943. KNA.
Kitching, Gavin. *Class and Economic Change in Kenya: The Making of an African Petite-Bourgeoisie*. New Haven: Yale University Press, 1980.
K'Ochieng', Appolo O. Personal interview by Paul Francis Omondi. 23 September 2020. Sega, Siaya.
Kohler, Oswin. "Die Ausbreitung der Niloten." Berlin: Beiträge zur Gesellungs- und Völkerwissenschaft, 1950.
Kritzinger, Johannes N.J. "Studying religious communities as agents of change: An agenda for missiology." *Missionalia* 23, no. 3 (1995): 366–396.
———. "Interreligious dialogue: problems and perspectives. A Christian theological approach." *Scriptura* 60 (1997): 47–62.
———. "A question of mission – A mission of questions." *Missionalia* 30, no. 1 (2002): 144–173.
———. "Faith to Faith – Missiology as encounterology." *Verbum et Ecclesia* 29, no. 3 (2008): 764–790. http://dx.doi.org/10.4102/ve.v29i3.31.
———. "Using Archives Missiologically: A Perspective from South Africa." In *Mission History and Mission Archives*, edited by Huub Lems, 18–42. Utrecht: Stichting de Zending der Protestantse Kerk in Nederland, 2011.
———. "Mission in prophetic dialogue." *Missiology: An International Review* 41 (2013): 35–49.
———. "Mission Theology and the Nature of God." In *Contemporary Mission Theology: Engaging the Nations*, edited by R. L. Gallagher and Paul Hertig, 80–93. Maryknoll: Orbis Books, 2017.
Kritzinger, Johannes N.J., and Willem Saayman, eds. *Mission in Creative Tension: A Dialogue with David Bosch*. Pretoria: SAMS, 1990.
———. *David J. Bosch: Prophetic Integrity, Cruciform Praxis*. Pietermaritzburg: Cluster Publications, 2011.
Lambert, Harold E. "Land tenure policy, Kenya." H. E. Lambert's memorandum on "Policy in regard to the administration of the native lands – note for discussion." 10 July 1946. PRO, CO 852/557/I6707/2.
Lambeth Conference. 1958: Resolutions, Lambeth Palace Library, London, 1958.

———. Resolutions, Lambeth Palace Library, London, 1968.

"Lambeth Quadrilateral". *Encyclopaedia Britannica*, 16 Mar. 2016. https://www.britannica.com/topic/Lambeth-Quadrilateral.

Lanternari, Vittorio. *The Religions of the Oppressed: A Study of Modern Messianic Movements.* New York: Knopf, 1963.

Lebaka, Morakeng E. K. "The value of traditional African religious music into liturgy: Lobethal Congregation." HTS Teologiese Studies/Theological Studies 71, no. 3 (2015): Art. #2761. http://dx.doi.org/10.4102/hts.v71i3.2761.

Leedy, Todd. "History with a Mission: Abraham Kawadza and Narratives of Agrarian Change in Zimbabwe." *History in Africa* 33 (2006): 255–270.

Leys, Colin. *Underdevelopment in Kenya: The Political Economy of Neo-Colonialism*, London: Heinemann Publishers, 1975.

Lieberknecht, U. *Gemeindelieder: Probleme und chancen einer kirchlichen Lebensäusserung*, Göttingen: Vandenhoeck & Ruprecht, 1994.

Lienhardt, Godfrey. "The Shilluk of the Upper Nile." In *African Worlds: Studies in the Cosmological Ideas and Social Values of African Peoples*, edtied by Daryll Forde, 138–163. Oxford: Oxford University Press/International African Institute, 1954.

Lindblom, Gerhard K. *The Use of Stilts, Especially in Africa and America, Also the Use of the Sling in Africa (Nilotes).* Stockholm: Riksuseets etnografiska avdeling, 1927.

Lochhead, David. *The Dialogical Imperative: A Christian Reflection on Interfaith Encounter.* Maryknoll: Orbis, 1988.

Lonsdale, John M. "A Political History of Nyanza 1883–1945." PhD thesis, Trinity College, Cambridge University, 1964.

———. "Political Associations in Western Kenya." In *Protest and Power in Black Africa*, edited by Ali Mazrui and Robert Rotberg, 589–638. New York: Oxford University Press, 1970.

———. "The growth and transformation of the colonial state in Kenya, 1929–52." Seminar Paper No.17, History Department, University of Nairobi, August 1980.

———. "Mission Christianity and Settler Colonialism." Unpublished paper, 1982.

———. "The Second World War and the Colonial State in Kenya." Presented to the Conference on "Africa and the Second World War." London: School of Oriental and African Studies, May 1984.

Lugard, Frederick D. to IBEA., 8 September 1894 (Ogot, Bethwel A. 1963, "British Administration in the Central Nyanza District of Kenya, 1900–60." *The Journal of African History* 4, no. 2 (1963): 249–273. www.jstor.org/stable/179537.Maddox, Gregory H. "*Njaa*: Food Shortages and Famines in Tanzania Between the Wars." *The International Journal of African Historical Studies* 19, no. 1 (1986): 17–33, 1986.

Mambo, George K. "The Revival Fellowship (Brethren) in Kenya." In *Kenya Churches Handbook: The Development of Kenyan Christianity, 1498–1973*, edited in David Barrett, et al., 110–117. Kisumu: Evangel Publishing House, 1973.

Matthews, Rev. H. *CMS Gleaner*, 1 October 1918, CMSA G3.

Matson, Albert T. "Uganda's Old Eastern Province and East Africa's Federal Capital." *Uganda Journal* 22 (1958): n.p. https://www.wdl.org/en/item/13797/view/1/53/.

Mattia, Joan P. "Walking the Rift: The Missionary Art of Bishop Alfred Robert Tucker." *Anglican and Episcopal History* 80, no. 3 (2011): 242–265. http://www.jstor.org/stable/42612605.

Maxon, Robert. "The Devonshire Declaration: The Myth of Missionary Intervention." *History in Africa* 18 (1991): 259–270. doi:10.2307/3172065.

———. *Struggle for Kenya: The Loss and Reassertion of Imperial Initiative, 1912–1923*. Fairleigh: Dickinson University Press, 1993.

Mbala, Nicholas O. Personal interview by Paul Francis Omondi. 11 August 2021. Aboke, Siaya.

Mbiti, John S. *Concepts of God in Africa*. London: SPCK, 1970.

———. *Introduction to African Religion*. London: Heinemann Publishers, 1975.

Mboya, Paul A. *Luo Kitgi gi Timbegi*. Kisumu: The Advent Press, 1938.

McGavran, Donald A. *How Churches Grow*. New York: Friendship Press, 1959.

———. "A Church in Every People." In *Worldwide Perspectives*, edited by M. Crossman, 224–227, Seattle: YWAM Publications, 2003.

———. *Bridges of God: A Study in the Strategy of Missions*. Eugene: World Dominion Press, 2005.

Meinertzhagen, Richard Col. *Kenya Diary 1902–06*. London: Oliver & Boyd, 1957.

Memorandum of Interview of Bishop Tucker and the Rev. J. J. Willis with the Group No. II Committee, June 26, 1906. CMSA G3.A7/05.

Memorandum on the Constitution of Churches, in the Mission Field 1901. (Memorandum 1901) G/C 9/2. CMSA.

Miles, Miranda, and Jonathan Crush. "Personal Narratives as Interactive Texts: Collecting and Interpreting Migrant Life-Histories." *Professional Geographer* 45, no. 1 (1993): 95–129.

Millar, Ernest. "Letter to Manley," 17 January 1916. CMSA G3 A7/.

Miller, Daniel. "A Theory of Virtualism." In *Virtualism: A New Political Economy*, edited by J. Carrier and D. Miller, 187–215. Oxford: Berg, 1998.

Minutes IV: Proposal of a Secondary School at Ambira. 25 July 1958. Omulo Private Archives. Marenyo, Siaya.

Missionaries and Native Clergy Register, 1804–1904. London, CMS, 1905.

Mitchell, Philip E. "Grouping of agricultural departments." Memorandum to Stanley, 9 March 1945. PRO CO 533/537/38628.

———. *African Afterthoughts*. London: Hutchinson, 1954.
Mojola, Aloo O. *God Speaks in Our Languages: The Story of Bible Translation in East Africa from 1844-2018*. Nairobi: Tafsiri Press, 2018.
———. *Bible Translation and Culture. Critical Intersections and Conversations*. Nairobi, Tafsiri Press, 2018.
———. *Utu, Ubuntu & Community. Reimagining and Celebrating the Web of Life and the Dignity and Worth of all Humans*. Nairobi: Tafsiri Press, 2020.
Mombasa Diocese Synod 7th session Minutes. July 1949. DMN Files.
Moris, Jon R. "The Agrarian Revolution in Central Kenya: A Study in Farm Innovation in Embu District." PhD thesis, Northwestern University, Illinois, 1970.
Mugo, Micere G. *African Orature and Human Rights*. Roma: Institute of Southern African Studies, 1991.
Munday, Jeremy. *Introducing Translation Studies: Theories and applications*. 3rd ed. New York: Routledge, 2010. (This edition was published in the Taylor & Francis e-Library.)
Municipal Corporations Ordinance of 1922, Section 43. Kisumu District. KNA.
Murray, Nancy. "Archdeacon W. E. Owen: Missionary as Propagandist." *The International Journal of African Historical Studies* 15, no. 4 (1982): 653–670. doi:10.2307/217849.
Mwangi, R. K. "Missio Dei: The Influence of early Keswick Theology of sanctification in socio-ethical life of the East Africa Revival Movement (EARM), 1930-2015, in the Anglican Church, Mount Kenya Region." PhD thesis, North-West University, Potchefstroom, South Africa, 2018. https://repository.nwu.ac.za/bitstream/handle/10394/31372/Mwangi.pdf?sequence=1&isAllowed=y.
Ndeda, Mildred A. J. "Nomiya Luo church: A gender analysis of the dynamics of an African independent church among the Luo of Siaya District in the twentieth century and beyond." *Missionalia* 31, no. 2 (2003): 239–277.
———. "Population movement, settlement and the construction of society to the east of Lake Victoria in precolonial times: the western Kenyan case." *Les Cahiers d'Afrique de l'Est / The East African Review* 52 (2019): 83–108.
Neill, Stephen. *Creative Tension*. Edinburgh: Edinburgh House, 1959.
———. *Christian Missions*. London: Hodder & Stoughton, 1964.
Ngere Group. Letter to Omulo for advice, 28 May 1951. Reuben Omulo Archives Marenyo, 1951.
Nicholls, Bernard D. Letter to Cecil T. F. Bewes, 18 December 1952. CMS AF59 G3/6/1 (also A5/6/4).
Nida, Eugene. *Toward a Science of Translating*. Leiden: E. J. Brill, 1964.
Nida, Eugene & Charles R. Taber. *The Theory and Practice of Translation*. Leiden: E. J. Brill, 1969.

Njoroge, Martin C., and Moses G. Gathigia. "The Treatment of Indigenous Languages in Kenya's Pre- and Post-independent Education Commissions and in the Constitution of 2010." 2017. http://dx.doi.org/10.7575/aiac.alls.v.8n.6p.76.

Nundu, Haggai O. *Nyuolruok dhoudi Mag Ugenya*. Nairobi: Kenya Literature Bureau, 1982.

Nyangweso. "The Cult of Mumbo in Central and South Kavirondo." *Journal of E. A. and Uganda Natural History Society* 10, no. 38 (1930): 13-17.

North Nyanza Rural Deanery Council Minutes. 11-12 August 1954. DMN Files, Butere.

Nyanza Rural Deanery Council Minutes. 12 November 1940. DMN Files, Ng'iya.

Nyanza Rural Deanery Council Minutes. 2 December 1942. DMN Files, Ng'iya.

Nyanza Rural Deanery Council Standing Committee Minutes. 17-18 November 1943. DMN Files, Ng'iya.

Nyanza Rural Deanery Council Minutes. 6 December 1944. DMN Files, Ng'iya.

Nyanza Rural Deanery Council Minutes. 22-23 August 1945. DMN Files, Butere.

Nyende, Simeon J. Interviews with Harry Reed 25 September and 29 October 1973, Gem. In Harry A. Reed, "Cotton Growing in Central Nyanza Province, Kenya 1901-1939: An Appraisal of African Reactions to Imposed Government Policy," 49. PhD Thesis, Michigan State University, 1975.

Nzioki, Elizabeth O. "The Development of the Anglican Church in Central Nyanza 1906-1963." MA thesis, University of Nairobi, Kenya, 1989.

Oates, Cedric O. Letter to A. B. Killick, 8 March 1943, and the Department of Agriculture's "Summary of Nyanza Rainfall," 7 May 1943. KNA.

Ochieng', Stephen A. Autobiography written in exile in Ghana. Reuben Omulo Archives, Marenyo, n.d.

Ochieng', William R. "Biography of Yona Omolo." In *Kenya Historical Biographies*, edited by Kenneth King and Ahmed Salim, 77-89. Nairobi: East African Publishing, 1971.

———. *A Pre-colonial History of the Gusii of Western Kenya: From A.D. 1500 to 1914*. Nairobi: East African Literature Bureau (EALB), 1974.

———. *An Outline History of Nyanza*. Nairobi: EALB, 1974.

———. *A history of Kadimo Chiefdoms Yimbo in Western Kenya*. Nairobi: EALB, 1975.

———. *People around the Lake*. London: Evans Brothers, 1979.

———. "Colonial Famines in Luoland, Kenya, 1905-1945." *Transafrican Journal of History* 17 (1988): 21-33. http://www.jstor.org/stable/24328689.

Ocholla, Andrew B. C. "Vyouj Cloveka a Jero kultur ve Vychodnoch Africe." MSc thesis, Praha, Dip. Prace, 1970.

Ocholla-Ayayo, Andrew B. C. *Traditional Ideology and Ethics among the Southern Luo*. Uppsala: Nordiska Afrikainstitutet, TSIAS, 1976.

———. *The Luo culture: A reconstruction of the material culture patterns of a traditional African society.* Wiesbaden: Frazsteiner Verlag, 1980.
Odaga, Asenath. "Education values of *Sigendini* Luo: The Kenya Luo Oral Narratives." MA thesis, University of Nairobi, Kenya, 1980.
Odinga, Oginga. *Not Yet Uhuru: An Autobiography.* Nairobi: Heinemann Educational Books, 1967.
Odinga, Raila A. *The Flame of Freedom.* Nairobi: Mountain Top Publishers, 2013.
Odonde, Jephthah. Letter to Omulo, September 1934. Omulo letters, Reuben Omulo archives, Marenyo.
Oduor, Gilbert O. Letter to Omulo, writing from at YMCA Royapettah, Madras - 14. 6 October 1951. Reuben Omulo archives, Marenyo.
Odwako, Elisham H. "The Church and Education: The Contribution of CMS in Western Kenya, 1905 and 1963." MA thesis, University of Nairobi, Kenya, 1980.
Ohanga, Apollo B. "Election Campaign Manifesto." Reuben Omulo Archives, Marenyo, Siaya, 1957.
Oliver, Roland. *The Missionary Factor in East Africa.* London: Longmans, [1952] 1966.
Oliver, Roland, and Gervase Mathew, eds. *History of East Africa Vol. 1.* Oxford: Clarendon Press, 1963.
Ogada, Odera. YKA Memorandum to DC/KSM, 1922. Owen Papers CMSA / Acc. 83/01.
Oginde, Joyce. Personal interview by Paul Francis Omondi. 11 August 2021. Aboke, Siaya.
Oginde, Fredrick. Personal interview by Paul Francis Omondi. 23 February 2021. Garissa, Kenya.
Ogolla, Janet O. Letter to Reuben Omulo from Mwatate, January 1958. Reuben Omulo Archives, Marenyo.
Ogot, Bethwell A. "The Concept of Jok." *African Studies* 20, no. 2 (1961): 123–130.
———. "British Administration in the Central Nyanza District of Kenya, 1900–60." *The Journal of African History* 4, no. 2 (1963): 249–273. www.jstor.org/stable/179537.
———. "Kingship and Statelessness Among the Nilotes." In *The Historian in Tropical Africa*, edited by Jan Vansina, R. Mauny and L. V. Thomas, 284–302. London: Oxford University Press, 1964.
———. "An African prophet -- the life and teaching of John Owalo." Unpublished manuscript, n.d.
———. *A History of the Southern Luo. Volume 1: Migration and Settlement, 1500–1900.* Nairobi: East African Publishing House (EAPH), 1967.

———. "Reverend Alfayo Odongo Mango 1870–1935." In *Kenya Historical Biographies*, edited by Kenneth King and Ahmed Salim, 98–111. Nairobi: EAP, 1971.

———. *Religion of the Central Luo*. Kampala; Nairobi; Dar-es-Salaam: East African Literature Bureau, 1971.

———. *A History of the Luo-speaking Peoples of Eastern Africa*. Kisumu: Anyange Press, 2009.

Ogot, Bethwell A. & Welbourn F.B. *A Place to Feel at Home*. Oxford: Oxford University Press, 1966.

Ogutu, Gilbert E. M. "A Historical Analysis of the Luo Idea of God 1500–1900." MA thesis, University of Nairobi, Kenya, 1975.

———. "Origins and Growth of the Roman Catholic Church in Western Kenya 1895–1952." PhD thesis, University of Nairobi, Kenya, 1981.

Okaro-Kojwang, K. M. "Origins and Establishment of the *Kavirondo Taxpayers' Welfare Association*." In *Ngano*, edited by B. G. McIntosh, 111–128. Nairobi: EAPH, 1969.

Okere, Gilbert. Personal interview by Paul Francis Omondi. 11 August 2021. Kagonya, Siaya.

Okero, Isaac E.O. Personal interview by Paul Francis Omondi. 16 November 2019. Nairobi.

Okero, Isaac E.O. Personal interviews by Paul Francis Omondi. 10 September and 3 December 2020. Nairobi.

Okot, J. p'Bitek. "Oral Literature and Social Background among the Acholi and Lang'o." Unpubl. BLit thesis, Oxford, St. Peters, 1963.

———. *Religion of the Central Luo*. Kampala: EALB, 1971.

Okonji, Flora. Personal interview by Paul Francis Omondi. 28 December 2019. Seme Kolunje, Kisumu.

O'kubasu, Wadore. Personal interview by Paul Francis Omondi. 16 August 2017. Nairobi.

Okwiri, Gero. Personal interview by Paul Francis Omondi. 23 September 2020. Uyoma, Siaya.

Olang', Festo. *Festo Olang' An Autobiography*. Nairobi: Uzima Press, 1991.

Oluoch, Jemima A. *The Christian Political Theology of Dr John Henry Okullu*. Nairobi: Uzima Publishing House, 2006.

Omachar, Barasa S. "The Contribution of the Church Missionary Society to the Development of Education: A Case of Ng'iya Girls School of Siaya County, Kenya 1923–1967." MA thesis, Moi University, Eldoret, Kenya, 2013.

Ombaka, James O. Personal interview by Paul Francis Omondi. 10 August 2021. Ulumbi, Siaya.

Ominde, Simeon H. *Kenya Education Commission Report* [Ominde Report], part 1. Nairobi: Government Printer, 1964.

———. *Kenya Education Commission report* [Ominde Report], part 2. Nairobi: Government Printer, 1965.
Omollo, Joseph. Interview in Kisumu, 26 July 1984. Quoted in Nzioki, *Anglican Church in Central Nyanza*, 171.
Omondi, Francis. "A Contextual Missiological Study of The Sheepfold Ministries in the Garissa and Tana River Districts of North-eastern Kenya." MTh thesis, South Africa Theological Seminary, Johannesburg, South Africa, 2018.
Omulo, Reuben O. Omulo Notes, Private Archives, Marenyo, Siaya, 1924.
———. Statement taken by Archdeacon W. E. Owen on 25 July 1927. CMSA Acc. 83/02.
———. General Letter, Kisumu. 16 December 1932. Marenyo, Siaya.
———. Letter to the DC Central Nyanza. 5 November 1952. AAC Lundha Church. Reuben Omulo Archives, Marenyo, Siaya.
———. Letter to the DC RE: Divorce Julia Athieno and John Adera, the Pastorate Standing Committee in August 1954. Omulo private Archives Marenyo, Siaya.
———. "Omulo 1954 Diary." Omulo Private Archives, Marenyo, Siaya.
———. "Omulo 1959 Diary." Omulo Private Archives, Marenyo, Siaya.
Omulo, Reuben and Nehemiah Mwanda. Ramula Pastorate Report "Course 2" 6 March to 9 April 1950. Reuben Omulo Archives, Marenyo.
Omulokoli, Watson. "The Historical Development of the Anglican Church Among the Abaluyia, 1905–1955." PhD thesis, Aberdeen University, Scotland, 1981.
Ong'ombe, Ochola. "Interview with Nzioki, Anglican Church in Central Nyanza," 181. 30 July 1984, Kisumu Town.
Onyango, Emily A. *Gender and Development: A History of Women's Education in Kenya*. Carlisle: Langham Monographs, 2018.
Opoku, K. S. "African Traditional Religion: An Enduring Heritage." In *Religious Plurality in Africa: Essays in Honour of John S. Mbiti*, edited by J. K. Olupona and S. S. Nyang, 67–82. Berlin: Mouton de Gruyter & Co, 1993.
Opondo, Paul A. "Fishers and Fish traders of Lake Victoria: Colonial policy and the Development of fish production in Kenya, 1880–1978." PhD thesis, Unisa, Pretoria, South Africa, 2011.
Osogo, John. *A History of the Baluyia*. Nairobi: Oxford University Press, 1966.
———. *Nabongo Mumia*, Nairobi: East African Literature Bureau, 1971.
Osodo, George. Personal interview by Paul Francis Omondi. 24 September 2020. Uriri, Siaya.
Otiende, John E., S. P. Wamahiu and A. M. Karagu. *Education and Development in Kenya: A Historical Perspective*. Nairobi: Oxford University Press, 1992.
Otieno, Alice O. Personal interview by Paul Francis Omondi. 22 and 25 September 2020. Yala Siaya.
Otieno, Joseph O. Personal interview by Paul Francis Omondi. 21 and 23 September 2020. Marenyo, Siaya.

Overdiep, Wim. *Het gevecht om de vijand. Bijbels omgaan met een onwelkome onbekende*. Baarn: Ten Have, 1985.

Overseas Studies Committee, Cambridge University. "Summer Conference on Local Government Problems in Africa." Cambridge: CUP, 1961.

Owen, Walter E. Letter to Heywood CMSA. G3 A 07/08, 1922.

———. Sermon, "Christianity and the Subject Races," as reported in the East African Standard, 17 June 1922. Owen Papers. Acc.83/Z2 (4).

———. "Memorandum on Native Education." DMN Files, 1923.

———. Letter to Kenya Secretary, C.M.S., 23 March 1923. Owen Papers. CMSA, Z1 file.

———. Letter to J. H. Oldham, 8 August 1926. Records of the International Missionary Council, London. CMSA Acc. 83 01.

———. Letter to Senior Commissioner in Nyanza, 24 June 1927. CMSA Acc. 83 01.

———. Letter to Heywood, 24 June 1927. CMSA G3 07/07.

———. Letter to Heywood in Mombasa, 27 June 1927. CMSA ACC 83/2.

———. Letter to Archbishop of Canterbury, 17 August 1927. CMSA Acc. 83 01.

———. Letter to Heywood for Archbishop, 27 August 1927. CMSA/Acc. 83/01.

———. "Empire and Church in Uganda and Kenya." *Edinburgh Review* (1927): 245.

———. "The Relationship of Missionary and African in East Africa." *Church Missionary Review* (1927).

———. Letter to Editor, East African Standard, June 1927. CMSA/ Acc. 83. 01.

———. Letter to Parkinson, 23 May 1931. CMSA Acc. 83 01. CO 533/410, PRO, London.

———. Letter to McKeag, 20 November 1931. PC/NZA.4/3/1, K.N.A.

———. Letter to chaplains' conference, 11 July 1933. Owen Papers, CMSA file Z1.

———. Letter to Pitt Pitts, 25 October 1933. CMSA G3/A5/O.

———. Letter to Hooper, 18 Oct. 1938. CMSA G3 07/08. Acc. 83/z.

———. "Outline of the History of the Kavirondo CMS Mission," 2. CMSA Acc. 83 Z2, n. d.

———. Memo, "Salaries of those who have been trained at Limuru," 1938. DMN Files.

———. Letter to Cash, 6 August 1940. Annual Report 1939–1940, in Owen Papers, Acc. 83/Z11 (5.

———. Letter to the Secretary of CMS in London, 9 August 1943. CMSA G3. 07/08 & Acc 83/z.

Owino, Meshark. "Colonial Neutralization of Indigenous African Military Institutions: The Case of the Jo-Ugenya to c. 1914." MA thesis, Egerton University, 1993.

Owiti, Abuga. Personal interview. 21 and 23 September 1994. Marenyo, Siaya.

Oyolo, Jeremiah. Ramula to Rural Dean K. E. Stovold 8 October 1949. Private archives Marenyo, 1949.

Spencer, Leon P. "Christianity and Colonial Protest: Perceptions of W. E. Owen, Archdeacon of Kavirondo." *Journal of Religion in Africa* 13, no. 1 (1982): 47–60. https://www.jstor.org/stable/1581117.

Pars, L. A. "Edward Carey Francis." *Journal of the London Mathematical Society* s1–43, no. 1 (1968): 368. https://doi.org/10.1112/jlms/s1-43.1.368.

Perham, Margery, ed. *Diaries of Lord Lugard Vol. 1: East Africa, November 1889-December 1890*. Evanston: Northwestern University Press, 1959.

Philp, Horace R. A. *A New Day in Kenya*. London: World Dominion Press, 1936.

Pickens, George F. *African Christian God-Talk: Matthew Ajuoga's Johera Narrative*. Lanham: University Press of America, 2004.

Pirouet, Louise M. *Black Evangelists: The Spread of Christianity in Uganda, 1891–1914*. London: Rex Collings, 1978.

Pleydell, Albert E. Annual Letter, 25 November 1910. CMSA G3. A7/08.

———. Annual Letter, Maseno, 13 November 1911. CMSA G3. A7/09.

———. "The Mass Movement in Kavirondo." *CMS Gleaner*, 1 October 1919.

———. Letter to Omulo, 11 June 1934. 32 Upper Abbey Road Brighton, St Paul's Theological College Archives Limuru.

Proceedings of the CMS, 1905–1906. CMSA G3.A7/05.

Provincial Commissioner Nyanza, Report 1904. KNA.

Proceedings of the CMS for Africa and the East, 1907–1908. CMSA G3.A7/05.

Proceedings of the CMS, for Africa and the East, 1922–1923. CMSA G3.A7/05.

Provincial Commissioner Nyanza 2/3. 1908–1915. KNA.

Provincial Commissioner Nyanza Province Annual Report 1912–1913. KNA.

Provincial Commissioner Nyanza 3/3/22, Indian settlements, May 8, 1913. KNA.

Provincial Commissioner Nyanza 1/1/4 109–09. KNA.

Provincial Commissioner Nyanza Provincial Report 1922. KNA.

Provincial Commissioner Nyanza Provincial Report 1926. Cmd. 2573. KNA.

Provincial Commissioner Nyanza. 4/3/1 KNA.

Provincial Unit of Research; Church of the Province of Kenya (PUR). *Rabai to Mumias. A Short History of the Province of Kenya 1844–1994*. Nairobi: Uzima Press, 1994.

Ramose, Mogobe B. *African Philosophy Through Ubuntu*. Harare: Mond Books, 2002.

Ratzinger, Joseph. *The Spirit of Liturgy*. San Francisco: Ignatius Press, 2000.

Ravenscroft, R. L. "The Role of the Archdeacon Today." *Ecclesiastical Law Journal* 3, no. 17 (1995): 379–392.

Reed, Colins. *Pastors, Partners, and Paternalists: African Church Leaders and Western Missionaries in the Anglican Church in Kenya, 1850–1900*. Leiden: Brill, 1997.

———. *Walking in the Light: Reflections on the East Africa Revival & Its Link to Australia*. Brunswick: Acorn Press, 2007.

———. "Denominationalism or Protestantism? Mission Strategy and Church in the Kikuyu Conference of 1913." *International Bulletin of Missionary Research* 37, no. 4 (2013): 207–212.

Reed, Harry A. "Cotton Growing in Central Nyanza Province, Kenya 1901–1939: An Appraisal of African Reactions to Imposed Government Policy." PhD thesis, Michigan State University, 1975.

Reiss, Katharina. "Type, Kind and Individuality of Text: Decision Making in Translation." In *The Translation Studies Reader*, edited by L. Venuti, 168–179. Translated by S. Kitron. London: Routledge, 2004.

Reiss, Katharina and Hans J. Vermeer. *Grundlegung einer allgemeinen Translationstheorie*. Tübingen: Niemeyer, 1984.

Report by General Secretary on His Visit to East and Central Africa in 1937. G/ADI/7.

Report of the Special Sub-Committee on the Training and Status of Missionaries. January 1902, G/AZ4.

Report of the Regional Boundaries Commission, (Kenya). 1962 Cmd. 1899, H.H. Johnston to Salisbury, 5 February 1900, FO 2/297, PRO. KNA.

Report of the Regional Boundaries Commission (Kenya). 1962 Cmd. 1899, 13–15. KNA, 1899.

Report of Uganda Bible Committee, 1908. CMSA. G3. A7/06.

Richard, Charles G. *Archdeacon Owen of Kavirondo*. Nairobi: The Highway Press, 1947.

Richards, Elizabeth. *Fifty Years in Nyanza 1906–1956, Nyanza Jubilee Committee*. Nairobi: ACME Press, 1956.

Roberts, D. F. "Some genetic implications of the Nilotic demography." *Acta Genetica et Statistica Medica* 6, no. 3 (1956): 446–452.

———. "Serology and History of the Northern Nilotes." *Journal of African History* 3, no. 2 (1962): 301–305.

Roscoe, Adrian. *Uhuru's Fire: African Literature East to South*. Cambridge: Cambridge University Press, 1977.

Ross, McGregor W. "1922: Kenya from Within." 87, Civil Case No. 626 of 1922. Chief Justice Sir Jacob Barth's judgment.

Saayman, Willem A., ed. *Missiology. Only study guide for MSA100-3*. Pretoria: UNISA Press, 1992.

Saayman, Willem, and Klippies Kritzinger, eds. *Mission in Bold Humility: David Bosch's Work Considered*. Eugene: Wipf and Stock Publishers, 1996.

Safholm, Per. "The Nilotic Religion." Fil. Lic. Thesis, Stockholm, 1958.

Salim, Ahmed I. *Swahili-Speaking Peoples of Kenya's Coast. 1895–1965*. Nairobi: EAPH, 1973.

———. *The East Africa in the Nineteenth Century unto the 1880s.* London: Heinemann and Paris: UNESCO, 1989.
Sanders, Edith R. "The Hamitic Hypothesis: Its Origin and Functions in Time Perspective." *Journal of African History* 10, no. 4 (1969): 521–532.
Sanneh, Lamin O. "Christian Mission and The Western Guilt Complex." *The Christian Century* (1987): 331–334.
———. *Translating the Message: The missionary Impact on Culture.* Maryknoll: Orbis Books, 1989.
Savile, Huge O. Letter to F. Baylis, Bristol, 29 March 1905. CMSA G3. A7/05.
———. Letter to the CMS Committee, Maseno, 16 April 1906. CMSA G3. A7/05.
———. Letter to Baylis, Maseno, 18 May 1907. CMSA G3. A/706.
Savile, Kathleen E. B. Proceedings of the CMS, 1905–1906. CMSA G3 A7/05.
Schiller, Laurence D. "Gem and Kano: A Comparative Study of Two Luo Political Systems Under Stress, 1880–1914." PhD thesis, Northwestern University, Evanston, 1982.
Schilling, Donald. "Local Native Councils and the Politics of Education in Kenya, 1925–1939." *The International Journal of African Historical Studies* 9, no. 2 (1976): 218–247. doi:10.2307/217565.
———. "The Dynamics of Educational Policy Formation: Kenya 1928–1934." *History of Education Quarterly* 20, no. 1 (1980): 51–76. doi:10.2307/367890.
Schreiter, Robert J. *Constructing Local Theologies.* 30th anniversary edition. Maryknoll: Orbis Books, 2015.
Seligman, Charles G., and B. Z. Seligman, *Pagan Tribes of the Nilotic Sudan.* London: Routledge & Kegan Paul, 1932.
Senior Commissioner Nyanza. Letter to Owen Kisumu 12 July 1927. Ref. No 2179/62.3 CMSA G3. 83/02.
Sessional paper No. 10 of 1965 (GOK): *African socialism and application to planning in Kenya.* Nairobi: Government Printer, 1965.
Shenk, Wilbert R. *Henry Venn, Missionary Statesman.* Maryknoll: Orbis Books, 1983.
———."Henry Venn and Mission Thought." *Anvil* 2, no. 1 (1985): 25–41.
Sheria za Kanisa juu ya Ndoa: Mukutano wa maaskofu wakiaanglicana wa Afrika mashariki- Canon of Marriage 1933. Conference of Anglican Bishops of East Africa. Reuben Omulo Archives. Marenyo Siaya, 1933.
Sicherman, Carol. *Ngugi wa Thiong'o: The Making of a Rebel. A Sourcebook in Kenyan Literature and Resistance.* London: Hans Zell, 1990.
Sifuna, Daniel. *Development of Education in Africa: The Kenyan Experience.* Nairobi: Initiative, 2000.
Smith, L. D. "An Overview of Agricultural Development Policy." In *Agricultural Development in Kenya: An Economic Assessment,* edited by Heyer J. et al., 111–151. Nairobi: Oxford University Press, 1976.

Smith, George. *A Short History of Christian Missions from Abraham and Paul to Carey, Livingstone, and Duff*. Edinburgh: T. & T. Clark Publisher, 1884.

Southall, Aidan W., ed. *Social Change in Modern Africa*. London: Oxford University Press, 1961. doi: 10.4324/9780429486449.

Sorrenson, M. P. K. *Origins of European Settlement in Kenya*. London: Oxford University Press, 1968.

Spear, Thomas & Isariah N. Kimambo, eds. *East Africa Expression of Christianity*. East African Studies. Columbus: Ohio University Press, 1999.

Spencer, Leon P. "Christianity and Colonial Protest: Perceptions of W. E. Owen, Archdeacon of Kavirondo." *Journal of Religion in Africa* 13, no. 1 (1982): 47–60. https://www.jstor.org/stable/1581117.

Stanley, Brian, ed. *Christian Missions and the Enlightenment*. Grand Rapids: Eerdmans, 2001.

———. *Missions, Nationalism and End of Empire*. Grand Rapids: Eerdmans, 2003.

Stanway, Alfred. Letter to Cecil Bewes, Maseno, 29 April 1946. DMN Files.

———. "Elementary Education in Nyanza Rural Deanery." n. d. DMN Files.

Stoke, Eugene. *The History of the CMS: Its Environment, Its Men, and Its Work*, 3 Vols. London: CMS, 1899.

Stovold, Kenneth E. Letter to the Pastorate at Ramula, 11 October 1949. Reuben Omulo Archives, Marenyo.

———. "*Hesabu ya Watu wa AAC Nyanza.*" June 1949. DMN Files, Maseno.

Steyne, Philip M. *Gods of Power: A Study of the Beliefs and Practices of Animists*. Houston: Touch, 1990.

Strauss, Claudia, and Naomi Quinn, eds. *A Cognitive Theory of Cultural Meaning*. New York: Cambridge University Press, 1997.

Strayer, Robert W. "Anglicans in Kenya: The Making of Mission Communities in East Africa." In *Anglicans and Africans in Colonial Kenya, 1875–1935*, edited by Robert W. Strayer, n.p. London: Heinemann Educational Books, 1978.

Swan, William. *Letters on Missions, by William Swan, Missionary in Siberia*. London: Westley and Davis, 1830.

Swynnerton, R.J.M. *A Plan to Intensify the Development of African Agriculture in Kenya*. Nairobi: Government Printer, 1954.

Taylor, John V. *The Growth of the Church in Buganda*, London: SCM, 1950.

———. *The Process of Growth in an African Church*, London: SCM, 1958.

The Anglican Church of Kenya Constitution 2002. Canon XXIII: OF MARRIAGE, 75–88. Nairobi: Uzima Press, 2002.

"The Canon Law of Marriage." Operational in Mombasa Diocese. Reuben Omulo Private Archives, Marenyo, Siaya, 1931.

"The Policy of the Alliance." No. 58 in J.W. Arthur Papers, Gen. 7864/3 Edinburgh University Library.

The Times. 24 October 24, 1964. Rt. Rev. R. P. Crabbe: "The Church in East Africa." 1964.

The Times. 27 February 1953. "Bishop of Mombasa." CMSA, 1953.

Thompson, David M. "British Missionary Policy on the Indigenous Church: The Influence of Developments in Domestic Ecclesiology and Politics." NAMP Position Paper 38, 1997.

Throup, David W. *Economic and Social Origins of Mau Mau 1945–53.* London: James Currey, 1987.

Translation Committee Minutes. October 1910. CMSA G3.A7/08.

Triebel, Johannes. "Mission and culture in Africa – A working report on Tanzanian experience." *Africa Theological Journal* 21, no. 3 (1992): 232–239.

Turaki, Yusuf. "Human Dignity and Identity and Reconciliation." In *Visions of Man and Freedom in Africa,* edited by M. Waiyaki, et al, 9–29. Potchefstroom: IRS. Series F1, No. 302, 1992.

———. *Christianity and African Gods: A Method in Theology,* Nairobi: IBS-Nig. Press, 1999.

Tucker, Alfred R. "Letter to Crabtree," 29 November 1904. CMSA G3. A7/04.

———. *Eighteen Years in Uganda and East Africa, 2 Vols.* London, Edward Arnold, 1908.

Tucker, Alfred R., and John J. Willis. "Memorandum of Interview of Bishop Tucker and the Rev. J. J. Willis with the Group No. II Committee." 26 June 1906. CMSA G3.A7/05.

Tutu, Desmond. *No Future Without Forgiveness.* London: Doubleday, [1999] 2003.

Uganda Notes, June, August, and September 1905. CMSA G3.A7/05.

Uganda Notes, November 1910. CMSA G3.A7/05.

Uganda Report, December 1906. CMSA G3.A7/05.

Urch, George D. "Education and Colonialism in Kenya." *History of Education Quarterly* 11, no. 3 (1971): 249–264. doi:10.2307/367292.

Van Zwanenberg, Roger M. A. "Colonial Capitalism and Labour." In *Politics and Nationalism in Colonial Kenya,* edited by B. A. Ogot, 21–52. Nairobi: EAPH, 1972.

———. "The Economic Response of Kenya Africans to European Settlement 1903–1939." In *Politics and Nationalism in Colonial Kenya,* edited by B. A. Ogot, 207–225. Nairobi: EAPH, 1972.

Vermeer, Hans J. "Skopos and Commission in Translational Action." In *The Translation Studies Reader,* edited by Lawrence Venuti, 227–238. London: Routledge, 2004.

Wagner, Gunter. *The Bantu of North Kavirondo.* Oxford: OUP, 1949. doi: 10.4324/9780429485770.

Walaba, Aggrey W. *The Role of Christian Missionaries in Socio-Economic Developments.* Eldoret: Bookshelf Publishers, 2009.

Walker, Robert H. "Appeal for Kavirondo." In CMS Report, 118–119, 1900.

Walliman, Nicholas. *Research Methods*. New York: Routledge, 2011. (This edition was published in the Taylor & Francis e-Library.)

Walls, Andrew. "The Expansion of Christianity: An Interview with Andrew Walls." *The Christian Century*, (2000): 792–799

Wanyanga, Sam O. *Triumph Through Faith: A Quest for Freedom and Rest – Story of Pastor Silfano Ayayo Mijema*. Dar es Salaam: Matokeo Publishers, 2017.

Warambo, Malaki W. O. Personal interview by Paul Francis Omondi. August 2019. Nairobi.

Ward, Kevin & Stanley Brian. *The Church Mission Society and World Christianity, 1799–1999*. Grand Rapids: Eerdmans, 2000.

Warren, Max A. C. *Unfolding Purpose: An Interpretation of the Living Tradition which is CMS*. London: CMS, 1950.

———. *Revival, An inquiry*. London: SCM, 1954.

———. *Crowded Canvas: Some experiences of a life-time*. London: Holder & Stoughton, 1974.

Wasawo, David P. S. "We Understand but Darkly: A Memoir." Unpublished, 2014.

Watts, Fraser. "Experiencing Liturgy." *Liturgy* 21, no. 3 (2006): 3–9. doi: 10.1080/04580630600642734.

Watts, T. A. Comments on "The Luo Customary Law of Land Tenure," a paper by Dr. G. M. Wilson. (Letter to Prov. Comm'r, Nyanza, Feb. 1955). Kisumu District Archives, 1955.

Weatherhead, Herbert T. C. "Pioneer Missionary Work in Kavirondo." In CMSA *Uganda Notes*, March 1909.

Welbourn, Fredrick B. *East African Christian*. London: Oxford University Press, 1965.

———. *East African Rebels*. London: SCM Press, 1966.

Wells, Samuel. *Improvisation: The Drama of Christian Ethics*. London: SPCK, 2004.

Wende Luo. (Hymnal) Edition of the Anglican Church of Kenya. Nairobi: Uzima Press, 1980.

Were, Gedion S. *A History of the Abaluyia of Western Kenya: c.1500–1930*. Nairobi: EAPH, 1967.

———. *Western Kenya Historical Texts: Abaluyia, Teso and Elgon Kalenjin*. Nairobi, EALB, 1967.

———. "The Western Bantu Peoples from A.D. 1300 to 1800." In *Zamani: A Survey of East African History*, edited by Bethwell A. Ogot and J.A. Kieran, n.p. Nairobi: EAPH, Longman Kenya, 1968.

Westerman, Diedrich H. *The Shilluk People: Their Language and Folklore*. Berlin, Deitrich Reimer (Ernst Vohsen), 1912.

Whisson, Michael G. *Some aspects of functional disorders among the Kenya Luo. Magic, Faith, Healing*, edited by A. Kiev. New York: Free Press, 1964.

Whisson, Michael G., and John M. Lonsdale. "The Case of Jason Gor and Fourteen Others: A Luo Succession Dispute in Historical Perspective." *Africa: Journal of the International African Institute* 45, no. 1 (1975): 50–66. www.jstor.org/stable/1158779.

White, Frank. Annual Letter, Maseno, 25 October 1911. CMSA. G3. A7/09.

Williams, Peter C. *The Ideal of the Self-Governing Church, W. Shenk, Henry Venn - Missionary Statesman*, Maryknoll: Orbis Books, 1991.

Williams, George B. *Report on the Sanitation of Nairobi, and the Townships of Naivasha, Nakuru and Kisumu*. Wellcome Foundation Library: WA 670, HK 4, 1907.

Wilson, G. Herbert. *Windlesham House School: History and Muster Roll 1837–1937*. London: McCorquodale & Co. Ltd, 1937.

Wilson, Gordon M. *Marriage Laws Customs, Maseno. Central Nyanza*, Nairobi: Government Printers, 1955.

Wilson, Godfrey. "An African Morality." In *Culture and Societies of Africa*, edited by P. Ottenberg, 345–364. New York: Random House, 1960.

Willis, Bailey. *Index to the stratigraphy of North America*. No. 71. US Gov't. Print. Office, 1912.

Willis, John J. "Christianity or Mohammedanism." *The Uganda Diocese CMS Intelligencer*, A.R. Tucker CMS Gazette 1090:305, 1904.

———. In *Uganda Notes*, August 1905, CMSA, G3/A7/P3.

———. Letter to Baylis, 4 November 1906. CMSA G3.A7/05, Kisumu.

———. "Willis Papers." 15 March 1908, 17 June 1908, 11 November 1908, 26 May 1909. London: Lambeth Palace Library Microfilm, CMSA G3.A7/08.

———. General Letter, 26 May 1909. "Willis Papers." CMSA G3. A7/08.

———. Annual Letter, 24 November 1910. CMSA G3. A7/08.

———. "The Appeal to the African." *Church Missionary Review*, January 1912. CMSA G3. A7/08, 1912.

———. "The Proposed Scheme of Federation." *Church Missionary Review*, January 1914. CMSA G3. A7/08, 1914.

———. "Buganda Teachers and Mass Movements." *Church Missionary Review*, 1918. CMSA G3. A7/08, 1918.

———. "An African Church in Building." London: CMSA. G3. A7/08, 1925.

———. Letter to Omulo from Leicestershire. 18 August 1938. St Paul's University Archives.

———. "Reflection in 1949: Uganda Revisited." Acc.120 F2 3.9.49, 1949.

Wright, Fredrick H. In *Uganda Notes*, September 1905. CMSA G3.A7/05.

———. Letter to Baylis, Maseno, 10 August 1909. CMSA. G3. A7/07.

———. General letter Kisumu, 30 August 1910. CMSA G3. A7/08.

———. Report in *Uganda Notes*, November 1910. CMSA G3.A7/05.

———. Annual Letter, Kisumu, 24 November 1910. CMSA G3. A7/08.

———. General letter from Kisumu, May 1912. CMSA G3.A7/07.

———. General Letter, Kisumu, 4 February 1914. CMSA G3. A7/07.

———. Letter to Senior Commissioners Kisumu, 8 February 1922. CMSA ACC 83/2.

Young, Frances. *The Art of Performance: Towards a Theology of Holy Scripture.* London: Darton, Longman & Todd, 1990.

Young Kavirondo Association Memorandum 1922. In CMSA /Acc. 83. 01, 1922.

Langham Literature, with its publishing work, is a ministry of Langham Partnership.

Langham Partnership is a global fellowship working in pursuit of the vision God entrusted to its founder John Stott –

> *to facilitate the growth of the church in maturity and Christ-likeness through raising the standards of biblical preaching and teaching.*

Our vision is to see churches in the Majority World equipped for mission and growing to maturity in Christ through the ministry of pastors and leaders who believe, teach and live by the word of God.

Our mission is to strengthen the ministry of the word of God through:
- nurturing national movements for biblical preaching
- fostering the creation and distribution of evangelical literature
- enhancing evangelical theological education

especially in countries where churches are under-resourced.

Our ministry

Langham Preaching partners with national leaders to nurture indigenous biblical preaching movements for pastors and lay preachers all around the world. With the support of a team of trainers from many countries, a multi-level programme of seminars provides practical training, and is followed by a programme for training local facilitators. Local preachers' groups and national and regional networks ensure continuity and ongoing development, seeking to build vigorous movements committed to Bible exposition.

Langham Literature provides Majority World preachers, scholars and seminary libraries with evangelical books and electronic resources through publishing and distribution, grants and discounts. The programme also fosters the creation of indigenous evangelical books in many languages, through writer's grants, strengthening local evangelical publishing houses, and investment in major regional literature projects, such as one volume Bible commentaries like the *Africa Bible Commentary* and the *South Asia Bible Commentary*.

Langham Scholars provides financial support for evangelical doctoral students from the Majority World so that, when they return home, they may train pastors and other Christian leaders with sound, biblical and theological teaching. This programme equips those who equip others. Langham Scholars also works in partnership with Majority World seminaries in strengthening evangelical theological education. A growing number of Langham Scholars study in high quality doctoral programmes in the Majority World itself. As well as teaching the next generation of pastors, graduated Langham Scholars exercise significant influence through their writing and leadership.

To learn more about Langham Partnership and the work we do visit **langham.org**

www.ingramcontent.com/pod-product-compliance
Lightning Source LLC
Chambersburg PA
CBHW061703300426
44115CB00014B/2543